The Business of Venture Capital

The Business of Venture Capital

Second Edition

Insights from Leading Practitioners on the Art of Raising a Fund, Deal Structuring, Value Creation, and Exit Strategies

MAHENDRA RAMSINGHANI

WILEY

Published by John Wiley & Sons, Inc., Hoboken, New Jersey.
Published simultaneously in Canada.

For general information on our other products and services or for technical support, please
contact our Customer Care Department within the United States at (800) 762-2974, outside
the United States at (317) 572-3993 or fax (317) 572-4002.

Wiley publishes in a variety of print and electronic formats and by print-on-demand. Some
material included with standard print versions of this book may not be included in e-books or
in print-on-demand. If this book refers to media such as a CD or DVD that is not included in
the version you purchased, you may download this material at http://booksupport.wiley.com.
For more information about Wiley products, visit www.wiley.com.

Library of Congress Cataloging-in-Publication Data:

Ramsinghani, Mahendra.
The business of venture capital : insights from leading practitioners on the art of raising a fund,
deal structuring, value creation, and exit strategies / Mahendra Ramsinghani. — Second edition.
    pages cm. — (The Wiley finance series)
  Includes index.
  ISBN 978-1-118-75219-7 (cloth); 978-1-118-92664-2 (ebk); 978-1-118-92661-1 (ebk)
1. Venture capital. I. Title.
  HG4751.R36 2014
  332′.04154068—dc23
                                                                    2014007536

Printed in the United States of America
10 9 8 7 6 5 4 3 2 1

In the memory of my parents

and

for Deepa and Aria, the light and the song

Contents

Foreword

I often get asked how I ended up becoming a venture capitalist (VC). My wife, Amy, likes to remind me that when I was an entrepreneur, I used to regularly give talks at MIT about entrepreneurship. I'd say—very bluntly—"stay away from venture capitalists." I bootstrapped my first company, and while we did a lot of work for VCs, I liked taking money from them as "revenue" (where they paid my company Feld Technologies for our services) rather than as an investment.

Feld Technologies was acquired about 20 years ago. Over the next two years, I made 40 angel investments with the money I made from the sale of the company. At one point in the process, I was down to under $100,000 in the bank—with the vast majority of our net worth tied up in these angel investments and a house that we bought in Boulder. Fortunately, Amy was mellow about this—we had enough current income to live the way we wanted, we were young (30), and generally weren't anxious about how much liquid cash we had.

Along the way, a number of the companies I had invested in as an angel investor raised money from VCs. Some were tough experiences for me, like NetGenesis, which was the first angel investment I made. I was chairman from inception until shortly after the $4m venture capital round the company raised two years into its life. Shortly after that venture capital investment, the VCs hired a new "professional" CEO who lasted less than a year before being replaced by a CEO who then did a great job building the company. During this period, the founding CEO left, and I decided to resign from the board because I didn't support the process of replacing this CEO, felt like I no longer had any influence on the company, and wasn't having any fun.

But I still wasn't a VC at this point. I was making angel investments with my own money and working my ass off helping get a few companies that I'd cofounded, like Interliant and Email Publishing, off the ground. I was living in Boulder at this point, but traveling continuously to Boston, New York, San Francisco, and Seattle, where I was making most of my investments. During this time, I started to get pulled into more conversations with VCs, helping a few do some diligence on new investments, encouraging some to look at my angel investments, and investing small amounts in some venture capital funds whenever I was invited to invest in their "side funds for entrepreneurs."

One of the VCs I overlapped with while in Boston was Charley Lax. Charley was a partner at a firm called VIMAC and was looking at some Internet stuff. I was one of the most prolific Internet angel investors in Boston at this point (1994–1995) so our paths crossed periodically. We never invested in anything together, but after I moved to Boulder, I got a call one day in early 1996, which went something like:

"Hey—I just joined this Japanese company called SOFTBANK and we are going to invest $500 million in Internet companies in the next year. Do you want to help out?"

Um—okay—sure. I didn't really know what "help out" meant, but on my next trip to San Francisco I had a breakfast meeting that ended with something like "welcome to the team."

I still didn't really have any idea what was going on, but I was making angel investments and having fun. And soon I was a "SOFTBANK Affiliate," a title that had a small monthly retainer, a deal fee for anything I brought in, and a carry on the performance of any investments I sourced. This was an informal enough arrangement for me to play around with it for a while.

I was in Boston the following week and met with two people who would become close friends to this day. The first was Fred Wilson, who had just started Flatiron Partners (SOFTBANK was an investor in Fred's fund), and the other was Seth Godin, the CEO of Yoyodyne. I vaguely remember a fun, energetic chat as we met a few people at Yoyodyne, ran through the products, and talked about how amazing the Internet and e-mail was going to be as a marketing tool.

My formal report back was short—something like "Seth's cool, the business is neat, I like it." SOFTBANK and Flatiron closed an investment in Yoyodyne a few weeks later.

Suddenly I was a VC. An accidental one. And it's been a very interesting journey over the past 17 years.

When I started investing as an angel investor, I often crossed the boundary between investor and entrepreneur. When I became a venture capitalist and started investing larger amounts in more companies, I continued to cross this boundary. It took a few years for this to catch up with me, but it finally smashed me over the head when I realized I couldn't effectively play the role of both the investor and the entrepreneur. I had to pick one.

Once I chose the role of investor, I also determined it was my job to completely support CEOs or founders. If I lost confidence in them for any reason, my first task was to confront them about it. If we could reconcile this, I'd continue to support them all the way and work for them. If not, it was my job as an investor to address my concerns at the board level.

Over the years, I have realized that it takes a mix of personal attributes and intellectual abilities to become a venture capitalist. While there are some great VCs, as with anything else, there are some awful ones.

Venture capital is a business where each investment teaches you something new—a lot can be learned by doing. In each of the books I've written, I emphasize the basic fact that a book provides only a basic framework, but each one of us has the ability to carve a different path in this universe.

In *The Business of Venture Capital*, Mahendra Ramsinghani has done an excellent job of this. As you read this book, either with the aim of becoming a venture capitalist or trying to understand the dynamics of the venture capital business, recognize that Mahendra has given you a framework for understanding how this all works. While VC personalities, styles, behavior, and effectiveness vary widely, Mahendra helps describe venture capital in a way that is comprehensive, yet easily understood.

—Brad Feld
Managing Director, Foundry Group
March 2014

Preface

"If you are under the impression you have already perfected yourself, you will never rise to the heights you are no doubt capable of."

— *Kazuo Ishiguro*, The Remains of the Day

In venture capital, what matters? Skill or luck? Maureen Wilcox could well be a very successful venture capitalist (VC). She bought two lottery tickets—one in Massachusetts and another across the state border in Rhode Island. Both tickets had winning numbers. Venture capital boils down to the ability of picking winners. Yet, no book can teach you how to pick winners or be a successful VC. At best, this is an attempt to develop and identify the framework for thought and action.

This book addresses the arc of a venture capital investment lifecycle. Fund raising, constructing a portfolio, identifying and investing in opportunities, roles of board members and more. My goal here is to inform, educate and, in some cases, even entertain. Over 50 leading experts have shared their views and practical advise. Findings from academic research papers have also been summarized. Dense formulas that contain Greek characters are not included, sorry nerds. Finally, I have also included lessons from my own experience of over a decade of investments.

Even as we live in the era of big data, nothing about venture capital investments is predictable or persistent. The correlation/causation debate continues. In analyzing performance of more than 2,300 funds between 1974 and 2010, over 250 funds returned more than 2X of paid in capital. These funds are in the $250 million size range. The number of funds above $500 million in size that returned 2X capital is meager: two funds. The bigger question practitioners need to ask—is 2X good enough a return? Over the 2000–2010 decade, venture capital shrinkage or right sizing has occurred across the board. The number of active venture firms dropped by 50 percent.

Average fund sizes declined from $170 million (2000) to $140 million (2012). Smaller venture funds of less than $50 million have dropped by 70 percent between 2000 and 2012. Yet some micro venture capital funds in the $35 million size category are trending upward of 5X cash-on-cash returns. If smaller fund managers are better at picking the right companies, why is this universe shrinking? In analyzing exit values, of the 534 exits that occurred in the decade, 320 exits were less than $150 million in size and had consumed an average of $56 million. It is no wonder then that SuperLP Chris Douvos asks, show me the RTFE or return the fund exit. Investors want to see one big hit in any venture capital portfolio that has the potential to return the entire fund. One investor I spoke with described a 2X return over 10 years as utterly mediocre, and is no longer investing in the venture capital asset class. This sentiment is prevalent as institutional investors now seek proven and experienced venture investors. Size matters, performance even more.

The one question I struggled with was: what makes a great VC? Or is there even such a thing? Like mutual funds and Hollywood stars, venture capital funds tend to cycle in and out of popularity charts—what's hot today is out of favor tomorrow. Do great VCs consistently pick the next big winner? Do they host diligence sessions at vineyards and sail into the sunset on a 40-foot catamaran? Or is greatness defined by immense popularity within entrepreneurial ranks? Is greatness an accidental outcome in the garb of a narrative fallacy? Or is it a thoughtful plan executed with grit and determination? These questions remain—and then, there are a few stories that I have left out. For example, the one about a VC who planted a hidden camera in a portfolio CEO's house. Or the one about an uber-arrogant Sand Hill Road VC whose administrative assistant told me she had a burning desire to kill him. Such gossip stories do not further the intellectual debate and are better narrated after three drinks. But boy, are these good stories!

Coming back to the question of attributes of a great VC, I have included a few examples of those who chose to not accept the status quo. Brad Feld disrupted the way VCs treat and engage with entrepreneurs (with respect, for a start). He co-authored a series of books to empower entrepreneurs, (I am honored to have co-authored *Startup Boards* with him) and co-founded TechStars, a global accelerator network. Dave McClure of 500 Startups wants to build an entrepreneurial ecosystem in every continent. Or consider Andreessen-Horowitz (A16Z). Venture capitalists can use the 2 percent management fee income to fatten their wallets. The management fees for Andreessen-Horowitz's funds are used to build an army of more than 100 team members with the aim of serving entrepreneurs better. By choosing to drop this moral hazard, they have become the sought-after firm by investors and entrepreneurs alike. Even as Sand Hill Road VCs grumble that A16Z is overpaying high valuations, investors gladly invested yet another

$1.5 billion in 12 weeks. These are a few examples of those who chose to make a meaningful contribution to the entrepreneurial ecosystem, well beyond the carry and fees. These are the crazy ones. Such behavior requires dissolution of ego and greed and calls for a sense of service and humility—all of which seem in short supply. My hope is that as practitioners we find our own meaningful ways to fuel the forces of disruption. Success then is aligned with something greater than material possessions—a legacy and a path worthy of emulation.

Part I of this book covers the process of raising a venture fund. The preliminary chapters describe the fund investment cycle, roles of various team members, in any fund and the economics of fees and carried interests, or profits. Part I aims to help decipher the investor universe, fund diligence, the legal terms, fund structures and more.

In Part II, the process of sourcing investments, structuring and negotiating term sheets, adding value as a board member and monitoring portfolio companies is covered. Finally, the last chapter touches upon the foibles of human psychology. I have relied on the insightful and often hilarious and humbling works of David McRaney, author of *You Are Not So Smart: Why You Have Too Many Friends on Facebook, Why Your Memory Is Mostly Fiction, and 46 Other Ways You're Deluding Yourself*. He writes, "You want to believe that those who work hard and sacrifice get ahead and those who are lazy and cheat do not. This, of course, is not always true. Success is often greatly influenced by when you were born, where you grew up, the socioeconomic status of your family, and random chance." Which brings us to the final question – how does luck factor in the venture capital universe?

We started with Maureen Wilcox who bought lottery tickets for both the Massachusetts lottery and the Rhode Island Lottery. Incredibly, she managed to choose the winning numbers for both lotteries but didn't win a penny. In a strange twist, the numbers she picked for Massachusetts lottery were the winning numbers for the Rhode Island lottery. And vice versa. Good picking skills—very lousy luck. That makes her a bad VC, doesn't it?

On the other hand, Evelyn Marie Adams won a $4 million lottery and four months later won another $1.5 million. Even luckier was Donald Smith. He won the Wisconsin State lottery three times in three consecutive years. Chris "SuperLP" Douvos often describe VCs as those with a lottery and a dream. If you think of this business as a game of luck, you should buy 40 lottery tickets instead of this book. If you wish to hone your skills, read on.

Acknowledgments

In preparation of this book, some of the world's leading venture practitioners offered their wisdom and insights. Their names are sprinkled all over this book. Without their participation, support, encouragement, threats, and sometimes the much-needed kick-in-the-rear, this would have remained just another idea. A mere acknowledgement, then, seems inappropriate. Deep gratitude would be more like it. And of course, while all the great ideas and insights are theirs, any mistakes are mine.

After the first edition was released, I was humbled with the positive responses that came from readers across the United States, Europe, and Asia. Thank you to those who took the effort to share your feedback and reviews.

Finally, the world of venture capital would be bereft of its glory, but for the entrepreneurial force. I bow deeply to that force, because it all starts with those "crazy ones" who believe they can change the world.

San Francisco
April 2014

One

Raising the Venture Fund

Raising the venture fund, especially first-time funds, is not for the faint of heart. Institutional investors or limited partners (LPs) look for the following:

- Performance track record and background of fund managers
- Investment strategy and its relevance to (a) managers' expertise and (b) market conditions

The LP universe is diverse. It includes pension funds, endowments and foundations, corporations, private family offices, and individuals. The motivations for each are primarily financial returns and asset diversification. LPs expect venture returns to be at least twice those offered by liquid securities, such as public market indices. Top quartile venture returns average upward of 20 percent of the internal rate of return (IRR).

According to Preqin research:

- Fifty-two percent of venture funds complete their fund-raising in 12 months. Others spend as much as 24 to 36 months on the road.
- Of the funds that successfully got off the ground, only 7 percent are first-time funds.
- About 70 percent of the funds successfully reach or exceed their targeted fund amount.

Placement agents are able to offer market intelligence and accelerate the fund-raising process via LP relationships for newer funds. Some LPs shun the venture asset class, as it is harder to establish determinants of consistent performance. Others play with only a select group of top-tier venture funds. Some choose to invest in a fund of funds or move over into other subclasses of private equity, such as middle market buy-out funds.

Part I covers the process of raising the venture fund. We look at how practitioners can find an entry point into the world of venture capital. Those brave enough to raise their own funds can gain a better understanding of the universe of institutional investors. Their asset allocation strategy and fund due diligence criteria are covered in this section.

CHAPTER 1

The Basics

"The key to making great investments is to assume that the past is wrong, and to do something that's not part of the past, to do something entirely differently."
—Donald Valentine, Founder, Sequoia Capital[1]

A day in venture capitalist's (VC's) life is like that of an entrepreneur—venture capitalists have to pitch a thousand pitches to institutional investors to raise their fund and execute a predetermined plan. If the plan goes well, rewards are distributed; egos are stroked and champagne flows. The partners then go back and raise another fund. If the plan goes really well, which is rare, the partners retire, join local nonprofit boards, or spend time aboard a fancy yacht. A VC's profession is driven by three primary functions: raise the venture fund, find investment opportunities, and generate financial returns.

RAISE THE VENTURE FUND

VCs raise money from financial institutions (called limited partners, or LPs in industry jargon) such as pension funds, foundations, family offices, and high net-worth individuals. (See Figure 1.1.) Investment professionals or general partners (GPs) develop an investment strategy. Based upon this thesis, its timeliness and robustness, investors commit capital to the venture fund. Investors or limited partners seek a blend of strong investment expertise, a compelling investment strategy, and supportive market conditions. Target returns for investors are typically in the range of 20 percent or more on an annualized basis.

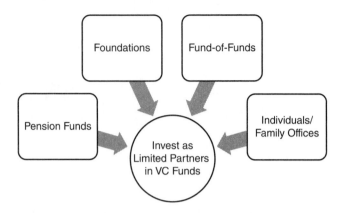

FIGURE 1.1   Limited partners (LPs) in a venture fund.

The fund-raising process can be long and arduous, taking as much as 18 months, and is often compared to an uphill crawl on broken glass. Many a VC is humbled in this process and can empathize better with entrepreneurs when financial institutions do not return their calls, do not ask them to pitch their fund strategy in seven minutes, offer no feedback, and go dark.

A venture fund is a close-ended fund. Once the target amount is raised or the fund is subscribed, no new investors are admitted. The life of such a fund is typically 10 years.[2] The fund is dissolved after the 10th year or when all portfolio investments have been liquidated.

Successful firms do not necessarily wait until liquidation of the previous fund; they raise their next fund as soon as the majority of the capital of the current fund is invested or designated as reserved for existing portfolio companies. Leading venture firms raise a fund every three to five years. Typically, funds are labeled with Roman numerals, such as ABC Ventures Fund I, II, III, IV, and so on. Roman numerals are a soft indicator of a venture fund's ability to survive and to generate returns across the various economic cycles. A firm's true measure of success is its ability to generate consistent returns over multiple economic cycles.

FIND THE RIGHT INVESTMENT OPPORTUNITIES

Once the fund-raising process is complete, VCs are under pressure to deploy the capital. During this investment period, as seen in Figure 1.2, any fund actively seeks Facebook-like opportunities to generate target returns. Investment periods can be three years to five years. In this period, the start-ups come in—the mating dance begins. The pitch deck, term sheets, valuations, and boards

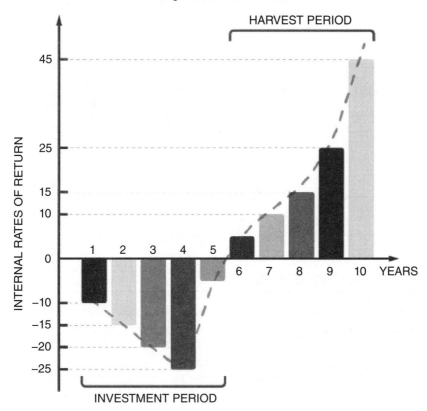

FIGURE 1.2 The J curve of venture fund investments.

are negotiated. A venture fund has to build a portfolio of companies that promise strong returns. Each portfolio company should demonstrate the potential to generate a return that equals a multiple of 8 to 10 times the capital invested. On a portfolio-wide basis, venture funds target a 20 percent annualized rate of return or a minimum of two to three times the invested capital.

A typical portfolio size for any fund can be 10 to 30 companies, based upon the sector and stage of investment. In technology sectors, the capital needs are lower, risks are deemed higher, and growth rate of companies is faster. In comparison, life science companies need larger amounts of capital and time to reach maturation. Hence, a technology venture fund may have as many as 30 companies in its portfolio, whereas a life sciences fund may have a dozen companies.

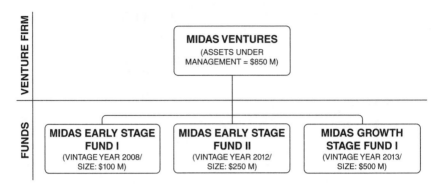

FIGURE 1.3   A successful venture firm raises several funds over time.

After the portfolio is constructed and the fund has been committed, a venture firm gets ready to raise another fund. (See Figure 1.3.)

GENERATE FINANCIAL RETURNS

As they say in the venture industry, any fool can write a check and make an investment; it is the returns that count. Fund returns, measured by internal rate of return (IRR) are a function of two factors: time and capital. The faster a portfolio company is sold, for as high an amount, the higher the IRR. This is often where things can get tricky. A speedy exit involves selling a start-up, and this can clash with the realities of market conditions and lofty entrepreneurial ideals.

Ideally, the exits should occur within three to four years from the date of investment, but only very few follow this hypercurve. Exit horizons are six to eight years, possibly longer based on market conditions. Delays create immense pressures on the fund managers as future fund raising can be jeopardized if the timing is not aligned. The graveyards are littered with plenty of start-ups, as venture capitalists fail fast and move on. If a start-up cannot achieve liftoff quickly, it often ends up in the "living dead" section of the portfolio.

Let us look at some attributes of the business of venture capital:

- **It's a risk–reward game:** The risks of a start-up investment are significant. Almost 80 percent of all investments fail. Venture fund portfolios are inherently risky, as the bets are on unproven technologies, shifting markets, and first-time CEOs. While entrepreneurs pitch start-up dreams, any VC can see the obvious upside—yet they are making a mental list of

TABLE 1.1 The Advantages of Shorter Holding Periods

Company	Capital Invested ($M)	Realized Value ($M)	Holding Period (years)	Gross IRR (%)
Company 1	1.0	5.0	2	123.6
Company 2	1.0	5.0	6	37.9

all the reasons why this start-up will fail. In other words, sizing up the risks and points of failure is essential.

Any venture fund's portfolio will eventually end up with a mix of a few huge successes, some middle of the pack, and some flameouts. Typical rule of thumb is that one-third of the portfolio generates 5 to 10 times the invested capital; one-third will generate 1 to 3 times or so. The final third of the portfolio will be relegated to the "experience" bucket as total losses. Yet at the point of investment, the expectation is to generate a 10-times return in three to five years.

- **Time is not your friend:** The longer a start-up takes to reach a critical value milestone, the more concerned investors become. After all, the one metric that venture funds and professionals live by, IRR, drops rapidly over the passage of time.

   Consider a simple example in Table 1.1. A VC invests $1,000,000 in a start-up in year 1 and generates $5,000,000 in year 3. The IRR yields a healthy 123.6 percent. Now, instead of year 3, assume that the exit occurs at the same value in year 6: the IRR drops down to 37.9 percent.

   Table 1.2 depicts how VCs demonstrate their performance to institutional investors. Notice that most portfolio companies are reduced to a single line statistic, measured primarily by multiple of capital invested and gross IRR.

TABLE 1.2 Fund Performance

Company	Capital Invested ($M)	Realized Value ($M)	Unrealized Value ($M)	Multiple of Capital Invested	Gross IRR (%)
Barn burner	2.0	180.0	—	90×	144
Middle of the road	1.5	0	$6.0	4×	NM
Also-ran	3.0	—	$1.5	0.5×	NM
Dry hole	2.5	0.1	—	—	NM

NM = Not meaningful.

- **Portfolio management:** All VCs love all their portfolio companies as they love their children, and they have many children, as many as 10 or more companies for any fund's portfolio. Even then, the relationship is a bit odd, like that of a friendly farmer feeding and nurturing a turkey for Thanksgiving slaughter. Josh Koppelman of First Round Ventures says, "You've heard the story of the chicken and the pig when it comes to making breakfast. Both the chicken and the pigs are involved, but the pig is fully committed. There's a little bit of truth to the fact. The VCs are the chickens in this relationship."[3]
- **VCs only make money *after* their investors make money:** A venture capitalist makes money in two ways: a base salary and a percentage of the profits (called "carry" or "carried interest"). Typically, funds make 20 percent of the profits generated on any exits. Some funds, thanks to their performance and brand, command as much as 30 percent. Most funds are structured so that the profits are distributed after they have covered *all* the previous losses in the fund. A successful firm raises multiple funds over time: those who cannot perform are relegated to the annals of history as unfortunate victims of Darwin's laws.

ROLES AND RESPONSIBILITIES

In any venture firm, the cast of characters includes the general partners (GPs, managing directors or managing GPs), vice presidents, principals, associates, and analysts. Investment professionals are responsible for making investment decisions, managing the portfolio, and generating returns. Associates and analysts often support the lead investors in due diligence or portfolio-monitoring activities and eventually rise up to leading investment decisions.

The primary responsibilities of the investment team differ along the lines of seniority. On any typical day, the GPs would juggle a number of activities: negotiating terms for investment opportunities, participating in boards of current portfolio companies, responding to any LP/investor requests, and putting out a few fires along the way. On the other end of the spectrum, an entry-level analyst is expected to source investment opportunities and screen these for further deliberations.

Roles such as venture partner and entrepreneur-in-residence positions are created to host proven entrepreneurs. Such professionals may source investments that fit within the fund's investment strategy or offer sector expertise to assist other partners in making decisions. Newer titles have evolved as fund operations have become more focused. For example, in larger funds, roles such as director of business development or head of deal sourcing have emerged.

The administrative team, also referred to as the back office, is responsible for the day-to-day operational and financial aspects. Operations teams manage activities such as payroll, taxes, and investor communications. Depending on the size of the fund, this team may include an office manager, chief financial officer, chief operating officer, and others such as legal counsel, marketing, and human resources.

The typical compensation package includes a salary, annual performance bonus, and a share of the profits, called "carry," or carried interests.

COMPENSATION

To better understand the compensation and financial economics, take the example of a $100 million fund. VCs are compensated by two methods: (1) management fees and (b) share of profits called carried interests or carry.

Investors pay an annual management fee, typically 2 to 2.5 percent of the committed capital per year. The investors also keep 80 percent of the profits, and the fund managers take home 20 percent. The carry model of one-fifth profits evolved from the time of the Phoenicians (1200 A.D.), who commanded 20 percent of profits earned from trade and shipping merchandise.[4]

Thus, for a $100 million fund, annual fees of 2 percent yield $2 million each year. The fees provide for the day-to-day operations of the firm and are used to pay for salaries, travel, leases, and legal expenses. The compensation packages are determined by the professional's responsibilities and experience. One of the perks of being a VC in Silicon Valley includes the privilege of not getting your cars towed. (See Figure 1.4.)

The primary expenses in any fund are salaries. The majority of this budget is allocated to investment professionals (general partners and members of the team, which could include associates and analysts) and the rest of the world (comptroller, operations, and back office). The budget also includes fees (legal, audit, and in some cases, specialized due diligence), travel, and miscellaneous operating expenses.

The typical compensation package includes a salary, bonus, and a share of the profits, the carry. The compensation varies by size of the fund; thus, in a $20 million fund, the scales may differ as compared to a fund with $1 billion under management. For a $20 million fund, the average annual fee income is $400,000, and this is typically split between two professionals. Larger funds have the ability to pay packages as described in Table 1.3.

FIGURE 1.4   In Silicon Valley, the perks of being a VC.

TABLE 1.3   Typical Compensation ($000)

Title	Salary	Bonus	Carry	Total
Managing GP	700	350	101	1,151
Partner	350	130	20	500
Principal	206	75	6	287
Venture partner	185	40	12	237
Analyst	100	10	0	110

Compensation is determined by the size of the fund.

TABLE 1.4 Sample Carry and Vesting Schedule

	Carry	Y1	Y2	Y3	Y4	Y5	Y6–Y10
Managing director 1	8%	20%	15%	15%	15%	15%	20%
Managing director 2	7%	20%	15%	15%	15%	15%	20%
Principals, associates, and staff	5%	20%	20%	20%	20%	20%	

Carried Interests

Carried interests, or carry split, can occur on the basis of experience and performance. In the example presented in the Table 1.4, carry is determined by roles and responsibilities. The vesting schedule is often spread out over (1) the investment period, or the first five years, and (2) the harvesting period, or years 6 through years 10, when the portfolio is being divested. To keep professionals engaged, carry is often released at the end of the life of the fund.

Pace of vesting is tied to investment period of the fund. Typical investment period is four to six years. Vesting schedules can match investment period on a straight-line method vesting yearly in equal shares. A 20 percent withholding released at final dissolution of the fund induces professionals to remain engaged throughout life of the fund.

Vesting clawback occurs when a partner gives up their carried interest for cause or disability per standard industry practices.

COMMUNISM, CAPITALISM, AND PARTNERSHIP OF EQUALS

Benchmark Capital is a partnership of equals. Matt Kohler, 31, Benchmark's newest member, gets an equal share of carry, as does Bob Kagle, who founded the firm 15 years ago. This philosophy fosters a team-oriented approach to the business—internal competition is eliminated. When this structure was announced by Benchmark, another venture capital industry veteran protested that such behavior is tantamount to "communism." Bruce Dunlevie of Benchmark promptly pointed out that the guy who said that "must have been a senior partner."[*]

At Bessemer Venture Partners, a balanced approach to financial rewards, performance feedback, and team spirit has fostered an environment where "not a single partner has left the firm."[**]

[*]Randall E. Stross, *eBoys: The First Inside Account of Venture Capitalists at Work* (New York: Crown Business, 2000), 89.

[**]Source: David Cowan, speaking at VCJ Alpha Conference (Half Moon Bay, CA, October 2013).

NOTES

1. "VC Titans Tom Perkins and Don Valentine Articulate What Makes a Good VC." Disrupt SF 2013 Conference Web site. Sept. 11, 2013. http://techcrunch.com/2013/09/11/vc-titans-tom-perkins-and-don-valentine-articulate-what-makes-a-good-vc.
2. While venture capital funds are structured as finite partnerships with a life span of 10 years, extensions of a year or two are standard, depending on the portfolio status.
3. Author interview, January 2012.
4. Lauren Fedor, "A History of Hedging," *Wall Street Journal*, June 12, 2010.

CHAPTER 2

Getting In

"A bit of advice
Given to a young Native American
At the time of his initiation:
As you go the way of life,
You will see a great chasm. Jump.
It is not as wide as you think."

—Joseph Campbell

When Jan Garfinkle decided to be a venture capitalist (VC), she polished her resume and approached several early-stage venture funds. Every fund turned her down. Garfinkle had spent 20 years in various operational capacities and had cut her teeth primarily at two venture-backed cardiovascular device companies. A large publicly traded company acquired both these companies, leaving Garfinkle a bit richer, wiser, and hungrier. She joined these start-ups after the initial idea had been vetted and the strategic direction of the company was being crystallized.

Early in her career, Garfinkle joined Advanced Cardiovascular Systems (ACS) as an associate product manager; the company was seen as the forerunner in over-the-wire angioplasty—a technique that reopens narrowed or blocked arteries in the heart (coronary arteries) without major surgery. The founder of the company, John Simpson, once remarked, "When we started the company, there was no interventional cardiology device sector."[1] C. Richard Kramlich, founder of New Enterprise Associates (NEA), one of the world's leading venture capital firms with over $10 billion under management today, had then invested in Advanced Cardiovascular Systems. Kramlich once said of ACS, "The procedure was entirely noninvasive . . . the body didn't have to go through the trauma it once had to endure."[2]

At Advanced Cardiovascular Systems, Garfinkle spent six years in marketing and sales of angioplasty systems. When Eli Lilly came knocking and acquired the company, the foundation stone for Guidant Corporation was laid. "We were the largest single shareholder in [Advanced Cardiovascular Systems]. . . . The company did extremely well,"[3] Kramlich would say. That was more than 25 years ago, when Garfinkle was at the threshold of her career. To be in an NEA-backed start-up was certainly fortuitous for Garfinkle's career path.[4]

Like all good serial entrepreneurs, Garfinkle moved on to John Simpson's next company, Devices for Vascular Intervention. The same founder who had built Advanced Cardiovascular Systems was now leading the charge in the next wave of the cardiovascular sector. Devices for Vascular Intervention laid its bets on atherectomy—a procedure to remove plaque from arteries. Here, Garfinkle wrote the first business plan, and over the next six years, as director of marketing and clinical research, she dove deeply into the universe of regulatory trials and approvals. Again, Eli Lilly had been watching closely and came knocking at the door. These two companies acquired by Eli Lilly became the foundation for Guidant Corporation, which was eventually spun off by Eli Lilly as a separate company and listed as GDT on the New York Stock Exchange (NYSE). Boston Scientific acquired Guidant in 2006 for $27.2 billion. At that time, the vascular intervention business was valued at $4.1 billion.[5]

When venture firms turned her down time and again, Garfinkle decided to do what any entrepreneur does—never take no for an answer! She decided to raise her own fund and launched Arboretum Ventures, a fund focused on early-stage health care and medical device companies. Having lived close to Nichols Arboretum in Ann Arbor, and with her own DNA of a nurturing type, she found the name to be the appropriate encapsulation of her philosophies and style.

Like Garfinkle, John Hummer, cofounder of Hummer Winblad, interviewed at five venture firms. "All five turned me down—on the same day," reminisces Hummer with a smug smile. He went on to start his own fund. "I climbed in from the window, as most do to get in this business of venture capital," comments the towering Hummer, who once was a professional basketball player.

Most venture professionals agree that there is no straight path into the business of venture capital. You have to climb in from the window, if that's what it takes! Jan Garfinkle and John Hummer were able to raise their own funds; for others, the starting point is often at an entry-level position.

ENTRY-LEVEL POSITIONS: ANALYSTS AND ASSOCIATES

Daniel Axelsen is an associate with New Enterprise Associates, one of the leading venture firms on Sand Hill Road. After spending two years in the investment banking industry, he moved to NEA, where he is focused on enterprise software investments. "Having worked on some major acquisitions, such as 3PAR's acquisition by HP, I acquired a strong set of skills in industry analysis and financial modeling," he says. Axelsen has honed his expertise further to seek investment opportunities in evolving markets. He has dived into the early-stage universe and speaks fluently on trends such as cloud computing, security, and bitcoin. "I was stunned to see how hard working most partners are at our firm," he says. To newcomers seeking to dip their toe in venture capital, he says, "You have to prepare for a set of radically different tasks each day. Don't let anyone tell you this is easy. And you learn quickly to not take the first opportunity that walks in the door, but rather analyze the universe for the best."

Getting into a Sand Hill Road firm takes a bit of luck, experience, and skills; Axelsen was able to score a position with a top tier venture firm. Yet for others, the challenges of getting in can be significantly higher.

Take the example of a pre-MBA analyst position posted at Bessemer Venture Partners, one of the longest-standing venture capital firms in the country (the firm started in 1911). More than 650 resumes, 42 first-round interviews, and 7 second-round interviews later, one offer was made. That's about 0.15 percent odds for an entry-level position! Such odds are daunting for any aspirant. Yet other positions on LinkedIn attract a large number of applicants, as many as 300 for each position. Figures 2.1 and 2.2 show samplings of demand for positions where as many as 300 to 700 applications are received.

FIGURE 2.1 Over 300 applications were received for investment professional position at Omidyar Network, an impact investment fund.

FIGURE 2.2 Over 700 applications were received for a private equity consultant role at Kurt Salmon consulting firm.

A TYPICAL VENTURE CAPITALIST'S (VC'S) RESPONSIBILITIES

A typical position description for venture practitioner would read as follows:

Key Tasks and Responsibilities: Participate in and contribute to all aspects of the investment process with responsibility for all quantitative and qualitative analysis of portfolio companies and funds.

Analysis: Qualitatively and quantitatively evaluate potential transactions, including performing detailed sector and company research and analysis. Conduct due diligence and assist with deal execution and transaction management. Carry out portfolio company analysis, including valuations and financial modeling. Prepare materials for the investment committee and other internal meetings. Interact with external consultants and advisers as required regarding analysis. Assist with closing administration.

Structuring and Execution: Participate in the development of appropriate deal structures in close liaison with legal team. Work with the legal team to prepare and coordinate the execution of agreements, offer letters, purchase agreements, and other legal and transaction documentation.

Postinvestment Monitoring: Familiarity with board member roles and corporate governance. Keep up-to-date on portfolio performance and address any specific requests for action or approval. Prepare returns forecasts, commentary, and other investment information for limited partners meetings.

Deal Sourcing, Marketing, and Fund-Raising: Conduct desk research for marketing, deal sourcing, and fund-raising. Build strong relationships with GPs/investors/consultants/advisers. Undertake warm/hot calling and cold calling (all usually as part of a team focused on a specific geographic area, industrial sector, or transaction type).

Skills: Solid knowledge of relevant (health care, energy, technology) sector. Transactional experience and analytical abilities. Advanced financial, business modeling, and writing skills.

Competencies: Results driven, ambitious, and highly motivated. Strategic and commercial acumen. An entrepreneurial approach, initiative and adaptability. Team player with a strong work ethic. Well informed on market trends and key players. Excellent networking skills.

Brant Moxley, managing director at Pinnacle Group International, an executive recruiting firm that focuses on private equity and venture capital career opportunities, says, "The demand is staggering—there are ten times the number of applicants for every job opening in the venture capital arena. Strong operating experience, demonstrated technical and financial skills, or experience in the investment banking business may also be a badge of honor at the entry level. What I find fascinating is while everyone wants to get in the business of venture capital, not many understand what it takes to stay in the business."

A pre-MBA position is, by design, established for two years. "Ninety percent of the time, these positions are not partner tracks. At best, an analyst would stay with the firm for three years, instead of the usual two," declares Moxley. C. Richard Kramlich of NEA once remarked, "Below the surface there's a huge amount of turnover."[6]

Bessemer has had six full-time analysts, and five have been involved in entrepreneurship in one way or another. Sarah Tavel of Bessemer writes, "People who do tend to rise to the top during the selection process do so because of their passion not just for venture capital, but for the entire ecosystem."[7]

When Bill Gurley graduated, he wanted to be a VC. He went to New York for the first time in his life to beg for meetings with VCs and was told "Don't even think about it, kid. Go work for 20 years, and then come back." Gurley went on to become one of the biggest sell-side analysts on Wall Street, quickly narrowing his focus to "this thing called the Internet, which no one knew anything about at the time." Microsoft founder Bill Gates recommended Gurley for his first venture job with Hummer Winblad. Gurley jumped at the opportunity, and said yes before even hearing the entire offer.[8]

John Doerr of Kleiner Perkins Caufield & Byers (KPCB), once remarked, "I cold-called Silicon Valley's venture groups, hoping to apprentice myself to one."[9] His cold-calling efforts did not get him a job at KPCB, but eventually, after five years at Intel, Doerr would land at this firm. Brooks Byers, who had asked Doerr to get some experience, famously invited him for a 5:30 A.M. jog to see how motivated he was. Doerr was at the track the next morning and landed the role.

Like Doerr, Robert Nelsen chased Brooks too, but found his calling elsewhere. "I remember cold-calling Brook Byers, founder of Kleiner Perkins Caufield & Byers about a hundred times. . . . I was always interested in venture capital," says Nelsen. Nelsen went on to be the cofounder of ARCH Venture Partners, which has now grown to manage $1.5 billion in assets. In his 20-year investment career, Nelsen has led nine companies to valuations of $1 billion or more. "Venture capital was my first career choice. I got a guide—this *Pratt's Guide to Venture Capital Sources*—to find out about this business," he says. In his first year of business school, Nelsen read about the launch of ARCH and approached the founder, Steve Lazarus.

"I told Steve I would work for him for free." Nelsen started with ARCH as soon as he finished college.[10]

"Back in the 1980s, I heard once that all venture capitalists operated from 3000 Sand Hill Road," says David Cowan. The ultimate Mecca of any wannabe VC, Sand Hill Road is a small strip that houses venerable names in the venture business: Kleiner Perkins Caufield & Byers, New Enterprise Associates (NEA), Sequoia, Draper Fisher Jurvetson (DFJ), Battery Ventures, and Canaan Partners. Cowan who had a brief two-year stint at Oracle, was eager to explore possibilities in the venture universe. One fine afternoon he drove to Sand Hill Road and walked unannounced into one of the venture firm's offices. The lady at the front desk was firm: "No, we don't have any openings." But Cowan persisted. "I am sure you know a few firms who would be looking." The lady pulled out a copy of the *Western Association of Venture Capitalists* directory and circled a few names. "I wrote letters to five firms. Two of the five offered me a position," recalls Cowan, who has been with Bessemer Venture Partners for more than 20 years.

Cold-calling a venture capital firm rarely works—especially in the modern day. "I don't think that approach will work today—the business is much more complex and competitive," warns Cowan.[11] What may work is likely a Web presence. Famously, Union Square Ventures recruited a two-year rotational analyst position by not seeking resumes but asking for "Web presence." Union Square defined Web presence as "anything accessible via a URL. It could be a blog, a social networking profile, a portfolio, a company, a social bookmarking archive. . . . It is whatever you think best represents who you are online."[12]

At the entry-level position, differentiators can be few and competition fierce. A Web presence can be a head start in building your path into a venture career.

INTERNSHIPS AND CAMPUS RECRUITMENT

Many venture firms offer internships but rarely conduct campus recruitment drives. Rajeev Batra, partner at the Mayfield Fund, says, "When I was finishing up my MBA at Harvard, I was approached by a few venture firms. I did not even realize I was being interviewed till we met for the third time." Batra had a few entrepreneurial gigs; a Ph.D. in electrical engineering demonstrated his domain knowledge. "In my B-school [business school] essay, I had written that eventually, I wanted to be a venture capitalist when I grow up," he says.[13]

Candidates often underestimate the power of internship opportunities. Many practitioners would be open to a thoughtful e-mail or a call along the lines of "Hi, I am graduating next year and wanted to explore a summer internship. I have studied your investment thesis and have identified

AN BFHUIL SE FLUIC, AMACH?

Terry McGuire, a VC of 25 years and chairman emeritus of National Venture Capital Association, is the cofounder of Polaris Ventures, a firm that manages $3 billion and has invested in more than 100 companies.

After college, he spent a year in Ireland and learned to speak Gaelic. Coincidentally, at his first job interview, the interviewer spoke fluent Gaelic. He muttered, "An bfhuil se fluic, amach?", which is Gaelic for "Is it wet outside?" McGuire promptly responded in Gaelic. The two hit it off, and McGuire landed the job.*

But was it just a stroke of luck? It certainly helped that McGuire was the president of the Harvard Business School Venture Capital Club. "It's a combination of training, the network, and opportunity that presented itself," says McGuire.

McGuire went on to start Polaris Ventures after a seven-year stint at a Chicago-based venture firm.

---

* *Source:* Steve Arnold, Jonathan Flint, and Terrance McGuire, "Polaris Venture Partners," in *Done Deals—Venture Capitalists Tell Their Stories*, ed. Udayan Gupta (Boston: Harvard Business School Press, 2000), 281.

a few opportunities that may be of interest. Let me know if I can come by and discuss these." That kind of an opening gambit is bound to get a response.

MIDLEVEL POSITIONS: PRINCIPALS AND MDS

For experienced professionals, the Kauffman Fellows Program—a two-year hands-on training program designed by the VCs for the VCs—can be a launch pad. Bryan Roberts, a partner at Venrock, found his mentor and career in venture capital thanks to the Kauffman Fellows Program. "I liked science and business and wanted to explore the intersection of these two fields—venture capital seemed interesting. I called HBS's [Harvard Business School's] career office as I was finishing my Ph.D. in chemical biology, and I was told about the Kauffman Fellows Program." Roberts was invited for a matchmaking event where 30 finalists were competing for 10 opportunities. "Tony Evnin, who started health care investing at Venrock over three decades ago and one of the first investors in the arena, showed up there and at the end of the day, offered me a job," recalls Roberts. "I didn't know anything then. . . . I was really lucky that I landed with a good person and a good firm."[14] Evnin may have picked his protégé well. Of the first four investments led by Roberts, three companies went public and the fourth was acquired for $1.1 billion.

"A good mentor in this business can be a huge asset," advises Brant Moxley. "But realize that in a classic venture firm, the senior partners do not have all the time to mentor juniors. A junior is like a remora—they just have to find the right feeding ground," he adds with a chuckle.[15] Moxley manages placements for a number of venture funds, funds of funds, and related asset classes. "It's okay to be a remora," he says.[16]

Punit Chiniwalla pursued the coveted Kauffman Fellows Program, which eventually helped him land smack in the center of the hypercompetitive venture universe of Sand Hill Road. Chiniwalla had made his first investment at a university venture fund, even before he had graduated from business school. This experience, combined with a Ph.D., enabled Chiniwalla to land in the Kauffman Fellows Program. The much-sought-after program, whose mission is to "identify, develop, and network emerging global leaders in venture capital,"[17] is a near-guaranteed entry ticket into the world of venture capital.

While working full-time at a venture capital firm, each Kauffman Fellow engages in a 24-month hands-on apprenticeship that includes professional coaching in seven modules, mentoring by seasoned venture partners, and triennial sessions of industry and leadership curriculum. The program claims that the fellowship's value can be measured along three axes of investing: apprenticeship, leadership development, and being a part of a global network.

Each year, about 20 to 30 fellows are picked from a pool of about 200 applicants. The application process is a two-step dance, which is rigorous by any measure. The written application and the interview—reviewers include leading VCs—look for a prior track record of accomplishments that are significant. Entrepreneurial background trumps operational background; in fact, it trumps everything else.

At the interview stage, the universe of 200 applicants narrows down by about a third. Candidates fly in to one of the two hot spots, Silicon Valley or Boston, and are grilled by panels of four to five VCs. The next stage is the finalist stage, where candidates who cross the finish line are then matched with firms who are seeking to bring on fresh talent. If any firm does not pick up a finalist, the process ends. For those selected, the sponsor venture capital firm pays the $60,000 tuition in addition to the salary for the two-year internship. These would-be Fellows are assigned mentors from established venture firms who, over the course of a two-year period, will provide insights and formal training into the art and science of venture investing.

Some of the common characteristics of Fellows include "a bias toward entrepreneurs; deep scientific, technology, or business domain expertise; an aspiration to contribute to the building of companies, either as an investor or as a start-up leader; an appetite for risk, ambiguity, and unstructured environments; and humility, empathy, a sense of service, and unquestioned integrity."[18]

INTERVIEWING FOR YOUR VC POSITION

Preparation:

- Research the venture firm's profile. Understand the sector and stage of investments, assets under management, and its latest fund size.
- Look up the key portfolio companies, and map their progress. Have these companies signed up strategic partnerships? Have they raised follow-on rounds of capital?
- Research any major exits.
- Read the founders' and senior partners' blogs. Understand their mind-set and philosophies well.

Examples of questions you can ask the venture firm:

1. What is the fund's investment strategy?
   - Of course, you have done your homework, checked out the Web sites and online data sources. You know the firm's history and the background of the founders.
   - Research one or two specific investments, and assess the competitive universe of similar investments made by other venture firms. Dive into the investment rationale and find out why this opportunity was chosen over others.
   - Ask how the fund's investment strategy has evolved over time. What challenges has the fund faced, if any, in sourcing opportunities? In raising capital?
   - Find out the life cycle of the current fund, that is, recently raised, partly invested, and with three more years to go in the investment cycle. All venture funds have a three- to five-year investment period from the time the fund is raised. Thus, depending on the timing of your entry, you could be involved in making investments, managing the portfolio, or preparing for the next fund raise.

(Continued)

INTERVIEWING FOR YOUR VC POSITION: (*Continued*)

2. What is a typical day at the firm? To whom would I report, and what self-development opportunities exist for an entry-level person?
   ■ Look for opportunities where you will participate in all facets of the business.
3. Is this a collaborative environment or a field of cowboys who thrive going solo? How do the team members collaborate with each other, especially when the portfolio companies are in trouble? When has the firm let go of any staff and why?
   ■ Look for troubling situations and how were these handled by the internal team: be prepared to get smooth talked. You will rarely hear honest statements like "We screwed up on that investment" or the GP "screams his head off and throws things all around, muttering obscenities." Talk to the industry peers and CEOs of portfolio companies, if you can, to get a true sense of the culture of the firm.
   ■ Can you see yourself having fun with this team? A beer on Friday night?
4. How will my performance be measured? Will we have clear milestones established? Will I be able to measure my own progress?
5. At what point will I be eligible to be on a partner track? Often the position description will state if it's a partner-track position.

HONING INVESTMENT EXPERTISE WITHIN ALLIED FIELDS

Getting in to a top-tier venture fund is tough. Yet practitioners have found ways to meet their career goals by starting in an allied universe. These pathways are not as competitive, and each one has its pros and cons. As they say, there is no straight path into venture capital.

Corporate Venture Capital and Angel Networks

About 6 to 8 percent of all venture capital investments in United States come from corporate venture capitalists (CVCs). Besides a financial return, corporations invest in start-ups to gain a view of the newest new thing. Corporate venture capital funds are sponsored by the mother ships to help generate financial returns. Allied objectives for CVCs include identifying novel technologies to enhance revenue streams and amplify a corporation's competitive position. Other corporate objectives include validation of new market segments, as well as leveraging relationships between the corporate venture capital portfolio and corporate business units. About 60 percent of corporations invest in venture funds as LPs, and 90 percent of CVCs invest directly in start-ups. Getting in a corporate venture capital firm of repute such as Google Ventures or Intel Capital can be a strong starting point for practitioners. Angel networks also offer excellent opportunities to entry-level candidates and are forgiving playgrounds where skills can be honed.

Institutional Investors

Opportunities in institutional investor universe can be a starting point. Pension funds—both private and public—fund of funds, university endowments, foundations, and insurance companies have to deploy assets in the universe of venture funds. Family offices also offer a strong starting point for practitioners. These are addressed in greater detail in Chapter 4.

Service Firms and Media

Investment banking firms, law firms and marketing firms have seen talent transition in to venture capital. Others who have leapt into the venture world include technology reporters.

From Entrepreneur to VC

The recent wave of investors has come from a demonstrated entrepreneurial background. Having started a company, raised capital, and generated an exit eminently qualifies you to serve other entrepreneurs well. But that does not guarantee success.

Table 2.1 illustrates the pros and cons of each pathway.

TABLE 2.1 Entry Points in Venture Capital

Pathway	Opportunities	Challenges
Entrepreneurial/ start-ups	Engage with entrepreneurs. Ability to understand value drivers, technology challenges, and team dynamics.	Impatience with other portfolio entrepreneurs. Temptation to jump in and drive when companies underperform. Sector expertise can be narrow. Pace can be too slow. As one entrepreneur turned VC remarked, "As a CEO, I was used to six emergencies before 9 A.M. As a VC, I am getting lazy."

(Continued)

TABLE 2.1 (*Continued*)

Pathway	Opportunities	Challenges
Corporate venture capital/ angel networks	Develop investment experience, sharpen due diligence abilities, and establish track record of investments.	Differing agendas and conflicts. Investment activities may be limited by corporate agenda or angel interests. Speed of decision making can be a concern.
Institutional investors	Ability to understand the LP/investor perspectives. Build relationships and have knowledge of new funds. Ability to time the entry.	Risk of being perceived as an asset manager versus an investor. Number of investments may be limited. Process is often slow and involves buy-in from various stakeholders.
Service providers	Ability to function as a resource to entrepreneurs.	Lack of domain expertise, of deeper understanding of financial dynamics.

SENIOR PARTNER VERSUS JUNIOR ASSOCIATE

Often, those at a junior level may wonder if entrepreneurs will engage with them. The debate is rife with opinions of a thousand bloggers: entrepreneurs should only talk to those professionals who can make decisions. While various blogs emphasize the important attributes of the investor's stature, experience, decision-making abilities, or getting the deal done, to get to the decision makers, the starting point is often a junior person.

Paul Graham of Y Combinator writes, "Junior persons scour the Web looking for start-ups their bosses could invest in. The junior people will tend to seem very positive about your company. They're not pretending; they want to believe you're a hot prospect, because it would be a huge coup for them if their firm invested in a company they discovered. Don't be misled by this optimism. It's the partners who decide, and they view things with a colder eye."[19] Peter Thiel, investor and entrepreneur points out that the junior person is often an advantageous starting point for entrepreneurs.

> *Tactically, the first thing to do is find someone who does need to make investments. That can mean finding a senior associate or a principal for your first pitch, not a senior partner. This contravenes the conventional*

wisdom that holds that you should not to pitch junior people. ("Don't pitch someone who can't write a check themselves.") That wisdom is wrong. Junior people will give entrepreneurs a fair shake because they need good deals to their name. If they don't find those deals, they won't become senior, and they very much want to become senior. So seek these people out: –they are motivated in a way more seasoned VCs are not. . . . No senior VC needs to do an investment. You should never forget that. Any senior VC that you're talking to is already wealthy and has many famous deals to show for it. Your company is probably not going to make a material difference to him and but does present a significant chance of adding to his workload and failure rate; there will therefore be a certain amount of inertia against the deal . . . on average most deals don't pan out but do take time.[20]

In short, a junior person's role in a firm cannot be underestimated, as he or she is often the first point of contact with an entrepreneur.

WHAT ABOUT LUCK?

For a few chosen practitioners, the entry into venture capital was not an up-hill crawl or a series of grueling interviews. It was a calling—a blaring siren. Bryce Roberts was planning to go to law school and in the interim decided to start a ski company in Jackson Hole, Wyoming. "One of my neighbors, a venture capitalist, invited me to sit in on pitch meetings and offer feedback," he says. Roberts went on to be the cofounder of O'Reilly Alphatec Ventures, which has led investments in a number of prominent technology start-ups.

Jack Ahrens, cofounder of TGap Ventures, has been in the venture business for over 30 years. While he was employed at a bank in Illinois, one afternoon he stumbled upon an internal memo that suggested his department was being shut down. "I was irritated and told my boss I would be leaving." His boss promptly jumped in: "We have a venture capital arm—what if we made you the president and gave you a raise?" "I took it—I barely knew what the heck venture capital was, but here I am some three decades later," says Ahrens. In these three decades, Ahrens has led over 35 successful exits, including 20 IPOs. Interestingly, neither Roberts nor Ahrens has the desire to grow his fund size beyond what is manageable. My own observation is that if they wished, they could easily raise a lot more capital and increase their fund size, but so far they have curbed any such inflated ambitions. For those who followed their calling, the ability to find strong investment opportunities, generate returns, and stay on the growth trajectory is not difficult.

There is no way of knowing whether you are a natural, as Sanford Bernstein puts it. Bernstein, founder of the investment banking firm Robertson Stephens, had invested in venture funds for 20 years. "Some do it, some can't, and like with athletes, there is no way of telling 'till they take the field," he once remarked.[21]

To prove they are good athletes, VCs need to pick good investment opportunities. John Doerr used to say that training a new VC was not unlike preparing a fighter pilot for battle. It takes six to eight years, and you should be prepared for losses of about $20 million.[22] Yet in its first fund, HummerWinblad invested in 17 companies, of which 16 yielded a positive return. Jan Garfinkle's Arboretum Ventures Fund I had two exits in quick succession that yielded strong returns—comfortably landing the fund in the top quartile.

It does help to have a reasonable measure of luck on your side. When Jan Garfinkle decided to raise her first fund, Arboretum Ventures, she met a leading LP over Chinese food to discuss her game plan. The LP committed, and the fortune cookie, now pasted in Garfinkle journal, said, "You will soon get something you've always wanted."

David Cowan of Bessemer Venture Partners adds it all up nicely: "The one most important quality of a successful venture capitalist is *luck.*"[23]

NOTES

1. David Cassak, "John Simpson: Reluctant Entrepreneur," *In Vivo: The Business & Medicine Report* 21, no. 3 (April 2003), accessed January 13, 2011, www.denovovc.com/press/denovo-simpson.pdf.
2. Peter J. Tanous, *Investment Visionaries: Lessons in Creating Wealth from the World's Greatest Risk Takers* (Upper Saddle River, NJ: Prentice Hall, 2003), 69.
3. C. Richard Kramlich, "Venture Capital Greats: A Conversation with C. Richard Kramlich," interview by Mauree Jane Perry, 2006, accessed January 13, 2011, http://digitalassets.lib.berkeley.edu/roho/ucb/text/kramlich_dick_donated.pdf.
4. NEA was then a mere $125 million fund. Today, NEA's committed capital exceeds $11 billion.
5. "Boston Scientific Announces Offer to Acquire Guidant at $80 per Share," news release, http://bostonscientific.mediaroom.com/index.php?s=43&item=376.
6. Gary Rivlin, "So You Want to Be a Venture Capitalist," *New York Times*, May 22, 2005, accessed January 13, 2011, www.nytimes.com/2005/05/22/business/yourmoney/22venture.html.

7. Sarah Tavel, Adenturista blog, accessed on July 3, 2010, www.adventurista.com/2008/04/vc-pre-mba-hiring.html.

8. Michael Carney, "At Benchmark, Good Judgment Comes from Experience, Which Comes from Bad Judgment," July 26, 2013, Pando daily Web site, http://pandodaily.com/2013/07/26/at-benchmark-good-judgment-comes-from-experience-which-comes-from-bad-judgement/.

9. John Doerr, "Kleiner Perkins Caufield & Byers," in *Done Deals—Venture Capitalists Tell Their Stories*, ed. Udayan Gupta (Boston: Harvard Business School Press, 2000), 374.

10. Robert Nelsen (ARCH Venture Partners) in discussions with the author, December 2010.

11. David Cowan (Bessemer Venture Partners) in discussions with the author, December 2010.

12. Union Square Ventures, "We're Hiring," accessed November 23, 2010, unionsquareventures.com/2008/02/were-hiring.php.

13. Rajeev Batra (Mayfield Fund) in discussions with the author, December 2010.

14. Bryan Roberts (Venrock) in discussions with the author, December 2010.

15. A remora, also called a suckerfish, grows to about three feet in length. Using its suction cups, it attaches itself to a larger fish, typically a shark. The relationship, termed as *commensalism*, is a one-way benefit to the remora with no distinct advantage to the shark. The remora hitches a ride and feeds off the shark's leftovers. In fact, there is a controversy as to whether a remora's diet is primarily leftover fragments or its host's feces.

16. Brant Moxley (Pinnacle Group) in discussions with the author, July 2010.

17. Punit Chiniwalla in discussions with the author, September 2010.

18. Society of Kauffman Fellows, "Frequently Asked Questions," accessed January 13, 2011, www.kauffmanfellows.org/faq.aspx.

19. Source: http://paulgraham.com/startupfunding.html

20. Blake Masters, "Class 8 Notes Essay—The Pitch," May 2, 2012, http://blakemasters.com/post/22271192791/peter-thiels-cs183-startup-class-8-notes-essay.

21. Gary Rivlin, "So You Want to Be a Venture Capitalist."

22. Ibid.

23. Seth Levine's VC Adventure blog, "How to Become a Venture Capitalist," accessed on November 23, 2010, http://www.sethlevine.com/wp/2005/05/how-to-become-a-venture-capitalist.

CHAPTER 3

Building Your Career as a Venture Capitalist

"In California, you need a license to drive a car or buy a gun, but not to be a venture capitalist."[1]
—Marc Andreessen, cofounder, Andreessen Horowitz

There are no barriers to entry, indeed, to get into the business of venture capital at all.

As the industry evolved in the late 1970s, most venture professionals came from technology, business development, finance, and investment banking backgrounds. Don Valentine, founder of Sequoia Capital, started his career in the semiconductor industry. Tom Perkins, founder of Kleiner Perkins Caufield & Byers (KPCB), started at Hewlett Packard as the administrative head of its research department. In recent times, venture capitalists (VCs) have come from varied backgrounds; for instance, Sir Michael Moritz, chairman of Sequoia, was a journalist with *Time* magazine. David Cowan of Bessemer Venture Partners started after he received his M.B.A. degree, and he has been making successful investments for two decades. Entrepreneurs like Marc Andreessen, Ben Horowitz, Brad Feld, and Peter Thiel went on to launch venture funds after the maturation of their own start-ups.

An entrepreneurial background and operational expertise qualifies a practitioner to serve the portfolio company better than those who do not. But that's not necessarily an indicator of success. Fred Wilson of Union Square Ventures has no entrepreneurial background. He has invested in some of the leading technology start-ups and has enjoyed stellar returns.

INTELLECTUAL STIMULATION AND FINANCIAL RETURNS

Leading venture capitalists agree that they were attracted to the industry for intellectual stimulation, financial gain, freedom/autonomy, and the thrill of building companies.[2]

Intellectual Stimulation

A career in venture capital investing is "the most fun you can have with your clothes on," says Deepak Kamra, of Canaan Partners.[3] A day in the life of a VC is full of stimulating conversations with entrepreneurs who are changing the world. At various points in their start-up journey, entrepreneurs seek investors to validate their concepts. Often, seasoned entrepreneurs will drag an investor out for coffee to test their assumptions. Amid all these caffeine-laden dreams, the investor is exposed to a steep learning curve of technological changes, the shifting sands of market dynamics, sources of opportunity, and competitive constraints. For those who thrive on comfort in ambiguity, a rapid pace, head-butting with type A entrepreneurs, and "those crazy ones," the career path of venture capital offers it all. Elizabeth "Beezer" Clarkson, managing director of SAP Ventures, says, "We forget how unusual this career is. We are privileged. Other sectors seem pale in comparison when we look at the range of energy and creativity that flows to us. It can be addictive."

For those seeking financial gain primarily, this path may not be optimal, at least in the short run. Venture capital is an "antifragile" career with fundamental asymmetry. In his book *Antifragile*, author Nicholas Naseem Taleb defines asymmetry to be when you have more upside than downside and tend to gain from volatility, randomness, stressors, errors, time, and uncertainty. Venture capitalists thrive on information asymmetry. They have a ringside view of the technological future, and the companies they have funded are often the ones to become the next-generation behemoths. Financial gains are expected as a by-product of value creation, but only after asymmetry is identified and realized within a short span of five to seven years.

Mentor Capitalists

Those who have had a successful entrepreneurial journey often see the venture as a pathway of imparting their lessons to the next generation. "At a certain point in your career, it is more satisfying to help entrepreneurs than to be one," says Marc Andreessen, cofounder of Andreessen Horowitz.[4] Scott Weiss joined Andreessen Horowitz after selling his company, IronPort Systems, to Cisco. "Being a venture capitalist gives me the opportunity to mentor and offer direction to the entrepreneurs. They trust my judgment because I have been down this path before," he points out. Scott built IronPort Systems to $200 million revenues in the tough recessionary post-dot-com era and six years later sold it to Cisco for $800 million. His prior experiences at Microsoft and Hotmail helped shape his own entrepreneurial path. Several practitioners agreed that the VC career path allows them to live vicariously through supporting other entrepreneurs.

Small Part of Something Big

"See, venture capital is reducible to a few words. You have to be interested in managing change, and you have to recognize that change is *necessary*,"[5] says Donald T. Valentine, founder of Sequoia Capital. When a paradigm shift occurs in any technological ecosystem, it is more likely that a venture capital investor is stoking the entrepreneurial fire. Schumpeter described forces of creative destruction, where industries are decimated when innovative trends occur. On the other side, the forces of creative construction, entrepreneurs and venture capitalists, are at work. To be a part of creating of that new *new thing* can be immensely satisfying.

APTITUDES AND ATTITUDES OF SUCCESSFUL PRACTITIONERS

Successful practitioners are not necessarily great entrepreneurs or operators – rather, they are students of markets, are patient, and treat this as a team sport. Christopher Rizik, a former VC who now manages a fund of funds, says:[6]

A good VC has three qualities: First, have a good sense of the world around you and how it is changing. After all, we put money behind ideas that change the world—the demographic, technological—unfilled needs. You have to be open and curious to look out into the future.

The second quality is patience—nothing will be as fast as you want. A smart practitioner never panics or gives up when companies hit a bump. Those who are patient will not only profit but will ultimately succeed at the expense of those who panic. Patience should be married with intelligence—if you can no longer achieve the end game, it takes discipline to walk away and say, we are just not going to get there. Swallow hard and realize you just lost a few million.

Finally, the third quality is to be fair with one and all. What goes around, comes around—in the end, the best VCs are people who were fair, were smart and treated everyone well. People seldom want to work with those who are out only for themselves.

Ability to Pick the Right Investments

The ability to pick the right investments typically comes after making a lot of bad investments. It's like the quote: Good judgment comes from experience, and experience comes from bad judgment. "Good instinct, well-honed by experience, makes a good venture capitalist. The most difficult part is dealing with uncertainty,"[7] says C. Richard Kramlich, chairman and cofounder of New Enterprise Associates. Some attributes that define good practitioners include the following:

- *Market trends:* The foremost and primary criteria, a practitioner's ability to understand how markets are evolving and where investment opportunities lie, is the essence of this business. Arthur Schopenhauer once wrote, "Everyone takes the limits of his own vision for the limits of the world." Good practitioners are able to recognize their limits. Equally important is the ability to time the market. "The pen computing fiasco occurred in the 1990s—it was like the iPad era, yet 20 years to early. You had a battery life of 20 minutes, and a steam crank on the side," says Marc Andreessen.[8]
- *Management teams:* A practitioner is a good judge of human character and entrepreneurial abilities. "We see a lot of executives who have a vision. Our job is to decide if it really is a vision or a hallucination,"[9] said Frank Caufield, partner emeritus, Kleiner Perkins Caufield & Byers.
- *Judgment:* "A lot of good venture capitalists have 'situational awareness'— they can walk into just about any kind of meeting and, in about five minutes, figure out who's doing what to whom and exactly what the issues are, sort of cut through it and figure out what's going on. You can look at a given situation and project its trajectory reasonably well,"[10] says James R. Swartz, founder of Accel Partners. And good judgment comes with experience. "It really pays off to come into venture capital after you've had a fair amount of experience doing something else. I think it's a business that you're probably better off entering in your thirties and forties than you are entering it in your twenties, because you need to build a frame of reference by which to judge people and to judge opportunities and to be able to judge markets and what's going on in the economy,"[11] says Reid Dennis, founder, Institutional Venture Partners.
- *Speed:* "Having a great brand is a good start. Speed of decision making is equally important," says Jeff Clavier of SoftTech VC.[12]
- *Optimism:* "You have to believe that the world can change . . . be optimistic and at the same time, be realistic and guarded, not romantic,"[13]

says Terry McGuire, cofounder, Polaris Ventures, and emeritus chairman of National Venture Capital Association. "You've got to be a good listener. I find if the venture capitalist does all the talking, he doesn't learn very much about the people he's thinking about investing in. Very important to listen . . . and judge who looks and feels like they have the makings of making a real company. Eventually, it becomes instinct if you do it often enough," says Paul "Pete" Bancroft, former CEO of Bessemer Securities and former chair of National Venture Capital Association.[14]

VC = Value Creation

"I don't think there is a good predictor that just because someone has an operating or entrepreneurial background that they are going to be a good venture capitalist. Conversely, if you don't, it doesn't mean you are not going to be a good venture capitalist," Marc Andreessen, cofounder for the leading venture firm Andreessen Horowitz said, while speaking at a Stanford Entrepreneurship forum.[15] The partners at Andreessen Horowitz have deep entrepreneurial and operational experience. "Venture capitalists should guide companies based on real-world experience. If you had a good marketing job, that beats an MBA. An MBA is a little bit general for the venture business. The partners at our firm can say to entrepreneurs 'we've been where you're going' and really mean it,"[16] says William K. Bowes Jr., founder, US Venture Partners.

Having relevant real-world entrepreneurial experience qualifies an investor to understand the challenges of any start-up better. It's a necessary condition, but not a sufficient enough condition to be a successful venture capitalist. "Fred Wilson of Union Square Ventures does not have an operational bone in his body—yet he is so effective in helping companies," says Bijan Sabet, a venture capitalist with Spark Capital.[17]

The primary goal for any VC is to create value for their entrepreneurs and their investors. "We are in the business of helping a company achieve critical path milestones. Being able to determine what is critical path is a matter of survival: Our job is to be insanely rigorous about what the critical path is. A definitive characteristic about a venture capitalist is being analytical about these milestones,"[18] says James Bryer, Accel Partners, and former chair, National Venture Capital Association.

Successful VCs have an entrepreneurial mind-set, the ability to understand the basics of value creation. Yet, the background of some of the leading VCs demonstrates no clear pattern. You could have strong operational expertise. Or not.

CAN'T WE ALL AGREE WITH EACH OTHER?

Consider these two diametrically opposite views on being a VC:

"I think you become a venture capitalist by being a great entrepreneur. As a successful entrepreneur, you can better figure out how to serve entrepreneurs in their mission. So those folks in the business school who figured they, like roll out of the womb born as a venture capitalist, I don't think they're going to be great venture capitalists. I think they should go get a job at a high technology company or a start-up. And then see if they want to step back from where the real action is into the world I work in, which is much more indirect and supporting entrepreneurs."

—John Doerr, Kleiner Perkins Caufield & Byers (KPCB)*

"As I was finishing up my MBA, I was told, 'You don't have anything to bring to the table. The last thing a CEO wants is some snot-nosed MBA telling him how to run his business. So go get some real experience.' I had to reject the prescription and carve my own path. Operational experience is a short-term advantage. It helps a venture professional to assess and manage investment opportunities but only in their sectors of expertise."

—David Cowan, Bessemer Venture Partners, In disucssion with author, December 2010.

---

* Stanford University's Entrepreneurship Corner, John Doerr, "How to Be a Venture Capitalist," http://ecorner.stanford.edu/authorMaterialInfo.html?mid=1281 (accessed November 26, 2010).

David Cowan rejects the notion that even entrepreneurial experience is a prerequisite. "Entrepreneurs have expertise in certain domains. But in venture, domains shift all the time. And when exposed to any opportunity, those with operating expertise tend to try and fix things—that can, at times, be counterproductive," he says. Rightfully so; several practitioners who had very strong entrepreneurial backgrounds concurred that the hardest part for them was to transition from being a player to being a coach—to let go and let someone else run their own company. They get impatient and question the pace of execution or the direction. Entrepreneurial success for VCs, if not modulated, can translate to being a royal pain in the rear for portfolio company CEOs.

Gibson Myers, emeritus partner, Mayfield Fund, supports that view. "Some people are just operating people. It's a whole different world to go to work, make things happen. And those people don't transition to venture capital very well, because they want to operate. In venture capital, you're one or two steps removed from that, and you're advising. You have a relationship. You have a bunch of companies. You can't spend the time,

A 20-YEAR-OLD VC

For a 20-year-old student, Alex Banayan leads an unusually busy life. As an associate VC with Alsop-Louie Partners, he meets young entrepreneurs with start-up ideas looking for venture funding. So how did Banayan, who is a University of Southern California (USC) junior and not even old enough to take the finance course at his school, end up getting the job as an associate VC? To set some context, the success of Mark Zuckerberg and Facebook has lured venture capitalists to scout for 20-something, college-going entrepreneurs for the next big idea. Alsop-Louie Partners, a firm founded in 2006 and managing $150 million, wanted someone to track for them upcoming start-ups across Los Angeles. VCs prefer young connectors, as youth attracts youth better as compared to 40- to 50-something venture capitalists. Stewart Alsop, General Partner, says he hired Banayan because he saw something in the 20-year-old that was, to him, more important than tech expertise: hustle and self-confidence.

The group of five "student VCs," Banayan and four others, follow start-ups on campuses of MIT, Stanford, and USC. The firm groups these students into two categories, geeks and gadflies. Banayan is a born gadfly or someone who upsets the status quo by posing upsetting or novel questions. A year and a half after signing, he's still searching for the elusive first deal.

Banayan wants to change the world. "I hate when people call me *ambitious*," he says, speaking with Scott Cendrowski of Fortune magazine.* Life is not about a position, but a purpose. Jobs come and go, but if you stay true to your purpose, you'll find the true meaning of life." And this VC practices humility. "Being humble is a state of gratitude in which you acknowledge that all the opportunities available to you today are thanks to the tracks laid out by the people who came before you," he writes in TechCrunch.** Banayan, who describes himself as an underdog, doesn't drink and doesn't party because he wants to focus on his career. His larger vision is to create a community, something like the Khan Learning Academy, in which would-be entrepreneurs get advice from people who have already become successful.

---

* Fortune, http://money.cnn.com/2013/06/13/technology/alex-banayan-vc.pr
.fortune/index.html
**http://techcrunch.com/2012/06/10/how-i-became-a-19-year-old-associate-vc/

so some just don't like it for that reason, or don't make it as a venture capitalist."[19]

Michael Moritz of Sequoia Capital does not have either entrepreneurial or operational expertise. He was a business journalist with *Time* magazine and crossed paths with Don Valentine, founder of Sequoia while he was working on a book.

Generalist versus Specialist: Jack of All and Master of All

While there is no good predictor of what makes a good VC, some patterns are obvious. Those without substantial start-up or operating experience can be successful in the profession. Yet here are some more contradictory observations—generalist versus specialist—both from very successful VCs: "Back in the 70s when I started, you could be a generalist and be successful in this business. As the business has evolved over the past 50 years, it has become a lot more focused around certain sectors, and now you need to be an expert in a few areas that matter," says Frank Caufield of KPCB.[20]

While domain expertise may be good, it certainly is not of significant importance in the long run. Your performance eventually matters. "In my 20-year career as a venture capitalist, I have invested in all kinds of domains and companies. For long-term success in this business, you have to think more generally and push yourself out of your comfort zone. You should be willing to reinvent yourself," says David Cowan.

When Seth Levine is not managing his investments at the Foundry Group, he writes on his blog VC Adventure. He writes:

> The core of being a good VC is the ability to move from one thing to the next, often completely disconnected thing, quickly and without slowing down. Rare is the time when I sit down and spend a few hours doing something (anything) without interruption; so much so that I generally interrupt myself these days if I'm spending too much time on any one thing, but mostly because in any given day things just seem to come up constantly. With something like eight companies that I actively work with these interruptions are all over the map—I may be helping one company sell its business, another raise capital, another plan for a strategic offsite and another with an executive search. Keeping all of this straight in my head is a bit of a task, as is shifting gears from talking about the tax considerations of a particular merger structure with one company to looking at moving into a new vertical market for another.[21]

Levine says that a good practitioner needs to have some ADD—attention deficit disorder. In his blog, he jokes that ADD may be a necessary and a much-desirable condition to be a good VC.

Tenacity: Be an Unstoppable Force

If you look at successful venture practitioners such as David Cowan; Jan Garfinkle, who started Arboretum Ventures; or Vinod Khosla, they all exhibit one special characteristic: tenacity. Never take no for an answer!

Once Cowan was headed to enjoy a business school break in Greece. When he reached the airport a few hours before his international flight, he discovered that his passport had expired, just the day before.[22] Cowan decided to, against all odds, make an attempt to renew his passport and catch that very flight. Most international travelers would fret, fume, and head back home or to the bar.

WHAT MAKES A GOOD VC? ABILITY TO GROW.

"Being a venture capitalist requires a varying degree of skills. At a seed stage, the skills required are different from say, investments at a mid- or later stage. At the seed stage, we have a founder. The venture practitioner needs to have the ability to understand risk, validate ideas, and connect these to the market. Exploration and validation are key steps at this stage. A start-up is a no-name entity—the credibility and track record of the venture practitioner can be a tremendous asset in recruiting management talent and customers. Talent that can grow the company is usually in high demand and otherwise would not be available.

"In the early stage, the practitioner's ability to help the start-up to find customers is very important. The Fortune 100 companies—those marquee customers that all start-ups seek—unfortunately avoid start-ups. They are trying to minimize the number of vendors and stick with the proven ones . . . even if you get your foot in the door, these companies need time and ability to assess the new product. It's a significant commitment . . . these are extremely busy executives and asking them to check a new product out requires strong suite of skills.

"As the company evolves further, the ability to syndicate the investment becomes critical. Other investors will look at how you are putting the investment rationale and leading the round."
—Promod Haque, managing partner at Norwest Venture Partners, in discussions with the author, November 2010.

Cowan hopped into a cab, rushed to the passport office, filled out an application form, and realized he did not have the required photographs. He rushed out to take pictures, then headed back to the passport offices . . . he waved his arms . . . renewed his passport, and made a mad dash back to the airport. He found that his flight to Dallas, which would connect him to Athens, had just left Logan airport. But wait . . . he discovered that he could hop on another flight to Dallas. En route to Dallas, he even asked the flight attendant whether they could "fly faster." Like a photo finish of a marathon runner, he got on the Athens flight seconds—yes, seconds—before the gates were being closed. And when he did board the flight to Athens, he laughed out loud in triumph.

At every step, every person Cowan encountered—cab drivers, flight agents, passport officers, photographers, over 15 people—said, "You will never make that flight." And Cowan just kept on pursuing his goal with unwavering determination. That should give you an insight into how little he cared about public opinion or protocols. Or indulged in self-pity or remorse. Those who have read Cowan's blog [23] on this incident compare it to an episode of the famous Fox TV series *24*. Others say that this is a story for your grandchildren. "Amazing," "What a beautiful story," and "You had me cheering for you all the way" were some of the other responses to his blog. The entrepreneur in Cowan is evident—get to the destination against all odds.

At Wharton, the admissions officer did not think Jan Garfinkle would be well suited for an M.B.A. Her background in engineering was not aligned with the mainstream approach of economics. And in those days, Garfinkle was the only female student in engineering and one of the few who wanted to pursue an M.B.A. Despite Garfinkle high scores on the GMAT, he suggested she should try her hand at something else. She ended up on the waitlist. A disappointed Garfinkle headed out for a brisk jog and after 30 minutes returned to the admissions office to give it one more shot. Garfinkle, who has mastered the gentle art of being assertive without being obnoxious, reaffirmed her desire to join Wharton and requested that the admissions officer reconsider. "He looked at me, bewildered, and then said, okay, well, come back tomorrow and we will get it done," recalls Garfinkle, who went on to earn her M.B.A. at Wharton. She would go on to meet the future CEOs of Guidant and Medtronic through a summer internship at Eli Lilly and Company, and both would play an important role in the development of Arboretum Ventures—her venture fund. Garfinkle's career path would likely have headed in a different direction if she had given up.

And Vinod Khosla would have stayed in Pittsburgh if he were not persistent. While studying at Carnegie Mellon University, he was eager to reach the Silicon Valley. "The draw of the Valley for me is an entrepreneurial draw unlike anything else about United States," he says. He applied to the Stanford Graduate School of Business but was turned down. "They asked me to get some work experience. I did get a job in Pittsburgh and applied again, and of course, they turned me down again,"[24] Khosla would recount. "I yelled and screamed at the director of admissions. To get me off his back, he put me on the wait list." At his third attempt, Khosla was getting disheartened. "Over the summer, I got to know everyone at the admissions office; they became my friends. But even then, the director did not let me in. The day before registration, I called him and said I am leaving Pittsburgh tomorrow morning. You like it or not, I am showing up at your door," he would recall.

The director finally caved in, and within a few hours, Khosla packed up and left Pittsburgh. "I had no place to go, so the admissions office staff put me up for a month," he remembers. And thus, he came to the Valley and founded a blazing start-up called Sun Microsystems and, after a successful stint at KPCB, launched his own multi-billion dollar fund—Khosla Ventures.

WHAT MAKES A GOOD VC? BRAINS, ENERGY, PERSONALITY . . .

"For a venture capitalist, I think you want brainpower and you want energy and you want personality.

"You want somebody who is going to attract people, because a good entrepreneur has more than one choice, typically, of where he gets his venture capital. He's not just looking for the money, if he's good and smart. He'll look for, what can you do for me? How can you help? And typically, he also is thinking, do I really want to work with this person on my board? Or am I going to be constantly answering nit-picking questions? Does this gal get the big picture? Will I be comfortable? Will we have a good time together? Because one of the things we stress whenever we talk to entrepreneurs—we want to have fun!

"It goes without saying you want somebody dead honest, and you want somebody that's got really good ethics, and you want somebody who's got a strong sense of pride in getting the job done.

"And then I didn't mention the analytical side—the analysis is not so much a paper analysis—although that's important in figuring out what the market is and what your odds are of filling a need and all that, what the size of the market is. All that's important."

—William Draper, III, founder of Sutter Hill Ventures

Source: William H. Draper, III, "Early Bay Area Venture Capitalists: Shaping the Economic and Business Landscape," oral history conducted by Sally Smith Hughes in 2009, Regional Oral History Office, The Bancroft Library, University of California, Berkeley, 2008.

THE CHALLENGES OF A VC CAREER

Steve Jobs of Apple fame does not seem to be impressed by VCs and once said VC "sounds like a bullshit job to me."[25] Ironically, this was reported by none other than Michael Moritz, who was then a journalist and now is a venture capitalist and chairman of Sequoia Capital. Of his own experiences as a VC he would say, "Every day is composed of a hundred soap operas— it's an exhilarating place to live and work."[26]

As a venture capitalist, you are not creating anything new, but rather fueling the creation of new innovations and businesses. Often regarded as a commodity, a VC is often compared to a role of a slick, glorified financier – most of whom take credit for the entrepreneur's successes and hide their losses or blame it upon others. On the other hand, some practitioners find a way to take credit for all successful outcomes. Here are a few challenges of being a VC:

- *Emotionally and intellectually demanding, a business of thousand "Noes"*: The business calls for a mental tenacity—not becoming exhausted by the times you must say no to entrepreneurs, turn people down, or turn someone's great idea down without being abrasive. To handle multiple investment opportunities and complex situations; to maintain your drive and discipline; to prioritize tasks; and to be comfortable with ambiguity are the hallmarks of this profession. "I have stopped trying to manage my calendar," says Jack Ahrens, a VC for 30 years. "Rather I keep a prepared mind for emergencies that may arise on any day."
- *Churn*: Once you get in, staying in the business of venture capital is easy only as long as you can generate superior returns. Successful practitioners continuously need to adapt themselves to economic cycles. Be prepared to be voted off the island—your numbers will tell you when it is your turn to leave.
- *Performance of partner*: The one and only measure of the business is financial returns. Returns are a function of capital invested and time. Time is your enemy. As the clock keeps ticking, the measure of performance—internal rate of return (IRR), which is a function of time—keeps dropping. Worse, in bad markets and recessionary times, the ability to exit an investment slows down, not to mention the potential value of the return. But investors really don't care for any excuses. As Roelof Botha of Sequoia Capital said regarding what keeps him up at night, "Suffice it to say that you're only as good as your next investment."[27]
- *Performance of firm*: In a world of one-hit wonders, consistency matters. Top-tier venture capitalists who generate returns get to raise their

BEING REASONABLY NICE CAN BE A COMPETITIVE ADVANTAGE.

"I've heard entrepreneurs say 'I don't want to talk to that firm because they are such jerks.' In almost all cases, these are well-known, older firms who come from the era when capital was scarce.

"Every experienced entrepreneur I know has a list of 'toxic' VCs they won't deal with. There are still plenty of VCs to pitch to get a fair price for your company and only deal with decent, helpful investors. It sounds kind of crazy, but being a reasonably nice person has become a competitive advantage in venture capital."

—Chris Dixon, Andreessen Horowitz

Source: "Being Friendly Has Become a Competitive Advantage in VC," Chris Dixon (blog), http://cdixon.org/2010/01/29/being-friendly-has-become-a-competitive-advantage-in-vc/.

next funds quickly and charge higher profits—as much as 30 percent, as opposed to the standard 20 percent. Marc Andreessen once said, "I don't believe there is such a thing as a VC industry. There are about 40 firms that really do well as investors and over 600 firms that will break your heart as an investor. A handful of firms generate all the returns and a lot of firms want to generate those returns."[28]

- *Market forces:* At times, changes in market trends can hurt highly specialized firms. Not too long ago, clean-tech investments were at an all-time high. As the waves receded, the green practitioners had to tweak their resumes. Some repositioned themselves as generalists. Others went back into the technology sector and sought "clean web" opportunities.

THE BUSINESS OF HOME RUNS

"Only a small number of start-ups are meant to be successful. The same goes for venture firms. I expect most VCs to fail. The entire business is about finding exceptional, awesome companies. If you find one of them every five years, nothing else matters."

—Mike Maples, Floodgate Fund

Source: Tarang Shah and Sheetal Shah, *Venture Capitalists At Work* (APress, 2011).

Often, when technology/software investments are on the upswing, life science sectors take a beating. Technology sectors have a shorter path to exit, while the time horizon of life sciences investments is longer, often mired with technological, regulatory, and financial risks.

- *Patience in financial returns. What, no carry?:* Of the 8,000 practitioners in the business in the United States, very few have seen any financial profits, or as they say, a "carry check." In other words, most practitioners have survived on salaries coming from management fees. This is yet another cause of heartburn for limited partners (LPs), who think such perverse incentives are misaligned.

- *Intellectual honesty (or lack thereof):* Any LP will regale you with stories of bad VC behavior. But at its very core, what irritates these investors is how VCs play around with numbers to bloat their performance. It's an age-old tactic: slice and dice the data to make sure your performance looks good, and then find the next sucker who can invest in the fund. VCs, with their inflated egos, hubris, and biases rarely do a mea culpa. No VC in his or her right mind will say, "We lost your money and we learned a few lessons." Often, VCs blame someone else for poor performance. Several LPs used terms like "disingenuous." FLAG Capital, a fund of funds summarized it as the Lake Wobegon[29] effect, where in a VC land, all the women are strong, all the men are good looking, and all the children [add venture capitalists here] are above average.

The VC business is subject to pressures from multiple ends: the supply of capital, the availability of investment opportunities, liquidity time frames, and regulatory dynamics. Elizabeth "Beezer" Clarkson, managing director of SAP Ventures, says, "Often, you don't know if it's you or its luck. Having humility is essential." In any career where those two imposters of fame and fortune prevail, you can be assured of petty politics, backstabbing, and opportunistic behavior. As they say, the business of venture capital is not for the faint of heart.

At its core, venture capital is truly an apprenticeship business. It takes years of mentoring to learn how to assess investment opportunities, set pricing and strategy, build and motivate management teams, deal with inevitable and unpredictable threats to the businesses, source additional capital and strategic partners, and finally, divest (for better or worse) these illiquid investments. "The good ones view it as a calling, not a career," says Diana Frazier of FLAG Capital Management, a fund of funds with investments in some of the leading venture funds.

Singer Bob Dylan once said, "I accept chaos. I'm not sure it accepts me." That sums it up nicely—you can accept venture capital, but will it accept you?

NOTES

1. Marc Andreessen, "A Panorama of Venture Capital and Beyond." Stanford University's Entrepreneurship Corner, May 13, 2010, http://ecorner.stanford.edu/authorMaterialInfo.html?mid=2457.
2. Geoffrey H. Smart, Steven N. Payne, and Hidehiko Yuzaki, "What Makes a Successful Venture Capitalist?" *The Journal of Private Equity* 3, no. 4 (Fall 2000): 7–29, doi: 10.3905/jpe.2000.319948.
3. Author interview, October 2010.
4. CNNMoney, "The Keys to Andreessen Horowitz's Success," YouTube video, February 6, 2012, www.youtube.com/watch?v=PbW-1k3ZOA4.
5. Donald T. Valentine, "Early Bay Area Venture Capitalists: Shaping the Economic and Business Landscape," an oral history conducted by Sally Smith Hughes in 2009, Regional Oral History Office, The Bancroft Library, University of California, Berkeley, 2010.
6. Christopher Rizik, Renaissance Venture Fund, in discussions with the author, December 2010
7. C. Richard Kramlich, "Venture Capital Greats: A Conversation with C. Richard Kramlich," interviewed by Mauree Jane Perry on August 31, 2006, in San Francisco, California, National Venture Capital Association, Arlington, Virginia.
8. PandoMonthly, "A Fireside Chat with Marc Andreessen," available at "PandoMonthly San Francisco with A16Z's Marc Andreessen, the Full Interview," streaming video, October 4, 2013, http://pandodaily.com/2013/10/04/pandomonthly-san-francisco-with-a16zs-marc-an-dreessen-the-full-interview.
9. Peter Tanous, *Investment Visionaries* (Upper Saddle River, NJ: Prentice Hall, 2003).
10. National Venture Capital Association, "Venture Capital Oral History," project funded by Charles W. Newhall III, interview conducted and edited by Mauree Jane Perry, 2006.
11. Reid Dennis, "Early Bay Area Venture Capitalists: Shaping the Economic and Business Landscape," interview conducted by Sally Smith Hughes in 2009, Regional Oral History Office, The Bancroft Library, University of California, Berkeley, 2009.
12. Jeff Clavier, SoftTech VC in discussions with the author, September 2013
13. Terry McGuire, cofounder, Polaris Ventures, in discussions with the author, December 2010.
14. Paul Bancroft III, "Early Bay Area Venture Capitalists: Shaping the Economic and Business Landscape," interview conducted by Sally Smith Hughes in 2010, Regional Oral History Office, The Bancroft Library, University of California, Berkeley, 2010.

15. Stanford University's Entrepreneurship Corner, Marc Andreessen, "A Panorama of Venture Capital and Beyond," accessed January 13, 2011, http://ecorner.stanford.edu/authorMaterialInfo.html?mid=2457.
16. William K. Bowes, Jr., "Early Bay Area Venture Capitalists: Shaping the Economic and Business Landscape," interview conducted by Sally Smith Hughes in 2008, Regional Oral History Office, The Bancroft Library, University of California, Berkeley, 2009.
17. Bijan Sabet, speaking at VCJ Alpha East in Boston, April 2013.
18. Gupta Udayan, *Done Deals—Venture Capitalists Tell Their Stories* (HBS Press, 2000).
19. Gibson S. Myers, "Early Bay Area Venture Capitalists: Shaping the Economic and Business Landscape," interview by Sally Smith Hughes, 2008, accessed January 13, 2011, http://digitalassets.lib.berkeley.edu/roho/ucb/text/myers_gib.pdf.
20. Frank Caufield (partner emeritus, KPCB), in discussions with the author, August 2010.
21. Seth Levine, "How to Become a Venture Capitalist," *VC Adventure* (blog), May 20, 2005, www.sethlevine.com/wp/2005/09/attributes-of-a-good-venture-capitalist.
22. David Cowan, "Heracles' Marathon to Olympus, Athena Awaits," *Who Has Time for This?* (blog), November 3, 2005, http://whohastimefor-this.blogspot.com/2005/11/heracles-marathon-to-olympus-athena.html.
23. Ibid., accessed December 12, 2010.
24. Vinod Khosla, "Career: Learning from Failure Early On," Stanford University's Entrepreneurship Corner, accessed January 2, 2011, http://ecorner.stanford.edu/authorMaterialInfo.html?mid=19.
25. Michael Moritz, *Return to the Little Kingdom: How Apple and Steve Jobs Changed the World* (New York: Overlook Press, 2009), 89.
26. Michael Moritz, *Inside the Minds: Venture Capitalists*, ebrandedbooks.com, 2000.
27. Blake Masters, "Peter Thiel's CS183: Startup—Class 7 Notes Essay," April 26, 2012, http://blakemasters.com/post/21869934240/peter-thiels-cs183-startup-class-7-notes-essay.
28. Marc Andreessen, "A Panorama of Venture Capital and Beyond." Stanford University's Entrepreneurship Corner, May 13, 2010, http://ecorner.stanford.edu/authorMaterialInfo.html?mid=2457.
29. A fictional town in the U.S. state of Minnesota. Garrison Keillor made this term popular, as he reports the news from Lake Wobegon on the radio show *A Prairie Home Companion*.

CHAPTER 4

The Universe of Limited Partners

"My life is very monotonous," the fox said. "I hunt chickens: men hunt me. All the chickens are just alike, and all the men are just alike. And, in consequence, I am a little bored."
—Antoine de Saint-Exupéry, *The Little Prince*

Venture capitalists (VCs) hunt institutional investors (called limited partners, or LPs), and entrepreneurs hunt VCs. If VCs understand the universe of LPs and the constraints and drivers of various LPs, the fund-raising process may become less boring for the hunter and the hunted. Potential investors in venture funds, or LPs, include institutional investors (e.g., pension funds, foundations, endowments, banks, and insurance companies) and family offices, including high-net-worth individuals (HNWIs). As seen in Figure 4.1, typically, the bulk of capital for venture funds comes from pension funds. While considering an investment in a venture capital fund, each LP assesses the opportunity based upon the following:

- *Asset allocation strategy:* A set of investment principles and portfolio construction guidelines designed to generate an overall target rate of return for the LPs. Venture capital is treated as a subasset class of private equity that falls under alternative assets.
- *Investment criteria:* The factors that help LPs choose target investments within each of the asset classes.
- *Investment process:* Timelines and steps each LP needs to follow to make an investment decision within each asset class.

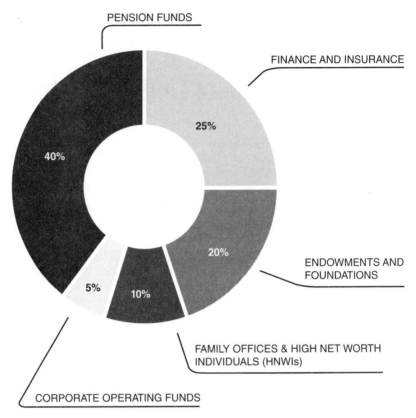

PENSION FUNDS

FINANCE AND INSURANCE

25%

40%

20%

5%

10%

ENDOWMENTS AND
FOUNDATIONS

FAMILY OFFICES & HIGH NET WORTH
INDIVIDUALS (HNWIs)

CORPORATE OPERATING FUNDS

FIGURE 4.1 The LP universe: typical sources of capital for venture funds.

All LPs aim to minimize risk and aim for a target financial return. For any venture fund, targeting the right mix of LPs is a bit like matchmaking; understanding the array of potential investors and their decision-making process is the first step in raising the fund in an efficient manner. For example, a first-time fund launched by first-time managers is more likely to raise capital from individuals and family offices and will seldom get the attention of institutional investors. In this chapter, we look at why this occurs and understand the allocation strategies of the various LPs. This may help develop a framework for targeting suitable LPs. For any venture fund, it is prudent to know that your competition does not come necessarily from other venture funds, but rather from other asset classes that offer a better risk-adjusted return to the LPs.

AN OVERVIEW OF ALTERNATIVE ASSETS

The four major asset classes are stocks (public equities), bonds (sources of fixed income), alternative assets (private equity, venture capital, hedge funds, real estate), and cash. Based on global economic trends, investors establish asset allocation strategies to adopt optimum allocation percentages in each of these asset classes.

Asset allocation, a prudent method to manage risk and returns, is driven by each investor's appetite for risk, rewards, and liquidity. Consider Figure 4.2. Venture capital is a subasset class of private equity and falls under the alternative investment asset class, and for most LPs, it is a smaller fraction of the overall portfolio.

Alternative assets are alternatives to equity and include a growing array of options, listed in Table 4.1.

Certain types of alternative assets, such as private equity/venture capital, are illiquid and do not provide the same advantages as do equities and hedge funds. Investor capital remains locked in for longer periods, which can be as long as 10 years in private equity and venture capital, and interim resale is not efficient. The concept of liquidity affects allocation outlays, and often investors seek an illiquidity premium, a higher return from this asset class.

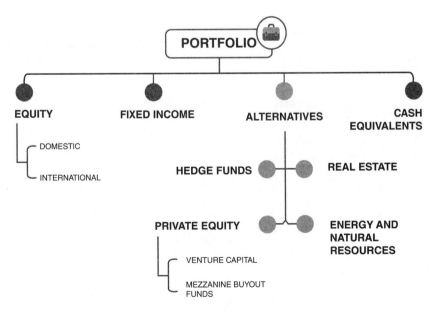

FIGURE 4.2 A typical Institutional Portfolio.

ASSET ALLOCATION AND IMPACT OF ALTERNATIVES

If an investor had allocated 60 percent in stocks and 40 percent in bonds, an average annual return would be 4.8 percent. If the allocation is diversified across the globe, the return would increase to 7.1 percent. If the alternative assets are added to the portfolio, the return falls to 8.21 percent.

Risk-adjusted performance is measured by Sharpe ratio as seen in Figure 4.3.

Source: State Street Center for Applied Research and The Fletcher School at Tufts University, By The Numbers: The Quest for Performance www.state-street.com/centerforappliedresearch/doc/CARFletcherPaper.pdf (Accessed on April 5, 2014).

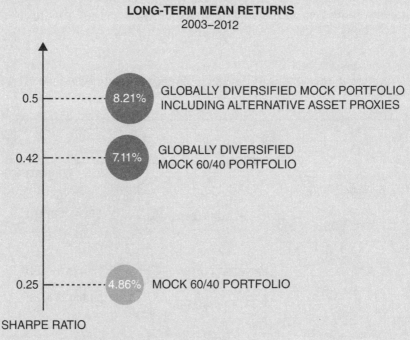

LONG-TERM MEAN RETURNS
2003–2012

FIGURE 4.3 Impact of asset allocation on returns.

TABLE 4.1 The Alternative Investments Universe

Class	Subasset Class	Investment Goals
Private equity	Venture capital, leveraged buyout funds (LBOs), distressed debt, mezzanine funds, special situations, and international private equity	Higher returns and diversification
Hedge funds	Global macro, absolute return, market neutral, long/short, 130/30, event driven, and derivatives	Higher returns and diversification with better liquidity as compared to private equity
Real estate, infrastructure	Real estate investment trusts (REITs), private real estate funds	Diversification
Commodities	Energy, oil, gas, timber, agriculture, and managed futures	Returns/cash income streams from other assets

Liquidity allows an investor to get out of investments without much friction, a concept that has continued to be debated through the years. In 1964, noted economist John Maynard Keynes stated that there is an "antisocial . . . fetish of liquidity" that drives investment institutions to concentrate their holdings in liquid assets. He added, "there is no such thing as liquidity of an investment for the community as a whole."[1] David Swensen, chief investment officer of Yale University, echoes Keynes's view. He wrote, "Investors prize liquidity because it allows trading in and out of securities. Unfortunately, liquidity tends to evaporate when most needed."[2] Examples of the stock market crash in 1987 and 2008 are indicative of this challenge, when liquidity evaporated.

Liquidity creates fickleness and generates infidelity, which hurts long-term asset classes such as private equity and venture capital. "The spectacle of modern investment markets has sometimes moved me towards the conclusion that to make the purchase of an investment permanent and indissoluble, like marriage, except by reason of death or other grave cause, might be a useful remedy for our contemporary evils. For this would force the investor to direct his mind to the long-term prospects and to those only," writes John Maynard Keynes.[3] Unfortunately, neither marriage nor investment is treated as permanent in current times.

Besides liquidity risk, other factors that impact investment flow in private equity and venture capital asset classes include higher fees and expenses, tracking valuations, regulatory challenges, and limited control over investment decisions.

Despite these drawbacks to alternative assets, market surveys affirm that alternative assets are an attractive and growing asset class. Enhanced returns, improved diversification of their investment portfolios, and a hedge against inflation risk are primary advantages of this asset class. Investors see alternative investments as a way of lowering the overall risk of their portfolios without giving up the opportunity for substantial returns. Average allocation to alternative assets is about 20 percent, with private equity and venture capital approximately at 7 percent.

Investors expect private equity and venture capital portfolios to deliver as much as 4 percent above the public equity markets. Table 4.2 shows typical median returns by asset class. Venture returns are included in private equity asset class.

While venture capital has gained LP interest and allocations have increased over the years, the asset class faces fierce competition from other classes within the alternatives universe. Chris Douvos, an LP in several venture funds, draws an interesting and humbling analogy. "If public markets are like an ocean—multitrillions of dollars at work—and private equity is a bath tub . . . say $300 billion a year . . . venture capital is like a small sink."[4] Dick Kramlich, founder of NEA, once said, "As an industry we are only raising 20 to 30 billion dollars each year, while private equity as an industry is raising 300 billion dollars. And there's two trillion dollars' worth of hedge funds. All of these resources are within the same purview . . . and there's a whole different definition of how rates of return are obtained and who you compete with."[5]

As Timothy Recker, former Chairman of Institutional Limited Partners Association, says, "The investment options for institutional investors are growing. Venture practitioners tend to be an insular group and negotiate their place within the private equity/venture capital category. I think they

TABLE 4.2 Median Returns of Public Pension Funds by Asset Class

Asset Class	1 Year (%)	3 Years (%)	5 Years (%)	10 Years (%)
Public equities	21.4	8.8	−0.8	8.9
Fixed income	9.0	8.2	7.6	6.5
Hedge funds	6.2	4.8	0.8	5.3
Private equity	**6.7**	**14.8**	**4.0**	**11.5**
Real estate	11.1	9.4	−1.4	8.1
Total investment portfolio	15.5	9.4	1.9	7.7

Source: Preqin, as of September 2012.

could easily price themselves out of the alternative class if they put the blinders on and do not aim to compete with other alternatives."[6] Any competitive class that offers better liquidity, a lower fee structure, and equal or higher returns can easily displace venture capital. Chris Douvos extends the competition beyond alternatives in different geographies. "As an asset allocator—in the 80s and 90s, venture capital asset class was like 'emerging growth' asset class, wrapped in an easy-to-understand legal and regulatory structure. And there was no choice but venture. Today, I could commit to emerging markets and generate good returns—the monopoly of venture has gone."[7] For most institutional LPs, venture capital is an asset subclass, a small percentage of their entire portfolio.

SOURCES OF CAPITAL: LIMITED PARTNERS

Capital flows into venture capital funds from pension funds, university endowments, foundations, finance companies, and HNWIs. While pension funds are the largest contributor, these are also conservative with respect to venture capital allocations. Endowments and foundations are comparatively more aggressive and allocate larger portions to venture capital asset classes. Finance companies function as specialized intermediaries and follow the guidelines established by their sponsors. A fund of funds (FoF) is established as an intermediary to allow larger institutional investors to research, access, and manage venture capital investments. Within all these players, some have a stronger penchant for private equity (PE) and venture capital and will often deviate from the aggregate.

Pension Funds

By far, the largest source of capital for the venture capital universe is pension funds. A public entity or a private corporation establishes a pension fund to manage employees' investments. Employees set aside a certain amount of their paycheck in a separate account, with the goal of saving for and enjoying their years of retirement. Employers, with an objective of attracting the talented employees and incentivizing savings, match the employee contribution into the pension plan. Thus, the two sources of cash inflows into pension funds are a sum of contributions made by individuals and employers. With a larger pool of employees, the steady trickle of contributions grows to a significant amount over time. The goal of any pension fund is to provide financial security to the employees and their beneficiaries. The pension fund is typically a separate entity and is governed by a board of trustees.

The typical asset allocation strategy for this pool of capital depends on the cash needs of the pension plan. Pension fund cash outflows are a factor of the benefits paid to retirees. Consider the California Pension Retirement System (CalPERS), the largest public pension fund in the United States, which had over $200 billion in assets in management.[8] CalPERS has more than 1.6 million beneficiaries who receive pension and health care benefits every month. A pension fund's investment team has to juggle these cash inflows and outflows. Since a pension fund needs to pay retirees a set amount each month, the demands on its cash position are high, and thus the fund allocates a higher proportion of its assets to public equities, where liquidity is higher. A typical pension fund will allocate around 10 to 15 percent of its assets to alternative assets, which include hedge funds, natural resources (such as oil and gas partnerships), private equity, and venture capital. Table 4.3 shows the typical asset class allocations of public pension funds in the United States and the expected rate of return for these asset classes.

Pension plans are divided into defined benefit (DB) and defined contribution (DC) plans. DB plan sponsors promise a specific cash benefit to an employee upon retirement, with the benefit depending on years of service and salary grades. In the United States, state government pension funds typically offer DB plans. Under DC plans, also called 401(k) plans in the United States, the plan sponsor agrees to make contributions only to the employee's pension fund.[9]

The distinction between DB and DC plans has important consequences for asset allocation. For DB plans, the combination of the sponsor's contribution policy and asset allocation strategy must be designed to fund the sponsor benefits as they become due. This translates to long-term liabilities. In recent years, the number of DB plans in the United States has steadily declined as

TABLE 4.3 Asset Allocation of Public Pension Funds in the United States

Asset Class	Typical Allocation (%)	CalPERS (%)	Expected Return (%)
Equity—domestic and international	52	54.6	7.5–9.5
Fixed income	28	23.1	4.5–7.5
Real estate	5	7.1	8.0
Alternative assets	14	13.9	6.0–8.5
Cash/cash equivalents	1	1.3	3.5
Weighted average expected return			7.0

Source: Karl C. Mergenthaler and Helen Zhang, "Public Pension Funds: Allocation Strategies," J.P. Morgan, accessed January 23, 2011, www.jpmorgan.com/tss/General/Public Pension Funds Asset Allocation Strategies/1289431691010.

more and more employers see pension contributions as a large expense that can be avoided by disbanding the DB plan and instead offering a DC plan.

For DC plans, however, there is no similar issue of asset-liability matching. The sponsor has no obligations beyond the prespecified contributions. Instead, the theoretically optimal investment policy for DC plans depends on the participant's preferences with respect to risk and return and the composition of assets held in other accounts.[10]

Besides cash flow demands for retirees, other constraints that affect pension funds include growing health care costs, legislation, and political dynamics. Several U.S. state governments have taken measures to manage the growing costs of health care and manage long-term liabilities so that pension assets are preserved and a steady income stream is generated to pay for the retiree benefits.

In many cases, the government mandates investment activities and prescribes language requiring that pension funds "maximize returns without undue risk of loss."[11] Pension funds are also subject to political pressures, and political interference can severely affect a pension fund's viability. All these factors impact the pension fund's ability to make investments in venture capital funds.

Endowments and Foundations

A university's cash inflows are a sum of student fees, grants, and contributions. On average, student fees and grants constitute 48 percent of a university's revenues; as these sources are uncertain, universities seek to insulate their position by creating endowments.[12] Less than 10 percent of revenues at Yale University have resulted from tuition, but more than 40 percent of the university's operating income comes from its endowment.[13]

An endowment generates investment income and provides a cushion against any potential uncertainties. With it, a university can focus on its primary goals of providing education and conducting research (or building a football stadium, depending on priorities)—activities that further social causes and knowledge. The grants and contributions are fickle and insufficient—neither of these are tantamount to predictable revenue streams. Research grants largely depend on government and political priorities, which change on the whim of the ruling parties. In his book, *Pioneering Portfolio Management,* David Swensen, chief investment officer of Yale University, points out that in 1755, the Colony of Connecticut refused to give Yale an annual grant due to the college's religious character, under the guise of rising wartime expenditures. He writes "institutions without permanent financial resources support day-to-day operations with funds from transient sources, limiting an organization's ability to shape its future."

Donations received by universities or other nonprofit entities such as cultural and religious institutions are set aside in endowments to accomplish certain investment objectives. Donors frequently specify a particular purpose for gifts, creating endowments to fund professorships, teaching, and lectureships; scholarships, fellowships, and prizes; maintenance; books; and other miscellaneous purposes.

Typical asset allocation for U.S. college and university endowments is shown in Table 4.4. Yale endowment's asset allocation has increased steadily in private equity over a 25-year period.[14]

More than 90 percent of endowments typically spend around 5 percent of their assets each year. They use these cash outflows for university operations or capital expenditures. Due to limited demands on their cash outlays, endowments are better suited for investments in alternative strategies. In comparison with pension funds, *endowments have invested as much as four times the percentage of their assets in alternative assets.* In a perfect world, endowment funds can potentially last forever, while pension funds can run out of money owing to demands of current liabilities.

Like endowments, foundations are a significant force in the world of private equity. Foundations exist to support charitable and nonprofit causes. Governed by federal laws and regulated by the United States Internal

TABLE 4.4   Yale Endowment's Asset Allocation: Private Equity Slice Grows Steadily

Asset Class	1985 (%)	1995 (%)	2010 (%)
Absolute return	0	20%[a]	19%
Domestic equity	65	30	7
Fixed income	15	20[b]	X[c]
Foreign equity	10	10	9
Private equity	0	10	33
Real assets[d]	10	10	28
Cash	0	0	4[c]

[a] In 1995, Yale defined absolute return asset class as hedge funds.
[b] In 1995, the fixed income asset class was categorized as U.S. bonds.
[c] In 2010, bonds and cash are lumped into one category at 4 percent. No allocation was defined in fixed income.
[d] Real assets include holdings of real estate, oil and gas, and timber.

Source: Yale Endowment, "Yale endowment grows by 8.9%, a gain of $1.4 billion." *Yale News*, September 24, 2010, http://opac.yale.edu/news/article.aspx?id=7789.

Revenue Service (IRS), foundations are managed by their trustees. Foundations support programs that are likely not supported by federal or state grants, such as child care, arts and education, health care, climate and environment, and religious and social causes. The emphasis placed on health care by the Bill and Melinda Gates Foundation is one such example. Foundations offer grants to various nonprofit organizations to conduct these programs.

Over 75,000 foundations in the United States manage more than $500 billion in assets. Private foundations are established and endowed by corporations (e.g., Ford Foundation, W. K. Kellogg Foundation) or families or individuals (e.g., Bill & Melinda Gates Foundation) and fund programs that are important to the donors. To meet IRS eligibility, private foundations must grant as much as 5 percent of their assets each year. The balance, 95 percent, is invested using asset allocation strategies. Foundations have to report their financial information publicly, as IRS guidelines mandate this disclosure.[15]

Besides private foundations, other types of foundations include community foundations, which attract a large number of individual donors from a geographic region, and corporate foundations. Corporate foundations exist to further the cause established by the donor corporation and are funded from the corporation's profits. More than 2,000 corporate foundations in the United States hold more than $10 billion in assets.[16] Other forms of foundations include operating foundations, which conduct research or provide services, as opposed to grant-making activities.

Compared to an endowment, the short-term cash needs of a foundation are not as significant. Hence, the allocations toward long-term assets, such as alternative assets (which includes venture capital), tend to be higher in comparison to those of a pension fund.

Finance Companies

Within the LP universe, finance and insurance companies provide as much as 25 percent of the capital for venture capital and private equity. Finance companies are treated as a catchall category to ensure clarity of presentation in this book. These include banks, nonbank financial companies, fund of funds, and other entities like TIAA-CREF funds, investment trusts in which assets are pooled for investment purposes. Each finance company defines its own internal criteria, such as target returns, volatility, holding period/time horizon, which helps develop their asset allocation plan.

Consider GE Capital, Equity, the financial arm of General Electric that positions itself as an entity that "maximizes the return on GE's investment capital by combining deep equity investing experience with GE's industry expertise, operating experience and global reach." GE Capital, Equity has invested in over 500 LP funds and currently has over $5 billion of assets under management.[17]

Insurance Companies

Like pension funds, insurance companies manage a large amount of cash inflows and outflows. Any insurance company is in the business of managing risk. An insured party pays a premium at a fixed time interval—say, monthly, quarterly, or annually. Insurance companies invest the premiums, but the underlying driver is to meet a potential obligation that may occur in the future. If an accident occurs, the insured receives compensation. The business model of any insurance company can be reduced to inflows via premium payments and investment income. Underwriting expenses and incurred losses are primary outflows. The scope of the insurer's business and required guarantees drives the target rate of return. These factors determine an asset allocation strategy for any insurance company. A sample is presented in Table 4.5.

Insurance companies have a unique advantage as a business model: the customer pays up front and eventually, at some point in the future, may receive benefits. In some cases, all a customer may ever get is the proverbial peace of mind. The primary mechanism to generate investment income for insurance companies is management of *float*—the amount of money that floats with the insurance company as premiums arrive and sit around, waiting to be paid out in the event of any claims.[18]

Insurance companies need to maintain certain levels of capital; if they fail, regulators can swoop in. Solvency requirements are an important factor, and hence the need to maintain a certain level of cash is important. Thus, insurance companies have to model their cash needs based on an actuarial

TABLE 4.5   Asset Allocation for the Insurance Industry

Asset Class	Life and Health Insurance (%)	Property and Casualty Insurance (%)
Bonds	63.4	64.8
Equity	26.0	16.1
Cash	4.7	8.0
Other	5.8	11.1

Data Source: Research Report - 2010 Institutional Investment Report, The Conference Board (2009 data). www.shareholderforum.com/e-mtg/Library/20101111_ConferenceBoard.pdf accessed on January 6, 2012.

assessment of risk and liabilities. In any insurance company, the accounting and actuarial teams develop the overall plan that determines cash inflows and outflows. Inflows are predictable, but outflows are not entirely predictable.

Actuaries invest an enormous amount of time in modeling demographic patterns of fire, floods, accidents, and other acts of God to derive a corelationship between premiums and claims—or risks and rewards. Hence, insurance companies attempt to manage their cash positions and liquidity effectively because unanticipated events could occur and affect their solvency. Thus, asset allocation for insurance companies is heavily weighted in low-risk investments such as bonds. Venture capital investments are lower on the totem pole and fall in the "other" category for most insurance companies.

Family Offices and High-Net-Worth Individuals

As much as 10 percent of PE and VC assets come from family offices and HNWIs, as seen in Table 4.6. A family office is a private company owned and run by a single wealthy family that serves to manage the investments and trusts of the family. A single-family office (SFO) or a multifamily office (MFO), as their names suggest, are professionally managed investment services companies that serve wealthy families. One of the primary functions of a traditional family office is to consolidate financial management with a view to preserving wealth, generating returns, and minimizing the tax impact for any family's fortune. Small teams of confidantes, including professional investment managers, are responsible for managing the family's assets and the family office. Among the other major tasks handled by the family office are the management of taxes, property management, accounting, payroll processing, and other concierge-type services such as travel arrangements.

Family offices are classified as Class A, B, or C, depending on their administrative structure. Class A family offices are operated by an independent

TABLE 4.6 Typical Asset Allocation for HNWIs and Family Offices

Asset Class	Allocation (%)
Equity	35
Fixed income	30
Real estate	14
Cash	13
Alternatives	8

company with direct supervision from a family trustee or an appointed administrator. Class B family offices are operated by an accounting firm, bank, or a law firm, and Class C family offices are directly operated by the family with a small support staff.

MFOs consolidate activities for several wealthy families with the objective of minimizing operational costs. The Family Wealth Alliance estimates there are approximately 3,000 U.S.-based SFOs and 150 MFOs. SFOs manage assets ranging from $42 million to $1.5 billion. Total assets under advisement by MFOs are upward of $350 billion, with an average client relationship size of $50 million. Median asset size at any MFO is close to $1 billion.[19]

According to a study conducted at the Wharton School, the most important objective for the SFO is transgenerational wealth management.[20] Having an SFO also allows the family members to pursue their own careers, while enjoying the benefits of cost-effective money management. As the wealth comes from family business, 58 percent choose to focus on their strengths and remain involved in operating the businesses, and 77 percent are majority stakeholders in their holding companies.[21] This has implications from an investment decision-making perspective.

Capgemini World Wealth Report reports typical asset allocation for HNWIs and family offices. In comparison to endowment and foundation allocations, this category is conservatively slanted, with around 8 percent in alternatives. However, some family offices have a strong propensity to invest heavily in venture capital asset class.

The Hillman family office of Pittsburg, Pennsylvania played a significant role in the launch of Kleiner Perkins Caufield & Byers (KPCB) Fund I in the early 70s by investing as much as half of the entire fund. KPCB Fund I invested $8 million in 17 companies (including some very successful ones like Applied Materials, Genentech, Tandem Computers, and one not-so-successful company called "Snow-Job") and returned $345 million to its investors. The estimated 43X cash-on-cash return made the Hillmans very happy, thank you very much.

In Europe, 63 percent of SFOs perform asset allocation in-house versus 47 percent of SFOs in the Americas. Thus, investment decisions and process timelines may differ if professionals manage the office. Due to the size of assets and the conservative undertones, the decision-making cycle for investment in PE and VC is comparatively longer.

Family offices and HNWIs are a significant source of capital for venture funds. According to a Capgemini Merrill Lynch World Wealth Report, worldwide, wealthy families and individuals control about $42.2 trillion.

More than 100,000 individuals in the United States are estimated to have assets in excess of $10 million.

North America remains the single largest home to HNWIs, with its 3.1 million HNWIs accounting for 31 percent of the global HNWI population.

In terms of the total global HNWI population, it remains highly concentrated, with the United States, Japan, and Germany accounting for 53.5 percent of the world's HNWI population. The fastest growths of HNWIs are in Asia or "Chindia."[22]

Corporate Operating Funds

Corporate investments in venture funds make up a bare whisper of 2 percent of all capital flowing into venture funds. A number of corporations such as SAP, Dow Chemical Company, and IBM invest as LPs in externally managed venture funds. Others establish internally managed corporate VC funds, such as Google Ventures and Intel Capital, which invest directly in companies.

FUND OF FUNDS

The fund of funds (FoFs) is essentially a variant whereby institutional investors (particularly larger pension funds and foundations) seek to invest in venture capital funds using an indirect investment approach, as opposed to researching and investing in funds directly. As depicted in Figure 4.4, limited partners such as pension funds and foundations seek FoFs to deploy capital efficiently, as well as to maximize returns.

ICH BIN EIN VC: SAP AG VENTURES

SAP Ventures is the corporate venture arm of SAP AG, the German software giant with $16 billion in revenues. The venture arm manages more than $1 billion. The fund has invested in companies as well as 10 early-stage venture capital funds. Its fund-of-funds portfolio consists of funds like SV Angel, a seed fund; August Capital, a Sand Hill Road-based fund known for big data investments; and Data Collective, a seed fund. Internationally, Point Nine, a Berlin-based seed fund with a focus on SaaS, marketplaces and mobile investments and Magma, a Tel Aviv-based Israeli seed and early stage fund have received commitments from SAP Ventures. Elizabeth "Beezer" Clarkson, Managing Director of SAP Ventures says, "SAP's global software ecosystem and 50,000 customers bring a strong advantage to any fund or start-up relationship. We know enterprise software can impact a start-ups go-to-market strategy effectively."

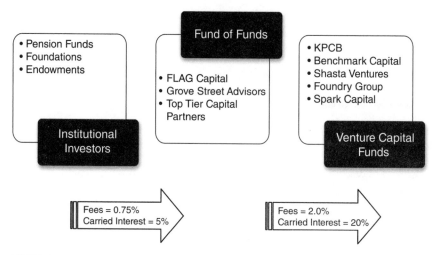

FIGURE 4.4   The fund of funds model

The FoF model emerged in the late 1980s to meet the asset allocation and diversification demands of larger financial institutions. A diverse set of FoFs has developed—from large, diversified global funds offered by Adams Street Partners, Credit Suisse, and Pantheon; to sector-focused investment vehicles from HarbourVest and Horsley Bridge; to smaller funds such as Switzerland-based LGT's FoF that targets middle market buyouts in Europe, and Cendana Capital, a FoF that focuses on micro-venture capital funds.

FoFs typically attract about 10 percent to 12 percent of all capital deployed within the private equity asset class, which is about $25 billion in any given year.

To institutional investors, FoFs offer the following advantages:

- *An efficient mechanism to access various asset classes/venture funds.* Institutional investors have optimum resources to research or manage certain asset classes. For example, a $50 billion pension fund may have less than 10 percent of its assets in private equity. This could be further sliced into mezzanine, buyouts, and venture capital. Apply another set of layers of risk diversification—sectors, geography, size, and vintage year—and what you have is a fairly complex matrix of relatively small investments. The ability to manage such investments effectively becomes a challenge for the pension fund managers. In such situations, FoFs allow for larger institutions to efficiently participate in the venture capital asset class without substantially increasing their overhead.

- *Access to high performing managers.* FoFs offer access to elite funds and have deeper knowledge of emerging funds with higher potential for performance. As FoFs are often keeping a close eye on the market dynamics, emerging managers, and high performers, FoFs are domain experts in such asset classes.
- *Diversification.* The universe of the private equity and venture capital fund managers evolves with the ebb and flow of economic trends and opportunities: venture, distressed, real estate, sector-focused funds, and turnaround funds. FoFs are attractive investment strategies because they enable investors to diversify and spread out risk over a range of different assets (e.g., a typical FoF will invest in 10 to 20 underlying funds, which in turn are investing in hundreds of portfolio companies).
- *Research and proactive relationship development.* While institutional investors may be experienced in private equity, they often lack the abilities or resources to conduct research and proactively build relationships. FoFs also offer specialized expertise to track and monitor industry trends, identify leading funds, build relationships with key managers, and staying current with investment terms.
- *Cost structure.* FoFs are cost-effective solutions for institutional investors because the due diligence, negotiations, and postinvestment portfolio management is outsourced to the FoF managers. A typical FoF fee structure is 5 percent carried interest combined with approximately 0.75 percent annual management fee. Institutional investors effectively pay two layers of fees in such a structure: one at the FoF level and another at the PE/VC fund level.

FoFs target their investments by region (e.g., United States, Europe, Asia) and subasset classes (e.g., venture, buyout, distressed, secondary markets).

FoFs raised approximately $30 billion in any year. The first FoF, a firm that would eventually become Adams Street Partners, raised a mere $60 million in 1976. Today, Adams Street Partners manages $20 billion and raises about $2 billion each year to be deployed in 15 to 30 new partnership commitments. Its target allocation typically includes 30 percent in venture capital, with the largest slice allocated to buyout funds 40 percent and the rest being set aside for mezzanine and distressed debt funds.

Some of the largest FoFs include Goldman Sachs and HarborVest Partners. Figure 4.5 shows typical asset allocation strategy for a leading fund of funds.[23]

FOF MODELS: VARIATION OF A THEME

Each FoF is designed to accomplish certain goals for its investors and for any venture fund seeking capital from these FoFs. It's important to identify how each FoF's fund strategy aligns with yours. Here are three FoFs all

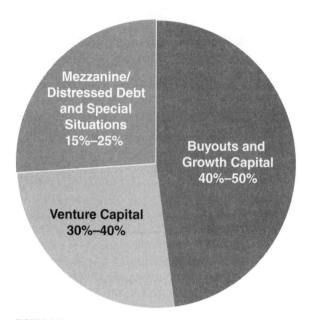

FIGURE 4.5 Asset allocation strategy for a fund of funds.

investing in venture capital funds, yet their investment strategy differs substantially. Table 4.7 compares these FoF models.

Targeting the Best in Class: Top Tier Capital Partners

Top Tier Capital Partners is a San Francisco-based niche-focused fund of funds. The firm makes primary and secondary investments in venture capital funds. Since its formation in 1999, the Top Tier Funds have raised $2.4 billion of investment capital and invested in 175 individual funds, representing 61 general partner groups.

The firm's investment process, experience, relationships, and reputation within the venture capital community has enabled a portfolio that includes the who's who of venture fund managers, such as Andreessen Horowitz, Accel Partners, Battery Ventures, KPCB, and True Ventures, among others.

The team of 10 investment professionals includes four managing directors, two principals, and two analysts with diverse but complementary backgrounds. This team is active on 54 fund advisory committees representing 29 venture capital firms.

Top Tier's venture capital history started with Philip Paul's fund and direct investments for the Hillman family in Pittsburgh, one of the first

TABLE 4.7 Comparing Fund of Funds

	Top Tier Capital Partners	Cendana Capital	Renaissance Venture Capital Fund
Assets under management	$2.6 billion	$88 million	$100 million
FoF investment strategy	Proven fund managers with differentiated strategy and established track record.	Proven entrepreneurs and seed investors	Proven fund managers with deep geographic ties and understanding of regional ecosystem
Average investment size in a fund	$25 million	$5 million to $10 million	$5 million to $10 million
Geographic focus	U.S. only, with higher concentration in California and New York	Silicon Valley and New York City only	Bicoastal funds investing in Michigan
Portfolio	25+ funds	10 funds	10 funds
Sectors of interest	Primarily technology, with select life sciences	Technology only	Technology and life sciences

investors in KPCB Fund I, and grew from the secondary purchases of the funds by Philip Paul into Paul Capital. Top Tier established its business at Paul Capital and spun out in 2011.

Laser Focused on Micro-Venture Capital Funds: Cendana Capital

Cendana Capital is a FoF focused on investing in institutional seed funds or micro-venture capital funds. Micro-venture capital funds (typically with a fund size of less than $100 million) target companies at a seed stage. According to some estimates, micro-venture capital funds are now deploying as much as $1.6 billion in start-ups. Michael Kim, who launched Cendana Capital, the first FoF in the micro-venture capital fundspace, has been a part of the Silicon Valley start-up ecosystem from the 1990s. He was a part of Morgan Stanley's M&A group on Sand Hill Road and president and chair of the Investment Committee of the San Francisco Employees Retirement System (SFERS), a $17 billion public pension fund.

At Cendana Capital, Kim aims to be selective, as micro-venture capital fund space is heating up. Having met around 250 fund managers worldwide in past three years, Kim has chosen to invest in only 10 funds.

"Most of the funds are managed by former entrepreneurs. Having spent the past decade as both an LP and GP, it is clear there are significant incongruities in how LPs and GPs seek to generate returns," says Kim.

Cendana Capital manages $100 million and deploys on an average position of $5 million to $10 million in micro-venture capital funds, and seeks to take a meaningful position in any micro-venture capital fund.

Spurring Innovation and Regional Growth: Renaissance Venture Capital Fund

Renaissance Venture Capital Fund (RVCF) is an FoF that invests in venture capital funds, with a focus on Michigan. Besides generating returns, the FoF aims to foster innovation by connecting its investors—primarily Fortune 500 corporations—with start-up companies.

RVCF's model works on raising capital from private corporations in Michigan and investing it in venture capital funds around the United States. RVCF then engages those portfolio venture capital funds with start-ups and upcoming entrepreneurs. While there is no geographic restriction on these funds, the fund's initial investment of $16.7 million has resulted in attracting upward of $300 million in 20 Michigan companies. RVCF's portfolio of venture capital funds comprises three Michigan-based funds and four out-of-state funds: one each in California, Illinois, Florida, and Houston.

"As fund-of-funds model evolves, two factors come into play—access to superior VCs and the ability to add value. Renaissance Fund is focused on creating value to our three constituents—our LPs, our venture funds and the portfolio companies," says Christopher Rizik, CEO of RVCF. Rizik has hired a full-time director of business development to help its portfolio venture capital funds and their companies to develop opportunities with the fund's investors with the goal of increasing interaction between the two communities.

While raising the Renaissance fund, Rizik had to bust silos: corporate treasury and pension sides of major companies responsible for prudent investing did not necessarily appreciate the strategic value to their organization brought by innovation and access to start-up company technology. But now, for the fund's corporate limited partners, driving innovation and corporate success is a part of the agenda. "Corporations need a line of sight in new technology developments and start-ups need access to Fortune 500 customers. One such customer can often change the course of any start-up's trajectory and turn failure into success," says Rizik. ArborMetrix, a health care data analytics company, was funded by RVCF's portfolio fund, Arboretum Ventures. It was able to gain access to one of RVCF's LP investors, Blue Cross Blue Shield of Michigan, which is an insurance provider. While the purchase decisions are based on merit of the technology, such relationships often reduce the sale cycle friction by as much as six to nine months; for start-ups, that's immense value.

The Renaissance model blends financial returns and geographic impact, a model that has generated a lot of interest: Renaissance regularly receives calls from other parts of the country hoping to replicate the Michigan model of driving entrepreneurship. One such example is the Cintrifuse fund of funds in Cincinnati, founded by an anchor investment from Procter and Gamble (P&G). P&G aims to develop Cintrifuse as an entrepreneurial hub with a venture capital component based on the Renaissance model. Cintrifuse has raised more than $50 million and has helped 32 companies to get started or grow in space.

What's attractive is that unlike government-sponsored funds, there are no restrictions on the amount of investment to be made locally. On the other hand, the Renaissance model follows the premise that there are enough opportunities, ideas, assets, and talent in their states, and there's no need to burden venture capital firms with rules and regulations. Rizik says, "We tore up the old arcane, protective rules of many similar funds and focused instead on aggressively bringing together the assets that made our region so special."

A fund like RVCF is critical for geographies seeking to support entrepreneurship and grow the number of innovative companies. Over the last 40 years, America's venture capital community has been a key driver of growth for innovation companies such as Google and Microsoft. A recent study by Global Insights shows that more than 21 percent of U.S. GDP comes from companies with a venture capital legacy. Venture capital–backed companies grow 50 percent faster and hire employees at eight times the rate of other companies.[24]

For this reason, many states are focusing on increasing the amount of available venture capital to drive innovation, employment, and growth. Over its lifetime, RVCF is projecting that it will attract over $1 billion in investment. Four years after its launch, according to the National Venture Capital Association, Michigan ranked 15th in venture capital investments among states, a remarkable improvement from its rank as 25th in the previous year. Over a five-year span, Michigan has seen a growth of 69 percent in venture capital compared to a national average of 3 percent.

COMPARISON OF LIMITED PARTNERSHIPS

In comparing the various LPs in Table 4.8, the allocation to alternatives varies, as does their primary driver for investments. Any venture practitioner seeking to raise capital needs to consider the size of an investor's alternative asset pool, decision-making criteria, and time lines of each investor.

TABLE 4.8 Comparing the LP Universe

Investor Type	Typical Percentage of Assets in Alternatives	Decision Maker(s)	Drivers	Constraints
Pension funds	14%	Portfolio manager, chief investment officer (CIO), investment committee; state treasurer may be the final signatory	Financial returns	Liquidity and risk management, size of investment staff, regulatory, political perspectives
Insurance companies	6%	CIO	Capital conservation	Liability, liquidity, solvency, regulatory
Endowments and foundations	51%	CIO	Financial returns	Size of investment staff; social and political views
HNWIs/family offices	8%	Managing director; family member may be the final signatory	Returns and relationships	Limited bandwidth; strategy and allocations are highly fluid
Corporations' operating funds	Opportunistic	Corporate development, CFO, or CEO	Insights into developing technologies and new revenue streams	Limited percentage allocation, board approvals; long-term participation is unlikely
Fund of funds	N/A	Managing directors	Financial returns, past performance, operational abilities	Existing relationships versus new fund opportunities. Available capital for new commitments

For any venture practitioner, it is imperative to understand the universe of alternative asset investors because each one has its own set of constraints. The largest percentage commitment of capital to venture capital comes from endowments and foundations owing to their relatively lower short-term cash needs. The smallest percentage commitment comes from insurance companies.

Good entrepreneurs handpick VCs who could be a part of their entrepreneurial journey, yet VCs don't apply the same filters when picking investors. Aydin Senkut of Felicis Ventures ponders "LPs don't often ask us if we are adaptable. Or if we can build a long-term platform that can withstand pressures. We aim to be an *antifragile* VC firm."[25]

NOTES

1. John Maynard Keynes, *The General Theory of Employment, Interest, and Money* (New York: Harcourt Brace, 1964), 139.
2. David F. Swensen, *Pioneering Portfolio Management: An Unconventional Approach to Institutional Investment* (New York: Free Press, 2000), 92.
3. John Maynard Keynes, *The General Theory of Employment, Interest, and Money* (New York: Harcourt Brace, 1964), 143
4. Chris Douvos, in discussion with the author, December 2010.
5. C. Richard Kramlich, "Venture Capital Greats: A Conversation with C. Richard Kramlich," interviewed by Mauree Jane Perry on August 31, 2006, in San Francisco, California, National Venture Capital Association, Arlington, Virginia (p. 69).
6. Timothy Recker (chair of the Institutional Limited Partners Association), in discussion with the author, December 2010.
7. Chris Douvos, in discussion with author, December 2010.
8. Asset Allocation, CalPERS, accessed on January 23, 2011, www.calpers. ca.gov/index.jsp?bc=/investments/assets/assetallocation.xml.
9. The ultimate value of the retirement benefit under a DC plan varies with the amount of contributions from the employer and worker as well as investment performance. DC plans differ on how much control the worker has over investment policy, but the worker usually bears most of the risks and rewards associated with variable investment performance.
10. Working Group Established by the Committee on the Global Financial System, *Institutional Investors, Global Savings and Asset Allocation* (Basel, Switzerland: Bank for International Settlements, 2007), accessed January 23, 2011, www.bis.org/publ/cgfs27.pdf.

11. Asset Allocation, CalPERS
12. David F. Swensen, *Pioneering Portfolio Management: An Unconventional Approach to Institutional Investment* (New York: The Free Press, 2000), 18.
13. Yale University, "The Yale Endowment 2009," accessed January 23, 2011, www.yale.edu/investments/Yale_Endowment_09.pdf.
14. YaleNEWS, "Yale Endowment Grows by 8.9%, a Gain of $1.4 Billion," September 24, 2010, Asset Allocation Data as of June 30, 2010, http://opac.yale.edu/news/article.aspx?id=7789.
15. IRS Form 990 offers annual financial information such as fair market value of foundation assets. For venture capital fund raising, this information can be researched online at sites like foundationcenter.org to qualify and target the appropriate foundations.
16. Joanne Fritz, "Corporate Foundation," accessed January 23, 2011, http://nonprofit.about.com/od/c/g/corpfound.htm.
17. GE Capital, Equity, "Info Center," accessed January 23, 2011, www.geequity.com/GEEquity/InfoCenter/infoCenter.html.
18. Warren Buffett loves such business models and has a significant stake in Mutual of Omaha, an insurance company. From 1967 to 2010, Berkshire Hathaway's float increased from $20 million to $65.8 billion.
19. The Family Wealth Alliance, *Seventh Annual Multifamily Office Study '10 Executive Summary*, accessed January 23, 2011, www.fwalliance.com/store/exec-summary-7th-annual-mfo.pdf.
20. "SFOs in Action: How the Richest Families Manage Their Wealth," *Knowledge@Wharton* (blog), May 14, 2008, http://knowledge.wharton.upenn.edu/article.cfm?articleid=1964.
21. The level of involvement in the family business, however, varies widely by geography. Only 40 percent of American families in the sample are involved in the family business, compared to 70 percent of the Europeans and 89 percent of those from other parts of the world.
22. Capgemini Consulting, World Wealth Report 2010, accessed January 23, 2011, www.us.capgemini.com/services-and-solutions/by-industry/financial-services/publications/world-wealth-report-2010.
23. "US Fund of Funds," accessed March 25, 2011, www.adamsstreetpartners.com/investment-programs/us-fund-of-funds.html.
24. Keynes, *The General Theory of Employment, Interest, and Money*.
25. Aydin Senkut (Felicis Ventures), in discussions with the author, October 2013.

CHAPTER 5

How Limited Partners Conduct Fund Due Diligence

"If it takes $10 million to make a good VC, that $10 million better come from the LP next door."

—Anonymous LP

Fund due diligence begins and ends with the team—the general partners (GPs). If the investment team has a strong performance track record and relevant expertise, and is pursuing a compelling strategy, fund raising can be a lark.

The due diligence process at the fund level is similar to that of due diligence in start-ups: source a few thousand opportunities, invest in a handful, and get returns from a few.

Limited partners (LPs) proactively seek prudent and experienced fund managers who can be good stewards of their capital and generate strong returns. But no LP hangs a sign at the door; rather, the communication channels are informal. Seasoned professionals, those top-quartile managers with demonstrated track records over multiple fund cycles, are sought after. Yet, others focus on the other end of the spectrum: emerging managers, who may bring a fresher approach, energy, and malleability to the mix. All fund-raising is at the mercy of markets—with Mr. Market on its side, even a mediocre group may have an oversubscribed fund.

A typical investment process for any LP seeking to invest in venture funds follows the following steps:

- *Sourcing and screening of fund managers:* The art of finding the right fund managers.

- *Fund due diligence:* The ability to assess the various risk-return measures for investing in such a fund.
- *Negotiations and closing:* Knowledge of various investment terms, the middle-of-the-road positions, and the ability to successfully close investments.
- *Postinvestment fund monitoring:* The ability to build an effective relationship with the fund managers, leading to open, honest, and timely communications.

This chapter looks at the various interconnected elements of fund due diligence, which includes performance, people (GP expertise, stability, and skills), and strategy (sector, market timing, and portfolio construction).

SOURCING AND FIRST SCREENS

While some seek to invest proven top-quartile established funds, others seek emerging managers. Some start the search with sectors and whittle down the universe of fund managers based on additional criteria. For LPs, the primary filter—performance—remains high on the list.

Lisa Edgar, managing director of Top Tier Capital Partners, a fund of funds, prefers to start her screening process with performance. "In an environment defined by change, it is important to assess the fund manager's ability to produce superior returns across various technological and economic cycles," she says.[1] Top Tier Capital Partners has established relationships with some of the leading funds.

A GP's ability to produce superior returns across various cycles is evident only after the venture firm has raised and invested a few funds. Georganne Perkins, managing director at Fisher Lynch Capital, a fund of funds (FoF), seeks proven GPs as well. "A roman numeral V or higher is a good start," she points out.[2] The V indicates the firm has invested capital over four previous fund cycles. Such a firm would have established a track record and a brand in the investment arena. Perkins, who formerly managed the private equity (PE) investment portfolio at Stanford University, reviews over 200 fund documents or private placement memorandums (PPMs) each year to invest in a handful of funds.

Most institutional investors typically see anywhere from 200 to 600 fund documents on a yearly basis. With such a high volume, the best way to stand above the ambient noise is to begin a relationship through an introduction. Without a warm introduction, fund documents that come in the door cold often head for the trash can, but the person who makes the introduction is equally important. A trusted relationship, ideally another peer-level limited partner, an existing GP, or a respected attorney, can make this path much easier. An inappropriate starting point could blow up this process very quickly. "For state pension fund managers, getting calls from politicians is typical, including calls from the governor's office. Those who use pressure tactics, despite stellar performance, are starting with a deficit," says Robert "Bob" Clone, who served as director of private equity for the State of Michigan and Indiana retirement plans, managing over $50 billion in assets.[3] Institutional investors often like to take it slow and warm up to a new fund manager over time, cautiously observing the fund's evolution and performance. G. Thomas Doyal, managing director of global private equity investments for a family office, says, "We watch managers over several years and multiple investment cycles before we are ready to engage." Doyal, who sees about 50 fund documents each year, reviews them only after a strong relationship has been established with the investment team. "It is very unusual for us to look at anything cold," he says.[4]

For newer managers, the ability to engage via an introduction and proactively build these potential institutional relationships is important. Providing meaningful updates on investments and performance can make the path easier. "Like any entrepreneur looking for the next best opportunity, we are always seeking the most promising managers of the future,"[5] advises Kenneth Van Heel, who manages $10 billion in assets as the head of the corporate pension fund for Dow Chemical Company.

Alex Bangash, an advisor to institutional LPs, has found the best managers by watching for those who become magnets for smart entrepreneurs. "How desirable is a VC [venture capitalist] to entrepreneurs? Do they want your service?" he asks.[6] Bangash is the founder of Rumson Consulting Group. The firm has helped clients invest over $1 billion in more than 50 funds, including some of the leading venture capital funds backing the marquee companies of the age. In the current day, the ability to attract the best-in-class entrepreneurs often sets the leading managers apart.

EVALUATING THE VENTURE FIRMS

Institutional investors evaluate venture firms on the two primary criteria: the fund managers' expertise and their investment strategy. Secondary criteria include investment terms and market conditions, as presented in Figure 5.1.

- *Fund managers' expertise:* As the foremost and primary criteria, limited partners seek to understand entrepreneurial/domain expertise. Performance is one of the foremost criteria.

■ *Investment strategy.* What is a fund's investment strategy, and how does it stand apart from the rest of venture funds? What unique factors/differentiators or "unfair advantage" does this combination of people and strategy bring to the venture capital arena?

While all the listed criteria are important, the diligence process seeks to find an answer to a fundamental question asked by Lisa Edgar: "Are we going to make money in this fund?"[7] Kelly DePonte of Probitas Partners, a leading placement firm, concurs: "The first question any LP asks of venture practitioners is quite simple: How can they make money for me?"[8]

In "What Drives Venture Capital Fund Raising?" authors Paul A. Gompers and Josh Lerner concluded that fund performance and reputation were the key determinants of fund-raising, in addition to macroeconomic and regulatory factors.[9] Beyond performance, the top due diligence criteria included team stability and a consistent investment strategy.[10]

This theme, performance is primary, recurs in various strands of academic literature. In a survey of investment criteria, over 200 U.S.-based LPs confirm the importance of performance.[11] In order of priority, the LPs started with internal rate of return with a minimum floor of 12 percent, and ideally closer to 30 percent, to be considered for investment. The returns are also typically tied to a benchmark index for comparing performance.

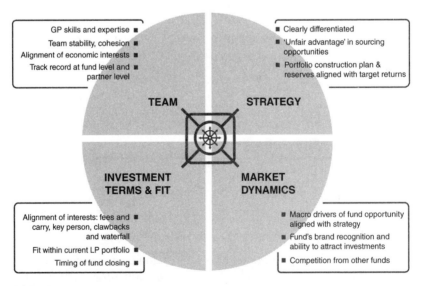

FIGURE 5.1 LP investment criteria.

FINALLY, A SOCIAL NETWORK FOR LPS

Trusted Insight is an institutional investor platform for alternatives, with more than 60,000 LP members in 98 countries. This platform allows LPs to share intelligence about fund managers in an open, honest way. A social network of LPs, Trusted Insight was launched by Alex Bangash to share LP expertise and due diligence across various sectors and geography. "We are targeting 100,000 LP members by 2014," says Bangash. Thirty thousand institutional investors engage with Trusted Insight each week. In terms of competition, Trusted Insight is going head-to-head with Bloomberg, which charges $24,000 per terminal per year. Trusted Insight is on its way to becoming the AngelList of LPs.

Source: Alex Bangash, in discussions with the author, September 2013

A performance of 400 basis points above the benchmark index, Russell 3000, or S&P 500 is often a threshold established by institutional investors. Other criteria included a consistent track record, diversification of the LPs, team experience, and fund strategy.

In their book *Beyond the J Curve*, authors Thomas Meyer and Pierre-Yves Mathonet propose qualitative scoring criteria, which ranks the fund management team and fund strategy as the top weighted factors, as shown in Table 5.1.

TABLE 5.1 Fund Selection Criteria

No.	Dimension	Weight (%)	Remarks
1	Management team skills	30	Investment and operational experience, sector expertise, regional connections, size of team, and complementary skills
2	Management team stability	10	Clear roles, responsibilities, decision making, historical relationships and stability, economic alignment of incentives, financial stability of fund, and succession planning
3	Management team motivation	10	GP commitment percentage, incentive structure, reputation, team independence, outside activities, and conflicts of interest

(Continued)

TABLE 5.1 (*Continued*)

No.	Dimension	Weight (%)	Remarks
4	Fund strategy	15	Sourcing, stage/sector, fund size, exit strategy, and overall strategy fit
5	Fund structure	10	Costs/fees, governance and compliance
6	External validation	10	Track record of previous funds, performance of comparable funds, quality of coinvestors and recurrence of investors
7	Overall fit	15	Considers the overall picture. For example, the fit between the team, fund size, and the strategy.

Source: Thomas Meyer and Pierre-Yves Mathonet, *Beyond the J Curve—Managing a Portfolio of Venture Capital and Private Equity Funds* (Chichester, UK: John Wiley & Sons, 2005), 221.

While conducting diligence on these selection criteria, wide ranges of attributes are reviewed, and these addressed separately in following chapters.

NOTES

1. Lisa Edgar (Top Tier Capital Partners), in discussion with the author, March 2011.
2. Georganne Perkins (Fisher Lynch Capital), in discussion with the author, January 2011.
3. Robert Clone, in discussions with the author, January 2011
4. Thomas Doyal, in discussions with the author, January 2011
5. Kenneth Van Heel (Dow Chemical Company), in discussions with the author, June 2010.
6. Alex Bangash (Rumson Advisors), in discussions with the author, October 2013
7. Lisa Edgar, "Are We Going to Make Money in This Fund?" *PEHub* (blog), September 7, 2010, www.pehub.com/81521/are-we-going-to-make-money-in-this-fund.
8. Kelly DePonte (Probitas Partners), in discussions with the author, December 2010
9. Paul A. Gompers and Josh Lerner, "What Drives Venture Capital Fundraising?" January 1999, available at http://ssrn.com/abstract=57935.

10. Private Equity International, *The Guide to Private Equity Fund Investment Due Diligence* (London: PEI Media, 2003), 91. The survey included responses from 313 institutions, 70 percent North America–based, with primary investing in PE and venture capital.

11. Sources of Capital for Michigan Venture Capital Firms and Entrepreneurial Companies. Research Report, Professor Zsuzsanna Fluck, Director—Center for Venture Capital, Private Equity and Entrepreneurial Finance, Michigan State University, 2007.

CHAPTER 6

Defining Your Fund's Investment Strategy

"I believe many strategies are the same, and rarely do funds have a truly ground-breaking investment strategy."
—Igor Rozenblit, LP with a multi-billion dollar fund[1]

An investment strategy—the very raison d'être of any venture firm—combines fund managers' skills and expertise with a given market opportunity to generate superior financial returns. Most venture capitalists use emergent strategies, in which the firm adopts a sandbox but also is flexible enough to deal with exceptions. Boundaries are adjusted periodically, and when exceptions occur, partners decide to invest based on the potential for return.

Strategy is important, but limited partners (LPs) are tired of, and somewhat irritated with, the me-too strategies that abound across the board. After all, what general partner (GP) does not want to invest in the next big thing? Chris Douvos, who has been an LP in several leading funds, notes, "In the venture business, we have a lot of smart people but not necessarily differentiated: *being smart is necessary, but not a sufficient condition*. Partners are often unable to demonstrate resonance between their backgrounds and their investment strategy."[2] Adams Street Partners, one of the world's largest funds of funds, seeks to find "the quality of the group's deal flow, with respect to intrinsic quality and competition for opportunities."[3] Chris Rizik, fund manager at Renaissance Venture Capital Fund, a fund of funds (FoF), takes the long view: "It all boils down to two things: the people and their investment strategy."[4]

A well-established strategy blends macro-sector-trends data with the fund managers' insights and analysis. Synthesizing this information, a fund manager points to the future, where opportunities may grow and generate significant returns. LPs seldom define the fund strategy. "The established venture firms and their skilled managers often set the investment strategy. I think it's much better for LPs to follow the established manager's thinking," says Alex Bangash of Rumson Group, who advises institutional investors on asset allocation. Yet, he cautions LPs regarding fund size. "The best performing funds of the past were smaller; say $50 million in size. Performance falls rapidly with fund size. In any other sector, with poor performance, you would get hanged in public."

A fund investment strategy includes the following:

- *Market opportunity, drivers of growth:* What are the key macrotrends that identify unsolved challenges? Is the universe large enough to source opportunities?
- *Competitive advantage in this market opportunity:* Does the fund have a significant unfair advantage in the domain? In Silicon Valley, funds like Accel, Andreessen Horowitz, and Greylock are sought after due to performance and brand gravitas. Consider the structural competitive advantage of Osage University Partners, a fund that has rights of first refusal to invest in leading university spin-offs.
- *Fund managers' background and relevant expertise:* Does the investment team have relevant background, or operational/entrepreneurial expertise? Funds like Andreessen Horowitz have redefined how venture firms add value to portfolio companies.
- *Capital efficiency, investment cycle, and target financial returns:* Is the capital sufficient to build a strong portfolio, including reserves? Does the approach allow for generating venture-like returns?
- *Risks and plan for mitigating these risks:* Rarely do fund managers address relevant risks within their team and investment strategy. Most fund documents contain a laundry list template of all risks, including acts of God.

Many fund managers fail to develop a compelling strategy that effectively combines all the above. "Having seen over 500 funds, I meet GPs who try to convince me that they have invented this asset class. These are savvy, smart people, but . . . if they only knew that I have seen the same pitch 300 times before. There are days when, as an LP, you feel like you are a pretty woman in a bar. Everyone is giving you his pick-up line, and it is tiring. You have great deal flow and great team dynamics . . . well, how very nice . . . now, are you going to tell me my eyes are pretty, too?" asks

Chris Douvos. Chris Rizik concurs: "GPs use words like proprietary and unique extensively—in the past 30 days, I have seen 10 funds that have no differentiators."

SECTOR-BASED STRATEGY

Certain sectors show promise at certain times, while others run out of favor. Consider the waves within the technology sector. As the bulky mainframe computer transitioned to the ubiquitous desktop, the ecosystem of hardware and software opportunities emerged. In the early 1980s, eager investors backed more than 100 hardware start-ups that focused on disk drives, desktop computers, and allied products. As the desktop wave descended to its nadir, the networking wave emerged, which led to the formation of Cisco, Juniper Networks, Bay Networks, 3 Com, and others.

Venture firms were evolving in the 70s and 80s, and with capital flowing rapidly in this asset class, a sector-based strategy was not as important as it is today. James Swartz, founder of Accel Partners, once remarked, "Biotech was just incredibly difficult. And services—I don't know, we just somehow gravitated to communications and software. I'd like to say we're brilliant and knew that was the way to go, but that wasn't it. We just felt more comfortable in our own skins doing those kinds of investments."[5]

As social media, games, and cloud computing are currently at their peak, leading investors have found opportunities within these sectors with the potential to generate strong returns.

Let us consider the inherent drivers of market opportunity. Do structural shifts in the market create new investment opportunities? Management guru Peter Drucker would say yes. Drucker defines systematic innovation as the "purposeful and organized search for changes, and . . . systematic analysis of the opportunities such changes might offer."[6] He outlines seven sources of innovative opportunity and agrees that the lines between these sources are blurred and overlap considerably (see Table 6.1).

Opportunity is embedded in four sources (the unexpected, incongruity, process needs, and structural changes), and three external factors (demographics, changes in perception, and new knowledge) are drivers of opportunity.[7]

It is not so much as identifying the market opportunity but rather tying the opportunity in a cohesive manner with the fund manager's expertise and their ability to execute the investment strategy. As Bob Dylan once sang in "Subterranean Homesick Blues," "You don't need a weatherman to know which way the wind blows."

TABLE 6.1　Drucker's Seven Sources for Innovative Opportunity: Can These Create Investment Opportunities for GPs?

Sources	Definition	Examples
Unexpected	Unexpected events, successes, or failures lead to opportunity.	Financial crisis and the rise of bitcoins, Airbnb, and the sharing economy
Incongruities	Discrepancy or dissonance between "what is" and "what ought to be"; composed of four areas: (1) economic realities of an industry (marketplace), (2) other realities of an industry (optimization of local, nonessential areas rather than system optimization), (3) customer expectations versus the industry perception of customer expectations, (4) internal incongruity with a process	Costs, processes, and quality of health care in the United States. Digital health tools create new opportunities.
Process Needs	Missing links or unmet needs in a process that could make the process cheaper, easier, or technologically or economically possible	Payment processing/credit cards/financial technology industry
Industry and market structures	Changes in industry or market such as new competitors, new customers, more differentiated products, new manufacturing or marketing processes, new substitute, or complementary products or services	Enterprise software shifts to cloud/software as a service (SaaS)
Changes in demographics	Changes in population structure, age structure, cultural composition, employment, education, and income	Aging population and health care needs
Changes in perception	Perceptional shift: "the glass is half full" versus "the glass is half empty"	Cleantech falls out of favor.
New knowledge	Discovery of new knowledge such as a new technology or materials	3D printing, touchscreens, Bluetooth LE, and the Internet of things

Source: Adapted from Peter F. Drucker, *Innovation and Entrepreneurship* (Oxford: Butterworth-Heinemann, 1985).

STAGE AND GEOGRAPHY

Other factors that impact investment strategy include geography (underserved regions yield opportunities due to pricing advantages) and the stage of investments (earlier stage companies need less capital but are riskier investments). Ultimately, an investment strategy is a combination of the fund manager's expertise, the market opportunity within the sector, geographic advantages, stage of investments, and the size of the fund. No single element stands out as much as the GP expertise. A few examples of fund strategies are laid out in Table 6.2.

Once a strategy is established, leading practitioners not only seek existing opportunities but also lead the formation of companies based on the white spaces, road maps, or the open avenues in the market.

White Space Investing: The Venture Practitioner as a Founder

Leading researcher John Seely Brown of Xerox fame defined white space research as "radical . . . lashing oneself to a problem and taking it wherever it goes. The only guide to where to go is the problem itself; if it takes you out of your discipline, you go with it. . . . Such research seldom happens at universities because peer review and tenure mechanisms tend to favor research that stays well within established disciplines."[8]

Several leading venture professionals have used this white space research strategy to proactively form start-ups. Ralph Waldo Emerson's credo resonates well with these mercurial minds: "Do not go where the path may lead, go instead where there is no path and leave a trail." John Jarve, general partner at Menlo Ventures, asserts, "More than half of the companies we finance come out of the research we do—Menlo is a very research-intensive firm." Jarve, who earned his master's of science in electrical engineering from the Massachusetts Institute of Technology says, "This is not something we hire somebody to do: we are pretty strong technically and analytically. Combined with our investment and market awareness, we often identify a new, emerging market, and choose to master it."[9]

At Bessemer Venture Partners, David Cowan leads the concept of developing investment road maps. While these road maps have their utility, it's a deeper understanding of technologies and the market challenges that help develop such a road map. Tom Perkins of Kleiner Perkins Caufield & Byers (KPCB) writes in his memoir, *Valley Boy*, that "the technical aspect didn't daunt me too much. I figured that I could learn it." While looking at Genentech, Perkins did not get into the scientific details, which he professes would have been over his head. Rather, he focused his questions along the

TABLE 6.2 Variations on a Theme: How Strategy Differs in Venture Firms

Fund	Market Opportunity and Drivers of Growth	Source of Investment Opportunities	Fund's Competitive Advantage	Sourcing Advantage	Capital Efficiency and Target Returns	Level of Competition from Other Funds
Arboretum Ventures, Ann Arbor, MI	Health care is a large, growing market fraught with inefficiencies and FDA regulatory challenges.	Universities in Midwest, research hospitals, corporations, and entrepreneurs.	Track record, team's expertise, and relationships with VCs across the country.	Underserved/ geographic.	Early-stage health care opportunities need at least $20 million and generate exits in the range of $150 million. Average span for exits is seven years.	Medium
Osage University Partners, Bala Cynwyd, PA	University research and development budgets are growing. Technology transfer offices are primary source of opportunities.	Top 10 universities with significant research budgets.	Sourcing tie-in with university technology transfer offices.	Contractual.	Variable. Ability to cherry-pick opportunities with lower capital needs and shorter investment cycle.	Low

Firm						
Foundry Group, Boulder, CO	Technology disruptions in social media, Web, human–machine interactions.	Rapidly evolving market space.	Relationships and network/entrepreneurial contacts.	Brand recognition of GPs. Launched tech stars in various leading cities (New York, Boston).	Lower capital needs to reach break-even. Target returns can be significant in short time frame.	High
Norwest Venture Partners, Menlo Park, CA	Global shifts in GDP growth, infrastructure, technology usage, and regulation.	Large—multistaged investments in multiple sectors and geographic arenas.	Brand and track record. Relationships.	Firm's network of relationships. Geographic spread.	Varied. Energy sectors demand higher capital with uncertain outcomes.	High

lines of equipment needs and steps to prove the technology. Perkins was playing the role of a classic project manager: setting goals, establishing time lines, and providing key resources—people and money.[10] Like most agile practitioners, he had mastered various technologies as they evolved: lasers, computers, and genetic engineering.

ROAD MAP INVESTING

"We at Bessemer try to take [the road map investing approach] more seriously than most," writes David Cowan of Bessemer Venture Partners.*

"Fresh out of business school, I joined Bessemer [in 1992] and proceeded to fall in love with every crappy pitch I heard. Fortunately, before I did any damage, my bosses intervened, suggesting that perhaps I should take a few months to Think Before I Fund. I developed a comprehensive list of 38 potential investment sectors of high technology, and I spent the next three months whittling it down to 5. I crossed off sectors, which required deep domain knowledge—sectors that were too early, too crowded, or too unproven. . . . I solicited advice from the smartest experts I could find. I went to conferences, surveying buyers," writes Cowan.

This resulted in sharpening the saw, which allowed him to focus, narrowing down his investment horizon to the data and communications subsectors.

"Each Bessemer investor's road map begins with an analysis of disruptive catalysts that have the potential to cause major displacements in our economy. Those disruptive catalysts might be technical (e.g., network vulnerabilities), demographic (e.g., aging U.S. population), regulatory (e.g., spectrum auctions or Sarbanes–Oxley), psychographic (e.g., consumer concerns about security), or geopolitical (e.g., China's reception to foreign investment)," he writes.

Cowan's road map lays out specific strategies, or "initiatives," to exploit the disruption. "For each of these initiatives [Bessemer] made one investment in the best team we could find attacking the problem—some were follow-on rounds . . . and some were new teams that we incubated in our offices." Creating a road map allows a practitioner to spot the growth opportunities and the cracks in the technology landscape.

Source: David Cowan, "Road Map Investing," *Who Has Time for This?* (blog), August 12, 2005, http://whohastimeforthis.blogspot.com/2005/08/road-map-investing.html.

For any venture practitioner, it is an important cranial exercise to assess the technological ecosystem and predict the harmonious interplay of the components. "While our competitors seemed happy to wait for fully fleshed-out business plans, and full teams, to walk through their doors, we were incubating our own new ventures, then building the teams to suit the needs. We had found a way to harness our impatience. I have never been good at just waiting," writes Perkins in his memoir *Valley Boy*.[11]

When Investment Strategy Shifts and Drifts

Mae West, the Hollywood star of yesteryear, once said, "I used to be Snow White, but I drifted." Any LP dreads strategy drift—those opportune moments when fund managers start to invest in everything else but their core areas of expertise. But a strategic shift, conducted between funds with a well-laid plan, can be beneficial.

"Even with a great road map, it's always necessary to maintain an open mind to great opportunistic investments," writes Cowan, who rues Bessemer's inability to exit telecom investments in the late 1990s.[12] Vinod Khosla exited the technology sector and burned the old technology investing road map to start afresh at Khosla Ventures, primarily to focus on investments in energy. Khosla established himself as a thought leader at the forefront of a new sector, challenging assumptions and engaging in strong debates with Princeton scientists on the future of biofuels.[13] As the cleantech sector lost its appeal, the firm shifted its focus to technology investments. Yet, several other firms who were firmly entrenched in the cleantech arena could not pivot and raise another fund.

Shifting strategies and developing new road maps are appropriate while raising new funds. But within an existing fund framework, if a fund manager attempts to shift the strategy substantially, the investors see it as a big negative. After all, the investors had bought an original thesis of investment, and unless the LPs approve the shift, the fund managers should resist the urge to tinker at such a grandiose scale.

"Strategy drift is an ongoing concern within the limited partner community. Opportunistic GPs get clever in their definition of how a certain company fits their strategy. This becomes a debate of definitions. I am always intrigued at a fund's success outside of the core fund strategy," says Kenneth Van Heel of Dow Pension Fund.

Every fund has a clause that allows the GPs to invest up to 10 percent of the capital in companies that are outside the core investment criteria. "In my world, GPs do not get credit for the success of these opportunistic outliers. Worse, if we see a pattern of successes only in the outliers, then the GPs have a bigger problem."

Brad Feld, cofounder of the Foundry Group, a venture firm based in Boulder, Colorado, writes, "Lots of VCs talk about their 'process,' 'investment thesis,' 'company building model,' 'value add model,' or other such cliche-ish phrase. Some of the great VCs really do have a mental model that they can articulate; the balance of the great VCs don't have one that they can (or choose) to articulate. However, most of the not-so-great VCs will have 'something else' that they use to frame their investing."[14]

Some leading professionals conclude that strategy in venture firms is ever evolving and opportunistic, at times developed to appease investors. Some say that performance trumps everything.

Igor Rozenblit, who managed investments for a European financial services firm, concluded that strategy did not matter to their firm. "Of the four criteria we used: strategy, track record, business sustainability, and alignment of interest—strategy was the least important. I believe many strategies are the same, and if a GP has truly ground-breaking strategy, he or she should go to Goldman Sachs, who is sophisticated enough to understand it and would gladly fund the whole thing. Our risk profile was to be on the lower side of the experimentation," he chuckles.

Gus Long says, "If a fund manager proposes a really novel strategy but the returns are mediocre, no investor will be interested. The novelty needs to be matched with performance."[15] Naturally, when a strategy is unproven, investors are unwilling to bear the risk.

NOTES

1. Igor Rozenblit, in discussion with the author, December 2010
2. Chris Douvos (TIFF), in discussion with the author, December 2010.
3. "For Fund Managers, Seeking the Highest Quality," Adams Street Partners Web site, accessed March 25, 2011, www.adamsstreetpartners. com/investment-interests/fund-managers.html.
4. Christopher Rizik (Renaissance Venture Capital Fund), in discussion with the author, February 2011.
5. James R. Swartz, interview by Mauree Jane Perry, 2006, "National Venture Capital Association Venture Capital Oral History Project," accessed January 30, 2011, http://digitalassets.lib.berkeley.edu/roho/ucb/text/swartz_james_donated.pdf.
6. Peter F. Drucker, *Innovation and Entrepreneurship* (Oxford: Butterworth-Heinemann, 1985), xiv.
7. Ibid.
8. John Seely Brown, *Seeing Differently: Insights on Innovation* (Boston: Harvard Business Press, 1997), xxv.

9. John Jarve (Menlo Ventures), in discussion with the author, December 2010

10. Tom Perkins, *Valley Boy: The Education of Tom Perkins* (New York: Gotham Books, 2007), 120–121.

11. Ibid., 131.

12. David Cowan, "Road Map Investing," *Who Has Time for This?* (blog), August 12, 2005, http://whohastimeforthis.blogspot.com/2005/08/road-map-investing.html.

13. Vinod Khosla, Timothy D. Searchinger, and R. A. Houghton, "Biofuels: Clarifying Assumptions," *Science* 322 (October 17, 2008): 371–374.

14. Brad Feld, "A Mental Model for VC Investments," *FeldThoughts* (blog), May 21, 2006, www.feld.com/wp/archives/2006/05/a-mental-model-for-vc-investments.html.

15. Gus Long, in discussions with author, July 2010.

CHAPTER 7

How Institutional Investors Evaluate Fund Managers

"Under the spreading chestnut tree I sold you and you sold me"
—George Orwell, *1984*

From any institutional investor's or limited partner's (LP's) perspective, a venture capital partnership is like being locked in a 10-year blind pool—a long relationship in which the investors have very little control, limited ability to exit the relationship, and no clarity of outcomes. Thus, investors seek proven fund managers. Figure 7.1 depicts the stacking order of professionals.

A proven fund manager is one who has generated consistent returns across multiple economic cycles. Few practitioners have demonstrated the ability to source opportunities, invest capital over multiple rounds, add tangible value as a board member, and generate exits. Such a proven manager is a much sought after star in the venture capital business. Proven managers do not have to amplify or sell their background, expertise, or scientific domain knowledge. LPs don't really care how they got there as long as they rack up the returns. Rookies eager to enter the business have to establish their credentials.

If a newcomer has entrepreneurial experience—started a company, raised multiple venture rounds, and led the company to an exit—the fundraising path becomes a bit easier. A demonstrated nose for choosing good investments is what matters.

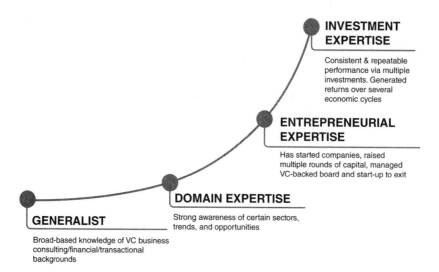

FIGURE 7.1   GP expertise: Show me the money!

"If you belong in the 'first-time manager/first-time fund' box, what are the investors going to base their decisions on?" asks Kelly DePonte. Some investors are blunt and discourage rookie fund managers. "After all, why should you train to become a venture capitalist on my nickel?" Others are quick to point out that it takes about $10 million of investor capital to train a general partner (GP). "I'd let the other LPs pay for this education," they say. "Experienced managers who have attained returns over multiple funds are attractive to any LP," says DePonte.[1]

Some key criteria for evaluating fund managers and the investment team include the following:

- *Performance:* Does the individual have an investing track record? Are the managers proven top-quartile performers? Emerging? Or somewhere in between?
- *Team Skills:*
  - What are the operating qualifications and background? Has the individual played relevant role in an operating capacity?
  - What is the individual's domain expertise: Is she a generalist or a specialist? Can she spot a trend or analyze opportunities?
  - Does the individual have any experience as board member? If yes, describe the person's specific value/role.
  - What is the role and investment focus of each individual? In larger multisector/multistage firms, this criterion has higher importance.

THE FUND MANAGEMENT TEAM DYNAMICS: STABILITY, SKILL SET, AND ALIGNMENT

Investors assess the team stability, alignment, and dynamics using a number of techniques. Team stability—the ability of the partners to work together through thick and thin—is considered a substantial risk with unproven managers or newer funds. Alignment of interests shifts when senior managers choose to retain most of the profits, leading to potential break-ups of younger partners. Finally, how the members of teams align with each other with respect to roles and responsibilities is a key question LPs often ask.

Here, we describe stability, alignment, and skill sets (soft skills, specialists, and social networks) to help develop deeper insights into a fund manager's due diligence.

Stability and Alignment: Will the Family Stay Together?

Newly minted partnerships are seen as risky. Team cohesion or stability risk is paramount in such firms. If partners cannot get along and quit for any reason, it can be a death knell for the fund. LPs frequently assess each individual's background and expertise, and more importantly, how these cohesively tie together to form a symphony.

Redundant skill sets or incompatible personalities are red flags. But while functional attributes can be easily ascertained, no LP can predict whether a marriage can last. Thus, the first-time funds have to demonstrate track records as well as intangible elements like cohesion and stability.

To assess team cohesion, LPs look at the following:

- *Alignment of incentives:* Compensation structure, responsibilities, and rewards for each team member.
- *Duration of relationship*: How long they have worked together and the circumstances or crises that have strengthened these relationships.
- *Alignment with LP's financial goals*: Fund managers own capital or "skin in the game"—the amount of fund managers' investment as a percentage of their net worth.
- *Distractions*: Sources of other income, time horizon to retirement. One LP rued that "Some GPs never die—they just keep coming back in some shape and form."

As Clint Harris, managing partner at Grove Street Advisors, puts it, "One of our team members has an insight into things like whether the junior members in a fund are talking to headhunters. If they are responding to

ROCK STAR PARTNER COMES ON BOARD

GPs need to treat their partners with respect both on and off stage. At a recent meeting, I complimented a senior partner for having attracted a star. He leaned forward and whispered, "You don't understand, he is our servant."*

---

* From an anonymous LP with investments in over 50 venture funds and over $1 billion under advisement. Author interview, October 2013.

---

calls, then you know there is something wrong. . . . The team member can make five phone calls and he will get an honest answer very quickly. . . . "[2]

Stability and alignment of interest are closely tied—should a senior partner be unwilling to share meaningful portions of carry, the junior team members will often vote with their feet and head for the door.

Table 7.1, a format developed by Pension Consulting Alliance (PCA), demonstrates alignment of interest of various principals in an early-stage fund. Red flags include the following:

1. No significant capital contribution from fund managers.
2. Disproportionate carry allocation, especially to senior partners.
3. Excessive compensation from other sources.

"When we formed Shasta Ventures, the three cofounders knew each other very well, but had never worked under the same roof. We undertook

TABLE 7.1   Sample Format: Assessing Alignment of Interest

Principal Name	Expected Capital Contribution	Carry Points (20%)	Total Annual Expected Compensation from This Fund	Total Annual Expected Compensation from Other Sources	Carried Interest Compensation if Fund Meets Objectives
Managing director 1	$450,000	10%	$400,000	None	$10,000,000
Managing director 2	$450,000	8%	$300,000	None	$8,000,000
Principal	$100,000	2%	$200,000	None	$2,000,000

intense efforts to understand how we would function as a team. We discussed, agreed upon, and wrote an operating manual, which includes everything from carry distributions down to managing travel decisions and dinner tabs. These aspects were finely calibrated—we were deliberate about this, and the LPs could appreciate it. Seeing this level of preparation, the LPs were comfortable that we could keep the fund together," says Ravi Mohan, cofounder and managing director, Shasta Ventures, a Silicon Valley–based early-stage technology venture firm.

Identifying Complementary Skill Sets

Venture capital investments call for a varied skill set in a team: raising capital, sourcing investment opportunities, adding value as board members, and leading exits. These skills are prefaced by entrepreneurial expertise, technological strengths, and the ability to perceive future market trends and maintain an even keel in somewhat ambiguous and rough times. LPs also closely look at the duration and the intensity of GP interactions—as investment professionals, not golf buddies.

Table 7.2 shows a complementary skill set of a team at an early-stage health care fund. Note the ability of the managing directors to attract junior as well as senior partners across two separate fund cycles.

The Importance of Soft Skills

In a survey of more than 145 leading VCs (venture capitalists), leading practitioners agreed that listening skills were considered more important for success in venture capital than quantitative skills.

The skills that were rated most important were as follows:

- Listening skills
- Ability to recruit talented management
- Qualitative analysis skills
- Coaching/counseling/advising skills

"You've got to be a good listener. I find if the venture capitalist does all the talking, he doesn't learn very much about the people he's thinking about investing in. Very important to listen . . . and judge who looks and feels like they have the makings of making a real company. Eventually it becomes instinct if you do it often enough," remarked Paul "Pete" Bancroft, former CEO of Bessemer Securities and former chair of National Venture Capital Association.[3]

Financial and technical skills were rated least important by practitioners, while possessing a CEO perspective was considered a valuable asset.[4]

TABLE 7.2 Complementary Skills in a Venture Firm

Title (Years with Firm)	Fund-Raising	Early Stage Investments	Operating Qualifications	Board Positions	Exits
Managing director 1 (Founder—8 years)	Successfully led raise of two prior funds totaling $100 million	Completed 20 investments over 8 years	Over 20 years, launched 20+ products in medical device companies; marketing, clinical research, and sales expertise	Seven board positions	One exit; as operator, two start-ups were acquired by publicly traded company
Managing director 2 (8 years)	Codeveloped investment strategy; supportive role	Completed 20 investments over 8 years	Nine years in consulting services; investment banking expertise	Five board positions	Two exits: one IPO and one acquisition
Principal (4 years)	N/A	Completed three investments over 4 years	Eight years in large automotive company; product development, manufacturing, and strategy	Three board positions	N/A
Venture Partner 1 (1 year)	N/A	N/A	Former CEO of publicly traded company	Three positions	Two exits as CEO of venture-backed companies
Venture Partner 2 (1 year)	N/A	N/A	Thirteen years as cardiac surgeon; development of medical devices and FDA regulatory trends	Observer	N/A
Associate (2 years)	N/A	Completed due diligence for two investments	Investment banking with a bulge bank	Observer	N/A

While conducting reference checks with portfolio company CEOs, LPs are able to identify GP strengths in these areas.

LPs also are able to grasp a deeper sense of the culture of the firm. "Naturally, GPs project that all is great within the firm, but while talking to associates, I get a different picture. I have learned how to get to the bottom of that quickly," explains Chris Rizik. Bob Clone, who has made investments in funds across the country, would set aside time to speak with the front-office staff, including the administrative staff and the receptionist. "These people may seem irrelevant but are on site every day. They see the entire family at work—the senior partners, and the junior partners and how they interact with entrepreneurs. And they are candid in sharing the true picture."

Generalists versus Specialists

In a study, Paul Gompers, Anna Kovner, and Josh Lerner demonstrated a strong positive relationship between the degree of specialization by individuals at a firm and the firm's success. A specialist investment professional in a specialist firm will outperform a generalist. The poorer performance by generalists appeared to be due to both an inefficient allocation of funding across industries and poor selection of investments within industries, concluded the authors. In other words, the generalists made bad choices across the board. But if you put a specialist individual in a generalist firm, the performance was weak.[5] Thus, the LP emphasis on domain expertise is intuitively high. Another interesting study of 482 venture practitioners in 222 first-time venture funds asserts the same proposition: *The specialists outperform the generalists.* The specialists were superior, especially when it came to early-stage investments. The study also concludes that the two strongest predictors of fund performance were entrepreneurial experience and domain expertise.

Yet the predominance of MBAs in the business of venture capital is evident. In 80 larger venture capital firms, of the 615 general partners, 58 percent had MBAs. Of these, 64 percent came from Harvard, Stanford, and Wharton.[6] But an MBA is not necessarily an indicator of strong performance. On the contrary, a research study shows that funds with more MBAs on board performed poorly as compared to others. "We found at least one place where having an MBA can be a disadvantage," summarized the authors.[7]

Social Capital: Who You Know Matters

Social capital in the venture capital arena can help a practitioner access opportunities, conduct due diligence, syndicate investments, and accelerate exits.

Do strong networks among venture capitalists improve their bargaining power over that of entrepreneurs? According to a study, yes indeed![8] LPs watch for syndication networks and ascribe an intangible value to a VC's networks.

For any LP, venture capital networks are an indicator of sector expertise and financial strength. Needless to say, the stronger networks were able to extract value from a pricing perspective; lower valuations were evident in more densely networked markets. Empirical evidence that better networked VCs enjoy better performance has already been established,[9] but lower valuation at the point of entry was also identified as a function of networks.

"My success, frankly, was mostly due to two things: One, as a CFO . . . I was a corporate finance expert at a time when biotech and medical devices were becoming very capital-intensive models. . . . I had an expertise that the industry needed; and I had these great relationships with [venture funds]. Everybody needs an angle, so that was my angle; I knew people,"[10] Alan Frazier, the founder of Frazier Healthcare Ventures, once remarked.

Steve Bird of Focus Ventures writes on the importance of networks in the business of venture capital:

> *"Quality of management" really means the quality of the relationships that GPs build over years in the business. Management means forging relationships with other top VCs that allow both parties to repeatedly form syndicates on the best deals. It means building a network among the entrepreneurial community so that the GP hears about a revolutionary technology when it's still in the lab, not after the company has landed its first round of financing. It means knowing important customers, suppliers, and scientists that can help a fledgling company reach its first quarter of profitability. And it means building trust with the broader financial community so that when the time comes for a portfolio company to get a loan, raise more capital, or go public, company management doesn't have to re-create the wheel.*[11]

I'M JUST A DUMB ACTOR WITH A LOT OF MONEY

Ashton Kutcher and A-Grade Investments

Ashton Kutcher's investments include Skype, Spotify, Airbnb, Foursquare, Fab, Uber, and Flipboard. He was one of *Time Magazine*'s Top 100 Most Influential People in 2010. In the same year, Katalyst Networks, a content company that he cofounded, was named as one of *Fast Company Magazine*'s Top 10 Most Innovative Companies. That's better than most VCs.

Kutcher's connection with tech investments can be traced back to his University of Iowa days when he was planning a major in biochemical engineering. He dropped out to pursue his career as a model after winning the "Fresh Faces of Iowa" competition. A few years down the line, he became more actively interested in tech investing. "I realized that the Internet was getting fast enough to allow for the growth of streaming video, and I started getting into that, and into digital analytics," he says, speaking with ZDNet. "Along the way, I came across a lot of other interesting start-ups—especially in social media, which appealed to me because it fostered communication between people, and allowed new and novel ways to market ideas, products, movies, and music."[12] His early forays in tech investing, Ooma and Blah Girls, were failures. But his active participation got him the attention of Silicon Valley heavyweights like Marc Andreessen. Andreessen encouraged him to put some money on Skype, then valued at $2.75 billion, which was considered high, but Ashton Kutcher was a happy man after Microsoft bought Skype for more than $8 billion. Kutcher has built his network of *interesting and really smart people* and hence gets to see things really early.

His due diligence approach is simple. Speaking with *Esquire,* he said "I have this kid who collects information from the Internet for me. Every once in a while something happens—when Apple went vertical with maps, Amazon acquired a maps company (3D mapping company UpNext). That might mean an open market segment for map APIs that can go cross-platform . . . that information can be really valuable when companies are pitching my fund."[13]

He cofounded A-Grade Investments and has invested $200 million in as many as 33 Silicon Valley start-ups. A-Grade Investments looks at consumer-facing software technologies, the density of the problem solved by the company, extraordinary entrepreneurs who are passionate with a lot of perseverance, and their technical know-how.

Kutcher is a part of the advisory board of Fab.com. With Airbnb, he's an "ally and a trusted advisor" and will help them out in a community engagement capacity. Adam Goldstein, cofounder of San Francisco–based travel start-up Hipmunk, says, "He's got a great product sense, and really clever branding and marketing ideas. I've gotten more out of the meetings with him than almost any other investor."[14] Another of his investments UberMedia, has released A Plus, a free program for desktop computers, which focuses on everything

(Continued)

I'M JUST A DUMB ACTOR WITH A LOT OF MONEY: (*Continued*)

Ashton—his Twitter updates, photos, the material he endorses, his own Twitter feed, and more. When was the last time you saw a portfolio company do that for a VC?

"For me, the most entertaining evening would be to go sit with entrepreneurs and talk with them about how they're building their companies" says Kutcher. "I am just a dumb actor with a lot of money."[15]

Source: Various media interviews with *Esquire*, *ZDNet* and *Money Morning;* see referenced end notes for further details.

I STILL HAVEN'T FOUND WHAT I'M LOOKING FOR

As a rock star, Bono, the U2 front man, continues to perform at sold-out concerts worldwide. His band has been inducted into the Rock and Roll Hall of Fame, has won 22 Grammy Awards, and has sold over 150 million records in its 35-year career. As an activist, he's no lightweight, either: He has been a Nobel Peace Prize nominee, was the 2005 *Time* Person of the Year, received the Amnesty International Ambassador of Conscience award, and is a passionate advocate for debt and HIV/AIDS relief—these are just a few among his many causes and citations.

He certainly looks and acts like a rebel, although his brand of rebellion defies our expectations of how a rocker should behave. He is still married to his high school sweetheart. They have four children. His band showed capable management and business savvy, unlike many artists, by retaining control of most of its catalog.

Bono continues to defy convention by indulging in his latest un-rock star-like behavior as managing director and cofounder of Elevation Partners, a venture capital firm that invested in companies like Facebook and Yelp. For a rebel-rocker-activist, such straitlaced, numbers-crunching, right-wing capitalist principles run counter to the free-wheeling, make-love-not-war themes that have been a winning formula of his success as an artist.

But the question that begs attention is, what would a Monday morning meeting at Elevation Partners look like? Does Bono attend the annual LP meetings and sign autographs? Do LPs question his portfolio value-add or attribution? Some questions will remain unanswered.

Most LPs would prefer to invest in managers who have a track record in the financial world, not Hollywood. Ashton Kutcher and Bono can claim to have both. Evaluating such fund managers may require more than just the ability to read internal rate of return (IRR) tables.

NOTES

1. Kelly DePonte (Probitas Partners) in discussions with the author, September 2010
2. AltAssets, "Institutional Investor Profile: Clint Harris, Managing Partner, Grove Street Advisors," September 4, 2002.
3. Paul Bancroft III, "Early Bay Area Venture Capitalists: Shaping the Economic and Business Landscape," interview by Sally Smith Hughes, 2010, accessed January 13, 2011, http://digitalassets.lib.berkeley.edu/roho/ucb/text/bancroft_pete.pdf.
4. Geoffrey H. Smart, Steven N. Payne, and Hidehiko Yuzaki, "What Makes a Successful Venture Capitalist?" *The Journal of Private Equity* 3, no. 4 (2000): 7–29.
5. Paul Gompers, Anna Kovner, and Josh Lerner, "Specialization and Success: Evidence from Venture Capital," *Journal of Economics & Management Strategy* 18, no. 3 (2009): 817–844.
6. *Young Venture Capital Society Newsletter* 1, no. 2.
7. Rebecca Zarutskie, "The Role of Top Management Team Human Capital in Venture Capital Markets: Evidence from First-Time Funds," *Journal of Business Venturing* 25 (2010): 155–172.
8. Yael V. Hochberg, Alexander Ljungqvist, and Yang Lu, "Networking as a Barrier to Entry and the Competitive Supply of Venture Capital," *Journal of Finance* 65, no. 3 (2010): 829–859. The authors conclude that there is less entry in venture capital markets in which incumbents are more tightly networked with each other. And the relationship factor seems to work both ways: a venture capital firm is significantly more likely to enter a market if it has previously established ties to incumbents by inviting them into syndicates in its own home market. In other words, VCs will not cooperate with an outsider until they have quid pro quo access to the outsider's markets.
9. Ibid.
10. Alan Frazier, "Venture Capital Greats: A Conversation with Alan Frazier," interview by Carole Kolker, 2009, accessed January 13, 2011, http://digitalassets.lib.berkeley.edu/roho/ucb/text/frazier_alan_donated.pdf.
11. Steve Bird, "Private Equity ... or Personal Equity? Why Who You Know Still Drives Venture Capital Returns," July 7, 2005, accessed February 20, 2011,

www.go4venture.com/content/Case%20for%20Late%20Stage%20
VC%20(July%202005).pdf.

12. David Shamah, "How can startups get their first VC investment? Ashton
Kutcher has some tips," originally for *Tel Aviv Tech*, May 20, 2013,
accessed on ZDNet, www.zdnet.com/how-can-startups-get-their-first-
vc-investment-ashton-kutcher-has-some-tips-7000015604/ accessed on
January 4, 2014

13. Tom Chiarella, "The All New Ashton Kutcher Story!" *Esquire*, February 14,
2013.

14. David Zeiler, "What Ashton Kutcher Can Teach You about Tech Investing,"
Money Morning (Web site), June 19, 2013, http://moneymorning.
com/2013/06/19/what-ashton-kutcher-can-teach-you-about-tech-
investing/ accessed on January 12, 2014

15. Tom Chiarella, "The All New Ashton Kutcher Story!"

CHAPTER 8

Fund Size and Portfolio Construction

*"I agree that two times two makes four is an excellent thing;
but if we are dispensing praise, then two times two makes five is
sometimes a most charming little thing as well."*
—Fyodor Dostoyevsky, *Notes from Underground*

Fund size is determined by the portfolio construction and capital needs to maintain fund ownership. Fund size is also determined by target sectors—life sciences, especially, tend to be capital intensive. Institutional investors, especially those managing multibillion dollars, prefer to invest in funds than are at least $100 million in size. This allows them to maintain efficiency and manage relationships appropriately.

Portfolio construction design factors in the size and timing of investments with the view to balancing cash flows and minimizing risk. Portfolio construction design involves the following:

- Total number of companies, typically a range, say 8 to 12. For technology funds, this range tends to be higher, at 20 to 30 companies.
- Average total investment amount per company, typically no more than 10 percent of the fund.
- Average investment amount at the point of entry. Typically, this would be one-third of the average total investment per company. Capital is reserved for future rounds of investment.

- Average target ownership at time of exit, and target exit values leading to target internal rate of return (IRR) estimates.
- Stage of investment—seed, early, or growth. These stages require different amounts of capital and offer differing risk-return profiles. Amount of investment by stage of company, reserves of capital for future round, and anticipated timing should be estimated.

The size of the fund vis-à-vis the investment strategy is an important consideration for institutional investors. Consider a portfolio construction strategy of a Midwest-based early-stage life sciences company. At Arboretum Ventures I, a fund of $20 million was established to focus on the health care sector. This fund size would allow investments of up to $2 million in 8 to 10 early-stage companies. In comparison, a technology fund is expected to invest in as many as 25 to 30 companies, as the sector is capital efficient. On the other end of the spectrum is a large fund such as Norwest Venture Partners (NVP). NVP targets multistage (venture and growth stage) companies across the globe.

While the life of the fund is legally established for 10 years, the capital is deployed during the investment period, typically the first five years. Fund managers actively seek to invest and build the portfolio during this period. The goal is to generate returns rapidly, say, within four to six years from the time of investment. However, technology investments have shorter market cycles and follow established patterns of capital needs, company maturation, and exit timing. On the other hand, medical devices and biotech investments require larger amounts of capital and have longer maturation timelines.

From these parameters, fund managers need to ensure the following portfolio construction attributes:

- *Source efficiently:* The quality of an existing portfolio determines the probability and timing of the raise of the next fund. Venture investors normally invest in about 1 percent of the companies they review. This means that the practitioners will need to review an average of 1,000 companies, if not more, to achieve the desired portfolio size of, say, 10 companies. That is an average of one company a day! Thus, the territory must be fertile with entrepreneurial opportunities. Casting a wider geographic net is essential if the ecosystem is barren.
- *Build a quality portfolio:* Ideally, in about four to five years from launch of the fund, a fund's portfolio is fully constructed. Toward later years, GPs seek opportunities where an exit is likely to occur within a shorter time frame. For emerging managers, the ability to find a company that yields a strong 10X-like exit in a three- to five-year window is critical. Without strong realized returns, the fund runs the risk of staying stunted.

- *Prepare for losses:* A good portfolio manager knows which companies to keep and which ones to let go. Many a GP has struggled with portfolio companies that cannot meet their value-creation milestones, or generate target returns in a time span of, say, five to seven years. The faster you recognize those losses, the faster you can redirect your time and resources to suitable portfolio companies. In constructing the portfolio, GPs often fall in love with their own cooking and ignore obvious signs of a downward trajectory. A number of factors—ego, saving face, good capital following bad—can stall this process and become a sinkhole. As David Cowan says, "Just focus on your top five—the rest is distraction." The harder part of the investor's discipline is to know when to quit. A seasoned practitioner, Seth Rudnick of Canaan Partners, points out that risk is inherent in this business and calls for a disciplined balance that any limited partner (LP) would expect.

  Despite all the foresight and hindsight that you can muster, you can still go wrong. And that is the difficulty of being in this business. The environment, markets, technology, regulatory agencies are all drivers of risk. You have to constantly scan all of those things and adjust anticipated outcomes. If you see a portfolio company consistently stumble, as a board member you may feel compelled to continue to work on that company. But as a venture investor you may ponder 'I can't make this work anymore and should let it die. I should rather turn my efforts to something I can make work.' And that's hard for practitioners. The intrinsic belief to throw a little more energy and a little more time into it may not necessarily save the company.[1]

- *Time is your enemy:* Portfolio companies always take twice as much capital and twice as long to exit. Early-stage companies rarely meet milestones as planned and always burn cash faster than anticipated. If the capital markets are frozen and no exit is foreseen, raising additional capital can be difficult. Most early-stage investors are wary of "future financing risk," where they have lost preferences and ownership position in portfolio companies. External factors and market conditions are bound to augment this risk. Establish a contingency plan. Institutional investors seek real-life experience where fund managers were able to protect their investment in such circumstances. Staging and prudent management of reserve capital ensure that milestones are met and the overall ownership is preserved until exit.

- *And finally, not all exits will be equal:* Not all exits are going to be IPOs, as much as you wish. Staged investments minimize risk but also reduce the potential returns.

SMALLER IS BETTER

"Take a typical $400 million fund. To get a 20 percent return over six years, you have to triple your capital, turning $400 million into $1.2 billion. It's going to take longer than six years, and you have to add management fees and carry, so that $400 million fund roughly has to return $1.5 billion to the investors to get a 20 percent return. On exit, that fund will own at most 20 percent of a company. That means that a $400 million VC fund has to create $7.5 billion of market value to return $1.5 billion to its LPs in order to deliver a 20 percent return."
—Josh Koppelman, First Round Capital

A fund's portfolio is a demonstration of fund managers' ability to execute upon their own vision. "The portfolio is your strategy in action: you can touch the portfolio, taste it, and see it. I spend a lot of my time visiting portfolio companies. I can tell when something is going well, and the portfolio companies share the value of VC and how it is actualized. This is the prism: I see the whole symphony being played out, and hopefully it is a harmonious interplay of the various elements," says Chris Douvos, who has been an institutional investor for over a decade.

Lisa Edgar of Top Tier Capital Partners summarizes the art of portfolio management succinctly:

As experienced LPs, our decision-making process relies upon pattern recognition in order to identify the characteristics of success and of failure—something [general partners] GPs should be able to do, too. What I'm looking for is the fund manager's view of which companies look like winners and which companies aren't quite cutting it, so that they can manage the portfolio to support only those that deserve additional capital. I understand this is an extremely difficult exercise— especially for very early-stage companies or when the outcome is truly binary, like with many health care investments. I would suggest that picking the winners from the losers—and more importantly, effectively managing the fund's capital—is specifically the role of the GP (and for which the limited partners pay a management fee). . . . I want to know how the VC's micro views on each company and macro view of the exit environment is directing overall capital allocation. That's what we call 'portfolio management,' and to LPs, effective portfolio management is one of the core criteria we use to evaluate managers.[2]

FIT WITHIN THE LP'S CURRENT PORTFOLIO

Any institutional investor manages a number of portfolio relationships. Capital is allocated in various asset classes to balance risk and returns. In *Beyond the J Curve: Managing a Portfolio of Venture Capital and Private Equity Funds*, authors Thomas Meyer and Pierre-Yves Mathonet point out that institutional LPs typically follow either a combination of a top-down approach or a bottom-up approach.[3] In a top-down approach, an LP would start with picking a sector (technology or life sciences), geographic region (Silicon Valley, Beijing, Israel), fund style (private equity [PE], venture capital, buyout), and stage (early, mezzanine, multistage).

A bottom-up approach is opportunistic and starts with identifying suitable funds, conducting a thorough analysis, performing due diligence, and completing the investment. Most LPs tend to blend these two approaches. "We look at every prospective deal in two ways: first in isolation, to see that it stands on its own merits; and secondly we see how the deal fits in the context of our existing portfolio. We obviously do not want to load the portfolio with a lot of [GPs] pursuing the same strategy, but there are areas where we are actively seeking greater levels of exposure," says Peter Keehn, head of alternative investments, Allstate Investments, managing $120 billion in assets.[4]

The matrix of relationships is vast and intricate, as seen in Figure 8.1; thus, any GP ought to qualify a target LP vis-à-vis his or her current portfolio.

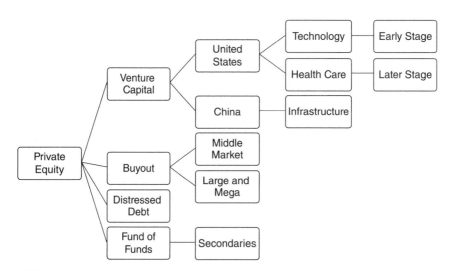

FIGURE 8.1 Sample LP's PE portfolio—A crowded dinner table.

While no LP publicly discloses their portfolio, Kenneth Van Heel suggests a simple approach: "We are trying to build our relationships, like everyone else. If I get an e-mail asking whether we are looking to invest in early-stage technology funds, I would have little hesitation in responding with candor."

Bob Clone, who managed a portfolio at a $50 billion state pension fund, noted: "We design our portfolio, but in general, we have always found room to accommodate a good opportunity. We have a top-down approach with subgroups within private equity such as venture, buyout, mezzanine, distressed debt, and growth equity. When we add a new fund, my allocation moves from 9 percent to 10 percent, so it does not make a significant difference. But if we are overweighed in a sector, say, I have eight biotech funds, we are not going to go for the ninth, obviously. We do watch allocations within each subgroup to ensure we are balanced."

Chris Douvos points out the challenges of new entrants in any LP's portfolio: "All my GPs are like my children: I love them all, but they all keep me up at night for different reasons. But I have a limited amount of money. At my dinner table, I can ladle out only so much soup. If you want to come for dinner, I have to send one kid off to college or juvenile hall—my table is a crowded one. If you are doing the same old thing, it's not compelling. What is it about your voodoo that would make me send one of my kids packing?"

Any institution invests a considerable amount of time in building a portfolio of relationships. In surveys of top 100 leading institutional investors, only around 40 percent were open to considering new relationships.

"Investors have invested the effort, completed the due diligence, and committed to the marriage," says Gus Long. The easier thing for any investor to do is to commit additional capital to an existing relationship, often called a re-up. A new manager means more work, more risk, and more uncertainty for any institutional investor. Thus, for most new fund managers, the competition is not from other new funds competing to get in, but from the existing relationships—or, as Douvos puts it, a crowded dinner table.

MARKET TIMING

Any investment strategy is based on a premise that the market conditions are ripe, ready to be exploited by entrepreneurs and the venture capitalists (VCs). But if the institutional investors are unable to react, the window of opportunity often closes. Institutional investors are often weary of new market opportunities and move slowly and cautiously. Market timing is critical when it comes to fund-raising. Investors are quick to point out that "Why should I invest in your fund?" is not a question that is as important as "Why now?"

Why should I invest in your fund now? How is your investment strategy relevant in the present market conditions?

"From time to time we have a market-driven and opportunistic approach within our generally structured portfolio architecture"[5] remarks Christophe Nicolas, executive director, Morgan Stanley Alternative Investment Partners, a fund of funds that manages over $6.5 billion. Figure 8.2 shows how various subasset classes within private equity compete for investor capital.

In favorable market conditions, if the institutional investors seek to rebalance their portfolios or reduce their commitments, it is likely that a fund manager may not have much traction in fund-raising discussions. "We have exited our relationships on several occasions when we are over weighted in certain categories. At times, we find that the number of relationships cannot be monitored effectively," says Van Heel. On other occasions, fund managers tend to be highly opportunistic in timing the raise of a new fund. "I get a chuckle when I receive a new fund documents right after a big exit has occurred. The performance looks fantastic, but most of us look past the short-term good news," quips one institutional investor.

For any fund manager getting ready to raise his or her next fund, market timing is important, but the amplitude of these shifts needs to be closely timed with LP sentiment. Successful fund raising is tied to performance as well as macromarket conditions.

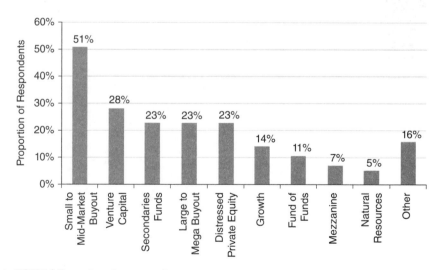

FIGURE 8.2 What the LPs seek.

Source: Preqin, 2013.

WHY LPS TERMINATE EXISTING RELATIONSHIPS

Catherine Crockett, founder of Grove Street Advisors, a fund of funds (FoF) with more than $6 billion under management, says, "Terminating a relationship is the hardest part." Crockett and her team screen more than 500 fund managers and deploy $500 million in any given year.

The primary reasons for terminating a relationship are performance, partners' motivations, and fund size.

- *Fund performance:* When performance falters, the decision is easy. No re-ups; it is an easy good-bye.
- *Partners' motivations and alignment:* As partners become successful, they lose their motivation—bloated senior partners with decreasing appetite should stay on the couch, not feature prominently in the private placement memorandum (PPM). They are not an asset in this business.

"It's a swell offer, Brad, and you're a great guy, but I've just got out of a bad limited partnership, and I'm not ready for that kind of commitment yet."

Ensuring that the rewards are shared with all investment committee and junior members is important. Finally, partners need to stay current with the market and technology developments.

■ *Fund size:* Successful funds grow too big too fast. LPs worry that with bloated funds, finding the right investment opportunities and generating returns will be harder. Small is beautiful, indeed. While success breeds success, as more LPs try to kick down the doors, the smarter LPs quietly exit through the side doors.

In a dynamic world, markets change, and the ability to generate returns changes. "If the three variables, investment team, investment strategy, and the market environment, are static, it is easy to make re-up decisions. But these are in a state of perpetual flux," says Lisa Edgar of Top Tier Capital Partners.

Fund-raising is an extremely competitive exercise. Consider the fact that more than 400 funds were seeking aggregate commitments of $80 billion.[6] Only about a third of the population will be able to attract capital. Thus, any fund manager needs to establish strong differentiators.

First-time funds have limited probability of raising funds with institutional investors, but they are looked on favorably by some fund of funds. History shows that fund managers who started small, raised capital from high-net-worth individuals and local foundations, and built a track record were able to achieve liftoff. The LP courtship process is a long and slow dance. As most LPs say, introductions are the best way to start. The role of a placement agent can be critical. For new managers, the typical time line from the first touch to a commitment is about 12 months or as long as three years.

A new fund is always scrutinized to the highest degree. The amount of diligence is an order of magnitude higher: track record, references, and such. "We put every piece of relevant information in the data room and let the LPs slice it any way they want," says Ravi Mohan of Shasta Ventures. "We did not pick a list of references but rather said, here are *all* the people we worked with. We did not cherry-pick—we let them decide who to call." In the end, it paid off. Shasta Ventures raised its Fund I in six months. The fund was oversubscribed.

Finally, success begets success. Benchmark Fund I generated an envious 92X cash-on-cash multiple. The fund raising timelines for Benchmark Fund II were probably shorter as compared to their first fund.

NOTES

1. Seth Rudnick (Canaan Partners), in discussions with the author, September 2010
2. Lisa Edgar, "Are We Going to Make Money in This Fund?" *PEHub* (blog), www.pehub.com/81521/are-we-going-to-make-money-in-this-fund.

3. Thomas Meyer and Pierre-Yves Mathonet, *Beyond the J Curve: Managing a Portfolio of Venture Capital and Private Equity Funds* (West Sussex: John Wiley & Sons, 2005).

4. AltAssets, "Institutional Investor Profile: Peter Keehn, Head of Alternative Investments, Allstate Investments, LLC," June 29, 2006, accessed February 20, 2011, www.altassets.com/private-equity-features/by-author-name/article/nz8835.html.

5. AltAssets, "Investor Profile: Christophe Nicolas, Executive Director, Morgan Stanley Alternative Investment Partners," December 8, 2009, accessed February 20, 2011, www.altassets.com/private-equity-investor-profiles/article/nz17499.html.

6. Preqin Investor Outlook: Private Equity, "The Opinions of 100 Leading Private Equity LPs on the Market and Their Plans in 2011."

CHAPTER 9

Performance Analysis

"This is the excellent foppery of the world, that,
when we are sick in fortune,—often the surfeit
of our own behavior,—we make guilty of our
disasters the sun, the moon, and the stars, . . ."
— Shakespeare, *King Lear*, act 1, scene 2

Investors assess performance primarily at the fund level and compare any fund's performance against a set of benchmarks. Let us look at the various aspects of performance assessment and the challenges therein. But before we dive into fund-level performance, let us start with individual-level performance.

INDIVIDUAL PERFORMANCE AND ATTRIBUTION

At the heart of it, the business of venture capital is akin to skydiving—small teams form pretty patterns, but each diver has to hold his or her own. Splinter groups are formed frequently. While some glide along, navigating the strong winds, others often crash. The rest of the divers can do little to prevent a crashing partner, so they move on and form a different pattern. Inherently competitive at an individual level, this business is one of hero worship and also-rans, where personal brands often tend to rise above the brand of a firm.

When it comes to individual attribution, practitioners often add a string of successes to their bios. For presentations to limited partners (LPs), the individual performance of practitioners is typically presented with one-page

TABLE 9.1   Sample Format: Individual Performance of a Practitioner

Name of Portfolio Company (Date of investment)	Investment Amount and Syndicate Investors	Investment Thesis	Current Status
SpiderCloud Wireless Inc., Santa Clara, CA. (Feb. 2013) Information technology	$55 million Charles River Ventures, Matrix Partners, Opus Capital	Indoor mobile-broadband networking gear for wireless operators. Helps solve network overload problems caused by handheld devices. Carriers like AT&T can meet the growing demand for mobile broadband on corporate campuses.	Closed a recent Series B round of $25 million. Company was recognized in *Wall Street Journal* as a Top 50 VC-backed company. Likely exit via a trade sale to Cisco or Juniper Networks.
ExactTarget, Indianapolis, IN. (May 2009) Information technology	$70 million Battery Ventures, Scale Venture Partners, TCV	Technology tools for e-mail and social media marketing	Company has raised $155 million and is IPO ready, although market challenges prevail. On a rapid growth path, completed three acquisitions in past 12 months.

case studies of each portfolio company. Table 9.1 depicts another sample format, a summary table that constitutes the list of portfolio companies managed by each professional.

Individual performance is measured along the following axes:

- Number and types of opportunities sourced and led or co-led.
- Amount of capital invested from fund.
- Amount of capital syndicated from other investors, including description of the firms.
- Number of boards participated.
- Exits and returns.

When it comes to individual attribution, fund managers should not only resist the urge to cherry-pick the best opportunities but also be prepared to share details of all the investments. "Cherry-picking can hurt your credibility: we live in a world where we are a few degrees away from ascertaining the facts," says Christopher Rizik, fund manager at Renaissance Venture Capital Fund, a fund of funds. For investors, it is not just a listing of opportunities that matters, but the general partner's (GP's) role in value creation. Attribution challenges can also cause internal competition within a firm and destroy its chemistry. In a business where hero worship trounces teamwork, it is easy to see why a partner would want to be on the board of a fast-rising portfolio company. In one firm, a newer partner, seeking instant attribution nirvana, assigned himself to the board of a rapidly growing portfolio company, edging the younger partner out. This business calls for a sharp mind, not sharp elbows—the younger partner eventually left the firm and took his skills elsewhere. The opportunity that was once rising soon cratered. Investors are all too familiar with such clever maneuvers. "Attribution ambiguity can be sorted out quickly; in most cases, the person who sourced the opportunity and nurtured it would be the first board member. We also talk to all the CEOs of portfolio companies to verify the fund managers' claims. In these discussions, the CEOs also help us understand who was a true value creator versus who showed up for the Christmas parties," says Kenneth Van Heel.

LPs are watchful of poor performance as well. If a partner's performance is uninspiring, LPs candidly share their concerns with the stronger partners and even establish preconditions for investments. This leads to elimination of weaker partners much in advance of the LP commitments. In one example, a new fund was set up by a number of practitioners who had worked at other brand-name firms. But when potential LPs really dug in and got off-the-record evaluation, the luster faded. In fact, these individuals had been pushed out of their firms. "These GPs were not the stars they made themselves out to be," remarked Clint Harris of Grove Street Advisors, a fund of funds, in an interview with AltAssets.[1] Despite this, a number of LPs had quickly lined up at the new fund's doors, eager to throw money at these underperformers, according to Harris.

FUND-LEVEL PERFORMANCE

LPs assess investment track records rigorously at the fund level as well as the contribution of each investment professional. Fund performance is measured using two primary metrics: internal rate of return (IRR) and cash on cash (CoC) multiples. While Table 9.2 shows fund-level performance in a stand-alone format, LPs typically assess stand-alone and benchmarked comparisons; but it is the LP who prefers to choose the benchmark. (See Table 9.3, in which all are early-stage funds with a U.S. regional focus.)

TABLE 9.2 Sample Fund Performance: Stand-Alone Format

Company	Date of Investment	Date of Realization	Total Capital Invested ($M)	Total Realized Proceeds (A) ($M)	Unrealized Value (B) ($M)	Total Value = A + B ($M)	Multiple of Invested Capital (×)	Gross IRR (%)
Realized investments								
Saver	Dec 08	Nov 09	$18.6	$60.0	—	$60	3.2	38.1
Distracter	Jan 09	Jun 10	$8.20	$1.0	$3.1	$4.1	0.5	NM
Total			$26.8	$61.0	$3.1	$64.1	2.39	24.2
Unrealized investments								
Potential	Mar 09	N/A	$5.0		$9.0	$9.0	1.8	9.2
Middle path	Jun 09	N/A	$8.20		$4.1	$4.1	0.5	NM
Total			$13.2		$13.1	$13.1	0.99	NM
Total fund investments			$40.0	$60.0	$17.1	$77.1	1.92	24.2

(NM = Not Meaningful)

TABLE 9.3 Sample Fund Performance: Benchmarked Format

Fund	Vintage	Fund Size ($M)	Type	Regional Focus	Called (%)	Distributed (%) DPI	Residual Value (%) RVPI	Multiple (X)	Net IRR (%)	Benchmark IRR (%)	Quartile	Date Reported
Avalon Ventures VI	1991	9	Early stage	U.S.	100.0	748.0	0.0	7.48	47.7	25.3	1	31-Mar-10
Avalon Ventures VII	2004	75	Early stage	U.S.	94.6	1.2	95.6	0.97	-1.2	-4.6	2	31-Dec-09
Avalon Ventures VIII	2007	150	Early stage	U.S.	36.5	0.0	378.5	3.78	182.0	-10.9	1	31-Dec-09

Source: Adapted from Preqin for illustrative purposes only.

LPs slice performance data in a number of ways, but it all begins with the returns. "Instead of giving us the aggregate performance numbers, it would be a lot easier if they gave us the cash flows for each portfolio company," says Bob Clone, who has managed over 75 GP relationships. LPs often grumble about the fact that data is not shared to the level of their satisfaction. The Institutional Limited Partners Association (ILPA) has developed reporting guidelines and templates for fund performance that addresses these challenges.[2]

Investors assess general performance metrics as well as specific data points. These data points are sliced in a number of different ways to understand the risk and GP's ability to adhere to the stated strategy.

- *Sourcing:* Did the opportunity originate through your proactive efforts? Or through a proprietary set of relationships? How well did the opportunity fit within the core investment criteria of the fund?
- *Investment analysis:* For established funds, LPs look into returns and analyze these by fund, year, industry subsectors, stage of investment, lead/co-lead roles and board representation. "At times, a fund's track record may be due to a 'one-off' event—we seek consistent performance over economic cycles," says Van Heel. A one-off event, also called a one-hit home run, occurs when one portfolio company generates the majority of the returns for the entire portfolio. "This business is about home runs indeed, but we aim to dissect the overall approach and strategy of the fund. At times, we remove the outliers from the venture fund portfolio and stress test it to see how the rest of the portfolio stacks up. And during the frothy times, we even take it one step further—we set aside the top two and bottom two outliers to see how resilient the returns are." Chopping off each end of the spectrum allows a rigorous investor to review the portfolio in a more balanced light. Several LPs agreed that this approach is used to stress test the returns. Others do not necessarily subscribe to this approach. "You are investing in VC for their best performing companies: the returns come from the top decile, whether it is in a fund, firm, or the industry. There is no consistency of return," says Perkins of Fisher Lynch Capital. Some LPs also seek to assess the loss ratio: the amount lost vis-à-vis the size of the fund. This ratio is a factor of sector and stage; for example, an early-stage technology fund would have a loss ratio of as much as 50 percent. A later-stage health care fund would be looking at a lower loss ratio. "Anything above 20 percent would make me nervous," says Igor Rozenblit, an institutional investor who invested in a venture fund that had a loss ratio of 3 percent.

Investors seek all these data points to predict a GP's ability to deliver consistent returns. "We use a number of data points—we start with our own internal notes, look at fund quarterly reports, web research, conferences, and portfolio company meetings—it is multidimensional. This assessment improves our ability to predict a firm's potential to earn the desired return," says Lisa Edgar. Predicting future performance is a harder challenge for any investor, but GPs need to be prepared to address what will make them successful in the current times. "If you don't have credible answers on how you plan to consistently generate returns, don't even bother knocking on any doors," says Gus Long of Stanwich Advisors.

COMPARISON BENCHMARKS

Investors compare fund performance with the aggregate returns generated by an entire venture capital asset class. For example, if a fund is of a certain vintage year and has generated 24.2 percent IRR, then an investor would stack these up against the appropriate benchmarks.

While selecting benchmarks, a number of self-selection caveats crop up here:

- *Vintage year:* A fund manager may be tempted to assign a vintage year when she started raising the fund as compared to when the final close occurred.
- *Universe of benchmarks:* The data source matters, as does the selection of benchmarks. Several data providers, including Cambridge Associates, Preqin, and Venture Economics, gather returns data. The universe of benchmarks can get equally large. Clever fund managers could position themselves as shining stars in any one of the following categories:
  - All private equity funds
  - All venture funds
  - All early-stage venture funds
  - All early-stage technology venture funds
  - All North America early-stage technology venture funds of the correct vintage year
- *Realized versus unrealized value:* The data can become muddier as you try to compare apples and oranges. Unrealized returns often translate to risk: values of shares held in any private companies often swing wildly.
- *Veracity of data/self-reporting:* As this industry calls for self-reporting, the skeptical LPs pointed out that on an industry-wide basis, the bad managers and the best managers never report their data—only the mediocre do. Diana Frazier of FLAG Capital management, a fund of funds, says, "The best managers do not bother submitting their

data to any databases." Thus, this creates another layer of complexity in trying to assess true performance of the vintage year. Rozenblit says, "We never used any public database due to the veracity issues. We had built our own internal assessment tools, which would give us some very powerful insights. I believe most LPs have similar internal tools." Rozenblit's firm receives at least 200 PPMs each year. His analysts would key in data from all investments from these 200 firms, building a substantial database, which could be sliced and analyzed in a number of different ways. Rizik suggests intellectual honesty:

MEASURES OF PERFORMANCE: IRR, COC, TVPI, OR DPI?

An informal survey conducted by McKinsey found that only 20 percent of executives understand the critical deficiencies of IRR.[3]

IRR has its allure, offering what seems to be a straightforward comparison of, say, 30 percent returns with 8 percent. IRRs appear favorable but do not consider reinvestment risks and the redeployment of capital in other investment opportunities in the calculation for investors.

Because IRR is expressed as a percentage, a small investment can show a triple-digit IRR. While this looks attractive at the first glance, a larger investment with a lower IRR can be more attractive on a net present value (NPV) basis. To interpret IRR as an annual equivalent return on a given investment is easy and intuitive, but this is only true if there are no interim cash flows. This may be the case with most venture investments, but in any biotech or a pharma exit, where earn-outs are negotiated, the IRR may become misleading quickly.

FLAG Capital Management, a fund-of-funds (FoF), points out that LPs often gauge fund performance by analyzing some nebulous combination of IRRs (dollar-weighted returns, which are influenced by the timing and magnitude of cash flows) and cash-on-cash investment multiples, either total value to paid-in capital (TVPI) or distributions to paid-in capital (DPI). Each can tell a different story and is important in its own right. But none is sufficient by itself to tell the whole story.[4]

Source: McKinsey Quarterly and FLAG Capital Management (see end notes for specific details).

"Make it simple: show me every investment you have made. If we smell any issues, it becomes a nonstarter. GPs should be forthcoming on the history."

PUBLIC MARKET EQUIVALENTS

While IRR and CoC are primary measures, public market equivalent (PME) measures a venture capital fund performance against an investment in S&P 500, an index of public market performance. If PME of a venture capital fund is greater than 1, then the investors did better than investing in publicly traded stocks.

Professor Steven Kaplan of University of Chicago Booth School of Business studied the various venture capital data sources such as Preqin, Cambridge Associates, and Venture Economics. He concluded that Preqin and Cambridge Associates data sets are closer to the actual data observed by institutional LPs, who manage their data sets in Burgis. Burgis data sets are much cleaner because they are derived entirely from institutional investors (the limited partners, or LPs) for whom Burgis's systems provide record-keeping and performance-monitoring services. This feature results in detailed, verified, and cross-checked investment histories for nearly 1,400 private equity funds derived from the holdings of more than 200 institutional investors.[5] Comparing data from Burgis over the years, Table 9.4 presents some the findings. Venture capital outperformed S&P 500 public markets index on an average across the three decades, and did so handily in the 1990s, while in the 1980s was a whisper better.

PUBLIC VERSUS PRIVATE : WHY PME MATTERS

PME is the simplest and the most effective measure of venture capital performance. Consider an example where an investor deploys $100 million in a venture fund and receives $200 million. In comparison, if $100 million were invested in S&P 500 during the same period, the investor would have received $207 million. Thus, gross PME = $200/$207 = 0.97, and net PME = $180/$207 = 0.87. In this case, the investor lost money by investing in this venture capital fund.

TABLE 9.4   Do Venture Capital Funds Outperform Public Markets?

Vintage Years	No. of Funds in Dataset	Capital Realized (%)	IRR*	Multiple of Capital	PME
Average	775	85.8	19.3	2.46	1.45
2000 s	423	33.0	0.3	1.07	0.95
1990 s	251	97.8	38.6	3.76	2.12
1980 s	101	100.0	15.8	2.37	1.08

Source: Robert S. Harris, Tim Jenkinson, and Steven N. Kaplan, "Private Equity Performance: What Do We Know?" *Journal of Finance* (July 2013).

*IRR presented is weighted average (capital committed for each fund as a proportion of the total commitments for each vintage year).

THE QUEST FOR THE ELUSIVE TOP QUARTILE MANAGERS

For all venture funds, being in the top 25 percent of their class is a coveted position. LPs and GPs alike view this golden spot most favorably. Studies show that top quartile public equity (PE) funds sustain their performance and produce returns of 50 percent greater than public benchmarks.[6] In one study, top quartile PE funds generated annual returns of 39 percent over a 25-year period—more than triple the returns for the S&P 500 (12.1 percent) and the NASDAQ (12.3 percent) in the same period.[7] Table 9.5 and Figure 9.1 further demonstrate the variance between the top and the bottom ends of the spectrum. Despite the fact that the data in Figure 9.1 is from 2001, the point illustrated is that the IRR variance due to manager selection is far more significant than any other metric. With such a wide variation, it is evident why LPs seek the best in class.

With stellar returns, it is no wonder that PE/venture capital is an extremely attractive investment—and that investors are looking for the crème de la crème of the universe to maximize returns. David Swensen of Yale University writes, "Selecting top quartile managers in private markets leads to much greater reward....The first quartile venture capitalist surpasses the median by 30.1 percent per annum, providing a much greater contribution to portfolio results."[8]

According to Kelly DePonte, the priority among investors is access to high-performing funds.[9] But the top funds are inaccessible for the vast majority of investors. A handful of funds have generated superior returns in a consistent fashion. The biggest beneficiaries of this performance have been larger institutions—the public and private pension funds, endowments, and foundations—which have seen their PE investments beating public market indexes.

A multibillion dollar French institutional investor, a financial powerhouse of sorts, came to Silicon Valley eagerly seeking relationships with

TABLE 9.5 The Best versus the Worst: Performance Variance in Venture Funds

Vintage	IRR Maximum	IRR Minimum
2003	21.1	–4.6
2002	43.2	–27.7
2001	29.0	–100.0
2000	29.0	–25.4
1999	18.0	–40.6
1998	1,025.1	–46.1
1997	213.0	–35.0
1996	133.3	–33.3
1995	447.4	–19.9
1994	73.2	–23.2
1993	87.4	–14.8
1992	110.4	–20.1
1991	346.4	1.2

Source: Preqin Median Benchmarks, all regions, Venture, as of September 2009, calculated for 648 funds. Returns net of management fees, expenses, and carried interests.

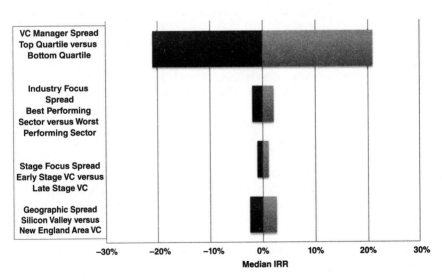

FIGURE 9.1 Manager selection and return variance: Manager selection trounces everything else.

Source: General Motors Investment Management Company.

a top quartile fund, but did not get much love: "After a number of calls, the top tier venture fund agreed to meet with us. All they would share is *a statement of net returns*. No details of portfolio companies or the amount invested, nor gross returns. Nor would we get any additional materials for due diligence. This fund was obviously trying to be efficient on the due diligence process as well as hiding the fee income. Their take-it-or-leave-it attitude was indicative of the demand-supply situation."[10] The French investor passed on the opportunity to invest in this top quartile fund.

ALL THE MANAGERS ARE ABOVE AVERAGE

According to FLAG Capital Management, being in the top quartile is akin to the Lake Wobegon effect, where all the managers are above average. "Like most LPs, I am still waiting for the 'other 75 percent' to show up—none of us know where to find them," quips Chris Rizik, fund manager, Renaissance Venture Capital Fund, a fund-of-funds.

To position themselves in the top quartile, 77 percent of PE firms were found to change key data inputs such as the selection of the reference benchmark and the definition of the fund's vintage year.[11] In this vein, one LP sardonically pointed out, "Sure—any fund can be in the top quartile when you self-select the benchmark and compare with funds that have all exits that occurred on a Monday in the month of October when the full moon was shining at its brightest."

The criteria for establishing performance benchmarks are riddled with inconsistencies and ambiguity, with measurements to identify top quartile private capital funds varying widely. While public equity fund managers can look to indexes such as the S&P 500, private fund managers do not have the luxury of straightforward benchmarks. FLAG Capital Management further points out in its newsletter that "Top quartile can mean a net IRR of 25 percent for its latest fund in its class" or a fund whose "CoC multiple" is in the top quartile of its fund class. But the dimensions can get tricky when you consider more subtle criteria. For example, funds with very attractive rates of return may have inferior CoC multiples if they have been flipped quickly. Funds may also have impressive projections on performance but no cash distributions. A venture firm may have a range of strong performing funds and one poor fund that, if excluded, can boost the other funds and bring it into the coveted top quartile position. In fact, omission of certain investments from the historical track record to boost performance indicators is a common tactic practiced among funds.[12]

With the imperfect state of performance benchmarking in the PE industry, investors cannot always make accurate investment decisions. Oliver Gottschalg, cofounder of the consulting firm Peracs, has put it this way: "Being in the 'top quartile' somewhere, somehow is not a meaningful criterion to assess the quality of a GP."[13] Assessing performance is as much an art as it is a science. With these challenges, it is imperative for the LPs to demand better measurements.

But as FLAG Capital correctly points out, the top performers have no motivation to offer their performance data. And those at the bottom of the pile hide the data to avoid any further embarrassment. What we have left is data from a pile of middle-market players. Any LP struggles with this conundrum— you could end up with "tallest among the very small." You can sense the challenges in the following excerpt from *Insights,* a FLAG Capital newsletter:

> *A serious problem in establishing benchmarks is the sourcing and aggregation of financial data because of the lack of transparency and publicly disclosed information from private companies. Often, this data is embedded in quarterly reports typically only sent to a select batch of people. Another source of information is through voluntary disclosure from the fund managers themselves or through performance reporting by clients or advisory services. The existing benchmarks professional investment advisors often compile are also flawed, as a large share of their funds tend to be from higher quality managers that the firm goes on to recommend to clients. Another inherent problem is that data from large institutional investors, such as pension funds, are often compiled from a sample of disproportionately large funds.*
>
> *Whatever the source, significant biases adversely affect frank attempts to benchmark the data. Sources dependent on accessibility and selective contributions lead to nonrepresentative sampling of the universe of PE funds. Finally, incentives to report are also misleading.*
>
> *Consider the choices top-performing managers have. There is no incentive to contribute fund data to the index, which only serves to raise the benchmark and makes the performance of the fund look less stellar compared to its peers. On the other hand, poorly performing fund managers also have no incentive to disclose data to a third party because they are highly unlikely to raise another fund. As one LP remarked, "Two poorly performing funds, and you are out of the game."*
>
> *Existing barometers for investors are therefore the best of what's available, but they should be approached with a grain of salt. Performance evaluation is still important; the key is to be cautious on selection of benchmarks, especially if self-selected by GPs. LPs dig deeper into manager track records, identify quantitative and qualitative indicators of performance on an absolute and relative level, and monitor the fund diligently beyond static indicators, such as the seemingly inviolable top-quartile benchmark.[14]*

NOTES

1. AltAssets, "Institutional Investor Profile: Clint Harris, Managing Partner, Grove Street Advisors," September 4, 2002, accessed February 20, 2011, www.altassets.net/features/institutional-investor-profile-clint-harris-managing-partner-grove-street-advisors.html

2. These can be accessed at http://ilpa.org/ilpa-standardized-reporting-templates.

3. John C. Kelleher and Justin J. MacCormack, "Internal Rate of Return: A Cautionary Tale," McKinsey Quarterly, October 20, 2004, accessed February 20, 2011, www.cfo.com/printable/article.cfm/3304945.

4. FLAG Capital Management, "Behind the Benchmarks: The Art of Private Capital Performance Assessment," November 2009, accessed February 20, 2011, http://www.flagcapital.com/media/3870/insights_2009_november_-_behind_the_benchmarks.pdf

5. Robert S. Harris, Tim Jenkinson, and Steven N. Kaplan, "Private Equity Performance: What Do We Know?" (July 2013). Journal of Finance, forthcoming; Fama-Miller Working Paper; Chicago Booth Research Paper No. 11–44; Darden Business School Working Paper No. 1932316. Available at SSRN: http://ssrn.com/abstract = 1932316 or http://dx.doi.org/10.2139/ssrn.1932316

6. Oliver Gottschalg and Robert M. Ryan, "Advanced Private Equity Benchmarking," Private Equity International, February 2008, accessed February 20, 2011, www.peracs.de/report/PEI_61_Guest5.pdf.

7. Private Equity Growth Capital Council, "Private Equity FAQ," July 2008, accessed February 20, 2011, www.pegcc.org/just-the-facts/private-equity-frequently-asked-questions.

8. David F. Swensen, Pioneering Portfolio Management: An Unconventional Approach to Institutional Investment (New York: Free Press, 2009), 75.

9. Kelly DePonte, "Lack of Access to Top Funds Is No. 1 LP Concern," Venture Capital Journal, May 1, 2007, accessed February 20, 2011, www.probitaspartners.com/pdfs/Lack_of_Access.pdf.

10. Anonymous institutional investor, in discussions with the author, September 2010.

11. FLAG Capital Management, "Behind the Benchmarks".

12. Ibid.

13. Ibid.

14. Ibid.

CHAPTER 10

Emerging Managers: A Promise of the Future

"Our best investment ever was in a first-time fund."[1]
—Sergey Sheshuryak, Adams Street Partners, a fund of funds (FoF)

Chamath Palihapitiya, employee number 40 at Facebook and the founder of venture fund The Social+Capital Partnership, is hailed by many as an unconventional venture capitalist. Institutional investors might label him as an emerging manager. Palihapitiya, who stood 39th on a list of Silicon Valley's 100 most influential people in 2012, was born in Sri Lanka.[2] His family immigrated to Canada to escape a civil war. Soon after obtaining a First Class Honors degree in Electrical Engineering from the University of Waterloo, he moved to California. Prior to launching his venture fund Social+Capital, he held senior management positions at AOL and Facebook. He joined Facebook when it had just over 50 million users and left with 750 million users. While at Facebook, he was making personal bets on start-ups such as gaming company Playdom and software company Bumptop. His bets started to pay off: Disney bought Playdom and Bumptop was sold to Google. The payout from these investments and Facebook planted the seeds for a career path as a venture capitalist (VC).

"The best VCs are like the best entrepreneurs—they can raise money quickly. Chamath has deep product-market skills, which were further honed as employee number 40 at Facebook," says one institutional investor. Palihapitiya's angel investment chops, and his own commitment to invest roughly $60 million or about 20 percent of the capital, got his fund launched.

Unlike a typical venture capital firm, which usually comprises several managers financed by a passive group of institutional investors, Social+Capital operates like an investor collective. Palihapitiya pays himself a fixed salary with no incentives. His philosophy is that traditional venture capital places a lot of emphasis on bonuses, which is driven by people who are giving money. That traditional structure, he argues, tempts fund managers to chase big fund-raising rounds and deals with quick exits. On the contrary, the fixed salary plus the fact that he's risked a lot of his own money helps him stay focused on the long term and make investments in areas that he really believes in. Palihapitiya sees himself as an activist investor who wants to break away from traditional venture capital methods, which, he perceives, are broken and opaque. Speaking at the national conference, Palihapitiya ruffled a few feathers by claiming that start-up quality is at an all-time low and people are not focusing on solving "real" problems. His mantra is that venture capital, when properly deployed, can solve the world's biggest problems and fill up the void of what he believes are shrinking scientific ambitions worldwide. Social+Capital mostly limits itself to investments in three sectors—health care, finance, and education services. Palihapitiya is particularly bullish on health care and wants to cash in on the $5 trillion promised under the Affordable Care Act. A passionate poker player, he recently made news by participating in the world's first $1 million poker tournament. His Tweet—"I change lives. I also have a jet"—sums him up well.

Yet for most institutional investors and limited partners, Palihapitiya would qualify as an emerging manager—or a practitioner who has yet to demonstrate superior returns in a consistent fashion. Take the example of Steven Lazarus, founder of ARCH Venture Partners. When Lazarus started to raise ARCH Venture Partners Fund I, investors would say, "Your track record is all ahead of you."[3] Those investors threw Lazarus in the emerging manager box and dismissed him. ARCH Fund I celebrated four IPOs as well as four acquisitions and generated 22 percent internal rate of return (IRR).[4]

The changing industry offers new opportunities for investors to access investments outside the mainstream venture capital universe. For investors, striking a balance between established fund managers and tilting slightly in favor of emerging managers is increasingly becoming the norm. In building more mixed portfolios with funds managed by premier names, as well as funds managed by emerging managers, investors can build dynamic and diversified portfolios and ensure risk-adjusted returns over the long run.

Several criteria are often used in identifying emerging managers.[5] According to Kelly DePonte, at one end of the spectrum they may be "first-time fund, first-time investors"—a group of professionals who lack significant investment experience. They may also be a group of individuals who have experience, but no track record working as a cohesive team. There could also be spin-offs of existing, more established funds. Partners who have raised money on a deal-by-deal basis and built their track records would be appropriate candidates for raising funds.

But limited partners (LPs) prefer experienced investors who have played the game well. As Gus Long of Stanwich Advisors points out, "First-time fund is acceptable, but not a first-time investor." As venture firms grow, partners run into incentive sharing and succession issues.[6] These issues may cause the stronger partners to split and form new firms, where they are in better control of their destiny, the brand, and the economics.

Finally, women or minorities who have been traditionally underrepresented in the venture capital and private equity (PE) markets are often dubbed as emerging.

WHY LPS SEEK EMERGING MANAGERS

Emerging managers compensate for their perceived shortcomings in many ways, offering a unique edge for investors.

A Futures Option

Kenneth Smith of Park Street Capital says, "My primary approach to emerging managers is to identify those super-performers who will be hard to access in later funds."[7] Often hungrier, they have a passion for investing in new platforms or in emerging markets such as Brazil and China. Grove Street Advisors has developed a simple yet effective technique to build an emerging manager portfolio (see Figures 10.1 and 10.2): make small bets and build up the position as the performance improves. Crockett explains, "We were fortunate to have backed Granite Global Ventures (GGV). Grove Street was an early investor in GGV-Fund I, which backed leading companies in China, like Alibaba. The timing could not have been better for both GGV and Grove Street."

Creativity, Hunger, and Performance

Kelvin Liu of Invesco, a fund of funds (FoF), writes that "since they do not have historic challenges of poor performance, they are able to pursue unique investment strategies."[8] As mavericks in the capital markets, they often have stronger motivations.

According to Hany Nada, cofounder of GGV, "when we started GGV-I, it was the aftermath of the dot-com crash in 2001—one of the toughest

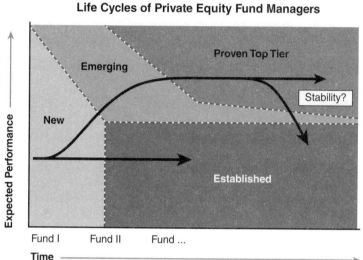

FIGURE 10.1 FoF allocation for an emerging manager portfolio.
Source: © Grove Street Advisors. Reproduced with permission.

periods to launch a new fund. Our compelling investment strategy was an important factor, but the only reason we made it during the tough economic times was because we were 'all-in'—a 110 percent commitment in making this fund successful. We had burnt all boats and there was no plan B. The LPs could sense this commitment," he says.

As a result, emerging managers are more fiercely driven toward achieving high performance and results right out of the starting gate and evolve to be nimble in their decision making. With entrepreneurial sensibilities, they

FIGURE 10.2 Concentrating capital with top performers.
Source: © Grove Street Advisors. Reproduced with permission.

often seize the market opportunities that their more established colleagues would balk at. In many ways, they run faster and have less to lose and more to gain from investing smarter than the bigger players.

Underdogs looking to prove themselves, they are often more flexible in working with investors, resulting in a greater alignment with investor interest. LPs and investors often take bigger percentage shares in their funds—larger than the typical 10 percent cap. Empowered, investors can then wield influence on decisions, terms, and fees.[9] "We don't mind being a disproportional part of the fund—in some cases we invested, say $5 million in a $40 million fund, and in others, we have about $19 million in a $50 million fund," says John Coelho of StepStone Group.[10]

Often, emerging managers integrate a different cultural mind-set. Much more open, some share their views in blogs and live a transparent life. Their way of doing business makes their more established counterparts look downright prosaic and even backward.

The general misperception of emerging managers is that they lack the experience and track record. Within the institutional LP community, the perceived risks in investing in emerging managers are high as these are perceived as ill-equipped, untested, and unseasoned neophytes. Rumson Capital Advisors, based in Princeton, New Jersey, observed that less than 7 percent of new firms generate returns in the top quartiles.[11] In essence, they were dismissed as minor league players in the world dominated by juggernauts.

All these qualities—smaller fund size, a taste for nontraditional investment strategy, drive, and innovation—are elevating emerging managers among those investors looking for a different path toward success.[12]

FORTY-SEVEN EXITS AND $4.3 BILLION OF VALUE, ALL IN SEVEN YEARS

In a short span of seven years, Aydin Senkut of Felicis Ventures has invested in some of the leading companies in the world and has 47 exits creating upward of $4 billion in value. This performance has catapulted him to become one of the top 10 up-and-coming VCs in the Forbes Midas List, featuring the who's who of the VC universe.

"As immigrants, we have to work hard to fit in, we try harder," says Senkut, who was born in Istanbul and speaks five languages including Turkish, Portuguese, German, and French. As Google's first international product manager, he launched the company's first 10 international sites, and played a key role in Google's translation service. Later, he moved to international business development. Seven years

(Continued)

FORTY-SEVEN EXITS AND $4.3 BILLION: *(Continued)*

later, he called it quits and founded Felicis Ventures, with a modest $4.5 million to invest.

In a period of seven years, Felicis invested in more than 90 companies and now manages over $110 million in assets. Four years after its first angel fund, Felicis raised a super-angel fund of $41 million, which was oversubscribed by 30 percent. Two years later, Senkut got back in the market and raised a boutique fund of $70 million, which was 42 percent oversubscribed. With 47 exits of an aggregate enterprise value of $4.3 billion, Senkut has established his mark in the early stage arena.

HOW INVESTORS RANK EMERGING MANAGERS

Rarely does an LP make an investment decision solely on the fact that a general partner (GP) is emerging—it may get a GP's foot in the door, which is a good start. A pecking order, as seen in Figure 7.1, establishes the probability of raising an institutional fund.

The primary risk that any LP faces with emerging managers is career risk. After all, why would LPs risk the embarrassment of losing their capital (and their job) with an unproven manager? "It's a lot safer to invest in Fund V," says John Coelho of StepStone Group.[13] Factors that impact LP decisions include the following:

- Ability to distinguish between market hype and market reality
- Strong knowledge base/domain awareness
- Differentiators of the fund strategy
- Sustained differentiation: Barriers to entry from other competitive investors
- Team dynamics and cohesion

And the signal-to-noise ratio in this category is significant. "Over the past eight years, we have seen 1,100 emerging manager funds and have invested only in 36," says Amit Tiwari, director at Invesco Private Capital.[14] Some managers deliberately slot themselves in this "emerging" category to gain attention from LPs, a ploy that is not necessarily advantageous. After being hounded by one firm for too long, an LP acerbically commented: "You have been emerging for too long—just call me back when you have actually *emerged*!"

INSTITUTIONAL ALLOCATIONS FOR EMERGING MANAGERS

Emerging managers tend to be sought out by high-net-worth individuals, family offices, and government funds, rather than by some institutional investors.[15]

The FoFs are often more open to emerging managers and have specific mandates (see Figure 10.3). Major institutional investors, such as California Public Employees' Retirement System (CalPERS) and California State Teachers' Retirement System (CalSTRS), actively invest in emerging manager-led funds. The effort is dubbed as "building investment portfolios that tap into the changing demographics and talent emerging in California and the nation."[16] For investment authorities at CalPERS and CalSTRS, the decision enables beneficiaries to access an untapped and dynamic market. Russell Read, CalPERS chief investment officer, noted that "it's easy to miss emerging firms that are still struggling to raise capital. . . . Most large firms started at the small end of the market and we want to find them on the small end of their asset class. Then we won't have to stand in line for their services on the big end later."[17] In LP surveys, 42 percent of the world's top 100 LPs were open to considering first-time funds. In partnering with emerging managers, investors have touted many benefits—early access to industry leaders, gains from better returns, higher rates of proprietary deal flow, and a management focus on maximizing profits rather than on increasing assets under management.[18]

Pension programs have demonstrated staunch support for minority representation among their emerging funds. Thus, the definition of *emerging* has

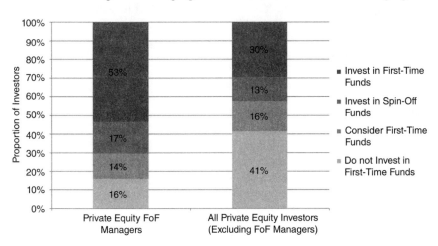

FIGURE 10.3 LPs' preference for investing in first-time funds.
Source: Preqin

expanded to include demographic factors as well as performance. CalPERS's alternative investment management (AIM) program explicitly states that its goal is to invest in women-owned or minority-owned funds. The partnership between CalSTRS investment authorities and Invesco Private Capital was formed to invest $300 million over a five-year period on behalf of the state teachers' pension fund. Kristine Brandt, director and CEO of Invesco, said, "The economy is more and more global these days, so you have to have that global mind-set. . . . If there isn't diversity [within the general partner], then where is that diverse thought coming from? In order to build better companies, in order to come up with the next best widget, I really think that diversity is required."[19]

A TALE OF TWO EMERGING MANAGERS

Two funds were born, in the same vintage year and the same geographic region, yet their paths diverged. And both are off to a strong start.

When a state's economic development agency offered to commit to two early-stage funds, as many as 12 funds applied. The two funds that made it to the finish line received 25 percent of their fund commitments from the state government. The ultimate kicker: the state had capped its return to 1.5X of its invested capital. Thus, as seen in Table 10.1, any other limited partner could gain additional pro-rata share of the excess return above 1.5X.

This is an excellent example of how a state government can stimulate the development of early-stage venture capital. In such a model, the state's ability to cap its returns stimulates the private sector to participate aggressively.

Assume a $15 million fund generates $45 million, or a 3X multiple of cash return. The fund has a $5 million commitment from the state capped at 1.5X.

TABLE 10.1 Capped LP Returns Sweeten the Launch for Emerging Managers

	Returns	
	1.5X Capped	Uncapped
Return of capital	$15,000,000	$15,000,000
Profits	$30,000,000	$30,000,000
LPs share of carry at 80%	$240,00,000	$24,000,000
State's share	$2,500,000	$8,000,000
Balance to rest of LPs	$21,500,000	$16,000,000
Excess returns to LPs	25.58%	None

Once the state receives $7.5 million, the investors can share the rest of capital, which can augment their returns by 25 percent.

As a result, the two funds, Huron River Ventures and Michigan Accelerator Fund, were able to attract investors and launch their funds. Their strategies differed enough to help the state achieve its goals of investment returns and economic diversification.

Both focused on seed stage investments. While Huron River Ventures targeted technology investments, Michigan Accelerator Fund was seeking medical devices, health care, and diagnostic opportunities.

The funds had strong teams with a blend of entrepreneurial, investments and transactional expertise. At Michigan Accelerator Fund, John Kerschen brought his mergers and acquisitions expertise. Having completed more than 75 completed transactions at upward of $500 million in aggregate transaction value, he had a strong understanding of how acquirers look at opportunities. His partner, Dale Grogan, complemented him through his start-up expertise and having raised more than $30 million for start-up and early stage VCs. At Huron River Ventures, Ryan Waddington had deep domain expertise in energy, technology, and over 15 years had made over 20 seed investments. Tim Streit had earned his stripes at J.P. Morgan Chase and executed transactions valued over $10 billion.

Geographically, the two were spread out over a 120-mile radius and were aligned to take advantage of opportunities in the region. With the University of Michigan in Ann Arbor, Huron River Ventures was able to invest in a start-up that spun out of the university. For Michigan Accelerator Fund, Grand Rapids offered a number of health care opportunities because of its vibrant ecosystem. Both have built strong portfolios—and the jury is still out on results—but without the stimulus provided by the state, these fund managers would have had a much longer, harder journey.

THE GLOBAL EMERGING MANAGER: 500 STARTUPS

Dave McClure, founder of 500 Startups, may soon have to change the name of his fund to 1000 Startups. In three years, he has invested $50 million in more than 500 companies across 40 countries, which translates to more than 150 investments a year. McClure argues that while his approach is unconventional, he and his team firmly believe that a high-volume strategy with a large sample size can give more consistent results, although outcomes may be small.

Dave McClure wants to be for technology start-ups what Billy Beane is for baseball. Like Beane, who by using statistical analysis, redefined how baseball players are picked, McClure wants to create and exploit newer metrics to distinguish top performers from average performers. Instead of making several million-dollar investments in few start-ups, 500 Startups wants to make smaller investments into a lot of start-ups.

Initial investment sizes max out at $250,000. The idea here, according to McClure, is to fail more cheaply. With a 70 to 80 percent failure rate in software start-ups, the goal is to fail fast and fail cheap. In addition to smaller investment sizes, the firm minimizes risks for its limited partner investors by diversifying across industries and geographies.

Companies from Japan, Brazil, China, Taiwan, Vietnam, Chile, Mexico, Switzerland, Ghana, Jordan, Israel, Ukraine, and Spain have received funding. However, 50 percent of the capital is earmarked for U.S. tech investments with a particular emphasis on Silicon Valley, 25 percent for the rest of United States, and the balance is invested globally.

500 Startups invests in businesses serving a clear customer need with a simple, scalable business model. For example, about 20 companies in the portfolio are food companies. The mantra for investing in food tech is simple: "Everyone eats, everyone is online." In addition to looking at a simple business model, McClure and his team ensure that the company has a functional product and the team has substantial technical and marketing skills. This unconventional approach has already resulted in several successes.

The firm has raised its second fund with $44.1 million in capital commitments and aims to invest in 300 or more start-ups. The first fund closed at $29.6 million and invested in 263 start-ups.

The fund and the accelerator are managed by 25 employees, including 14 noninvestment staff. George Kellerman, chief operating officer, says that 500 Startups' model aims to take entrepreneurship culture to all parts of the world and not restrict it to the Silicon Valley. "There are undiscovered entrepreneurs across the furthest reaches of the globe. We want to go to the talent, not expect them to come to us," he says. The brand is gaining momentum, and at its most recent accelerator batch, the seventh since inception, more than 1,200 start-ups applied and 30 were selected. The sourcing advantages are obvious, and so is the value-added support provided by the 200 or more mentors. "Speed matters, and yet we have to maintain the quality," says Kellerman. Twenty-four exits have occurred thus far. With exits on the rise, limited partners may soon see 500 Startups as institutional grade fund, not just an emerging manager fund.

NOTES

1. AltAssets.com interview, 2008.
2. The Silicon Valley 100, *Business Insider*, www.businessinsider.com/
   the-silicon-valley-100-2012-1?op=1.

3. Robert Finkel and David Greising, *The Masters of Private Equity and Venture Capital* (New York: McGraw-Hill, 2009), 210.

4. Steven Lazarus, "From IP to IPO, Key Issues in Commercializing University Technology," in "The VC View, " supplement, *Intellectual Asset Management Magazine*, March 2005, accessed March 12, 2011, www.archventure.com/archview.html.

5. Kelly DePonte, "Emerging Managers: How to Analyze a First-Time Fund," accessed February 20, 2011, www.probitaspartners.com/pdfs/emerging_manager_due_diligence_2005.pdf.

6. Grove Street Advisors, "Case Study 1," May 10, 2001, accessed February 20, 2011, www.grovestreetadvisors.com/news/gsa_case_study_01.pdf.

7. Kenneth Smith, speaking at Venture Alpha West, October 2013 conference.

8. Kelvin Liu, "The Growing Importance of New and Emerging Managers in Private Equity," accessed February 20, 2011, www.institutional.invesco.com/portal/.../II-IPCEM-IVP-1-E%5B1%5D.pdf.

9. Ann Grimes, "New Kids Arrive On the Venture-Capital Block," *Wall Street Journal,* February 25, 2005, accessed February 20, 2011, http://online.wsj.com/article/0,,SB110928737299763683,00.html.

10. John Coelho, speaking at Venture Alpha West, October 2013 conference.

11. Ann Grimes, "New Kids Arrive on the Venture-Capital Block."

12. Ibid.

13. John Coelho, speaking at Venture Alpha West, October 2013 conference.

14. Amit Tiwari, speaking at Venture Alpha West, October 2013 conference.

15. Jean-Pierre Pipaud, "Emerging Managers: Elizabeth Flisser, Capital Z Asset Management," *Emerging Managers Incubation* (blog), September 22, 2008, http://emerging-managers.blogspot.com/2008/09/emerging-managers-elizabeth-flisser.html.

16. "CalSTRS AND CalPERS Unveil Emerging Managers and Financial Services Database," January 17, 2007, accessed February 20, 2011, www.calstrs.com/newsroom/2007/news011707.aspx.

17. Ibid.

18. Women in Investments, Alternative Investment Management Program (CalPERS) presentation, February 10, 2009, www.calpers.ca.gov/eip-docs/ . . . /womens . . . /wiic-private-equity.pdf.

19. Sara Behunek and Mary Kathleen Flynn, "Closing the VC Gender Gap," *The Deal,* July 2, 2010, accessed February 20, 2011, www.thedeal.com/newsweekly/dealmakers/weekly-movers-and-shakers/closing-the-vc-gender-gap.php.

CHAPTER 11

The Venture Capital Firm, Operations, and Culture

"I think of venture capital business as a series of individual personalities, as opposed to a series of firms."[1]
— James Breyer, Accel Partners, Former Chairman,
National Venture Capital Association

A *venture firm* is a catchall phrase that encapsulates at least two separate entities—the general partnership (typically structured as a limited liability company in the United States) and a limited partnership. The general partnership is an entity that employs fund managers and earns annual management fees and carried interests. The limited partnership structure allows several investors to have a "limited" liability to the extent of their ownership in the fund, which is managed by the general partner, as seen in Figure 11.1.

More on fund governance and operations is dealt with in later parts of this chapter. Let us first look at the DNA of any firm.

THE DNA OF A FIRM

Like any start-up, the firm needs to define its operations and build its brand identity. However, many firms believe that a Web site and some fancy logos are sufficient to create their brand identity. In an era when entrepreneurs have choices, the venture firms need to weigh the importance of branding

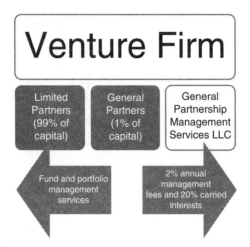

FIGURE 11.1   Venture firm and its entities.

their venture firm appropriately. The venture firm can develop into three archetypes:

- A group of cowboys
- An agency
- A service platform

The Firm as a Group of Cowboys

Most firms operate as a crude aggregation of cowboys: Each partner does his or her own thing. Each partner works solo to find opportunities and bring these to the table. On Monday morning, at the partner meetings, each cowboy tries to show other cowboys what a great catch he or she has brought to the table. Often a fight erupts to establish the hierarchy. The smarter partners often pre-empt such brouhahas by working behind the scenes, gathering the votes, and eliminating any objections. The discussions are often perfunctory and awkward.

At its core, these cowboys need each other to raise money, because limited partners invest in teams, not solo performers. So the soloists pretend to be a part of a symphony and raise the fund, and then promptly go back to doing what they do best—being cowboys.

Down the road, when these opportunities start to struggle, the other cowboys may have that "I told you so" look on their face. Cowboys are now forced down this lonely path of trying to resurrect the dying opportunities. Others watch, sigh, and move on.

WHO IS MY CUSTOMER?

Most venture firms struggle with a differentiated brand identity. Should they try to cater to their investors by demonstrating their successful investments? Or should they try to attract the best founders and entrepreneurs? Both these audiences have radically different views on what is important for them.

Often, the CEOs of portfolio companies wonder why they do not get much help from the other partners in the firm. In a survey of more than 150 CEOs, the differences in the views of the CEOs and those of the venture capitalists (VCs) were indicative of the chasm that exists between the two.[2]

CEOs care more about partners than the overall firm and even less about the reputation of a firm's portfolio companies. However, most venture firms tout their past successes—IPOs or acquisitions—on their Web sites. Partners brag about the string of the investment successes, when CEOs don't necessarily care about them.

Limited partners (LPs) are concerned about succession and the strength of the overall firm. They seek a perpetual money machine generating superior returns, not afflicted by individual egos and limited life spans. But for entrepreneurs, the individual personalities and reputations matter, not succession issues. Entrepreneurs are attracted to the partners as much as the money. A firm's brand impacts their ability to attract the best and brightest founders. But entrepreneurs don't look at a firm's Web site as much as they consider what their peers and third parties think about the firm. Star power is the beginning: How the entrepreneurs benefit from the firm matters.

The Firm as an Agency

For Andreessen Horowitz, the model of the venture firm is simple: Be the change you wish to see in this world. The firm has modeled itself on and blended the values of a talent agency and two financial firms: Creative Artists Agency, the talent agency, and Allen & Company and J. P. Morgan, the financial firms. "We aspire to be like these firms. Allen & Company, a boutique investment bank that, since 1920s, has gone through generations of leadership and strategy but has preserved its culture and value systems— which is remarkable as a Wall Street firm. The original J. P. Morgan of the 1910–1920, era . . . played a fundamental role in financing the build-out of modern America," says Marc Andreessen.

SETTING THE SERVICES STANDARD

"We saw the opportunity to create the venture firm we as entrepreneurs would have taken money from, had it existed at the time."
—Marc Andreessen, Andreessen Horowitz

Source: CNN Money, Feb 6, 2013, accessed January 3, 2014, www.youtube .com/watch?v = PbW-1k3ZOA4.

Creative Artists Agency (CAA) is a Hollywood talent agency that is said to be the entertainment industry's most influential organization, managing some 1,400 of the top talents in the acting industry. Their partnership was based on teamwork, with proceeds shared equally. There were no nameplates on doors, no formal titles, no individual agent client lists. Practices followed the company's two "commandments": be a team player and return phone calls promptly. According to Andreessen, the period of CAA's growth from 1975 to 1990 under the leadership of its founder, Michael Ovitz, had an enormous impact on the talent management arena.[3]

Here are some lessons from these firms that have been incorporated into Andreessen Horowitz's operations:

■ *Focus on thought leaders and the best talent:* Over the years, CAA has kept its hold on the market by retaining the best clients in Hollywood. It has captured a near monopoly of A-list actors, directors, and writers. CAA is aggressive when it comes to attracting talent, just as Andreessen Horowitz may be when it comes to attracting talented CEOs. At times, if CAA couldn't get the actors they wanted, they would poach the agents who managed them, sometimes tripling their salaries, and got their clients along with them. Similarly, Allen & Company hosts an annual Sun Valley conference, which attracts the thought leaders in media and technology as well as politicians and policymakers. Its 2013 conference was attended by Rupert Murdoch, Bill Gates, and Mark Zuckerberg, to name a few.

■ *Create a one-stop shop:* CAA's original revenue model was to rely on commissions from clients. As the business started dropping for various reasons, it aggressively expanded to become a one-stop shop for the entertainment industry. Some of their services now include brand management, communications, market research, trend forecasting, and strategic marketing. CAA even helps its celebs to turn into Web 2.0 social mavens. Similarly, Andreessen Horowitz aims to serve the portfolio companies in a myriad of ways. When it comes to helping portfolio companies recruit talent, the firm has 11 recruiting experts on staff. Co-founder Ben Horowitz calls it "HR in a box," and the firm measures success on the "introduction-to-hire rate."[4]

■ *No-ego/team spirit:* CAA's corporate culture is a blend of Eastern philosophy and team sports. Team members are encouraged to suppress their individual ego for the benefit of the team. Every Monday morning, the 100 agents meet and share their own schedules and industry developments. CAA shuns the media and likes to operate under the radar. Allen & Company, one of the underwriters for the Google and Twitter public offering, does not even have a Web site. Andreessen Horowitz cannot avoid that Web presence (after all, Marc Andreessen invented the browser) and has a full-time partner to manage the media relationships for the firm and its portfolio companies.

The Firm as a Community Creator

For larger firms, the ability to deploy resources is easier. For smaller funds, the management fees often constrain the abilities to build a large team. First Round Capital took a different approach to tackling the issues. "We think of ourselves as building a community, not a portfolio. Historically, value-add was primarily delivered by a venture capital partner interacting with a CEO. We think far more value can be delivered by creating a community of founders, where each CEO in our portfolio can help the others, and each CTO, each CFO, each recruiter, each engineer," says Josh Koppelman.[5]

First Round has a team of six people focused full time on building products, events, and services to help connect the companies with one another. "If you are the SEO person at a start-up, your job is pretty lonely, and you don't have many peers to ask for help and advice. But we have over 30 people focused on SEO in our portfolio, and are building software—including an extremely active online network tool—to help them interact with each other. Now, every time we invest in a company, it actually adds value to our prior investments because there are new smart people who participate in the dialog, rather than subtract," points out Josh Koppelman.

Brett Berson, head of platforms at First Round Capital, says that such an online peer-to-peer teaching model changes the game. "Instead of knowledge accumulation, we are ensuring dis-intermediation. Let the best ideas come from the best people," he says. The platform, which includes a Yelp-like system for finding service providers such as accountants and lawyers, is helpful to portfolio companies. Portfolio CEOs, CTOs, and CFOs are all connected with one another and post topics for others to chime in on, such as how to motivate a distracted founder, structure a compensation plan, plan for ad optimization online, or assess the benefits of raising venture debt. "As a VC, we are now shifting to platform-as-a-service," says Berson.

The platform model is catching up. Sequoia Capital launched a similar open online platform called Grove, where entrepreneurs can share information and ideas on building start-ups. However, the usage in an open arena versus closed loop can be different. Finally, the platform is not a substitute for mentoring, which is often more effective in person.

GOVERNANCE OF THE FIRM

The governance of the firm primarily rests on the shoulders of the cofounders or the managing directors. Thus, prior to formalizing a partnership, the fund's founders need to agree on the various operational matters. These include details such as names of the individuals who will be the members of the firm and decision-making guidelines for all operational matters, such as the following:

- Employee matters: Compensation, hiring, and firing processes
- Investment committee composition
- Selection of venture partners and entrepreneurs-in-residence
- Service provider selection: attorneys, accountants/audit firms, marketing and PR-related activities
- Budgetary allocations

The firm cofounders can also develop guidelines for the following:

- Operations, ethics, and confidentiality matters
- Process of admission and selection of investment committee members

The cofounders can provide guidelines on board participation:

- Best-suited member versus one who sourced the opportunity
- Participation on conflicting company boards
- Public board's participation

The Firm's Operational Guidelines

The founding partners establish guidelines that ascertain how the following decisions are made:

- How are new individuals admitted or terminated from the general partnership membership?
  - Majority vote of number of current members
  - Majority vote by percentage of carry allocation

- Upon addition of new members, how will carry or economic interest of existing members be diluted?
  - Proportionally, all member shares are adjusted.
  - Selectively, a few member shares are adjusted.
- Will investment decisions require unanimous vote or a majority vote? How does the partnership agree to invest additional amounts in portfolio companies?
- Under what conditions can a member withdraw or be terminated?
  - Cause: negligence, breach of conduct, fraud, SEC or tax matters, personal financial situation, such as bankruptcy
  - Membership withdrawal in challenging circumstances—disability or death
  - Voluntary withdrawal

Under each of the conditions above, the withdrawn members' financial interests are reviewed:

- Retains carry interest as is liable for clawback
- Retains carry in existing investments, but no new carry is offered
- Forfeits carry completely
- Is liable for pro rata share of capital contributions
- Stays/resigns from portfolio boards
- Investment committee structure, decision-making criteria, and votes

Carried Interests

Not all limited partners (LPs) accept the *Benchmark Model* of equal carry for all members. Others feel that if members are not incentivized with a meaningful portion of the carry, they will not stay. Carry split, described in Table 11.1, can occur on the basis of:

- Investment expertise
- Seniority in the firm

An average cash value of carry is highly speculative and very few firms have actually seen carry profits in the past decade.

Of the 20 percent pool, typical carry at the general partner (GP) level would be, say, 5 percent, while at the entry level, an associate's share of carry would be less than 0.5 percent, if any. In some cases, firms allocate carry by each portfolio company. The lead partner who is on the board of a portfolio company may get a predetermined percentage of the carried interests.

TABLE 11.1 Sample Carry and Vesting Schedule

	Carry	Y1	Y2	Y3	Y4	Y5	Y6–Y10
Managing director 1	8%	20%	15%	15%	15%	15%	20%
Managing director 2	7%	20%	15%	15%	15%	15%	20%
Principals, associates, and staff	5%	20%	20%	20%	20%	20%	

Notes on vesting:
Pace of vesting is tied to investment period of fund. Typical investment period is four to six years. Vesting schedules can match investment period on a straight-line method vesting yearly in equal shares.
A 20 percent withholding released at final dissolution of fund induces professionals to remain engaged throughout life of fund.
Vesting clawback for cause, death, or disability occurs per standard industry practices.

FROM SAND HILL ROAD TO SECOND LIFE, BESSEMER GAINS AN ADVANTAGE IN VIRTUAL LAND

Bessemer Venture Partners is a global venture capital firm, with U.S. offices in Silicon Valley and Boston, and international offices in Brazil, Israel, and India. Now it is expanding once again, by opening an office in. . . Minecraft? That's right, BVP is taking a page out of the book written years ago by all those venture capital firms that hung shingles in Second Life (back when people used Second Life). Partner David Cowan pointed out that the "office" was originally opened as a way to communicate with an entrepreneur who is big into Minecraft (and has some relationship to the game's creators), but also as an effort to better connect with the broader gaming community. For example, the firm plans to hold office hours within the site, and even has used it for some intra-office communication. BVP Minecraft office was designed by Cowan's two school-age children. When asked why his children had interest in designing a BVP office in Minecraft, he replied: "I think a lot of parents are asking themselves why their children have interest in Minecraft." The virtual office even has a basement area "in memoriam" for dead companies and a server room, which in the age of cloud may be quaint, but its there for a nice reason.

—Dan Primack, as reported in *Fortune Term Sheet*, January 8, 2014

* To view the BVP Minecraft offices, see https://www.youtube.com/watch?v=3JQXdWtdsCQ.

Administration and Operations: The Back Office

Back- and middle-office operations are critical to a fund's success. Investors are paying more attention to the details; poor or insufficient back-office administration is often a reason for investors to forgo making an investment in the fund. Georganne Perkins of Fisher Lynch Capital, a fund of funds puts it bluntly: "If the GPs are equipped to handle other people's money, it can be a positive." Put another way, any start-up with the requisite technical and financial oversight and controls (a CFO) is attractive to any GP, and the same goes for any LP.

"Well designed back- and middle-office operations provide fund principals and investors with confidence that the data they are receiving is correct—data integrity—and may be used to base decisions on," says Harry Cendrowski, author of *Private Equity: History, Governance and Operations*.[6] Cendrowski is also the founder of Cendrowski Corporate Advisors, a back-office services firm that offers financial services, taxation services, and investor relations to a number of private equity and venture capital firms. According to Cendrowski, a back office can offer the following:

- *Financial reporting:* Fund and portfolio company financial reporting for LPs and fund managers, and monitoring of portfolio company performance, are provided.
- *Accounting:* Accounting services are a critical component of the back- and middle-office operations. Fund principals rely on the information generated in the accounting system for decision making (e.g., how much cash should be distributed to investors? what are the cash needs of the fund for future expenses?), inspiring investor confidence (are capital accounts properly stated and communicated timely?), and their own economic interests (are management fees properly calculated? are incentive allocations properly calculated?).
- *General accounting:* Bookkeeping functions, posting journal entries, account reconciliations, preparation of financial statements, management of operating cash, maintenance of the general ledger, including posting of all transactions, is necessary for proper financial and tax reporting.
- *Capital accounting:* Tracking cash intake, basis in entities, maintenance of investor capital accounts, and calculation of distributions is provided.
  - Maintenance of investor capital accounts is a critical function, as this is the primary measure on which investors rely in assessing their investment. It represents the investor's economic interest in the fund and is often the key component in determining distributions as well as profit and loss allocations.

- Components of investor capital accounts include the proper computation and documentation of capital calls and distributions. Computation and documentation of capital calls allows the fund to meet its obligations and commitments for fund expenses and portfolio investments. Computation and documentation of distributions is critical to investor confidence by indicating that fund principals are abiding by the terms of the operating agreement. In addition, fund principals need to know how much capital has been committed, how much has been called, and how much has been returned to investors.
- The proper allocation of economic and taxable profits and losses is another reason why proper maintenance of capital accounts is critical. Economic income affects the investors' right to distributions.

- *Business valuation:* A back-office interfaces with fund principals with respect to the valuation of portfolio investments. **Generally accepted accounting principles** (GAAP) basis financial statements must reflect investments at their fair value rather than historical cost. The back- and middle-offices may provide assistance in the valuation process and must ensure that the proper value is recorded in the general ledger. ASC 820–compliant (formerly FAS 157) mark-to-market portfolio company valuations for fund return calculations are essential.
- *Preparation of investor communications:* Fund return calculations, investment reports, and capital call notices are included in communications.
- *Audits and taxes:* A back-office coordinates the annual financial statement audit of the fund and is the primary contact with auditors. It is the source of all the information the auditors will be assessing in their examination. As such, it is critical that the back office not only is able to provide the necessary information in a timely manner but also is able to provide explanations and answer questions with respect to the information on the auditor's request. The back office is usually involved in the preparation of fund tax returns and investor K-1s. In addition, the back office is responsible for calculating and documenting tax basis— the fund's tax basis in its investments as well as the investors' tax basis in the fund. Some back offices extend their services into offering consultative services in the partners and principals' tax liabilities and goals, develop a plan to minimize their tax liabilities, and/or enhance after-tax return on investment.

Transferring responsibility for these activities to an independent third party reassures limited partners that they are receiving timely and accurate information. Administrative resources at the fund level are freed up, permitting managers to focus on scouting, screening, and harvesting deals. Costs to the firm are further decreased, as these operations are typically borne by the fund, not the general partners. Thus, it is in any general partnership's interest to establish strong business systems.

While building the firm's brand is critical, establishing the underlying fabric of economics, ownership, and culture requires a diligent approach. For many first-time funds, the fund-raising activity often commences prior to formal establishment of structures.

NOTES

1. Gupta Udayan, *Done Deals—Venture Capitalists Tell Their Stories* (HBS Press, 2000).
2. NVCA, Branding and Venture Capital: Research Preview, July 2013, Survey conducted by DeSantis Breindel.
3. Ibid.
4. Nicole Perlroth, "Forbes Q and A with Andreessen-Horowitz's [*sic*] Secret Agent," *Forbes*, February 2011, accessed on January 3, 2014, www.forbes.com/sites/nicoleperlroth/2011/02/04/forbes-q-and-a-with-andreessen-horowitzs-secret-agent.
5. Mark Boslet, "*The New Full Service VC*," *VCJ*, June 2013, https://www.fenwick.com/FenwickDocuments/VCJ%20June%202013_cover%20story.pdf.
6. Harry Cendrowski, *Private Equity: History, Governance, and Operations* (Hoboken, NJ: John Wiley & Sons, 2008).

CHAPTER 12

The Fund-Raising Process

*"Nothing in the world is worth having or worth doing unless it
means effort, pain, difficulty. . . . I have never in my life envied
a human being who led an easy life. I have envied a great many
people who led difficult lives and led them well."*
                                        —Theodore Roosevelt

Having reviewed the universe of investors, their investment criteria, terms,
and fund structure, we look at getting to the finish line—getting the fund
to a close—the process of admitting investors into the fund. Most funds
have a two-step closing process: a first close followed by the final close, unless of course you are Andreessen Horowitz, Foundry Group, or Greylock
and can raise the capital in a matter of few weeks.[1] After the fund has closed,
the exhilarating or exhausting process of raising capital comes to an end.

The process of closing, or the first close, as depicted in Figure 12.1, can
occur typically at about 40 to 70 percent of the size of the fund. For example, a $20 million fund can conduct its first close at $10 million or higher.
The final close occurs ideally within 12 months of the first close. Conducting
the first close allows a general partnership to start making investments and
collecting fees.

When sufficient financial commitments have been gathered, the attorney
sets a closing date. Prior to closing, the following preconditions must occur:

- *Private placement memorandum (PPM):* Finalize the PPM and supple-
  ments and circulate to all closing investors.

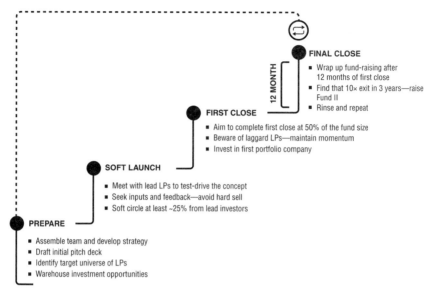

FIGURE 12.1 Steps to fund closing.

- *Subscription agreements:* For each investor, the subscription agreement is reviewed to ensure accuracy, completeness, and compliance with securities laws. The aggregate capital commitments are established for the first close.
- *Limited partnership agreement:* All negotiations with the limited partnership universe are completed and the final draft is circulated to all investors.
- *General partner agreement:* The general partner (GP) limited liability company (LLC) agreement, which is internal to the fund managers, is completed and circulated to all fund managers.
- *Side letters:* Any side letters that may have been negotiated must be completed and circulated with relevant investors.[2]

The steps to a close are typically led by an attorney/law firm, and after all limited partnership agreements have been executed by limited partners (LPs), the certificate of good standing is obtained by attorneys. This date of "good standing" becomes the closing date. Fund managers execute subscription agreements and accept closing subscriptions. Wire transfers are then completed and at times are held in escrow by attorneys until the full amounts are received from all LPs. The fund managers would execute the GP LLC agreements. This process requires much orchestration of several different elements, and a good attorney will offer a checklist at least 60 days ahead of closing. Such a checklist can help a GP to coordinate all the moving parts effectively.

BUILD YOUR TARGET LIST OF INVESTORS

Screening and targeting potential LPs, as described in Table 4.8) can significantly improve the GP's ability to raise a fund. Some concepts to consider while screening LPs are as follows:

- *Affinity for emerging managers versus established managers:* While some fund of funds (FoFs) have dedicated emerging manager programs, others seek established managers. One LP quips, "I don't see GPs who are still in kindergarten—they can call me after they cross Roman numeral IV," implying funds that have a track record of four fund cycles.
- *Size:*
  - Assets under management: If the target limited partnership is too large, for example, a $50 billion pension fund, a smaller fund of, say $100 million in size, may have a harder time convincing the LP to invest $10 million. Typical investment size for such a pension fund would be approximately $50 million or higher.
  - Minimum investment size: Larger limited partnerships seek to avoid a number of smaller transactions and thus improve internal efficiency in managing their portfolios.
- *Affinity to your stage of investments:* Some limited partnerships have found middle-market buyout to be a suitable strategy; conversely, others have found early-stage venture to be appropriate.
- *Sector of investments:* Is the LP looking to build a technology portfolio?
- *Past investments activity:* Has the target LP invested in similar funds? Average amounts? There is a caveat for emerging managers: if an LP has not invested in this asset class, be prepared to invest in a long education process. And frequently, after you educate the potential LP, you might find that this LP has decided against investing in this venture capital asset class—or worse, decided to invest in another, likely better performing fund. At least you earned some karma points from that LP!

Various customer relationship management (CRM) vendors, such as Salesforce.com, offer a customized tool for venture capital funds. These can be used to track and manage the fund-raising process. Depending on the brand, performance, and market conditions, the process takes up to 18 months. In Figure 12.2, the limited partnership outlay variation can be seen by size of funds. In any smaller early-stage fund, the population of high-net-worth individuals (HNWIs) is significantly large.

What should your limited partnership universe look like? A healthy practice is often to target certain kinds of LPs because of the inherent advantages

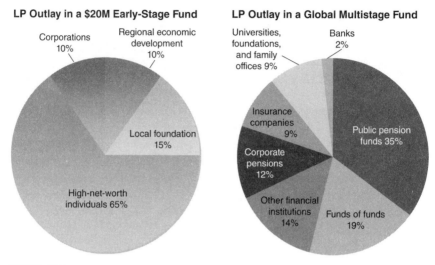

FIGURE 12.2   Limited partnership outlay varies by type of fund.

they offer. "We wanted to attract 20 LPs, which would include a healthy mix of fund-of-funds, foundations, family offices, pension funds. Eight months and 200 meetings later, that is exactly where we ended up," says Ravi Mohan, Shasta Ventures. Shasta's Fund I target size was $175 million and closed at $210 million in approximately seven months.

FUND MARKETING MATERIALS

A PPM, a rough equivalent of a business plan, a succinct presentation/slide deck, and a two-page executive summary are essential marketing tools. Any good PPM will have, at the minimum, the following key sections:

- Investment team—general partners' backgrounds
- Investment strategy
- Portfolio construction
- Performance—prior track record
- A brief summary of terms and conditions of the investment opportunity

These sections are critical, while other supporting sections, such as investment process and investment summaries of prior investments, are a welcome addition. Other mandatory sections include risk factors; tax and regulatory matters; and foreign securities laws, which are boilerplate texts of pure legalese, placed to protect both sides.

While the PPM is the backbone, an executive summary (ES) and a powerpoint pitch deck (PPT)—both drawn from the placement memorandum—are used as opening gambits with potential investors. According to Wilson Sonsini Goodrich and Rosati, a leading California-based law firm, omitting information can be just as damaging as affirmative misstatements.[3] Other issues to look for include the following:

- *Team*: Overstatement of qualifications of the team, time commitment, and track record, as well as prior experience, education, and other attributes.
- *Financial information*: Failure to distinguish between gross and net investment returns and valuations, failure to supply a complete listing of all investments as opposed to mere highlights.
- *Other material information*: Failure to disclose adverse facts related to lawsuits, regulatory actions.

The PPM averages about 50 pages to 75 pages in length and includes the following:

- Executive summary (3 to 5 pages): The primary reasons—the headliners—why any LP should invest in the fund:
  - Market opportunity
  - Background, history, and performance of the firm
  - Management team
  - Investment focus areas
  - Summary of terms
- Market opportunity and investment strategy (5 to 8 pages)
- Investment process (3 to 5 pages)
- Organization and management team (5 pages)
- Selected transactions/investment summary (5 to 8 pages, 1 page per transaction)
- Investment terms (10 pages)
- Risks and regulatory considerations (20 pages)

The bulk of the PPM—about 30 pages—is weighted heavily with investment terms and legalese. Any potential investor's attention needs to be drawn to the team, performance, and strategy sections. GPs should take extra care to ensure that the marketing documents are packaged elegantly, without heavy emphasis on visual sizzle and without any errors. "I have seen several fund documents with typos—it is not a good starting point," one Midwest-based LP pointed out.

PRESENTATION SLIDES

A fund presentation is no more than 12 to 14 slides encapsulated for a 15-to 20-minute presentation. "A pitchbook should *not* be longer than 15 pages," says John Crocker, Auximos Group managing director. "People show up with *War and Peace* and expect you to go page by page."[4]

By all means, avoid any adjectives, and resist the urge to overindulge in self-praise. Let the actions (numbers, outcomes) speak for themselves. Key points to highlight in a presentation would include the following:

- *Team:* Demonstrate expertise (number of investments, returns), strong interrelationships (cohesion), and complementary skills.
- *Investment strategy and market opportunity:* Demonstrate a compelling thesis that explains how this team, combined with the stated strategy and market conditions, is a well-timed opportunity.
- *Prior and new investments:* Demonstrate that the GPs can source at least six to eight good opportunities and syndicate these in the first five years. Note to GP: To invest in six to eight opportunities, a deal flow rate of 100X needs to be demonstrated.
- *Returns:* The team has the track record and/or the ability to make investments and generate superior returns. Demonstrate that you can find opportunities and invest at favorable terms leading to step-ups and strong exits.

MAKING THE PRESENTATION PITCH: DRINK
YOUR OWN KOOL-AID®

GPs should consider approaching LPs from a customer-centric view: the LPs should clearly see the benefit in investing in you. "VCs [venture capitalists] demand of their portfolio companies that the value proposition should be very customer focused. But GPs seldom approach LPs with a value proposition. If a GP can make it in the interest of that LP, they may actually want to invest in the fund. This simple perspective seems to be lost on a fair number of GPs," laments Chris Rizik, who raised two venture funds as a GP and now manages Renaissance Venture Capital Fund, an FoF

Really, that is your elevator pitch! That is a common reaction after LPs have suffered lengthy, boring presentations where GPs get into self-aggrandizing mode. Slide after slide of ennui where GPs get into "and let me tell you about this company . . . " mode has caused many LPs to wring their hands. GPs should start the meetings by asking how the LP would like to best use the allotted time. If given a chance to present your pitch, drink your own Kool-Aid. Remember when you chastised entrepreneurs about their presentations being long-winded and off point? Your pitch should be no more than a dozen slides and 15 minutes. This is so basic, but rarely happens.

"A GP should approach the LP exactly the same way they want an entrepreneur to approach them. I have been surprised how few GPs can actually eat their own cooking when it comes to making presentations," says Chris Rizik. A lengthy 40-slide presentation, macro trends, and off-point information do not further your cause. Having lived the life on the other side as a VC, Rizik is sympathetic about the challenges faced by any GP. Daniel Feder, Covariance Capital Management's senior investment manager, private equity and venture capital, says pitchbooks that are too long,

DON'T FALL ASLEEP, APPEAR BORED AND OTHER STRANGE REQUESTS FROM LPS

Reuter's peHUB published a list of top 10 Dos/Don'ts for fund managers when meeting with potential investors:

- Don't stretch a meeting to longer than 90 minutes. The sale is not made in the first meeting.
- Don't use superlatives in self-description.
- Do ask about the LP's investment program and approach. And appear interested in it.
- Do be clear about what you won't invest in and why. It's okay to have skepticism/self-regulation about areas outside your expertise.
- Do be as transparent as possible about your successes and nonsuccesses (AKA failures). Take appropriate credit for both sides of the equation.
- Don't just address the older members of your audience.
- Don't direct the first female in the room to "get you a cup of coffee with milk and sugar."
- Don't be late.
- Do exhibit a sincere passion for what you do. Make it seem like you'd still come into work every day, even if you didn't have carry.
- Do make sure that no one on your team falls asleep or appears bored during the presentation.

Source: Luisa Beltran, peHUB reporting from Venture Alpha East PartnerConnect panel, "Roadshow Workshop: Dos and Don'ts Advice from Top LPs," April 2013.

some as lengthy as 60 pages, make him "want to get out of this meeting." GPs can just provide handouts, Feder says. Firms shouldn't just stick to the pitchbook during meetings, he says. "Try to get off the pitchbook. I love that."[5]

Igor Rozenblit adds, "The goal of the meeting is for the LP to collect information from the GP. The GPs should not spend time telling us about their value-add to the portfolio. In my opinion, most LPs do not believe that GPs add any value; thus, GPs are better off focusing the time on answering LP questions during the meeting."

ATTRACTING THE LEAD INVESTOR: YOUR "NUT"

Many GPs start the fund-raising process by looking for the lead investor, an LP who can make the first significant commitment for the fund. If the fund managers are new to the game, this can be a significant challenge. Certain institutional LPs, particularly pension funds and FoFs, seldom consider investing in funds with limited track records. Endowments and foundations may be open to looking at the opportunity, but it all depends on the sophistication, nuances, and appetite of each LP.

Consider ARCH Venture Partners' ability to find a lead investor for their Fund I circa 1980. On a Saturday afternoon, Steven Lazarus, founder of ARCH, was able to pitch a vice chairman of an insurance company. This potential LP took a break during his tennis game and committed $4 million by the end of the hour-long meeting. "I had my nut and from that point the money rolled in," Lazarus would say.[6] ARCH raised $9 million for its Fund I. Newer funds are better suited in targeting a larger number of smaller investors, such as HNWIs individuals and family offices.

When it comes to fund-raising, the top quartile firms, of course, have a problem of meaningful allocations. In the brief windows of fund-raising cycles, the problem of excess prevails—how to choose from all those LPs kicking down the doors and ensure that a meaningful share is allocated to each LP. This is a problem that the mediocre firms would love to have! Recall that larger LPs, who typically have billions in assets under management, would be underwhelmed with a tiny share of a top quartile fund. Even if the top quartile fund doubles this capital in 10 years, the overall impact on the pension fund returns is minimal. A drop in the bucket doubles to two drops—still a minor variation. All LPs are waiting for that top quartile bucket to overflow. When funds reach that top-quartile hot fund stature, the fund-raising cycles become shorter and shorter as existing LPs tend to stay put and the new LPs compete to get in. Leading funds have no LP churn.

SNAGGING THAT LEAD INVESTOR: LESSONS FROM RICHARD KRAMLICH, FOUNDER OF NEW ENTERPRISE ASSOCIATES (NEA), A LEADING VENTURE FIRM

"So, let me get this straight. You're talking about us putting up a million dollars, right?"

Kramlich: *"Yes, sir."*

"You're talking about not telling us how you're going to invest it, is that right?"

Kramlich: *"Yes, sir, that's correct."*

"And you're telling me this money is going to be illiquid for 12 years, is that right?"

Kramlich: *"That's correct."*

"You're telling me, you all, as a group, have no track record, and you're not promising any rate of return, is that right?"

Kramlich: *"Yes, sir, that's right."*

So finally, this LP says, "Well, if you all feel comfortable taking the risk, I'll support you."

This LP invested $1 million in NEA Fund I.

Source: C. Richard Kramlich, "Venture Capital Greats: A Conversation with C. Richard Kramlich," interviewed by Mauree Jane Perry on August 31, 2006, in San Francisco, California, National Venture Capital Association, Arlington, Virginia.

On the other hand, several subpar or below-average firms are able to sucker in newer LPs at every fund-raising cycle.

A good lead investor can act as a source of other introductions, be a powerful reference, and greatly improve your chances of raising the fund. GPs should focus their early efforts on attracting such a kingmaker. But finding someone who will take a leap of faith with a newer GP team is not easy.

Once a lead investor has committed, the GPs ought to continue to attract those fast followers, and finally those laggards, who will come in days before the final close. The only proven way to attract these is to communicate effectively.

COMMUNICATE, CREATE, AND MAINTAIN MOMENTUM

The process of managing multiple relationships effectively and leading these to a closing point where they are ready to make a commitment is fraught with uncertainties and challenges. GPs who were successful pointed out that they followed some simple guidelines:

- *Communicate:* Any potential investors with whom you met would like to know how you are progressing with your fund-raising efforts. A steady flow of meaningful communication, timely but not excessive overload, can help a GP to gain ongoing mind-share with LPs.
- *Create momentum:* The ability to create momentum with LPs is an art form, akin to rolling a snowball downhill and making sure that it arrives at its destination in one piece. Tying momentum and communication together, an example could be, "In the past 90 days we have added commitments of an additional $10 million, raising our total commitments to $25 million. These commitments include a family office, several HNWIs, and a strategic corporate investor."

Take the example of .406 Ventures Fund I, which attracted $167 million in the tough economic environment. "About 90 percent of our fund was raised from institutions. It took one year to get it done from first close, 18 months from start to finish. LPs tested us at every step. We were politely persistent and created momentum. It is a lot of work and not for the faint of heart," says Liam Donohue, cofounder and managing director of .406 Ventures.

MAYBE YOU ARE JUST NOT READY FOR VENTURE CAPITAL

Consider how William H. Draper, III nudged a potential LP, who was firmly perched on a fence, to take the leap. "Maybe you're just not ready for venture capital," he said to a potential LP debating over a $10 million commitment. "Oh, no, no, no," the LP said. So all of a sudden, the cards turned and he signed it.* The LP committed, and Draper Gaither Anderson did not ever invest the entire $10 million. They invested $6 million and returned $750 million to their happy investors.

---

* William H. Draper, III, "Early Bay Area Venture Capitalists: Shaping the Economic and Business Landscape," oral history conducted by Sally Smith Hughes in 2009, Regional Oral History Office, The Bancroft Library, University of California, Berkeley, 2008, p. 31.

ANNOUNCING THE CLOSE

Foundry Group Fund III was much like Fund II—team, strategy and such. Journalist Mark Boslet of Thompson Reuters called it a "cut and paste" fund, where the Fund III PPM was a "cut and paste" of the Fund II documents. Foundry Group managing director Jason Mendelson took it a step further and even copied verbatim the blog announcing Fund II.

Getting to the close for any fund manager is easy—all it takes is the ability to indulge in self-flagellation, listen to a thousand noes, crawl uphill, and eventually find a lead investor. For any GP, this experience often trains them to empathize with entrepreneurs. By rudimentary estimates, less than 10 percent of first-time funds reach the finish line, while the other 90 percent abandon their plans and try their hand at something else.

LPs are much more responsive when a GP aims to be customer-centric (as in "What is in it for the LPs?") and concise. Offer middle-of-the-road terms. Let's take a look at the fund investment terms and understand these in the following chapter.

THE "CUT AND PASTE" FUND: FOUNDRY GROUP ANNOUNCES A SUCCESSFUL CLOSE OF FUND III

We are very happy to announce today the closing of our third fund, Foundry Venture Capital 2012, L.P. The fund is the same size as our last one: $225 million in limited partner commitments. We are pleased to be working with a great group of investors.

We will continue to do exactly what we have always done: invest in seed and early-stage investment opportunities in the software and IT space that are located across the United States. We'll also continue to pursue a strategy of Thematic Investing that has served us well over our investing careers.

We very much look forward to working with another group of great entrepreneurs and portfolio companies.

—Jason, Ryan, Seth, and Brad

P.S. For those of you keeping track this is the exact same blog post we used last time to announce our fund. :)

Source: Jason Mendelson's blog, *Foundry Group*, www.foundrygroup.com/wp/2012/09/raising-our-third-fund-foundry-venture-capital-2012-l-p/.

NOTES

1. In most cases, the soft efforts to begin the fund raise start 6 to 12 months ahead of the full-blown efforts. The media only shows the brighter side. And no fund managers in their right minds would profess to experiencing prolonged pain in this uphill crawl.
2. I am grateful to Wilson Sonsini Goodrich and Rosati PC (WSGR), a leading Silicon Valley Law firm, for this information.
3. "Due Diligence in the Preparation of Private Placement" memorandum, WSGR Fund Services Group.
4. Luisa Beltran, "GP Tips to Make Fundraising Easier: Don't Fall Asleep or Look Bored During LP Presentations," Reuters PEHub, April 4, 2013, accessed on January 6, 2014, www.pehub.com/2013/04/04/tips-gps-making-fundraising-easier-dont-look-bored-during-lp-presentations.
5. Ibid.
6. Robert Finkel and David Greising, *The Masters of Private Equity and Venture Capital* (New York: McGraw-Hill, 2009), 216.

CHAPTER 13

Terms of Investment: The Limited Partnership Agreement

"Terms are important but seldom the primary drivers of investment decisions. As they say, terms never make a poor firm look good nor make a good firm unattractive."
—Kelly Williams, President of GCM Grosvenor Private Markets (formerly Managing Director and Head, Customized Fund Investment Group, Credit Suisse, Fund of Funds)

A typical fund-offering document, called the private placement memorandum (PPM), includes the fund's investment strategy, the fund manager's background and expertise, and market opportunity. The fund's limited partnership agreement (LPA) is the document that contains legal terms that describe the fund control mechanics, management, investment, and distribution of returns.

KEY TERMS

A short summary of key terms is usually included in the fund documents and are presented here in Table 13.1.

The highly negotiated terms between any investors and fund managers are defined in Table 13.2.

The various financial and governance terms in fund are structured to meet the goals of both investors and fund managers, as shown in Table 13.3.

TABLE 13.1 Key Fund Terms

Fund size	$100 million
Commitments	Institutions: $5 million minimum
	Individuals: $1 million
Investment Size	Approximately $1,000,000 to $2,500,000 per initial investment. Maximum investment per company capped at 10% of the fund or $10,000,000.
Fees	2.5% reducing by 0.5% each year after year 5
Industry focus	Technology (enterprise, consumer, security) and digital health
Investment stage	Seed-stage companies with committed management teams and proven commercial viability
Geographic focus	Silicon Valley, primarily
Term	10 years. The fund will invest aggressively in the first 3–4 years and seek to realize returns on its portfolio investments in 6–8 years.
Investment structures	Priced equity rounds, capped convertible notes with warrants/ discounts
Investment term	Anticipated year 1 to year 4. Due to the stage of investments, the holding period may be up to 5–7 years or longer.
Portfolio construction and governance	Target portfolio will include a mix of start-ups with high-risk profiles (30%), medium-risk profiles (40%), and lower-risk profiles (30%). Governance and management of portfolio will be via board seats and active engagement with founders.

TABLE 13.2 Most Negotiated Terms in a Fund

Term	Definition
Carry	The percentage of profits, or "carried interests," shared by the investors and the fund managers. Typical carried interests are split 80% to the investors and 20% to the fund managers.
Management fees	The annual fees paid by investors to fund managers for operating expenses of the fund. Typical fees are 2.5% per annum of committed capital, paid quarterly.
Waterfall	The process and flow of sharing the returns.
Clawback	The process of recovering excessive profits, if any, from fund managers at the end of the fund life.

TABLE 13.2 (*Continued*)

Term	Definition
Key person	Key persons, or the investment team of the fund managers, are identified. Should these key people leave the fund or become unable to conduct their duties, the investors trigger the right to take action, including stop making investments.
Indemnification	The fund investors indemnify the fund managers if they lose their capital.
Side letters	Some institutional investors such as pension funds often ask for additional rights via side letters. Because these agreements are drafted on a case-by-case basis, these are called "side letters," as these are aside of the LPA

TABLE 13.3 Financial and Governance Terms

Terms	Goals
Fund size, term, management fees, minimum contributions, and GP commitment	Describes the basic financial structure
Drawdowns, reinvestments, investment limitations, defaults, coinvestments	Describes the flow of investment capital
GP investment committee	Determines how investments are made
Allocation of profits and losses, distributions, GP clawback	Describes the flow of returns from the GP back to the LP
Key person event, investment period termination or suspension, no-fault divorce or GP removal, for-cause termination or GP removal, transfer of LP interests and withdrawal, reports, parallel funds and successor funds, audit, LPAC	Describes the management and governance of the fund
Liability of LPs, indemnification, employee benefit plan regulations, public disclosure issues, tax-exempt investors, non-U.S. investors	Other legal, taxation, and regulatory matters are defined in these terms

FUND FINANCIAL TERMS

All investors seek a balance of financial and control provisions in the fund terms. With respect to financial terms, typical negotiation elements include the following.

Management Fees

- *Percentage:* Management fees are typically 2.0 to 2.5 percent per annum of committed capital.
- *Duration:* Fees ratchet down each year after the investment period, which is typically five years. Fund managers should establish a minimum floor to make sure there are adequate fees to support the portfolio management, accounting, and tax matters toward the end of the life of the fund.
- *Fees from multiple funds:* Investors insist that fees be reduced when a successor fund is formed. The fees are also typically reduced if the fund managers receive any compensation or fees from portfolio companies. If the fund managers manage an existing fund, investors often assess the existing fund's investment period, commitments, fees, and its impact on the proposed fund's fees. It is typical for fund managers to raise a new fund when an existing fund is about 70 percent invested.

As shown in Table 13.4, the amount of investable capital varies over the life of the fund as the structure and timing of fees vary.

TABLE 13.4   Fund Management Fee Vesting Scenarios

	Years 1–5	Year 6	Year 7	Year 8	Year 9	Year 10	Total GP Fees ($M)	Investable Capital ($M)
Scenario 1	2.5	2.5	2.5	2.5	2.5	2.5	**25.00**	75.00
Scenario 2	2.5	2.25	1.75	1.5	1.25	1	**20.25**	79.75
Scenario 3	2.25	1.8	1.44	1.15	0.92	0.73	**17.30**	82.70
Scenario 4	2.5						**12.50**	87.50

In Scenario 1, the fees stay flat at 2.5 percent of the committed capital. This is unlikely—a GP dream scenario—but is presented for illustration.
In Scenario 2, the fees drop by 10 percent after year 5, or the investment period.
In Scenario 3, the fees start at 2.25 percent and drop by 20 percent after year 5.
In Scenario 4, the fees drop to zero after year 5. This example is atypical and is extracted from a single LP (government-sponsored) fund PPM.

Seth Levine, managing director in The Foundry Group, a leading technology fund based in Colorado, says, "Good GPs [general partners] think of management fee as a loan against carried interest. Carry is paid on the full fund value, not net of fees. Any fees you take out are effectively loans against future performance."[1]

Financial Commitment of the General Partners

The industry standard for GP commitment to the fund is at the minimum 1 percent of the capital. Thus, for a $100 million fund, the managers are expected to invest at least $1 million. However, some managers are bold enough to take bigger bets, proving that they can eat their own cooking. Chamath Palihapitiya committed $60 million when he raised a $300 million Social + Capital Fund.[2]

Carried Interests and Performance-Based Triggers

The industry standard for carried interest split is 80/20, where the investors retain 80 percent of the profits and 20 percent profits go to the fund managers. In Tier One funds, where performance has been demonstrated over multiple funds and economic cycles, carried interests can be as high as 30 percent. However, this is rare, and most fund managers stay with the 20 percent structure. Often, emerging managers attempt to drop the carry to 10 percent to lure investors. This seldom impacts the ability to attract investors or hasten the capital raise process. Most institutional investors ignore such overtures and treat these as a deviation from the norm. At times, it is perceived as a sign of weakness.

Venture capital funds typically do NOT offer a preferred rate of return. This is a norm in private equity funds, where a return rate of, say, 8 percent is established. Often called a hurdle rate, this rate factors in the cost of capital over the time period.

More importantly, a cause of heartburn for LPs is the way fund managers calculate carried interest to their advantage. Take, for example, the calculation of carried interest. Carry should be calculated on the basis of net profits, not gross profits according to Institutional Limited Partners Association (ILPA) best practices. Put differently, fund managers should treat fees as a loan.

Separately, in a survey of 50 institutional investors, the largest issue for any LP is the calculation of carry: Is it calculated deal by deal or by fund level? Needless to say, LPs prefer fund level calculation of carry, which allows them to recover their capital first before any carry split.

EXAMPLE: CARRY CALCULATION: NET PROFITS VERSUS GROSS PROFITS

To illustrate the difference between net profits and gross profits, consider the following table:

Carry Calculated on the Basis of Net Profits and Gross Profits

	Net Profits ($M)	Gross Profits ($M)
Profits	$125	$150
GP carried interest at 20%	$25	$30
GP fees + carry =	$50	$55

For a $100 million fund, assume a management fee of 2.5 percent per annum over a 10-year period. Typically, the management fee steps down after the investment period, but for simplicity of calculations, let us assume a flat rate. Thus, $25 million in fees is paid to the GPs, which leaves investable capital of $75 million. Assume fund returns are $150 million. The difference between net profits and gross profits can be substantial. LPs look at the gross profit calculations unfavorably, especially for larger funds.

Several funds have developed a tiered carry structure. For example, the 80/20 split is effective until the investors receive three times the committed capital, over and above which the structure changes to 70/30. Such performance-based triggers are not an industry norm but are seen in hypercompetitive regions such as Silicon Valley or smaller micro-venture capital funds.

Waterfall

The waterfall defines how capital will be distributed as exits occur. The industry norm, as seen in the Table 13.5, is to first return the principal amount back to investors (also called "100 percent catch-up") before the fund managers share any profits.

Typically, distributions are made in the following amounts and order of priority:

1. First, 100 percent to all partners in proportion to their respective capital contributions until the partners have received cumulative distributions equal to the sum of their capital contributions; and

TABLE 13.5   Presenting Waterfall to Investors

Investor ABC: Waterfall/Carry Calculation (per Section X.X(x) of LPA)				
Partial Sale of (Company Name)	Investor ABC Pro Rata Share	All LPs	GP	Total
Distributable cash	200			
Return of capital	100			
Pre LP/GP split [A]	100			
After LP/GP split [B]	80			
Carry paid/(received) [A–B]	20			

2. Thereafter, the balance (a) 20 percent to the general partner (the "carried interest distributions") and (b) 80 percent to the limited partners in proportion to their respective aggregate capital contributions.

Investors are supportive of distributing carried interest to fund managers after the investors receive back their entire committed capital. Certain fund managers allocate carry on a deal-by-deal basis, and profits are distributed after each exit occurs. This creates potential challenges for the future when the final investments are liquidated. If, at a fund level, losses are generated, clawbacks are triggered where the fund managers have to pay back amounts to investors.

Clawbacks

One of the heavily negotiated provisions, clawbacks, occur when returns need to be paid back by the fund managers to the investors. When carry is distributed early in the life of a fund only to be followed by later losses, clawbacks ensure that investors get their 80 percent profits for the full portfolio at the end of the fund term. It is impossible to predict what the overall portfolio returns and fund profits will be at the end of the term. Overdistribution to fund managers is likely to occur if the early successes are offset by later failures. Thus, an LP can "claw back" the shortfall amounts from fund managers at the final liquidation.

Fund managers must take great care to plan for clawback possibilities. "I have known of managers that have to sell their houses due to clawbacks," says Kelly DePonte of Probitas Partners. "This is a Damoclean sword that hangs over every GP's head."[3] LPs prefer that an escrow account be established and combined with joint and several personal guarantees from all fund managers/carry recipients. The clawback conditions on taxes are obvious in that LPs shall not seek to claw back the income taxes paid by the GP on the carry earned.

Naturally, neither party looks forward to triggering this clause, but it is a necessary clause for investor protection. An escrow account is often a suitable middle ground, where a portion of distributions are set aside for such situations. With fund managers themselves, suitable agreements need to be established. If clawback liability is joint *and* several among the carry recipients, one partner can be liable for another partner's liabilities.

FUND GOVERNANCE TERMS

Fund governance or control provisions are often governed by a limited partner advisory committee (LPAC). It typically includes three to five larger investors in the fund. A balanced LPAC has representation of various constituents by size of investment or type of constituent (pension funds, endowments, HNWs, etc.). Bob Clone, who managed a portfolio of investments for a pension system in Michigan and Indiana, says, "In designing LPAC, while being one of the largest investors in a fund, we would always look for the interests of the smallest investor. At times, we would insist that the GPs invite at least one representative from the high-net-worth group to participate on the LPAC."

Responsibilities of the LPAC include, but are not limited to the following sections:

Investment Limitations

Investors limit the fund manager's ability by percentage of capital, geography, and type of security. For example, managers cannot invest more than 10 or 15 percent of fund commitments in a single company because it's a prudent risk management and mitigation strategy. Other constraints include geographic (e.g., fund managers cannot invest in portfolio companies domiciled outside of the United States or Canada) or types of securities. Fund managers cannot invest in publicly traded securities.

In several investor interviews, strategy drift was brought up as a minor irritant. Strategy drift occurs when GPs claim to make investments in a certain sector and stage but later shift away from the agreed-upon strategy. While most agreements allow for up to 10 percent of capital to be invested in such "opportunistic" investments, investors start to feel uncomfortable when a larger amount of capital starts to move into other categories. When any market forces cause shifts in strategy, fund managers are better suited in seeking LPAC approvals. When the clean-tech sector started to go out of favor and yet funds were bound by the agreements, fund managers started to push the envelope on investments. One institutional investor remarked, "You will be amazed what was being passed off to us as a clean-tech opportunity." Another said, "When the best returns for a GP come from the 'other' investment categories and not the primary investment thesis, it makes us wonder."

Conflicts of Interest

Can fund III make an investment in a fund II portfolio company? Under what circumstances will the investment be referred to LPAC for approval? Fund managers often find themselves in situations that may be perceived as self-serving. Some managers may have other sources of income, and may make personal investments in select portfolio companies or in companies outside of the fund. Such potential acts of conflict need to be approved or disclosed.

"Key Person" Provisions

If there are any changes in the core investment team personnel, the investors have the right to suspend the fund's investments or terminate the fund. The fund managers, on the other hand, have an interest in continuing the entity and investment activities. The following list some negotiation elements:

- Who are the key persons? What subset of partners is considered more important to execute the strategy? Are the LPs in agreement with the selection? It is critical for investors to identify the key persons and have adequate remedies if they are no longer managing the fund.
- What is defined as the trigger for such a clause? Death, disability, and failure to devote appropriate time are often standard trigger conditions. LPs prefer the suspension of investments to be automatic after a triggering event, unless a plan is approved by the LPAC to move forward with alternate personnel.

No-Fault Divorce

Investors can terminate the relationships with the fund without any particular reason or "fault" on either side. This certainly tilts the axis of power. Depending on the terms of the partnership agreement, the fund can thus be dissolved, the investment period can be stalled, and/or the GP can be replaced. While LPs seldom trigger this clause, it creeps up when issues such as GP misconduct or breach may have occurred. Tax/regulatory matters, felonies, bankruptcies, negligence, and breach of agreements by GPs can trigger this clause. "In my experience, a 75 percent to 80 percent LP vote is typical for a no-fault termination of the fund," says Howard Beber, a fund attorney at law firms of Proskauer Rose.

Indemnification/Standard of Care

This clause eliminates any liabilities for the fund manager for any act or omissions and prevents lawsuits. Exceptions include fraud, good faith, gross negligence, fraud, or willful malfeasance.

Confidentiality

Certain investors, such as state pension funds and university endowments, are subject to the U.S. Freedom of Information Act (FOIA) guidelines. FOIA is an information disclosure statute that encourages accountability through transparency. While FOIA laws vary from state to state, generally, in the venture capital context, certain information reported by a GP to a public plan LP can be the subject of a FOIA request. A newspaper reporter could submit a FOIA request to a public plan LP and subsequently publish sensitive fund or portfolio company information. To date, many states have modified their laws to protect portfolio company information from public disclosure. GPs also seek to limit details of fund investments in portfolio companies from becoming public as they could impact future financing and valuations. A variety of remedies exist, including limiting information to such LPs or, in extreme cases, barring such LPs from future participation in funds.

Other terms include the following:

- *Valuation matters:* LPAC adopts guidelines and weighs in on markups or markdowns of portfolio company valuation.
- *Side letters:* All LPs are equal, but some LPs are more equal than others. Side letters provide additional clarity or describe the specific agreement (above and beyond the standard terms) between the GP and the LP. LPs know that side letters are a common theme in the business. To avoid debates regarding the GP fee calculations, one LP proposed an elegant side letter asking, "The auditors have reviewed and ascertained that the GP fees have been calculated correctly."
- *Coinvestments:* LPs may negotiate coinvestment rights to have the ability to cherry-pick investment opportunities and invest more capital in promising companies. In doing so, LPs also gain insights into how the

GP chooses the opportunities, structures investments, and adds value as a board member. The process and timing of responses needs to be managed effectively by the GP: it is likely that the LP may not have the ability to conduct due diligence, invest in follow-on rounds, or respond within the allocated time frame. However, if an LP can bring some strategic insights to the company, it is often worth the time and effort for both parties. GPs also need to be cautious in that such an investment from an LP, especially a corporate LP with industry knowledge, does not scare off acquirers and impair the exit potential and value.

WHAT INSTITUTIONAL LPS SEEK

The Institutional Limited Partners Association represents 240 organizations that collectively manage over $1 trillion of private equity capital. ILPA has developed best practices for fund managers that focus on alignment of interest, governance, and transparency:[4]

- *Alignment of interest:* The GPs should focus on profit maximization and not merely management fees.
- *Governance:* The fund managers should put controls and adequate checks and balances in place so that investors' interests are primary at all times.
- *Transparency:* The fund managers should share financial performance, fee income, and returns calculations.

These practices are governed by the terms shown in Table 13.6.

TABLE 13.6 ILPA Best Practices vis-à-vis GP–LP Terms Summary

Driver	Terms
Alignment of interests between LP investors and GP fund managers:	
Does the GP have skin in the game?	Is the GP commitment significantly above or below industry standards? What is the GP's commitment with respect to his or her net worth?
Are the management fees structured appropriately?	Do the management fees adjust when successor funds are raised? How are the fees adjusted after the investment period?
Are there opportunities where a GP–LP conflict of interest may arise?	Can the GP coinvest its personal capital in select cherry-picked opportunities? Will this create a fundamental conflict in the portfolio? As one LP asks, "Why should a manager have side bets and other businesses?"

(Continued)

TABLE 13.6 (*Continued*)

Driver	Terms
Is the GP–LP profit-sharing structure designed appropriately?	Waterfall distribution and clawback provisions
Are all the GP management team members motivated to succeed?	Compensation, GP distribution of carry within its team, resources to operate the fund
What is the investment strategy?	Investment limitations by company, sector, pace of drawdowns, reinvestments, investments from multiple funds in same opportunity
Governance and controls of the fund and its management	
Does an LPAC exist? What are the roles and responsibilities of such a committee? Do the LPs have adequate information?	LPAC size, responsibilities, and frequency of meetings; reports, annual meetings, valuation guidelines
Standard of care: Does the GP allocate substantial time and attention to building and managing the portfolio?	Is the fund a GP's primary activity? Does the GP have other income streams, investments, or interests?
Do the LPs have options to limit the downside or exit the relationship?	No-fault divorce, key person event, key person insurance, termination of investment period, transfer of LP interests, and withdrawal
Transparency of financial information	
Transparency of GP income streams, portfolio quality	Fees and carried interest calculations, valuation and financial information, other relevant GP information, and protection of proprietary information

As the managing director of private equity for the University of California Regents, Timothy Recker manages a portfolio of venture capital and private equity funds. As the former chair of the ILPA, he worked on a number of issues to ensure that the interests of the two sides are aligned. "The ILPA has diligently worked to address a number of issues that make the GP–LP relationship stronger," he says.[5] According to industry surveys, as many as 58 percent of LPs may choose not to invest in funds that ignore the ILPA guidelines.

OFFERING SWEETENERS TO ATTRACT LPS: A DOUBLE-EDGED SWORD

Several GPs offer sweeteners to make the fund attractive to potential LPs, and some even attempt to create a sense of urgency.

Liam Donohue offers a good example of a sweetener. "We pooled our own capital, invested in five companies and offered to contribute this portfolio of five investments to the fund *at cost*. LPs got a sense of opportunities we can attract and realized that we were serious about getting in the business. We believed that this is a small price to pay. We could demonstrate we understood how to build a portfolio that aligns with our strategy. LPs know that it is easy to write about strategy in an offering document, but having actually 'walked the talk' and done it as a first-time fund, that level of thoughtfulness and sophistication allowed us to demonstrate that we can walk the talk," he says.[6] When one of the portfolio companies, HealthDialog, a health care analytics company, was sold for $775 million, the LPs received 2X in less than seven months.

Examples of sweeteners that have not yielded positive outcomes include offering portfolio companies from previous funds that may not have made any meaningful progress. In one example, fund III offered at least half a dozen companies from fund II to LPs at cost. This can irritate existing fund II LPs, who have borne significant risk. Future fund III LPs may also wonder how they might be treated when it comes time to raise fund IV.

WHAT MATTERS MOST

In a survey conducted by the Center for Private Equity and Entrepreneurship at Dartmouth's Tuck School of Business, about 100 GPs and LPs were asked to rank the most negotiated terms.[7] For GPs as well as LPs, the primary tension arises around the overall economics of the fund. LPs often get concerned when fund managers seek to prioritize their own interests above the LP interests. As Table 13.7 displays, key person provisions, clawbacks, and management fees were among the top negotiated terms.

Understanding key limited partner agreement (LPA) terms and knowing what to negotiate can help a GP accelerate the fund-raising process. Investors seek to ensure the alignment of interests. The fee carry, and other restrictive covenants, safeguard their investments and focus the GP toward long-term profit creation. LPs may have remedies, such as key person provisions, cause or no-fault fund terminations, or fund manager removal provisions. These remedies are rarely exercised yet provide a negotiating leverage and a safety cover.

TABLE 13.7   Most Negotiated Terms in Order of Priority: LPs and GPs

LPs—Most Negotiated	GPs—Most Negotiated
1. Key person	1. Clawbacks
2. Waterfall	2. Key person
3. Management fees	3. Management fees
4. Clawbacks	4. Carry
5. Side letters	5. Side letters
6. Indemnification	6. Waterfall
7. Carry	7. Indemnification

Note: Survey included 97 LPs and 117 GPs.

Selecting an experienced fund attorney to develop an appropriate negotiating plan is equally critical. "Choose your service providers wisely—the wrong choice can damage your prospects," says Kelly Williams of Credit Suisse. "We have seen some very good first-time funds but their legal counsel behaved poorly and it did not help the cause."[8] A good attorney knows the market trends of the terms, understands the value of attracting an institutional LP, and proceeds to guide the fund managers accordingly. In one example, a $30-plus billion institutional investor complained that a mature venture firm, now raising fund IV, had picked a small-town attorney with very little experience in negotiating LPAs. "We were utterly flummoxed," says this LP, "and wondered—were the GPs trying to save the fees? I mean, this inexperienced attorney created much angst at our end. They used improper terminology, did not know the market standards . . . it reflected very poorly on the GPs. In fact, nowadays, the first thing we look at in an LPA is the name of their legal counsel. If this is an experienced firm, well versed with private equity, it shows that the GP knows what they are doing."[9]

And if needed, a placement agent can (for a generous fee) introduce you to several investors. Often agents are invited to help top-off a fund, which may have reached 70 percent of the target raise. We the role of placement agents is addressed in the following chapter. Most industry veterans agree: LPs do not invest in funds based on terms (but they may choose *not* to invest if terms are too GP favorable). Rather, LPs make investment decisions based on the full package—team, strategy and past performance. As one investor remarked, "Show me an established firm with consistent top quartile returns and I will concede on most terms."

NOTES

1. Seth Levine (Foundry Group) in discussions with the author, December 2010

2. Evelyn M. Rusli, "In Flip-Flops and Jeans, An Unconventional Venture Capitalist," Dealbook, *New York Times*, October 6, 2011, accessed on January 6, 2014, http://dealbook.nytimes.com/2011/10/06/in-flip-flops-and-jeans-the-unconventional-venture-capitalist/?_r=0.

3. Kelly DePonte (Probitas Partners), in discussion with the author, August 2010.

4. ILPA, "Private Equity Principles 2.0," accessed January 17, 2011, http://ilpa.org/wp-content/uploads/2011/01/ILPA-Private-Equity-Principles-2.0.pdf.

5. Timothy Recker, in discussion with the author, December 2010.

6. Liam Donohue (.406 Ventures), in discussions with the author, December 2010

7. Colin Blaydon and Fred Wainwright, Tuck School of Business at Dartmouth, "Limited Partnership Agreement Project: Results of GP and LP Survey," accessed January 17, 2011, http://mba.tuck.dartmouth.edu/pecenter/research/pdfs/LPA_survey_summary.pdf.

8. Kelly Williams (Credit Suisse), in discussions with the author, February 2011.

9. Anonymous institutional LP, managing $30 billion in assets, in discussions with the author, October 2010.

CHAPTER 14

The Role of Placement Agents in Fund-Raising

"I'm no prophet. My job is making windows where there were once walls."

—Michel Foucault

Placement agents not only advise venture capital funds seeking to raise a new fund, but also broker much of the crucial interaction with institutional investors and key players in the private equity community. Expanding the investor base and accelerating fundraising efforts, placement agents often act as advisors and sounding board. Emerging managers as well as more established firms look to placement agents to gain access to new institutional investors and to streamline the logistics of the fund-raising operations. Beyond opening new doors for funds, agents also influence fund terms and offer advice on market terms and conditions.

Even though the best funds don't need placement agents, across the board, institutional investors prefer to interact with placement agents. A few reputed agents are able to build a matrix of institutional investor relationships and reduce the friction in the process as well. Igor Rozenblit, who led fund investments on behalf of a $2.5 billion European financial services company, says, "Many venture fund managers would not bother to do a primary assessment of our investment criteria and send us completely irrelevant fund memorandums. These would land in the dustbin quickly." Other institutional investors agreed. Edgar adds, "We get fund memorandums from all over the world—China, India, Brazil—and a lot of these are not even relevant, nor fit within our strategy."

Several institutional investors highlighted the role of a placement agent as being critical in the sourcing process. A placement agent brings expertise and a set of relationships, along with knowledge of market trends. These minimize the friction any fund manager may face while raising a fund.

Good placement agents are inundated with solicitations and are highly selective of engagements. For the right fund, placement agents will risk their reputation and invest significant time with the expectation of getting paid after the fund is closed. Kelly DePonte, partner with Probitas Partners, a leading placement agency, says, "I review 600-plus placement memorandums in any given year, and barely a handful will make the cut." DePonte's perspective comes from his interactions with leading institutional investors across the world who make multi-billion-dollar decisions. See Figure 14.1 on agents' views on key traits a fund manager is expected to possess.

Augustine "Gus" Long, partner at Stanwich Advisors, points out that a good placement agent functions as a proxy institutional investor. "If we cannot gather enough confidence and comfort in the fund manager, we do not engage," remarks Long, who managed a $1 billion fund of funds (FoF) prior to joining Stanwich Advisors. Rozenblit concurs that a good agent can make a significant impact for the right firm: "The top venture firms do not need agents, and on the other end of the spectrum, there are firms that are so bad that even a placement agent will refuse to touch them. There can be a few good venture firms in the middle who can benefit from placement agents." Thus, emerging managers with some demonstrated track record, and a compelling strategy, ought to consider whether a DePonte or a Long can make the uphill task easier.

Investment banks like Credit Suisse and UBS have divisions that offer placement agent services. These global entities, operating from many offices

FIGURE 14.1   Fund manager traits.
Source: Preqin

with dedicated staff handling multiple accounts for their private equity customers, can access a larger pool of investors quickly. In addition to investment banks, there are also other global investment placement and advisory firms that focus on providing placement agent service. Unlike investment banks, however, these large independent entities often work exclusively as placement agents. Smaller boutique independent firms also provide placement services, often focusing on a sector or geographical niche (e.g., the Middle East) or a select circle of investors. They may also specialize in specific types of funds (e.g., funds of funds and venture capital funds). "The big houses like Credit Suisse or UBS typically send institutional investors a book of deals in the market. You can pick a few and ask for more details. The good placement agents research extensively and listen carefully. More so, even before they sign up a client, they know who they will market it to," says Bob Clone, who managed a portfolio of funds at State of Michigan and Indiana Retirement Systems.

AGENTS BRING MARKET INTELLIGENCE AND RELATIONSHIPS

The right placement agent can make a significant impact during the fund-raising process by providing insights in market trends, identifying key relationships in institutional investor universe, and refining the strategy/pitch materials. "We spend tremendous amount of time getting fund materials ready, presentations and rehearsals to ensure consistency of communication. Getting an hour with a leading institutional investor is difficult, but when you do get it, we make sure that the fund manager can make the best use of it," says Gus Long of Stanwich Advisors.

Kelly DePonte points out the critical roles that a placement agent plays in supporting venture capital funds:

■ *Market intelligence and social capital:* Placement agents offer connections and a solid base of contacts for their clients, but they are much more than a glorified Rolodex or phone book of investors. Rather than serving as a static database of names for private equity funds, the best placement agents are aggressive trackers, watching the shifts in personnel, sniffing out sector trends, and monitoring investment appetite in the allocations of private equity. In hiring placement agents, funds gain more efficiency in their fund-raising efforts by benefiting from the agents' targeted approach rather than by relying on shallow leads and marketing plans.[1] Agents keep a constant check on the pulse of the market, honing long-term insight and an instinctual know-how on what relationships work or don't work. Placement agents also provide access to new investors and sources of capital. As one fund manager pointed out, when trying to raise a larger fund, you have to talk to new investors—strangers—and a placement agent can simplify this process

LET ME HELP YOU HELP YOURSELF

Placement agents allow fund managers to "focus on [their] core competency—deal making." Placement agents save a fund from being distracted on the lengthy and painful process of fund-raising—a necessary but often periodic step. "You only raise funds every four, five, six years, [so] you can't do it as well as a professional," said Doug Newhouse, whose fund was oversubscribed.* Placement agents are key strategists in determining the details of a fund-raising campaign, such as a target fund size, investor expectations on staffing and professional backgrounds, selection of the right legal team, and other launch details that might be overlooked, even by more experienced fund managers or fund managers overseeing multiple funds. They also play an indomitable role in marketing, giving advice on putting together a scalable mix of investors who not only are willing to commit but also have the resources to do so given a difficult market. With their close contacts, they often have a better sense of the investor market than does a venture capital fund manager. Also, in taking a lead negotiator role in interfacing with investors, placement agents can advise on the right timing for a launch by gauging the strengths and handicaps of investors. More importantly, placement agents can sustain the momentum in a marketing or fund-raising campaign. By moving swiftly in these areas, a fund is brought to a close much faster and avoids languishing and being dubbed unimportant or irrelevant by investors faced with a wide range of opportunities.

"The fund-raise process is a step function—the objective of the first meeting is not to get signed subscription documents—the objective is to get to the next step which is, on site for due diligence. For some institutional investors, it's three steps, and for some it's twenty steps—but you have to be ready at every step. A qualified team without the right form and delivery can kill the investment. There are groups that should get funded but do not because they cannot communicate their story effectively . . . that part of our preparation process is often painful, but that's where we make the biggest impact," says Gus Long of Stanwich Advisors.

---

* "What to Expect from a Placement Agent: Things You Should Know," Probitas Partners, as quoted in *The Definitive Guide to PE Fundraising*, PE Media.

- *A guide on fund terms and trends:* Finally, placement agents offer value to venture capital firms by keeping fund managers informed about fund terms and conditions before going to market. Agents are aware of institutional investor demands on economic and legal trends such as distribution waterfalls, no-fault divorce, clawback provisions, and more. From their interactions with investors, placement agents can predict how the investment market will react to fund terms and conditions as well as adapt to shifting economic and governance provisions. Venture capital fund managers should look for placement agents who can appropriately address the market to your fund type. Agents focusing on international funds can seldom assist a seed-stage fund. Besides possessing intimate knowledge of the investment community, agents bring the experience in conducting rigorous due diligence, preparing marketing and fund-raising campaigns, and effectively bridging partners and investors.[2] On the other side of the coin, as institutional investors become increasingly selective about the funds they invest in, the placement agent's role becomes more critical than ever in smoothing communication between general partners (GPs) and limited partners (LPs), particularly for emerging funds. While many LPs want to invest in safe bets and brand-name funds, they are also willing to invest in new funds if an accomplished placement agent brokers the deal. Placement agents are particularly supportive of new venture capital funds run by managers with a strong track record. Commenting on the deals between general partners and limited partners, Jeffrey Stern, a managing director with Forum Capital Partners, has said that new funds with experienced leaders are the kinds of firms that "make institutional investors perk up," and that "it's [the placement agent's] job to scout these firms for the investors"—striking the right balance between the positive return and inherent risks for investors.[3]

Igor Rozenblit, who represented a $2.5 billion European financial services company seeking investments in venture capital and private equity funds, would frequently interact with some of the top placement agents such as UBS, Credit Suisse, Lazard, and Park Hill. He says: "Some fund managers may not be good at exaggeration but the placement agents are gifted at it. Placement agents would usually puff things up—and the top worn-out clichés of placement agents ignored by most institutions include statements like, 'We have soft-circled about two-thirds of the fund . . . or this is the hottest fund to date' . . . and the best one 'It's going to be oversubscribed—we are closing tomorrow.'" Rozenblit quipped that agents who are too slick hurt the fund, or lose credibility for both parties. "In one case, we closed one month after *the final close*—the agent was not happy."

ETHICAL CHALLENGES

Incidences of abuse in the placement service industry, often from political insiders using their political affiliations, contacts, and celebrity reach to broker deals between investors and funds, have caused many headaches for the legitimate entities. Orin Kramer, head of New Jersey's Investment Council, has commented on some placement agents as "politically connected intermediaries . . . who are not really in the financial business," who cause a multitude of thorny ethical issues.[4] According to various news sources, New York, New Mexico, Florida, and Massachusetts have seen a rise in civil complaints regarding the management of pension funds and the use of placement agents with political connections and financial self-interest in brokering deals with investors.

For example, the Los Angeles Department of Fire and Police Pensions was shocked over the $150,000 fee received by Henry Morris, a former New York political advisor, who worked as a placement agent from Quadrangle Group LLC, for roping in $10 million for their investment fund. In New Mexico, firms that employed Marc Correra, son of a supporter of New Mexico Governor Bill Richardson, earned $15 million on investments to the state's endowment and teacher pension fund.[5]

Such examples illustrate how former politicians, campaign operatives, and other public officials are getting into the business and may raise legal issues. California has passed a bill to restrict the use of placement agents by requiring anyone who solicits investments from CalPERS and CalSTRS—the California state public retirement systems (with over $274 billion in assets under management)—to register as lobbyists. This effectively prohibits agents from receiving compensation from investment deals in state funds. Legislators pushed the bill in light of the case of a former CalPERS board member who garnered placement fees of more than $47 million from the state investment managers.[6]

Other private equity firms, such as Carlyle, became embroiled in a "pay to play" kickback controversy. In New York, the attorney general and the SEC accused Hank Morris, a placement agent hired by Carlyle and many other firms, of hatching a scheme that involved kickbacks from investment firms seeking allocation deals with the state's public pension fund. Carlyle, which manages $85 billion and had raised upward of $700 million from a New York pension fund, paid $20 million to settle kickback scandals.[7]

Some placement agents will continue to function as hired guns for private equity funds. Others play a legitimate role and reduce friction in an industry where constraints on time are high and the demand-supply ratio of capital is perpetually tilted. Caveat emptor—choose your partners with care.

NOTES

1. "What to Expect from a Placement Agent: Things You Should Know," Probitas Partners, accessed January 19, 2011.
2. "A Guide to Private Equity Fund Placement Specialists," Private Equity International (PEI) Media.
3. "Placement Agents Have Record Year as Private Equity Firms Fundraise," December 12, 2005. http://www.sterlinglp.com/news/index_3d02e514 .aspx.html accessed on December 12, 2010
4. Martin Z. Braun and Gillian Wee, "How Pension Placement Agent Exploited Political Ties (Update1)," Bloomberg.com, May 18, 2009, accessed January 19, 2011, www.bloomberg.com/apps/news?pid= newsarchive&sid=atwTqj6OjY7U.
5. Ibid.
6. Proskauer's Private Investment Practice Group, "United States: California Restricts Use of Placement Agents," *Mondaq*, October 11, 2010, accessed January 19, 2011, www.mondaq.com/unitedstates/article.asp? articleid=112514.
7. John Carney, "Carlyle Will Pay $20 Million in Pension Fund Kickback Scandal Settlement," *Business Insider*, May 14, 2009, accessed on January 6, 2014, www.businessinsider.com/carlyle-will-pay-20-million-in-pension-fund-kickback-scandal-settlement-2009-5.

TWO

Making Investments

The only measure of venture capital success is performance. The ability to pick the right companies that generate superior returns is paramount to any professional's success in this business.

The investment process—sourcing, due diligence, negotiation of investment terms, board roles and supporting entrepreneurs—is important, yet secondary. Investors primarily care about strong financial returns. While sourcing investment opportunities is a function of the firm's team expertise and relationships, the venture firm's brand as being entrepreneur friendly has also become an important factor. Investors, who are independent and act decisively, are responsive and treat entrepreneurs as equals attract strong opportunities. Eventually, a strong brand is built upon this foundation.

When it comes to due diligence, seasoned investors are students of the market; if the market is ready, they make quick decisions and actively invest in start-up opportunities that serve the market needs. Management team, product, features and competition are important attributes, yet the best investors rarely overthink and are comfortable in ambiguity.

Mike Maples of Floodgate Fund has invested in some of the leading technology startups in the Silicon Valley. He often completes his due diligence in 10 minutes. "The best deals we have done are the ones where we decided the quickest—which is counterintuitive to me. Ten minutes into a meeting with an entrepreneur, I stopped the presentation, raised my hand and said I want to invest. The company had momentum, an authentic entrepreneur and an awesome market."[1]

---

[1] Tarang and Sheetal Shah, *Venture Capitalists at Work: How VCs Identify and Build Billion-Dollar Successes* (New York: APress, 2011).

These five general criteria determine investment decisions:

1. Does the management team demonstrate integrity, a sense of urgency, knowledge and agility?
2. Is a clear market pain point identified? Has a value proposition established?
3. What are key risks and a plan for mitigation?
4. Are capital needs, efficiency and break-even taken into account? Does the company have financing from other sources?
5. Can this investment generate target returns within desired time frame?

Table P2.1 describes the various criteria in greater detail for investment consideration. Not all of these criteria are applicable to early stage companies.

TABLE P2.1:   Due Diligence—Key Criteria

Criteria	Definition	Remarks
Management Team Criteria		
Management team	Stage-ready and well-rounded team, committed and coachable.	Company should have attracted a strong team with clarity on skills for sales and marketing and product development. While each company has specific needs for talent, look for the individuals, their backgrounds, and a fit with their roles.
Internal systems	Financial, sales and operations systems are documented and managed effectively.	Company should demonstrate adequate internal systems such as (a) financial reporting, controls, and decision making, (b) sales and marketing systems, (c) product development road maps.
Overall milestones	On plan to meet its milestones. No material change in its business strategy or direction	Review company's product roadmaps and assess with the quarterly reports and actual progress. While deviations are a norm, ensure that the company is on or ahead of plan prior to considering follow-on funding.
Reporting and communication with investors	Monthly, quarterly reports are provided in a timely manner. Verbal updates or meetings are frequent.	Company's ability to keep investors updated on key developments via reports, communications and updates is important.

Criteria	Definition	Remarks
Financials		
Revenues	On plan or exceeding plan	Review financial milestones of revenues and gross margins. Stability of margins will be reviewed. These will be assessed in conjunction with other balance sheet–and cash flow–related matters to ensure the financial stability of the company.
Other	No significant debt or receivables; cash flows are sufficient.	
Investment Terms		
Size of round	Sufficient to help company reach the next milestone	Investment will be syndicated as a part of a larger round. Is this capital sufficient for meeting the stated milestones?
Position	Coinvestor or follower	Syndicate follow-on investments with external investors as a mechanism to validate risk mitigation.
Terms of investment	Case-by-case basis	Ensure that current terms of investment are suitable to ensure target returns.
Additional capital needs	Future capital needs and path to break-even are clear	Investment may be ideally suited in situations where companies demonstrate capital efficiency. If companies need substantial follow-on rounds, these would elevate the risk.
Risk Mitigation		
Syndicate investors	Additional investments from current investors or new investors	Assess various factors of risk mitigation such as (a) professional investment from venture funds at up-rounds, (b) growing demand of products/pipeline of orders, (c) diversity of customer base.
Purchase order pipeline	A meaningful pipeline of orders is at hand	

The role of an investor on a start-up board is to support the CEO as needed. In some cases, investor board members offer strategic insights, open doors to customers and attract key team members. CEOs especially value investor board members' roles when it comes to raising the next round. Building reserves to invest in follow-on rounds is important; yet knowing when to let go of the nonperformers is the harder part.

In Part II, we dive into the process of sourcing, diligence, and structuring investments. The post-investment phase of portfolio value-add, as a board member, is also reviewed. Finally, we look at the exit pathways. The last chapter of this section delves into the human psychology, the inherent bias and foibles of our behavior.

CHAPTER 15

Sourcing Investment Opportunities

"I want to find the next Facebook when it's just Mark Zuckerberg."

—Kevin Rose, Google Ventures[1]

K evin Rose, a partner at Google Ventures, has fine-tuned the art of sourcing investments in Silicon Valley. When he found out that mobile payments company Square was raising a round, he reached out to Jack Dorsey, co-founder of Square. But the investment round was full, and Dorsey said Square didn't need more investors. Rose noticed that Square did not have a video demonstration of the product. He quickly put together a video to demonstrate the product and showed it to Dorsey, just as an FYI. Impressed, Dorsey turned around and invited Rose to invest in the so-called full Series A round.[2]

Kevin Efrusy of Accel Partners was ranked in top five of the *Forbes* Midas List of venture capital investors. After all, he sourced this great investment opportunity called Facebook for Accel Partners. Efrusy, who had served two separate stints as an entrepreneur-in-residence at Kleiner Perkins Caufield & Byers (KPCB), had joined Accel with the primary directive—find the next big thing in social start-ups. While Efrusy was on the hunt, he found his target two years into his career at Accel. Chi-Hua Chien, a graduate student doing research for Accel, pointed out this opportunity called Facebook to Efrusy, who never gave up till he trapped this elusive beast.

"Social networks had this dirty name," he said in *The Facebook Effect*.[3] Facebook had more than 20 competitors when it was launched. Six months before its launch, Friendster, one of its competitors, had raised $13 million from top venture capital firms such as KPCB and Battery Ventures. Separately, the search giant Google had relaunched Orkut, another social-networking rival. And soon after Facebook's launch, MySpace boasted nearly five million users.

None of this competition slowed Efrusy—he called and e-mailed the startup relentlessly—and was stonewalled or turned down. "We will move heaven and earth to make this a successful company," Efrusy once told Mark Zuckerberg. But Facebook was not interested in talking to venture capitalists (VCs). "He was hounding us," one Facebook executive would recall.

Finally, Efrusy decided to walk over to Facebook's offices and entered a chaotic scene, where remnants of the previous night's liquor party were strewn all over. One person, struggling to assemble a DIY table, had blood oozing from his forehead. Efrusy promised Zuckerberg, who was nibbling on a burrito: "Come to our partners' meeting on Monday. We'll give you a term sheet by the end of the day, or you'll never hear from us again."

Over the weekend, Efrusy did some intense calling around to find out more about the Facebook phenomenon. On Monday morning at 10 A.M., Zuckerberg, wearing his flip-flops, shorts, and a T-shirt, showed up at Accel's offices with two cohorts. They didn't bother bringing any slides. Five days later, after much song and dance and pleading, Accel had closed on a $12.7 million investment at a $100 million pre-money valuation, owning a 15 percent stake in Facebook. Efrusy did not get a board seat. "It hurt my feelings," he would say. "But I understand."

Efrusy displays all attributes essential to source a good investment opportunity: rapid assessment, proactive contact, and a hunter-like tenacity. But it is not just Efrusy's qualities that count—the firm also matters. Accel Partners was founded in 1983, managed $6 billion, and helped entrepreneurs build over 300 successful category-defining companies. And Jim Breyer, a partner at Accel, is ranked high up on several investor lists. The venture firm's brand, track record, and the stature of Jim Breyer (who is firmly established in the "VC God" category) certainly had an overall impact on completing the investment.

But even more interesting is the fact that James Swartz, founder of Accel Partners, speaking prophetically of investing in new technological waves, once said, "The older generation . . . better just get the heck outta the way, or if you want to stay in the game, get a kid and let him do his thing."[4] Little did Swartz know that this Efrusy kid was already at work in sourcing the next big thing for Accel.

Hany Nada, cofounder of GGV, a $1 billion venture fund boasting of investments in Chinese giants like Alibaba, agrees. "I am 42 years old and I find that it is better to bring in the newer generation—they understand emerging technology trends better than I do."

DORM ROOM FUND: GET A KID AND LET HIM DO HIS THING

Facebook, Google, Microsoft, Dell, Napster—what do the founders of these companies have in common? They all started in a dorm room, their founders absconding from their classrooms. And how do you source these opportunities? Enter the Dorm Room Fund, a venture fund backed by First Round Capital, which is run by students for students. The fund provides student entrepreneurs with seed capital and mentorship right on their own campuses.

The Dorm Room Fund aims to be the first choice for student entrepreneurs who need capital. Started in Philadelphia, the fund is now present in eight U.S.-based universities, including Stanford, Massachusetts Institute of Technology (MIT), and Princeton.

First Round Capital selects the investor teams, and although these kids come from diverse backgrounds, they have a common passion—to help their peers start companies. Each investor team is pitched from student entrepreneurs, does due diligence and manages the deal flow on the campus. The student investor teams conduct weekly meetings, manage the voting structure and make investment decision, but they don't hold any board seats. The final sign off comes from First Round Capital.

First Round puts $500,000 in each university fund. The average investment size is $20,000 structured as an uncapped-convertible note, which is a form of debt that can be converted to equity at a later stage without a cap on valuation. Students don't have to worry about valuations and can focus on nurturing the business. In addition to funding, First Round Capital partners are available for consultations and conduct training sessions on investment philosophies. Gains, if any, are put back into the fund. There is no intervention in the investment process by First Round unless they come across something legally or ethically wrong. Nor are there any restrictions on the kinds of businesses to be developed, although with a $20,000 investment, most businesses tend to be technology start-ups. First Round doesn't hold any exclusivity for the next round of funding. Students are free

(Continued)

DORM ROOM FUND: (*Continued*)

to start conversations with other potential investors, although they are welcome to approach First Round if they need to. Incidentally Josh Kopelman, the Managing Director of First Round Capital, started his first company in a dorm room.

The fund is a win-win for both First Round and the students. First Round gets access to a pipeline of new businesses. At the same time, the student get access to First Round resources such as best practices for hiring, support in bringing advisors, and access to the press.

In addition to funding, Dorm Room Fund provides student entrepreneurs with resident advisors who act as mentors. The Dorm Room Fund has invested in 24 companies after reviewing more than 400 companies.

Source: Brett Berson, VP of Platform, First Round Capital in discussions with the author.

While the hypercompetitive universe of the Silicon Valley demands such Efrusy-like attributes, and the advantages of age in sourcing opportunities are undeniable, the rest of the world functions differently. Typical sources of investment opportunities lie embedded within the network—the social fabric woven over time that yields consistent quality referrals. Entrepreneurs or trusted peer investors are often the most qualitative and reliable sources. Other sources include incubators and accelerators, attorneys, angel networks, banks and nonbank financial institutions, and technology transfer offices. Figure 15.1 depicts the overall investment process, which commences with sourcing. Table 15.1 outlines these options in more detail.

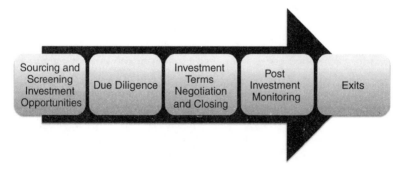

FIGURE 15.1   A venture fund's investment process.

TABLE 15.1 Sources of Investment Opportunity

Source	Advantages	Disadvantages
Accelerators and incubators/demo-days	Large volume of vetted opportunities. Best suited for seed investors	Overcrowding—the best start-ups are funded prior to demo-days. For some start-ups, valuation can get inflated very quickly.
AngelList/online matchmaking sites	Access to opportunities, no geographic barriers.	Stimulates herd mentality of stock market.
Peer investors/other venture practitioners	Speedier due diligence in trusted relationships.	Lame horses can be parlayed as great opportunities.
Attorneys, accountants, and consultants	Can provide some level of prescreening based on fund criteria and fit.	Caveat emptor: All clients who pay $300 an hour look great!
Banks/venture debt providers	Can mitigate risk; may have skin in the game.	Senior lenders have first lien on assets.
Serial entrepreneurs	Well-vetted ideas, better understanding of investor mind-set, recognition of challenges.	May not have any skin in the game.
Economic development/nonprofit professionals	Volume, access to a larger network.	Quality may be suspect.
Business plan competitions and venture forums	Prescreened and vetted, this may be a good source of opportunities for early-stage investors.	Watch for students who participate for the sake of participating and winning—not building a business.
University tech transfer offices, federal research labs	Diamond in the rough! May need to invest time to build the business strategy and team.	Watch for technology in search of an application.
Corporate spinouts	Potential for joint development, coinvestments	Market size may be limited. Patents may have limited shelf life.

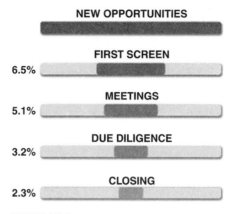

FIGURE 15.2 Typical sourcing, screening, and investment ratios.

As a rule of thumb, investors look at a very large volume of opportunities before they invest in any one. For Jim Breyer and Accel, the brand attracts a lot of volume. "We see ten thousand business plans a year, and we invest in about ten," he noted.[5]

Consider the statistics in Figure 15.2 representative of typical percentages of investment.

THE BEST SOURCE: THE NETWORK

In any business, it's primarily relationships that matter. But in the venture business, relationships can make or break a practitioner. For the handful of venture firms that have established brands, opportunities may arrive from a vast matrix of relationships: serial entrepreneurs, peer venture investors, attorneys, investment bankers, and service providers. Brad Feld of the Foundry Group had a 15-year relationship with Mark Pincus, the founder of Zynga. Feld and Union Square Ventures led the first round of investment in this start-up, and in four years, the company's valuation was well over $5 billion. Or consider Pierre Omidyar, founder of eBay. While seeking the first round of capital, Omidyar had a term sheet that offered at least 2.5X higher valuation, but he still chose to go with lower valuation offered by Benchmark Capital. Pierre knew Bruce Dunlieve, a general partner (GP) at Benchmark who had invested in his prior company, and he trusted the relationship. Thanks to the relationship advantage and gravitas, Benchmark netted $2.5 billion on its $5 million eBay investment.[6]

Networks function well within certain geographies. "Northern California is very network-centric, and it's relatively uncommon to find really high-quality investment opportunities in the straightforward way of going to conferences and having people submit things on your Web site. The really good deals go through a network because it's an extremely well connected, low-friction community," says William Elkus, managing partner of Clearstone Venture Partners, who counts PayPal and Overture among his past investment successes.[7]

For the rest of venture practitioners, the sourcing process is a lot of shoe-leather grunt work, often delegated to junior analysts: attending industry conferences, reading various publications, and initiating contact with company executives to build trust and initiate due diligence. One venture capitalist (VC) had a picture on the wall, which bemoaned "How many frogs should I kiss?"

Brent Ahrens of Canaan Partners summarizes: "This business is about deal flow and cash flow—if you can generate quality deal flow or raise cash from LPs [limited partners], you are good."[8]

The business calls for the perpetual development of the art of honing sourcing abilities. Regional venture conferences blend company presentations with the wisdom of reputed venture practitioners. While it is rare to find truly novel and groundbreaking opportunities at such events, this is fertile ground for most venture practitioners. However, LPs are seldom impressed to hear that your firm's sourcing strategy consists primarily of attending conferences. LPs often wish to know whether you have any unfair advantage or competitive threats in sourcing opportunities. Chris Douvos,

WHEN OPPORTUNITY MEETS THE PREPARED MIND

One evening, Don Valentine, founder of Sequoia Capital, was dining at a restaurant when he saw Steve Jobs and Mike Markkula together and sensed what was being discussed. He dispatched a bottle of wine with a note: "Don't lose sight of the fact that I'm planning on investing in Apple."

Valentine invested $150,000 shortly thereafter in Apple at a $3 million valuation.

Source: Michael Moritz, *Return to the Little Kingdom: Steve Jobs, The Creation of Apple and How It Changed the World* (New York: Overlook Press, 2009), 237.

SOURCING ADVANTAGE: TREAT EVERY ENTREPRENEUR WITH RESPECT

"My best opportunity ever in my 30 years of investing experience came from an entrepreneur I had turned down. He referred another entrepreneur to our fund, and we made an investment that turned out to be our best performer ever. I guess when we said no, we must have done it in a thoughtful way."

—Jack Ahrens, TGap Ventures

who has been an LP for more than a decade, says, "Some of the brand name funds have a deep network, which is very hard for new GPs to replicate. This network can be a significant advantage—you can validate ideas, launch products, and even engineer exits at the right time."[9]

When a successful entrepreneur reaches out to you and asks you to participate in his next big thing, you have arrived. That sourcing advantage can be immense. As Chris Rizik says, "What is it about you that acts as a magnet to entrepreneurs? Dumb money is found aplenty, everywhere."[10] As much as the network matters in sourcing, networks take time to get established. And there are disadvantages of relying too much on others: the best opportunities are rarely shared. For those starting fresh, often the best way to source a good opportunity is get out there and start hunting. Accelerators, demo-days, and angel networks are some good starting points to source opportunities.

ACCELERATORS AND DEMO-DAYS

Incubators and accelerators have waxed and waned with economic times—the term *incubator* used to bring visions of tall glass buildings teeming with young entrepreneurs chowing down on pizza and indulging in excessive caffeine. Accelerators, smarter versions of incubators, have sprung up in every corner of the world, and they bring in mentorship, smaller amounts of seed capital, and no emphasis on real estate.

According to Seed-DB,[11] a database of accelerators, there are over 170 accelerators worldwide, and almost 3,000 companies that have received approximately $2.73 billion in funding. Exits have occurred for 5 percent of these, or around 150, creating $1.76 billion in value. That translates to an average investment in these companies of approximately $900,000 and an average exit size in the $10 million range.

THE VC E-MARKETPLACE: ANGELLIST, KICKSTARTER, AND FUNDERSCLUB

A hardware start-up has several Sand Hill Road VCs eating out of their hands. Having launched their product on Kickstarter, they are collecting preorders at the rate of more than $20,000 a day. With $3 million in preorders at hand, VCs are begging to invest or otherwise get in on this opportunity. The pre-money valuation has risen into the obscene category. Without Kickstarter, this company would have been laughed out of any VC meeting with a terse comment: "We don't do hardware!" As Marc Andreessen correctly pointed out, software is eating the world.

Online portals like AngelList may have just begun nibbling at toes of Sand Hill Road. VCs are burying their heads in the sand (or silicon, depending on the geography). Foundry Group, a fund based in Boulder, Colorado, is one of the first VCs to look at this wave as an opportunity and has launched FG Angels, syndicating investments via AngelList.

AngelList processes as many as 500 introductions and moves $10 million each month. The amounts are small today, but that's how it started with online e-commerce purchases: Small amounts build trust for larger transactions. First we bought books online, and now we are buying cars, flat-screen TVs, and more. Similar paths may emerge with investing.

FundersClub, which brands itself as an online VC, has completed more than 30 investments. FundersClub is hyperfocused on start-ups based in Silicon Valley and brands itself as an online VC fund. These online models are gaining traction and will change the landscape of investments. Yet many investors scour these online portals to keep track of and source some of the better opportunities.

ANGELS

Fertile territories for opportunities for venture investors, angel funds, and affiliated forms of seed capital provide an early access to investment opportunities. Over 550 angel groups exist worldwide,[12] nearly 300 of which are based in the United States.[13] Angel investor groups are composed of wealthy individuals or high-net-worth individuals (HNWIs) who pool resources and investment expertise. Angels typically target early-stage entrepreneurs who need $100,000 to $1 million in equity financing. The number of active angels in the United States is reported to be upward of 125,000; of these, between 10,000 and 15,000 angels are believed to belong to angel groups.[14]

■ *Numbers:* An average angel group invests $1.9 million in approximately seven opportunities. About 42 members compose a typical group.[15]

- *Stage:* Twenty-six percent of angel investments are in the seed and start-up stage, while 56 percent are post-seed/start-up investing.
- *Returns:*[16]
  - The average return of angel investments is 2.6 times the investment in 3.5 years—approximately 27 percent rate of return (IRR).
  - Fifty-two percent of all the exits returned less than the capital the angel had invested in the venture.
  - Seven percent of the exits achieved returns of more than 10 times the money invested, accounting for 75 percent of the total investment dollar returns.

Angel groups have limited cash resources for administration and management. Before you build inroads to any angel investor network, consider the following.

- *Understand the overall process and the strength of the network:*
  - Does the network have good opportunities in the pipeline?
  - How is the prescreening conducted? Who conducts the due diligence?
  - Does each angel invest one off on his or her own, or are the investments pooled and negotiated as a group?[17]
  - Are there standard terms of investment? What, if any, sectors are preferred over others? Have the angels made any follow-on investments?
  - Have there been any up-rounds or syndications with venture capitalists? Any exits?
- *Limited bandwidth:* Angels have limited resources to invest, and an angel can lose interest fast after a few investments turn into tax write-offs. A measure of activity is the number of investments made in the past 12 months.
- *Limited sector expertise:* If an angel has expertise within a certain sector, that's a good start. Make sure you spend time with those who have domain knowledge and can share their experiences.
- *Get to know the big dog:* Every angel group has a big dog—the center of this universe or the smartest guy with the deepest pockets. In Silicon Valley, that would be Ron Conway. The big dog is essential to the longevity and cohesion of a group: Many angels typically follow the investment rationale of a big dog. Big dogs make a lot of investments and are astute in managing their portfolios and risks. By the same token, be wary of passive angels and tire kickers: many angels sign up as members but are rarely active. For example, 65 percent of the memberships in angel groups are latent angels, individuals who have the necessary net worth yet have not made an investment. Either they are too busy or just not interested or they are tire kickers, entertaining

themselves at the cost of entrepreneurs. Avoid these unconscionable devils at all costs.

- *Standardized terms:* Angel investment terms can be nonstandard. *In one survey, 78 percent of VCs said the number one reason that makes an angel-backed company unattractive to VCs is overly high, unrealistic valuations.* Fifty-eight percent of the respondents said angels' involvement had made a company unattractive. Angels also complicate negotiations and are viewed by venture capitalists as generally unsophisticated.[18] Opportunistic angels can stick an entrepreneur with investment terms that hurt both parties in the long run. In another study, it was evident that angel funding was helpful in survival of a company per se, but was not central in whether a company obtained follow-on financing.[19] Despite this, at least 49 percent of the venture capitalists coinvest with angels on most opportunities.[20]

- *Quality of the portfolio:* Are the investments progressing toward an exit? The ultimate test of any investment activity is future rounds from venture investors or, better still, exits. Only 45 percent of angel groups had coinvestment with venture capital firms. As we saw earlier, only 7 percent of investment opportunities returned 10 times the capital—or as they say, venture-like returns.

THE FOUNTAINHEADS OF ACADEMIA AND RESEARCH

According to the Association of University Technology Managers (AUTM), universities in United States invest upward of $60 billion each year in research, and create about 600 start-ups.[21] Granted that a fair amount of the investments would be in basic research, data indicates universities are a fertile domain for sourcing opportunities.

When it comes to mining universities, Robert "Bob" Nelsen of ARCH Venture Partners may have mastered the art of sourcing opportunities within university labs. When Nelsen met Mark Roth, a cellular biologist at the Fred Hutchinson Cancer Research Center, Roth was working on suspended animation—a technique to induce a hibernation-like state in animals by cutting off their oxygen supply. Most venture capitalists would flee such a discussion. Not Nelsen, who worked with Roth patiently for five years. Steven Lazarus, founder of ARCH and now its managing director emeritus, would say of ARCH's investment strategy, "This was not seed capital. In our case, we were identifying science literally at the site of inception, assessing whether it had commercial potential and then erecting a commercial entity around it—it was virtually [starting] from scratch."[22] As a result, Ikaria was formed with an initial investment from ARCH, Venrock, and 5AM Ventures. And Mark Roth,

SOURCING ADVANTAGE : HOW TO MONETIZE UNIVERSITY START-UPS

Osage University Partners has partnered with more than 50 universities, essentially acquiring each university's investment participation rights. Universities often take anywhere from 2 percent to 10 percent equity in a start-up. While a university can maintain its participation rights by investing additional capital at future rounds, it's rare that technology transfer offices actually exercise these rights. Quite simply, these are not investment entities but rather are focused on commercialization. Enter Osage. The partners at Osage built an index of start-ups from 50 top-flight universities that had licensed their technology to those start-ups but had not invested in them. What they discovered startled them: there was a very respectable 33 percent rate of return, which is better than most venture capital funds have generated.[23] A partner university allows Osage to invest in their start-ups. This helps maintain the same percentage of ownership as Osage invests cash in subsequent funding rounds. In return for assigning their investment rights to Osage, the universities share some of the fund's profits that take into account the success of each school's spin-out companies.

the scientist who could have easily been passed off as a mad scientist, went on to win the MacArthur Genius Award after the company was launched.

It is seldom the science that translates to opportunities—the business talent is a critical component of the mix. Many university start-ups flounder when founding teams lack a healthy balance of business acumen, as well as a sense of urgency.

Universities as a source of entrepreneurial talent is a much more fertile ground. When angel investor K. Ram Shriram bumped into two young kids called Sergey and Larry in an elevator at Stanford University, it was a chance meeting. Yet, he went on to be the first one to invest $500,000 and the term, "elevator pitch" was born. Sergey Brin and Larry Page's start-up, Google, catapulted K. Ram Shriram onto the list of *Forbes* billionaires.

CORPORATE RESEARCH

Research and development (R&D) spending by U.S. companies is at least four times that of university expenditures. In United States, the corporate annual R&D investments are more than $200 billion each year. According to Booz & Company, a consulting firm, the top 1,000 companies invest $500 billion each year globally.[24]

While these territories may seem fertile, most R&D investments occur to further productivity and profitability. Corporations have little expertise or motivation in spinning start-ups that eventually become venture backed. As such, corporations have a reason to be threatened by start-ups. Rather than promote start-ups, corporations tend to relinquish rights to a valuable IP.

Xerox is one example that comes up often, in view of missing the opportunity on the graphic user interface (GUI), which was monetized by Apple. To that point, it was Bill Gates, founder of Microsoft, who once famously called on Steve Jobs, "Hey Steve, just because you broke into Xerox's store before I did and took the TV doesn't mean I can't go in later and steal the stereo."[25]

A similar example of a missed opportunity originates from the merger of Pharmacia-Upjohn, two pharmaceutical giants. After the merger of Pharmacia and Upjohn, David Scheer, a venture catalyst who blended his knowledge of science and venture capital, was hired to scour some back-burner projects for potential development or divestiture. A compound caught David's attention. "Apo-I Milano protein was the most interesting," Scheer recalls. "We had vision that this project deserved a platform as the next frontier in the cardiovascular arena."[26] Scheer partnered with Roger Newton, the codiscoverer of Lipitor, the world's most successful cardiovascular drug, and launched Esperion Therapeutics. Esperion went public in five years and was acquired by Pfizer for $1.3 billion. Timothy Mayleben, the chief operating officer who led the company through multiple venture rounds to IPO, says, "Every investor in every round made strong returns." In the biotech sector, spin-out activities have occurred more frequently as compared to other sectors. While larger companies are sources of talent and know-how, limited start-up and venture activity of merit has evolved from larger companies. In select cases, and especially in the pharmaceutical sector, corporations can be a rich source of opportunities.

TRADE CONFERENCES

Trade conferences, where the cutting edge of developments can be seen, are often rich sources of opportunities for seeking investments.

Daniel Axelsen of New Enterprise Associates (NEA), a Silicon Valley venture firm, says, "Trade shows can be an ideal place to seek investments. I often go to a security conference and the buzz from a room full of engineers is palpable. The business unit heads and the geeks gather to share data and information. Such shows act as a fabric between the worlds of investors,

entrepreneurs, and large company executives." Arthur Rock, one of the early
investors in Apple, once went to a computer show in San Jose when nobody
really had a computer to show, but rather had parts of computers. And
while other booths were empty, there was a long line at the Apple booth.
Rock would recall, "Jesus, there's got to be something here."[27]

Leading investors walk the halls of trade shows to assess industry trends
and direction, meet with the technical thought leaders, and explore investment opportunities. Start-ups that may have achieved a certain stature or
size are often exhibiting their wares at industry trade shows.

At times, it may just be a serial entrepreneur wandering these halls,
looking for his next new thing. That's how William H. Draper, III came
across LSI Logic, a semiconductor company. Wilfred Corrigan, then CEO
of Fairchild Semiconductor, was itching to do something new. He met with
Draper at a convention and expressed his desire to start a new company.
Draper invested, and LSI Logic went public two years later. At the time,
NASDAQ billed it as the largest technology IPO.[28]

"A combination of factors is at play—attending conferences, listening
to the keynote speakers present new ideas, and looking at the new products
helps us to understand the problems these smart people are trying to solve.
We take that into consideration and try to define what really makes sense
for us to invest in," says Lip-Bu Tan of Walden International. "Ideally, for a
new market, there are no conferences. We find many of our most interesting
opportunities in tiny conferences, where there are 30 or 40 vendors, and
we're the only VC firm that's at the conference," says John Jarve of Menlo
Ventures.[29]

But while attending conferences is one way of seeking opportunities,
Tim O'Reilly, who organized such conferences frequently, had a head start
in sourcing when he partnered with Bryce Roberts to raise a venture fund.
"Tim is one of those rare businesspeople who not only takes the longest
and broadest possible view," the *Linux Journal* wrote of Tim O'Reilly,
who launched a series of publications and conferences around technology and innovation.[30] After hosting O'Reilly Media's first Open Source
event, O'Reilly garnered national publicity and since has held summits on
peer-to-peer technology, Web services, geek volunteerism, and Ajax. These
summits forge new ties between industry leaders, raise awareness of technology issues, and crystallize the critical issues around emerging technologies. And of course, they are a fertile ground for investment opportunities.
O'Reilly Media describes itself as "a chronicler and catalyst of leading-edge
development, homing in on the technology trends that really matter and
galvanizing their adoption by amplifying 'faint signals' from the alpha
geeks who are creating the future."[31] LP Chris Douvos says, "Tim is the
Obi-Wan Kenobi of the tech space . . . a great ecosystem exists around

him and entrepreneurs are attracted to this guru and the ecosystem."[32] So when O'Reilly and Bryce Roberts decided to raise a fund, O'Reilly Alphatec Ventures (OATV), Douvos jumped in with both feet and invested. OATV has a significant sourcing advantage, a first look at many new opportunities even before they become opportunities.

Practitioners can benefit from conferences primarily via gathering industry trends and interacting with thought leaders. Consider these as educational sessions. Every now and then, an opportunity might pop up that will merit an investment.

PITCH ME, BRO

Start-up pitch sessions and demo-days have become customary pegs in any technology ecosystem. Equivalent to a beauty pageant, entrepreneurs walk the ramp in 10 minutes or less, the VCs show the scorecard of a 5 or an 8 ("Never a 10, one VC told me—that would mean I would be hounded by the entrepreneur"), and the audience claps and moves on to the next pitch. As the pitches roll by, the VCs offer their feedback. "Sounds like a Swiss knife," they say to one idea. A Swiss knife is a technology with 23 or more features, very difficult to manufacture, and in VC jargon translates to "you are trying to do too much—let's get focused here." Entrepreneurs who could barely scratch the surface in two minutes, protest, "I have a lot more to say here . . ." but are gently ushered along into the Q-and-A session. "I applaud you for trying to change the world," says one VC. Ninety minutes later, the VC panel having shared its observations, the entrepreneurs leave the room with lots of advice and no cash. But for practitioners across the country, such events are a tactical mechanism of looking at opportunities. For entrepreneurs, this presents an opportunity to meet and pitch a VC, albeit under pressure. Any practitioner worth his or her expertise or money is invited to participate on such panels, where entrepreneurs seek attention and capital, not necessarily in equal parts. And then there are entrepreneurs who will stop at nothing at such events to get a VC's attention. "Someone started to whisper in my ear at a urinal—bad idea!" says Rick Heitzmann of FirstMark Capital (see Figure 15.3).[33]

These events offer prescreened opportunities to investors who may choose to follow up after these events and dig deeper into the investment thesis. Ask Rajeev Batra of the Mayfield Fund, who was featured on a panel called "Hand us the next killer Cloud App, and we will hand you $100,000." The event, organized by Salesforce.com, the leading customer relationship management (CRM) company, invited 40 companies to present to a VC panel, with leading practitioners from firms like Sequoia

FIGURE 15.3 Pssstttt . . . heard of "Lunar" power (seen at a VC event men's room).

Capital and Bessemer Venture Partners. Such pitch sessions are ideal opportunities to build your brand as a practitioner as well as to land the next big thing.

COMPETITIONS: FROM $40 MILLION MOONSHOT TO $10K

The Google Lunar XPRIZE, the largest international incentive-based prize of all time, aims to do something we haven't done as humanity since 1973: safely land on the surface of the moon. The prize aims to create a new "Apollo" moment for this generation and to spur continuous lunar exploration with $40 million in incentive based prizes. To win this money, a private company must land safely on the surface of the moon, travel 500 meters above, below, or on the lunar surface, and send back two "Mooncasts" to Earth. All of this must be completed by December 31, 2015. The race is on!

Of the 20 or so teams competing for this XPrize, not many may become venture-backed start-ups. But competitions are a proven mechanism to get the juices flowing and solve grand challenges, spur innovation, and improve our life conditions.

A McKinsey 2009 report on the impact of business plans stated that "as many as 60 prizes have debuted in the past decade, representing almost $250 million in new prize money. And the total funds available from large prizes have more than tripled over the last decade to surpass $375 million. The total prize sector could already be worth as much as $1 to $2 billion."

For business school students across the country, participating in and winning a business plan competition is a badge of honor. Some students have found these to help make some pocket change on the side. Several start-ups have been funded and launched successfully—thanks to such competitions.

Todd Dagres of Spark Capital found his Akamai opportunity when he was mentoring a team at the MIT $50,000 competition. Dagres, then at Battery Ventures, invested in Akamai, which went public.

When Jayant Kulkarni and Adam Regelman started Quartzy, a company dedicated to solving inventory management solutions for scientific laboratories, they participated in the Olin Cup—a business plan competition at Washington University at St. Louis. After winning the competition, they attracted two term sheets and closed a seed round shortly thereafter. Quartzy went on to win another business plan competition in New York City, and was accepted at Y Combinator. The company closed its Series A investment, led by Keith Rabois of Khosla Ventures.

For Scott Hanson, founder and CEO of Ambiq Micro, winning the DFJ-Cisco business plan competition was a pleasant surprise. He shook his head in disbelief. "Unbelievable," he muttered as he posed with Tim Draper, founder of DFJ Ventures, for photo ops and TV cameras in the heart of the Silicon Valley. Hanson had just beaten 16 teams from around the world to win a $250,000 seed investment. Six months after the award was announced, Ambiq raised a $2.4 million round led by DFJ Mercury. In total, the company has raised over $20 million to help develop the next generation of energy-efficient microcontrollers. Reducing energy consumption in phones, computers, and other computing devices by a factor of 5 to 10 times tipped the scale in his favor.

Draper said every single plan had a strong case to be the winner, and it was exceptionally difficult to choose just one.

COLD CALLING

While this may be the most painful part of any analyst's job, cold calling is now an essential mechanism to source opportunities in hypercompetitive markets. "I had barely started, but we were expected to cold call and source at least 25 opportunities each month," says an analyst at a leading Silicon Valley multistage venture fund. While some firms have found cold calling to be tactically advantageous, others have relied primarily upon their networks.

Most practitioners I talked to did not share stellar examples of opportunities sourced as a result of cold calls. In fact, many shrugged their shoulders, and one muttered, "I just need to make these calls . . . my senior partners say it builds my character, but it's just a waste of time. I know that if anything comes from it, it will be a pleasant surprise." Even the legendary investor of yesteryear, Arthur Rock, cold-called 35 companies—from airplane companies to battery manufacturers—and got turned down by all of them.[34]

YOU WIN SOME, YOU MISS SOME

As successful as some of these VCs may be, every practitioner misses a few good investment opportunities.

Venky Ganesan of Menlo Ventures recalls, "When Sean Parker said, 'Venky, I'm going to Boston to meet this young college student who wants

FIRST ROUND CAPITAL LOSES SOME AND GAINS SOME: TWITTER AND SQUARE

"I was user number 247 on Twitter. We were an investor in a company called Odeo, which was started by Evan Williams, (Twitter's cofounder) to build a podcasting service. We participated in the seed round . . . and when Apple launched a podcasting platform, Evan decided to return the money to the investors and bought everyone back. Then, he was working on this thing, T-w-t-t-r. He could not afford the domain with the vowels! . . . We offered them a term sheet—$500,000 at a $5 million pre-money valuation [meaning his firm would hold a 10 percent stake in the company]. Evan continued to fund it, and three months later, Union Square Ventures was leading the round at a $20 million valuation. It was four times the price we offered. . . . We could have participated. $500,000 in that round. . . . I have the e-mail pinned over my desk saying 'thanks but no thanks.'

"That led to one of our most spectacular successes. . . . Jack [Dorsey] was starting Square, and . . . I said 'Dude you got to give me a chance to redeem myself,' and over dinner Jack said, 'You thought that one was expensive?' [I said] 'No problem, we're in.' Square turned out to be a spectacular success for First Round Capital."

—Josh Koppelman, First Round Capital

Source: Josh Koppelman at Upround Conference, San Francisco www.youtube .com/watch?v=CaX_2n9iAxI.

to start a site focused on connecting college students with each other. It's called The Facebook. Would you like to meet the guy?' I said, 'Wait, college student . . . dropped out of Harvard . . . site aimed at college students, that thing is never going to make money.' I remember that moment every day."[35]

Bessemer Venture Partners and OVP Venture Partners are venture firms that have created the anti-portfolio showcasing their missed opportunities. The Bessemer anti-portfolio lists the investment opportunities that the firm missed—one of the few venture firms to make light of its opportunities lost, which include Google, Apple, and other legendary barn-burner investment opportunities.[36]

OVP Venture Partners, a venture firm based in Portland, Oregon, missed its opportunity to invest in Amazon.com. "If you are in this business long enough, you'll see some great deals walk through your door. If you are in this business long enough, you'll show some great deals the door. We try to limit our self-flagellation to one deal per fund."[37] OVP's Gerry Langeler suggests that "it takes a certain personality, one that many venture firms lack, to publicize your fallibility. . . . It indicates you're not some stuffy, highfalutin' group that's going to lord over your entrepreneurs," Langeler writes. "Business is fun. . . . you may not be able to laugh on most days, but if you can't laugh, find another line of work." And for the LPs who invest in OVP, such acts build "credibility that comes from candor and self-disclosure."[38]

Legendary investor Warren Buffett admired Bob Noyce, cofounder of Fairchild Semiconductor and Intel. Buffett and Noyce were fellow trustees at Grinnell College, but when presented, Buffett passed on Intel, one of the greatest investing opportunities of his life. Buffett seemed "comfortably antiquated" when it came to new technology companies and had a long-standing bias against technology investments.[39]

Peter O. Crisp of Venrock adds his misses to the list: One "small company in Rochester, New York [came to us, and one of our junior guys] saw no future [for] this product . . . that company, Haloid, became Xerox." They also passed on Tandem, Compaq, and Amgen.[40]

ARCH Venture Partners missed Netscape—that little project Marc Andreessen started at the University of Chicago. An opportunity that, according to Steven Lazarus, would have been worth billions! "We just never knocked at the right door," he would say. Eventually, ARCH decided to hire a full-time person to just keep tabs on technology coming out of the universities to "make certain we don't miss that door next time."[41]

Deepak Kamra of Canaan Partners comments on his regrets: "Oh, God, I have too many . . . this gets me depressed. A friend of mine at Sun Microsystems called and asked me to meet with an engineer at Xerox PARC who had some ideas to design a chip and add some protocols to build what is now known as a router. The drivers of bandwidth and Web traffic were strong market indicators, and he was just looking for $100,000. I really don't do deals that small and told him to raise some money from friends and family and come back when he had something to show."[42] That engineer was the founder of Juniper Networks. He got his $100,000 from Vinod Khosla. Khosla, then with KPCB, added an IPO to his long list of winners. Juniper slipped out of Kamra's hands because it was too early. And of course, those were frothy times when everyone was deluged with hundreds of opportunities each day.

KPCB missed an opportunity to invest in VMWare[43] because the valuation was too high: a mistake, according to John Doerr. Draper Fisher Jurvetson (DFJ) was initially willing but eventually passed on Facebook (ouch!), as the firm believed the valuation was too high at $100 million pre-money.[44] KPCB, not wanting to be left out of an opportunity like Facebook, invested $38 million at a $52 billion valuation.[45]

Tim Draper of DFJ, who earned his stripes with opportunities like Baidu (the Chinese version of Google), Skype, and Hotmail, turned down Google "because we already had six search engines in our portfolio." Several leading valley VCs like NEA and KPCB invested in Fisker Automotive, which consumed over $1 billion and teetered on bankruptcy. DFJ backed its competitor Tesla Motors, which is now traded publicly. DFJ missed Facebook but made it nicely on Tesla.

Angel investor K. Ram Shriram almost missed his opportunity to invest in Google when he turned the founders away. "I told Sergey and Larry that the time for search engines has come and gone. But I am happy to introduce you to all the others who may want to buy your technology."[46] But six months later, noticing an interesting pattern, Ram Shriram invested $500,000 as one of its first angel investors.

Nolan Bushnell, engineer and founder of Atari Computer, was not so lucky. "I turned down a third of Apple Computer for $50,000."[47] In 2013, Apple's market capitalization was over $450 billion.

Sourcing is a critical component of any fund's investment strategy and longevity. LPs are eager to find out if you have any unfair advantage in sourcing opportunities. When capital is available aplenty everywhere, why would entrepreneurs or syndicate partners call you?

Target the right sourcing arenas. If you are not fishing in the right pond, as Warren Buffett says, you could end up with a lot of frogs in your portfolio. Any GP needs to ask, "Can I find an opportunity that can grow or generate 10X within three to five years?"

If your networks are poor, you will attract subpar opportunities. "The ability to attract the best opportunities is closely tied to a brand—the aura of the venture firm, which is a by-product of historic performance.

You originate deals based upon the reputation of the firm—that's recursive. The better deals you've done, the better your reputation and the easier it is to find people willing to approach you. The reputation of your firm depends upon your success in marketing, but more important, it fundamentally depends upon the quality of the people. It's a complex set of dynamic variables," says William Elkus of Clearstone Venture Partners.

Proprietary relationship is a tired and overused term found in every fund document. LPs abhor it. Use it at your own risk and only when you can substantiate your unfair advantage in sourcing. "I give a lot more importance to sourcing, even more than the value-add claims of VCs as board members," says Erik Lundberg, chief investment officer of University of Michigan Endowment.[48]

Good practitioners track sources of good opportunities systematically. This effort seems painful at first, yet can be rewarding in the long run. A sourcing pipeline is not substantially different from any sales pipeline— if it is thin, you will be in trouble, sooner or later. Tracking tools also help to periodically assess the forest, the patterns of missed opportunities, strong sources, relationship dynamics. and more. In the world where data and analytics are at the core of decision making, such a tool becomes imperative.

The opportunities you attract are an indicator of your strategy, your brand, and your network. As Goldman Sachs's eighth commandment goes, "Important people like to deal with other important people. Are you one?"[49]

As we will see in the following chapters, sourcing is only a small part of the puzzle. Negotiating terms and closing in on the investment are equally important. As one GP quipped, "If sourcing was like dating, closing the investment is like a marriage—it is a commitment."

NOTES

1. J. O'Dell, "The Kevin Rose Reboot: Our First Look at Google's Newest VC," VentureBeat, April 14, 2013, accessed on January 6, 2014, http://venturebeat.com/2012/08/14/kevin-rose/view-all.
2. Reid Hoffman and Ben Casnocha, *The Startup of You: Adapt to the Future, Invest in Yourself, and Transform Your Career*, (New York: Crown Business, 2012), 122. (See Kevin's video of the product at www .youtube.com/watch?v=3BP5ax1qs5o.)
3. David Kirkpatrick, *The Facebook Effect: The Inside Story of the Company That Is Connecting the World* (New York: Simon & Schuster, 2010), 116–121. In recreating this section, I have relied extensively on this book.

4. James R. Swartz, interview by Mauree Jane Perry, "National Venture Capital Association Venture Capital Oral History Project," 2006, accessed January 30, 2011, http://digitalassets.lib.berkeley.edu/roho/ucb/text/swartz_james_donated.pdf.

5. TechCrunch, "Jim Breyer: 'We See 10,000 Media Business Plans a Year, and Invest in about Ten,'" November 19, 2011, accessed on October 2013, http://techcrunch.com/2011/11/19/jim-breyer-media.

6. Randall E. Stross, *eBoys: The First Inside Account of Venture Capitalists at Work* (New York: Crown Business, 2000), 216, 291.

7. William Elkus (Clearstone Partners), in discussions with the author, September 2008.

8. Brent Ahrens (Canaan Partners), in discussion with the author, September 2008.

9. Chris Douvos, in discussion with the author, December 2010.

10. Christopher Rizik (Renaissance Venture Capital Fund), in discussions with the author, February 2011.

11. Seed-DB, Seed Accelerators, accessed on October 5, 2013, www.seed-db.com/accelerators.

12. Data is from www.angelsoft.net, a leading software-as-a-service tool for managing angel networks.

13. Statistics from www.angelcapitalassociation.org.

14. Ibid.

15. Ibid. This is data from the year 2007: Substantial variations from these investment ranges have not been reported. Of course, we do not include super angels in these statistics.

16. "Exits from 539 angels [who] have experienced 1,137 'exits' (acquisitions or Initial Public Offerings that provided positive returns, or firm closures that led to negative returns) from their venture investments [between 1987 and2007], with most exits occurring since 2004." Robert Wiltbank and Warren Boeker, *Returns to Angel Investors in Groups* (Lenexa, KS: Angel Capital Education Foundation, November 2007).

17. A well-managed network has a streamlined decision-making and negotiation process, typically managed by one angel representative. If each angel is to decide on his or her own the terms, amounts, and so forth, the process can be fraught with challenges for both investors and entrepreneurs.

18. Tony Stanco and Uto Akah, *Survey: The Relationship between Angels and Venture Capitalists in the Venture Industry* (2005), The survey was sent to 2,156 VCs and angels; 14 percent responded.

19. William R. Kerr, Josh Lerner, and Antoinette Schoar, "The Consequences of Entrepreneurial Finance: A Regression Discontinuity Analysis" (working paper No. 10–086, Harvard Business School Entrepreneur-

ial Management), March 16, 2010. Available at SSRN: http://ssrn.com/abstract=1574358.

20. Tony Stanco and Uto Akah, *Survey*.

21. AUTM 2011 data.

22. Robert Finkel and David Greising, *The Masters of Private Equity and Venture Capital* (New York: McGraw-Hill, 2009).

23. Damon Darlin, "It Came From Their Lab. But How to Take It to the Bank?" *The New York Times*, March 12, 2011.

24. Barry Jaruzelski and Kevin Dehoff, "The Global Innovation 1000: How the Top Innovators Keep Winning," (*Booz & Company*, Issue 61, Winter 2010).

25. Quoted in *Mac Week*, March 14, 1989.

26. David Scheer (Scheer and Company), in discussions with the author, August 2008. "Cholesterol Champions," accessed December 26, 2010, http://pharmexec.findpharma.com/pharmexec/article/articleDetail.jsp?id=109681.

27. Arthur Rock, interview by Sally Smith Hughes, 2008–2009, "Early Bay Area Venture Capitalists: Shaping the Economic and Business Landscape," accessed January 30, 2011, http://digitalassets.lib.berkeley.edu/roho/ucb/text/rock_arthur.pdf.

28. William H. Draper, III, "Early Bay Area Venture Capitalists: Shaping the Economic and Business Landscape," oral history conducted by Sally Smith Hughes in 2009, Regional Oral History Office, The Bancroft Library, University of California, Berkeley, 2008. Accessed on July 3, 2010.

29. John Jarve (Menlo Ventures), in discussion with the author, September 2008.

30. Doc Searls, "A Talk with Tim O'Reilly," *Linux Journal*, February 1, 2001, accessed February 1, 2011, www.linuxjournal.com/article/4467.

31. "About O'Reilly," O'Reilly Media, accessed January 28, 2011, http://oreilly.com/about/.

32. Chris Douvos (TIFF), in discussion with the author, December 2010.

33. Robin Wauters, "Venture Capitalists Get Grilled (and Pitched at Urinals) at #*TCDisrupt*," *TechCrunch* (blog), May 26, 2010, accessed on December 12, 2010, http://techcrunch.com/2010/05/26/venture-capitalists-get-grilled-and-pitched-at-urinals-at-tcdisrupt.

34. Arthur Rock, in an interview by Sally Smith Hughes, http://digitalassets.lib.berkeley.edu/roho/ucb/text/rock_arthur.pdf.

35. Cromwell Schubarth, "New Menlo VC Venky Ganesan on Idolizing Warren Buffett and Avoiding 'The Social Network,'" *Business Review*, March 5, 2013, accessed on October 6, 2013, http://businessreview.org/new-menlo-vc-venky-ganesan-on-idolizing-warren-buffett-and-avoiding-the-social-network.

36. Bessemer Venture Partners, "Anti-Portfolio," Web page, accessed February 1, 2011, www.bvp.com/Portfolio/AntiPortfolio.aspx.

37. OVP Venure Partners, "Deals Missed," Web page, accessed January 6, 2014, www.ovp.com/deals-missed.

38. Scott Duke Harris, "The Venture Deals That Got Away," *Mercury News,* August 10, 2008, accessed February 1, 2011, www.mercurynews.com/ci_10156479?nclick_check=1.

39. Alice Schroeder, *The Snowball: Warren Buffett and the Business of Life* (New York: Bantam Dell, 2008), 320.

40. Peter O. Crisp, in an interview by Carole Kolker, "Venture Capital Greats: A Conversation with Peter O. Crisp," October 21, 2008, accessed February 1, 2011, http://digitalassets.lib.berkeley.edu/roho/ucb/text/vcg-crisp.pdf.

41. Robert Finkel and David Greising, *The Masters of Private Equity and Venture Capital,* 215.

42. Deepak Kamra (Canaan Partners), in discussions with the author, July 2008.

43. A virtualization software company formed in 1998, now a publicly traded company with over $2 billion in revenues.

44. David Kirkpatrick, *The Facebook Effect: The Inside Story of the Company That Is Connecting the World* (New York: Simon & Schuster, 2010), 120–122.

45. Scott Austin, "Kleiner Perkins Invested in Facebook at $52 Billion Valuation," *Wall Street Journal,* February 14, 2011, accessed April 2, 2011, http://blogs.wsj.com/venturecapital/2011/02/14/kleiner-perkins-invests-in-facebook-at-52-billion-valuation.

46. K. Ram Shriram, Keynote Speech, Michigan Growth Capital Symposium, University of Michigan, Ann Arbor, 2007. The full video can be found at iTunes: "Michigan Growth Capital Symposium 2007 Keynote Speaker—Ram Shriram, Founder Sherpalo Ventures."

47. TechCrunchTV, Andrew Keen talks with Nolan Bushnell, Author of "Finding The Next Steve Jobs," www.youtube.com/watch?v=dWpu62yEpTI, accessed on January 2, 2014.

48. Erik Lundberg (University of Michigan), in discussions with the author, December 2010.

49. Charles D. Ellis, *The Partnership: The Making of Goldman Sachs* (New York: Penguin, 2008), 188.

CHAPTER **16**

The Art of Conducting Due Diligence

"Conrad was a speculator . . . a nervous speculator . . . before he gambled, he consulted bankers, lawyers, architects, contracting builders and all of their clerks and stenographers who were willing to be cornered and give him advice. He desired nothing more than complete safety in his investments, freedom from attention to details and the thirty to forty percent profit, which according to all authorities, a pioneer deserves for his risks and foresight. . . ."
—Sinclair Lewis, *Babbitt* (1922)

Most venture practitioners would agree that "a pioneer deserves 30 percent to 40 percent profit . . . for his risks and foresight," although they may not necessarily agree with Conrad's style of due diligence. Yet due diligence in venture investments seldom follows a structured approach and often is conducted in a free-flowing manner.

Due diligence is the art of sizing up an investment opportunity—its potential and risk. Entrepreneur and venture capitalist (VC) Peter Thiel is the cofounder of companies like PayPal and Palantir. "Great companies do three things. First, they create value. Second, they are lasting or permanent in a meaningful way. Finally, they capture at least some of the value they create" he points out.[1] According to Thiel, durable start-ups create something new, or *go from 0 to 1*, instead of replicating an existing model, or *going from 1 to n*. Once a novel idea has been launched, the goal is to monopolize quickly and eventually, spread that monopoly into other parallel domains.

Identifying value creation and estimating its sustained advantage is the core of due diligence activity. Mitch Lasky of Benchmark Capital says, "I almost hesitate to use the word due diligence because it implies a certain methodical rigor—rather we ask, what are attributes of successful venture investments." For Lasky, these attributes include the following:

- *Quality of the entrepreneurs:* Do they have a sparkle, a sense of enthusiasm, penetrating intelligence, and courage? Even if they have not done it before, these qualities are essential.
- *Market:* Does this opportunity create disruption and outsized returns? Is the market ready for this product?

Note that early-stage investors seldom start with valuation or financial projections. "Valuation is down the list," Lasky says. And what about financials? Most practitioners, especially at the early stage of investing, seldom get caught up in the projections. It is certainly important to understand the highlights: capital needed to accomplish major milestones or reach break-even, year 5 revenue projections, or exit multiples. But the two criteria—management and markets—trump the financials by orders of magnitude. At Venrock, the underlying question asked of every opportunity is "Is there a glimmer of greatness in here?" Kleiner Perkins Caufield & Byers (KCPB) seeks "people, unfair advantage, clarity on risk, and home run swings."[2]

Warren Buffett summarizes his due diligence process with four simple criteria:[3]

1. Can I understand it? Buffett defines "understanding a business" as "having a reasonable probability of being able to assess where the company will be in ten years."[4]
2. Does it look like it has some kind of sustainable competitive advantage?
3. Is the management composed of able and honest people?
4. Is the price right?

If it passes all four filters, Buffett writes a check.

Venture capital due diligence focuses on three key aspects: management, markets, and technology. The best opportunities often have a healthy mix of all three.

THE DUE DILIGENCE CHECKLIST

The checklist in Table 16.1 can be used as a simple outline to assess any opportunity and develop the investment thesis.

TABLE 16.1 Due Diligence Checklist

Criteria	Description
Product or service	The product or service is described completely and concisely. The need for the product or service is evident. The stage of development—prototype, first customer, multiple customers—is identified. A development road map is included.
Customers, revenue, and business model	The customer value proposition is quantifiable, high, and recognizable. The market need is established, and the customer has an urgency to act. The product price points are identified, along with gross margins and costs.
Market size	The current target and addressable market size is estimated. It is a large and growing market, quantifiable to a certain degree.
Management	The key team member(s) have the expertise and skills needed to run this type of business. Is there clarity on additional hires and timing of recruitment? What are the significant holes in the team?
Competitors and competitive advantage	The product or service is better than the competition based on features and/or price. Is current and future competition identified and evaluated for weakness or significant barriers?
Capital efficiency and value creation	A reasonable milestone event chart with value drivers, date, and capital needs is identified.
Financials	Are plans based on realistic assumptions with reasonable returns? Does it contain reasonable, justifiable projections for two to three years with assumptions explained?
Exit assumptions	Is there a reasonable exit time frame? Is there some clarity on the target universe of buyers?

Table 16.2 is a generic checklist that elaborates on key checkpoints by stage of company.

Practitioners can focus on most important criteria of due diligence by stage of the investment opportunity. It is pointless dissecting detailed financials for a seed stage company. As Nassim Nicholas Taleb writes, "They think that intelligence is about noticing things that are relevant (detecting patterns); in a complex world, intelligence consists in ignoring things that

TABLE 16.2   Key Due Diligence Questions for Consideration by Stage

	Seed Stage	Early Stage	Growth Stage
Management	What is the founder's expertise and understanding of the market pain? Does management have the ability to let go and attract smarter people at the right time?	Based on market needs, can the management team take a prototype and develop a commercial product? Technology development? Sales? Financial?	Can the team achieve high growth, high margins? Explore geographic expansion? Manage resources—people and cash—effectively? What are the board dynamics?
Market	Is there a need in the market? Is it a growing market? Will the market expand to accommodate breakthrough products?	Gauge the ability to cross the chasm from early adopters to mainstream market.	Look for the arrival of me-toos, competitive pressures.
Technology	IP assessment. Freedom to operate. Laboratory scale data. Can you make it once?	What are the features and alignment with market needs? What are the market/customer level data? Can you make it many times?	Look at deployment and operational efficiencies. Can you make it consistently, with high quality, while maintaining costs?
Financials	Is this a shot in the dark? Look for milestones and capital needed to reach value creation.	What is the test pricing and what are the revenue assumptions, gross margins?	What is their margin erosion? What is the ability to improve or sustain gross margins? Assess detailed financial analysis of past (1) income statement, (2) balance sheet, and (3) cash flows.

THE SOCRATIC METHOD OF CONDUCTING DUE DILIGENCE

How would the Greek philosopher Socrates conduct due diligence?

Using the Socratic method, the process of diligence is not a pre-scribed format: it's a shared dialogue between the investor and the cofounders, and both are responsible for agreeing on the key challenges, opportunities, and milestones. VCs often ask probing questions to expose the risks and identify the assumptions that frame the thoughts of the cofounders. Yet, good VCs allow the cofounders to ask questions, as well. The process of excavating risks progresses interactively, and the conversation is open-ended. PowerPoint slides are a deterrent, and there is an immense premium in being in the flow of inquiry rather than using defensive arguments or ideological posturing.

Both parties account for their thoughts and beliefs. While knowing facts is important, how the two sides assess these facts is more important.

The stakes are high. Socratic diligence results in a productive discomfort.

Both sides acknowledge that there is ambiguity and uncertainty; the process does not yield clarity as much as agreement that we are surrounded by darkness. "I don't know" is a refreshingly welcome position, that if followed-through, may yield to surprising outcomes.

Above all, the method aims to keep both parties on a level playing field. The VC knows as much or as little as the entrepreneur. Yet most entrepreneurs assume that VCs have all the answers. It's up to the VCs to change this dynamic and create a level playing field.

are irrelevant (avoiding false patterns)."[5] The art of conducting due diligence is to know what to ask and, more importantly, how to ask. Due diligence meetings are not a grilling session where the VC lords over an entrepreneur. If the Greek philosopher Socrates would have done due diligence, every company would open up to new worlds of possibilities.

WHAT IS IMPORTANT: JOCKEY, HORSE, OR MARKETS?

In any investment opportunity, most venture capitalists concur that the jockey, or the management, matters more than any other criteria. The horse, or the technology, is another factor. Yet others believe that a large, growing market is the primary criteria. While this remains a much-debated subject, practitioners gravitate toward a combination of the three, and it all starts with a growing market.

John Doerr of KPCB postulates the value of management and sees the role of a venture practitioner as a glorified recruiter. Don Valentine, founder of Sequoia Capital, takes a contrarian view. For those who want to back smart people, the proverbial A team with a B market, Valentine has stated tongue-in-cheek, "I continue to encourage them in that direction."[6] Valentine's position "Give me a B idea with a huge market and I will find the best people. But give me the market first. *Please.*"[7]

The legendary Warren Buffett's observation mirrors the philosophy of picking the right market. "Good jockeys will do well on good horses, but not on broken-down nags. Managers are never going to make progress while running in quicksand."[8] Buffett goes on to point out that to the extent he has been successful, it is because he concentrated on identifying one-foot hurdles that he could step over, rather than attempting to clear a seven-footer.[9] "The market, like the Lord, helps those who help themselves," notes Buffett.[10]

But how does one spot the direction of the market? "A good practitioner needs to be a student of the market: one who can perceive where the market is going, the trends. Therein may lie an opportunity—you have to sniff it out. There's no single source for that information. As a venture capitalist, a lot of smart people come to you, and it's generally drinking in, reading, and talking to smart people. If you see something's happening and you can sense a trend, your next step is to find a company that is an emerging leader in an emerging sector. You have to catch the opportunity before it's obvious," says Todd Dagres, Founder, Spark Capital, and investor in Twitter.

Lip-Bu Tan of Walden International agrees: "You have to identify a big market that you can go after and systematically look for opportunities that would allow you to enter the market."[11] The right way to gather the data points is to be a student of the market—be on the street.

Market reports produced by leading research firms are good for only macro-level trends. For example, market research firm IDC forecasts that public cloud expenditures will reach $107 billion by 2017. In early stage venture investing, such lofty projections are doled out generously by entrepreneurs. Take the simple example of four research firms, each of which predicted the first year unit sales for the iPad. The iSuppli Corporation predicted 7.1 million units; Piper Jaffray predicted 5.5 million. Forrester Research was more conservative, at 3 million units, and Kauffman Brothers predicted a meager 2.5 million.[12] Apple sold a staggering 15 million iPad units in the first year of its sales.[13] A leading Sand Hill Road–based VC told me that when encountering such fancy numbers, he politely requests entrepreneurs to skip to the next slide—after all, everyone who walks in the door has a multi-billion-dollar market size.

TIMING THE MARKET

"Is it better to invest in someone who started a company in a mediocre year for returns and did well, or started one in a good year with mediocre results?

Most people say the first case. But results from academic studies show it is the second, because that indicates the founders have a better sense of market timing."[*]

—Graham Spencer, Google Ventures

"What did I learn from my worst investment? We learned that we have never made a bad investment where the technology did not work—the dynamics of market did not work. The timing of product availability and market demand needs to be simultaneous. Of the 500 companies we invested in, we have shut down at least 100 companies, as the expectations of success were no longer realistic."[†]

—Don Valentine, Sequoia Capital

---

[*] From Claire Cain Miller, "Google Ventures Stresses Science of Deal, Not Art of the Deal." *The New York Times*, June 23, 2013.
[†] Don Valentine speaking at Stanford Business School, accessed on January 2, 2014, www.youtube.com/watch?v=nKN-abRJMEw#t=368.

James R. Swartz, founder of Accel Partners, once said that good VCs can size up an opportunity in five minutes: "They have situational awareness. They can walk into just about any kind of meeting and, in about five minutes, figure out who's doing what to whom and exactly what the issues are, sort of cut through it and figure out what's going on. . . . You sort of look at a given situation and project its trajectory reasonably well."[14]

Good due diligence process helps a practitioner find the top risks and the upside of any opportunity. Steeped in shades of gray, any due diligence process offers some answers, but not all: Practitioners need to be comfortable with some degree of ambiguity. If you had all the answers, the opportunity would cease to exist.

Practitioners should be wary of analysis-paralysis and respect an entrepreneur's time, not make incessant or irrelevant demands. Rather, a practitioner needs to ask: What are the top three risks associated with this opportunity, and can I make an investment decision based on addressing these risks effectively? Entrepreneurs respect speed and decisiveness. In current times, the due diligence process need not be a long-drawn-out one. As Jim Plonka of Dow

THE BIG DATA APPROACH TO VC INVESTMENTS

Some believe that conventional factors such as luck and instinct still play a critical role when it comes to success in venture capital funding. Google does not believe in that model of investments. Its venture capital arm collects, collates, and analyzes data. Some of the parameters Google uses in its algorithm are timing of launch of the venture, past success record of founders, and location of the venture, say, in tech hubs such as San Francisco Bay Area.

The investment philosophy has its share of critics who argue that this approach will never capture the "chemistry" or "magic" of Silicon Valley. Google, on the other hand, is convinced about its data-driven investment strategy and insists that number crunching is one of its core strengths. "If you can't measure and quantify it, how can you hope to start working on a solution?" asks Bill Maris, managing partner of Google Ventures. "We have access to the world's largest data sets you can imagine. It would be foolish to just go out and make gut investments." Intuition still plays a role in the investment decision and can sometimes overrule results suggested by data. "We would never make an investment in a founder we thought was a jerk, even if all the data said this is an investment you should make," says Maris. "We would make an investment in a founder we really believed in, even if all the data said we're making a mistake. But it would give us pause."

Source: Claire Cain Miller, "Google Ventures Stresses Science of Deal, Not Art of the Deal," *The New York Times*, June 23, 2013.

Venture Capital says, "For any opportunity, I can get as much as 85 percent of the information needed to make a decision in 14 days or less."

In between the science of the deal and the art form, there lie several opportunities that make the conservative minds wonder who would ever invest in these companies? And why, oh why?

WHO INVESTS IN RAP MUSIC AND SHAVING BLADES?

Author and playwright William Goldman wrote "nobody knows anything" in context of the movie industry's inability to predict which movie will be a success at the box office. "Nobody, nobody, not now, not ever knows the least goddam thing about what is or isn't going to work out at the box office," he wrote.

Indeed, *Raiders of the Lost Ark* was turned down by every studio because it was considered to be "too over the top" or "too expensive to produce." The budget of the film was around $18 million. It grossed over $380 million and was nominated for nine Academy Awards. The list of such examples is long.

Unconventional as they may be, some investments may seem like the movie and can be dismissed as "too out there." From helping interpret rap lyrics to setting a new trend in coffee to smartly marketing razor blades, here are a few companies that made the cut for venture capital investments. If you think these investments are not changing the world, remember Goldman's line: Nobody knows anything about what is or isn't going to work.

Rap Genius

Rap Genius is a crowd-sourced hip-hop lyrics explanation site aimed at helping readers interpret the meaning of lyrics through annotations. Rap lyrics are full of slang, metaphor, and vague references. Users, reading lyrics on the Rap Genius Web site, can click on any line and an annotation explaining the lyrics pops up. Let us illustrate with the lyrics of a popular Eminem song "The Way I Am." When you click on the line "I'm not Mr. 'N Sync," you get a pop up with a two-paragraph annotation on the history on 'N Sync, Eminem's dislike for this group, the reasons for the same, and so on. The site has several features such as Rap IQ, or points to contributors for annotations and suggestions, and Rap Map, which uses Google Earth to show places mentioned in lyrics. The site has a verified accounts feature where established rap artists can sign themselves up to annotate and moderate their own lyrics. Andreessen Horowitz invested $15 million in Rap Genius. While the firm's partner Ben Horowitz is an avid rap lover, it's not just rap that got them excited on this one. He says, "Knowledge about knowledge over time becomes as important as the knowledge itself."

They see various different applications of Rap Genius in areas such as news, poetry, literature, religious text, legal texts, science papers, and many more areas. For instance, Rap Genius recently partnered with a cooking site to help its readers annotate recipes and how-to articles. When Marc Andreessen was building Mosaic, a browser that was later commercialized as Netscape, he had a vision that every Web page should have an annotation option. He couldn't pursue it then, but with Rap Genius that vision became a reality.

Blue Bottle Coffee

Blue Bottle Coffee, a specialty coffee retailer, has grown rapidly from its early days serving customers at a single location—the Bay Area farmers market. What makes Blue Bottle distinct from, say, Starbucks? To set some context,

Blue Bottle Coffee is also known as the "Apple of coffee." So while Apple had its Steve Jobs, Blue Bottle Coffee has founder and CEO James Freeman, who, with his focus on aesthetics and obsession for quality, makes sure his customers have a delightful experience each and every time. The company uses only organic, shade-grown, and pesticide-free beans. To make customers enjoy the taste and aroma of coffee at its peak, they ensure the coffee is served in less than 48 hours of after coming out of the roaster. Blue Bottle Coffee derives its name from the first coffee house in Central Europe, The Blue Bottle.

Its revenues come from not only the retail outlets, but also several wholesale customers and an online direct-to-consumer business. Blue Bottle Coffee received a funding of $20 million by a group of investors led by True Ventures, Index Ventures, and a serial entrepreneur who is the founder of the popular Fresh and Wild organic stores in London.

What caught the fancy of True Ventures is James's attention to detail, his vision, and his business sense. They see it as a new movement or a "third wave" of coffee, akin to microbrewery in beer, in which consumers looking for quality and a unique experience are moving to superior quality, crafty micro-roasters.

Dollar Shave Club

Dollar Shave Club, a company that started out selling replenishable razor blades, is a prime example of what is commonly referred in marketing textbooks as an example of the power of branding. When Michael Dubin, chief executive officer and cofounder, launched a YouTube video promoting his venture one year ago, he had no idea of what lay ahead of him. As the video went viral, he received 12,000 orders in the first two days, leading to a Web site crash. A year and a half down the line, Dollar Shave Club now has 200,000 subscribers. And yes, the immensely popular video has more than 11.5 million views to date.

Dollar Shave Club has several unique selling points such as price and convenience. But the main reason behind the brand's success so far has been an ever-increasing and loyal user base that prides itself on using Dollar Shave Club. No surprises here, as Dubin hails from a digital media and marketing background and has worked for clients such as Gatorade, Nike, and Nintendo. While his company is offering a subscription service, he dislikes the term and prefers to think of it as "membership commerce." In a short time, Dubin has expanded the 30-employee Venice company beyond razors, and it now also offers shave butter and disposable wipes for men. His ambition is to own the entire bathroom.

The company raised $9.8 million from Silicon Valley venture capital firm Venrock, KPCB, Forerunner Ventures, Andreessen Horowitz, Shasta

Ventures, Felicis Ventures, White Star Capital, and others. VCs are betting on the brand expanding beyond razors to become "the Internet's best men's company."

When we look at these companies, a simple question pops up: should a practitioner care about exits? While it is essential to ascertain a broad universe of potential buyers and the reasons why these players would buy a start-up, it is futile to sweat the details.

In an ever-evolving arena, where technologies and markets are in a constant state of flux, it is difficult to predict how two vectors will intersect. As Rick Snyder, former VC and now governor of Michigan, once famously remarked, "Forget exit strategy, most of these start-ups need an entry strategy."[15]

NOTES

1. Blake Masters, notes from Stanford class, Startup:CS183, as recorded by Blake Masters in Spring 2012, http://blakemasters.com/post/20955341708/peter-thiels-cs183-startup-class-3-notes-essay.
2. Vinod Khosla, "The Entrepreneurial Roller Coaster . . . High Highs & Low Lows," accessed February 6, 2011, www.khoslaventures.com/presentations/RCApr2003.ppt.
3. Peter Bevelin, *Seeking Wisdom: From Darwin to Munger* (San Marino, CA: PCA Publications, 2007), 220. Buffett mentioned these criteria at a press conference in 2001.
4. Warren Buffett, *The Essays of Warren Buffett: Lessons for Corporate America*, ed. Lawrence A. Cunningham, 2nd ed. (New York: L. Cunningham, 2008). Buffett defines "understanding a business" as "we have a reasonable probability of being able to assess where it will be in ten years."
5. Nassim Nicholas Taleb, *The Bed of Procrustes: Philosophical and Practical Aphorisms* (New York: Random House, 2010), 78.
6. Peter J. Tanous, *Investment Visionaries: Lessons in Creating Wealth from the World's Greatest Risk Takers* (Upper Saddle River, NJ: Prentice Hall, 2003), 79.
7. Ibid.
8. Warren Buffett, *The Essays of Warren Buffett*, 112.
9. Joseph Nocera, "Saint Warren of Omaha: It's Easier to Worship Warren Buffett Than It Is to Understand What Makes Him a Great Investor," *Money* (CNN Money Web site), July 1, 1998, http://money.cnn.com/magazines/moneymag/moneymag_archive/1998/07/01/244582/
10. Mary Buffett and David Clark, *The Tao of Warren Buffett: Warren Buffett's Words of Wisdom—Quotations and Interpretations to Help*

Guide You to Billionaire Wealth and Enlightened Business Management (New York: Simon & Schuster, 2006), 14.

11. Lip-Bu Tan (Walden International), in discussions with the author, December 2009.

12. Yukari Iwatani Kane, "First-Day Sales of Apple's iPad Fall Short of Sky-High Hopes," *Wall Street Journal*, April 6, 2010.

13. Steve Jobs, iPad2 keynote address, March 2, 2011.

14. James R. Swartz, "Venture Capital Greats: A Conversation with James R. Swartz," interview by Mauree Jane Perry, 2006, accessed January 13, 2011, http://digitalassets.lib.berkeley.edu/roho/ucb/text/swartz_james_ donated.pdf.

15. As quoted by Vic Stretcher, founder of HealthMedia. Rick Snyder's venture fund, Avalon Investments, led an investment in HealthMedia, a health care IT company and was acquired by Johnson & Johnson.

CHAPTER 17

Management Team Diligence

"The reasonable man adapts himself to the world, the
unreasonable one persists in trying to adapt the world to himself.
Therefore all progress depends on the unreasonable man."
—George Bernard Shaw, *Maxims for Revolutionists*, 1903

Subjectivity in conducting team diligence can often be crippling. Yet this is often the case in management team diligence. The attributes of strong management teams, or the proverbial jockey, are difficult to assess. Often practitioners have a short window of time.

ASSESSING INTANGIBLES

Attributes such as integrity, execution abilities, people skills, and the ability to attract a team of high performers cannot be assessed quickly. Let's look at these attributes in the context of venture capital investments.

Integrity

In selecting the jockey—the top executives—Warren Buffett's views are relevant and appropriate: "Somebody once said that in looking for people to hire, you look for three qualities: integrity, intelligence, and energy. And if they don't have the first, the other two will kill you. Think about it; it's true. If you hire somebody without the first, you really want them to be dumb and lazy."[1]

When assessing the management team of an early-stage start-up, integrity ranks first. Integrity boils down to the sum total of honesty in words and actions, an ethos that defines any individual. But there is no easy way to assess this attribute. Practitioners spend a substantial amount of time investigating business skills and technical expertise of entrepreneurs. The process is imprecise and involves referencing—multiple discussions with people who have interacted with the entrepreneurs in the past. It is usually during this process that one can discover the mind-set of any entrepreneur. It is easy to spot those who are the bookends of the spectrum—the strong, high-integrity individuals and the ones who are mired in sleazy dealings. It is the ones in the middle—those who manage to stay above the law but hide beneath a web of lies and inconsistent behavior—these are the ones who always get you! As Buffett says, those who do not have integrity but have intelligence can not only take advantage of you; they can even kill you!

Entellium, a Seattle, Washington–based developer of customer relationship management (CRM) tools, raised $50 million in venture investments over its eight-year history. But the CEO and CFO were cooking the books faster than they were raising venture capital. They overstated revenues by as much as three times for three consecutive years. An employee stumbled upon the actual revenue data while cleaning out a former employee's desk and discovered the fraud. The lead venture fund had invested as much as $19 million in Entellium. Fraud may be a rare occurrence in the venture capital arena, but when it occurs, it can damage the reputation of its investors.

Integrity and honesty are fundamental qualities of any management team but are much harder to assess. The easier conclusions are often the obvious—this team is hungry, has technical expertise, or business acumen. But if you see any shades of gray, try not to justify the investment. Consider walking away from the opportunity. Pete Farner of TGap Ventures says, "I use a simple test in assessing potential CEOs we would back—would I trust them enough to look after my own kids?" Such a high bar would eliminate the vast majority of riffraff quickly.

Team Building

Besides integrity, what are the other qualities to look for in any management team? "Do they understand their own limitations and weaknesses? Are they able to attract a team, and eventually, can they recruit their own CEO and replace themselves?" asks Lip-Bu Tan of Walden International. These qualities are fundamental but rare: after all, human beings suffer from insecurities. If they attract team members who are highly accomplished, they might end up looking small. Or get sidelined! The weak entrepreneurs often gravitate toward looking smart in a land of the small as opposed to looking stupid among giants. Those who are standing on the shoulders of giants are the ones who matter.

Consider William Shockley, who won the Nobel Prize for coinventing the transistor. Despite being a brilliant physicist, Shockley had no people skills and successfully alienated his two coinventors, thanks to his brash and abrasive style. His staff was subjected to lie detector tests, and he publicly posted their salaries. He was even passed over for promotion at Bell Labs. When he died, he was completely estranged from most of his friends and family—his children read about his death in the newspapers.[2]

When eight of Shockley's researchers, termed as the Traitorous Eight, resigned to start Fairchild Semiconductor, all he did was write *"Wed 18 Sept—Group Resigns"* in his diary.[3]

His communication skills certainly did not impress anyone.

Besides being a poor manager, Shockley's presentation skills were terrible. He read all his speeches in a monotone, was a poor writer, and "flogged metaphors" mercilessly. Larry L. King wrote of Shockley that he "made such an inept presentation that he could not have instructed us how to catch a bus."[4]

Joel Shurkin, Shockley's biographer, writes, "If Shockley had been a better manager, he'd be one of the richest people in the world today. He would have been the match for Bill Gates. He is the father of Silicon Valley; he knew more than anybody in the world the importance of these machines, these transistors; he knew that he was revolutionizing the world; he knew that if his company could control the direction that the transistor should go toward, that he would be very rich. Unfortunately, he was a terrible manager and he never had the chance."[5]

Shockley's inability to build teams is evident—despite being a brilliant technologist and a Nobel Laureate, he could not get over his fear and insecurities.

An investor needs to watch for traits that enable the founders or the core management team to attract star power. Most management teams will be replaced, either by choice or by sheer exhaustion, in the travails of the start-up journey. A simple question to consider is: Is this person honest and bold enough to replace himself or herself at the right time and even become redundant?

Execution: Lambs versus Cheetahs

Defined as the fine art of getting things done, execution abilities are one of the top criteria of management assessment. In an early-stage company, execution would be quite simply "the ability to define and meet value creation milestones using optimum resources." In his *New York Times* bestselling book *Who: The A Method for Hiring*, author Geoff Smart asks, "What types of CEOs make money for investors?"[6] Smart, who has frequently interacted with the venture capital world, grew up in a family in which psychology was discussed at the breakfast table. "My father was an industrial psychologist. So when I interned at a VC firm, I asked the partners what it takes to be a successful venture capitalist [VC]. And they said, it's all about management," he says. But Geoff found that despite all the emphasis on management, there was no clear methodology of assessing people. "If people are so important, why is it that we spend all of this time doing Excel models or market analysis?" he would ask. But Smart was told that the people part is intuitive and that there is no way you can evaluate people accurately. "Had I not had the contextual background of psychology, I would have taken everything that venture capitalists told me at face value."[7]

To assess CEO traits, Geoff teamed up with Steven Kaplan, a noted scholar on entrepreneurship and finance at the University of Chicago. The team went on to conduct the largest study of CEO traits and financial performance. The results were compelling and controversial. Data from 313 interviews of private equity (PE)–backed CEOs were gathered and analyzed. Taking these assessments, the authors matched the CEO assessments with actual financial performance. The *Wall Street Journal* ran a half-page article on the findings.

Smart points out that investors often have a tendency to invest in CEOs who demonstrated openness to feedback, possess great listening skills, and treat people with respect. "I call them 'Lambs' because these CEOs tend to graze in circles, feeding on the feedback and direction of others," he says. And he concludes that investors love Lambs because they are easy to work with and were successful 57 percent of the time.

But Smart found that the desirable CEOs are the ones who move quickly, act aggressively, work hard, demonstrate persistence, and set high standards and hold people accountable to them. (He called them "Cheetahs" because they are fast and focused.) "Cheetahs in our study were successful 100 percent of the time. This is not a rounding error. *Every single one of them* created significant value for their investors," writes Geoff.[8] "Emotional intelligence is important, *but only when matched with the propensity to get things done.*"[9]

Separately, Steve Kaplan's research led to the same conclusion. In the study "Which CEO Characteristics and Abilities Matter?," the authors assessed more than 30 individual characteristics, skills, and abilities.[10] Surprisingly, the study showed that success was not linked to team-related skills and that such skills are overweighed in hiring decisions. *Success mattered only with CEOs with execution-related skills.* The study asserted Jim Collins's

"Good to Great" description of Level 5 CEOs who have unwavering resolve, are fanatically driven, and exhibit diligence.

The essential lesson we derive from this study and from the Shockley example is that while technical expertise is important, marrying technical skills with short-term milestones and rapid execution is critical. As Peter Drucker says, effective executives "get the right things done"[11]—at the right time.

HOW TO ASSESS THE JOCKEY

Management due diligence is easy; just be prepared to invest, say, 200 to 300 hours in the process. In conducting CEO due diligence, investors from storied firms such as Accel, Bessemer, KPCB, Greylock, New Enterprise Associates (NEA), Sequoia, and Mayfield Fund shared information on how they assessed management teams of 86 portfolio companies.[12]

For example, William Hunckler, III of Madison Dearborn Partners invested 322 hours over six months. Hunckler invested more than 50 hours interviewing nine categories of references leading to detailed assessments of the team. Geoff Smart describes this approach as the "airline captain approach," one in which the pilot checks every parameter to ensure that a plane is safe to fly. Hunckler focused his attention principally on prior work assessment. Smart says, "The approach is common sense, but fewer than 15 percent of venture capitalists actually use this approach."

Eugene Hill of Accel Partners, another participant in the study, said, "Evaluating the management team properly and backing the right people is the difference between success and failure in this [venture capital] business."[13] Hill has a track record of accuracy that ranks him at the 92nd percentile. In total, he spent 126 hours on human capital valuation, spread systematically across various methods. He "spent 21 hours in reference discussions with people from 11 different categories of references. This was the highest number of different categories of all venture capitalists in the study. He said his analysis was based on 'mostly data' rather than gut intuition," wrote Smart.[14]

Various styles of assessing human capital include the airline captain approach, the art critic, the sponge, and the prosecutor. Of these, the airline captain approach, as Hunckler used, yielded a median internal rate of return of 80 percent. A high level of systematic and disciplined data collection and analysis of the management team members characterize this approach.

In contrast, as seen in Figure 17.1, the three primary alternative approaches achieved internal rates of return under 30 percent. While airline captains tend to achieve close to 90 percent accuracy in human capital valuations, art critics are lucky if they hit 50 percent. If you're an art critic, one of two CEOs will crash and burn. Recall Don Valentine, founder of

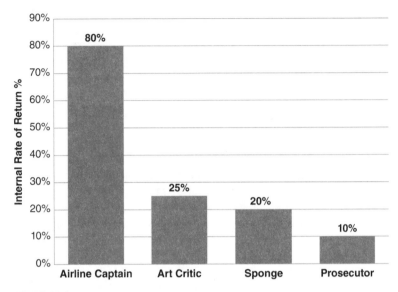

FIGURE 17.1   IRR and due diligence styles.
Source: Geoffrey H. Smart, "The Art and Science of Human Capital Valuation."

Sequoia Capital, who once remarked that if you can select people correctly 52 percent of the time, they ought to have a statue built for you. The moral of the story, the author concludes, is that gut checks are good, but a diligent checklist approach will avoid the plane crash.

- *Airline captain*: This method of assessing CEO candidates "resembles the way an airline captain assesses his or her plane prior to takeoff to decide whether it is safe to fly." It is the most effective method for yielding top results, but it is also time-consuming and intense.
- *Art critic*: An art critic glances at a painting and within a few minutes can offer "an accurate appraisal of the value of the work." But art critics in venture capital can be ineffective, especially when trying to value human capital. They "think that their years of business experience equip them to achieve an accurate assessment of people in a very short amount of time—that a person's human capital is as visible in its entirety as a painting on the wall," wrote Smart. "Art critics talk a lot about intuition, gut feel, and 'shooting from the hip.' Unfortunately, they also talk a lot about inaccurate human capital valuations and deals in which they lost 100% of their investment."
- *Sponge*: "Sponges are like art critics who need a little more data before making an assessment. Sponges do not perform a human capital needs analysis, but 'soak up' data through multiple methods of human capital

valuation—and then synthesize the information in their gut. As one sponge said, he does 'due diligence by mucking around.'" The sponge is proven as effective as an art critic.

- *Prosecutor*: "Prosecutors act like prosecuting attorneys." As they walk into the room to conduct an interview, they will indulge in theatrics, such as slamming a fist on the table, pointing a finger, and waving their arms. According to the study, "They aggressively question managers and attempt to 'pull the truth out of them.'. . . Prosecutors talk about 'testing' management on what they know. The problem with this method is that prosecutors only collect data on present behaviors—how managers respond to questions in the present, live, right now. In comparison, *past* behaviors are more indicative of future behaviors," concluded Smart. One of the least effective methods for CEO selection, this method is best used for interrogations of prison cell mates.

Venture capital practitioners typically conduct interviews based on the following categories:

- *Work sample:* This is the most heavily used means of interviewing: typically, VCs spend more than 60 hours per deal in work samples with management.

    In these direct interactions, VCs quiz the management team on various issues related to the business. They are called work samples because they allow the VC to view samples of how the managers think and work firsthand. The time that VCs spent in work samples was positively related to the accuracy of the human capital valuation in early-stage deals but negatively related to accuracy in later-stage deals. Why the difference? In early-stage deals, these discussions are more probing and often personal. In later-stage deals, formal presentations by managers coached by investment bankers can be as misleading as they are informative. The evidence suggests that work samples are not sufficient for achieving accurate human capital valuations.

- *Reference interviewing:* "Reference interviews are discussions with people who have observed the behavior of the target managers. There are several possible sources of reference interviews: personal references, supervisors, coworkers, industry players, current employees, suppliers, customers, lawyers, accountants, bankers, or other investors."

- *Past-oriented interviewing:* "Whereas the work sample relies on present or 'hypothetical' behavior, past-oriented interviews rely on *past* behavior." "This method," branded by Smart as the top-graded interview, "is based on the notion that past behavior is the best predictor of future behavior. Therefore, during past-oriented interviews, venture capitalists talk chronologically with individual managers about their entire career histories. This interviewing format has emerged as the most effective personnel assessment method in industrial psychology within the last five years."[15]

While these techniques of diligence have been practiced, here are the top three lessons any practitioner should watch for.

As venture practitioners, there is seldom enough time to understand the abilities and creative elements of any candidate. The biggest challenge is assessing the intangibles in a very short time.

A number of other personality tests exist, each of which has a varied set of inputs and outputs, all aimed at establishing a window into a person's emotional and intellectual construct. A few that are noteworthy include the Myers-Briggs Type Indicator (MBTI) and the Caliper Test.

The MBTI is a Jungian personality test that qualifies people into one of 16 types based on how they focus their attention, analyze information, make decisions, and orient themselves into the external world. For example, ESTJ, for extraversion (E), sensing (S), thinking (T), judgment (J), people

---

THE TOP THREE LESSONS FROM THE ART AND SCIENCE OF TEAM DILIGENCE

What VCs failed to assess:

1. Lack of general management/operations experience
2. Cannot work well with others
3. Sales/marketing skills

Top three reasons given by VCs for bad hiring decisions:

1. Speed: Sign that term sheet quickly and get the deal done. Pressure to invest due to competition or coinvestors.
2. Halo effect: What a rock star—great past performance or great technology! We just ought to be grateful to be a part of this investment.
3. Too many cooks: A number of syndicate partners, other team members, and no head chef.

Source: Geoff Smart, "The Art and Science of Human Capital Valuation," 1998, accessed February 6, 2011, www.ghsmart.com/media/press/human_capital.pdf.

would be defined as follows: "practical, realistic, matter-of-fact. Decisive, quickly moves to implement decisions. Organizes projects and people to get things done, focuses on getting results in the most efficient way possible. Has a clear set of logical standards, systematically follows them. Forceful in implementing their plans."[16] While the MBTI output paints a picture, it doesn't offer clarity as to whether an ESTJ is suited to be a venture capitalist.

For that reason, Don Walker, a senior partner at a Midwest venture firm, uses the Caliper Test for almost all hiring decisions. Caliper believes equating a person's interest with a person's ability is a flawed approach. You have a lot of wannabe CEOs, but do they have the requisite abilities? Most tests are also easily faked, according to Caliper. Obviously, if you ask the true-false question "I am a responsible person," the probability that anyone would select false is near zero. But Caliper Tests are structured to eliminate these challenges with a more sophisticated test design. Furthermore, the test recognizes that desirable qualities for certain positions may be handicaps for others: for example, impulsiveness and originality can be seen as evidence of weakness or instability. Keeping the perspective of the person as a whole and not his or her parts and not relying on past experience as a prime qualification are two essential ingredients of a good test design, but what tips Caliper over the edge to the more reliable side is its ability to match the person to a role.

Caliper has developed four categories and over 25 criteria that assess a person's ability to influence, build relationships, solve problems, make decisions, and organize. The test applies these criteria to specific job functions that determine whether the best match can be crafted. For example, a manager and a salesperson need varying degrees of certain skills. Caliper uses the term "ego drive" to define how much a person needs to be able to persuade others and gain satisfaction from the successful persuasion. The test also uses the term "ego strength" to refer to the degree a person likes himself or herself. Described another way, ego strength is an individual's ability to keep pushing when everyone says no. It is a strong sense of self: A CEO has good ego strength when he or she can take no for an answer yet keep moving in the right direction without flinching. Such events do not destroy the self-image but rather make a good leader hungrier for the next opportunity. This is the key to resilience. People who take rejections personally lose steam very quickly: Afraid of rejection, they find that it's better to not make the next call—they invite rejection, or worse, potential conflicts. On the other hand, "ego drive," the *ability to persuade* coupled with the intense *need to persuade*, can yield a highly productive person.

Caliper concludes that just drive is not sufficient to make a good salesperson. To be a good executive, you need to have a strong blend of these two criteria . . . a strong sense of self *and* the ability to persuade.

Of these three approaches, Smart's approach may be more relevant, thanks to Smart's contextual background in venture capital.

ANDREESSEN HOROWITZ ON THE ART OF CEO SELECTION

The art of CEO selection according to Ben Horowitz of the venture firm Andreessen Horowitz can be summarized in three words: direction, execution, and results.

DIRECTION: DOES THE CEO KNOW WHAT TO DO?

Strategy and decision making: Does the CEO know what to do in all matters all of the time? Can the CEO tie the strategy to a story—how is the world a better place, thanks to this company? A CEO can most accurately be measured by the speed and quality of her decisions. Great decisions come from CEOs who display an elite combination of intelligence, logic, and courage.

EXECUTION: CAN THE CEO GET THE COMPANY TO DO WHAT HE OR SHE KNOWS?

Execution and team building: Once a vision is set, does the CEO have the capacity, and can the CEO execute? Horowitz points out that capacity translates to having world-class, motivated talent. Building a world-class team and ensuring the quality of the team stays strong is important.

Effectively run the company: Very few CEOs get an A and fail to scale, because the skills required to manage a well-run organization are wide-ranging, from organizational design to performance management, incentives, communication, the whole gamut. The key question to ask is, "Is it easy for the employees to get their job done?"

RESULTS: DID THE CEO ACHIEVE THE DESIRED RESULTS AGAINST AN APPROPRIATE SET OF OBJECTIVES?

Were appropriate objectives established? Too low or too high? Horowitz warns against setting objectives for early-stage companies, as no one really knows the size of the opportunity. Finally, the size and the nature of opportunities vary across types of companies: Some are capital intensive, while others have measured growth and market adoption. CEOs will perform better on a test if they know the questions ahead of time.

Source: Ben Horowitz, "How Andreessen Horowitz Evaluates CEOs," Ben's Blog (blog), May 10, 2010, accessed February 6, 2011, http://bhorowitz .com/2010/05/30/how-andreessen-horowitz-evaluates-ceos/.

But in most venture-backed start-ups, while attracting top-level talent may be important, the stability of teams is entirely unpredictable. Churn of top-level talent occurs due to a number of reasons—the pace, the pressures, low cash positions, missed milestones—and thus, practitioners need to realize that while management teams are important, no one can predict when teams run out of steam and hit the bottom—or give up! Once Tim Draper, founder of Draper Fisher Jurvetson, asked an entrepreneur, "And what will you do if the idea does not take off?" asked Tim. The young entrepreneur said, "I will try something else—maybe find a job." At which point Tim said, "Entrepreneurs never give up." One significant risk every practitioner faces is when the CEO throws in the towel.

Professor Steven N. Kaplan of the University of Chicago Graduate School of Business studied 50 venture-backed companies that evolved from business plan to IPO and found that management turnover is substantial. Kaplan concludes that investors in start-ups should place more weight on the horse, as in the business, and not the jockey. And all the hoo-ha about quality of management may be important in the early stages, but it declines rapidly: Only 16 percent of the companies stress the importance of management expertise at the time of the IPO. Founders get slayed quickly along the way: Only 49 percent of the venture capital–backed founders stayed until the IPO.

Kaplan concludes: "Human capital is important, but the specific person appears less so. A business with strong non-people assets is enduring."[17] "The glue holding the firm together at a very early stage is composed of the patents, the stores, and the processes. Except, perhaps, for raw start-ups, VCs should bet on the horse. We see the jockeys changing, but we don't see the horse changing."[18]

PICKING MANAGEMENT VERSUS MARKETS

"I think choosing great people is much more difficult than picking great markets because we have always understood the technology and understood the markets. Picking great people is a less than 50 percent proposition, and if you are right 52 percent of the time, they ought to build a statue to you."[*]

—Don Valentine, Sequoia Capital

[*] Speaking at Stanford Business School, October 2011, accessed on January 2, 2014, https://www.youtube.com/watch?v=nKN-abRJMEw.

FAST ELECTRIC CARS, ROCKET SHIPS, AND MARS COLONIZATION— WOULD YOU INVEST IN THIS ENTREPRENEUR?

Born in South Africa, and a self-taught computer programmer, Elon Musk sold his first software at the age of 12, a space game called Blast Star, for about $500. He received a bachelor of arts in business from the Wharton School and bachelor of science in physics from the University of Pennsylvania. He enrolled at Stanford to get a Ph.D. in applied physics but dropped out after two days to fulfill his entrepreneurial dreams.

His first venture was Zip2, an online publishing platform for the media industry. Things were pretty tough in the beginning, and he didn't have enough money. He sold Zip2 to Compaq for $307 million, in which he made approximately $22 million. He cofounded X.com, offering online financial services and e-mail payments, which eventually went on to become PayPal. eBay acquired PayPal for $1.5 billion, and at the time of sale Musk was the largest shareholder, owning 11.7 percent.

For his final frontier, Musk founded his third company SpaceX or Space Exploration Technologies, a designer and manufacturer of advanced rockets and spacecraft, with $100 million of his own moolah. The ultimate goal of SpaceX is to enable people to live on other planets. In six years, SpaceX launched their first rocket Falcon 1 into orbit at a cost of roughly $7 million, which was a reduction by a factor of 10 over the prevailing costs at that time. Musk says he could bring down the cost by solving for existing inefficiencies within aerospace firms, such as risk aversion to using modern technologies and elimination of multiple layers of subcontracting.

SpaceX was awarded a $1.6 billion contract by NASA for 12 flights of their Falcon 9 rocket and Dragon spacecraft to the International Space Station, a habitable artificial satellite. Four years later, the firm made history with Falcon 9/Dragon as it became the first commercial company to visit the station.

Ken Howery of Founder's Fund is an investor in SpaceX and points out that "Elon plans on running SpaceX for the rest of his life. It will take him ten to twenty years to get a man on Mars. Potential investors thought we were crazy to back this rocket company, but we had followed it for six years. Elon had taken much risk out of it and even invested $100 million of his own. We won't see much competition anytime soon in this category."*

Musk is also the CEO of Tesla Motors, a publicly-traded company manufacturing electric cars. Tesla also sells electric power train systems to Daimler and Toyota. Musk is reported to have a 32 percent stake in Tesla and is the largest shareholder and chair for Solar City, the largest provider of solar power systems in the United States.

Musk has also unveiled a prototype for a "hyperloop," or a supersonic air travel machine to carry people from San Francisco to Los Angeles in 35 minutes. The proposed speed of up to 800 miles per hour is faster than most commercial airliners. This concept is aimed to make long-distance travel cheaper than any other means of transportation. Not many VCs are beating a path to his door as yet.

----

* Tarang and Sheetal Shah, *Venture Capitalists at Work* (New York: APress, 2011).

SERIAL ENTREPRENEURS VERSUS FIRST-TIME ENTREPRENEURS

All things equal, a venture capital–backed entrepreneur who has taken a company public has a 30 percent chance of succeeding in his or her next venture.[19] A failed entrepreneur is next in the pecking order, with a 20 percent chance of success, and a first-time entrepreneur has an 18 percent chance. Researchers assessed the cause of success and point out that successful entrepreneurs know how to launch companies at the right time—before the markets get crowded.

Market timing skill is more important than the novelty of the technology. Consider the fact that 52 percent of computer start-ups founded in 1983 went public. In contrast, only 18 percent of those started in 1985 went public. In less than 24 months, the probability of a successful outcome had changed by a factor of three! Interestingly, the same entrepreneurs who were able to time the market during their first start-up were able to time the market in their next start-up, as well. Thus, the entrepreneur's ability to time the market is indeed more important than other attributes. Those who can time market cycles several times are indeed smart: Luck is no longer a factor for such entrepreneurs.

However, with successful entrepreneurs, the hunger level may drop with success or age. Or worse, arrogance may set in.

WHAT ABOUT CHARISMA?

One of the early investors in Apple, Arthur Rock, recalls a meeting with Steve Jobs and Steve Wozniak:

> *Jobs came into the office, as he does now, dressed in Levi's, but at that time that wasn't quite the thing to do. And I believe he had a goatee and a moustache and long hair—and he had just come back from six months in India with a guru, learning about life. I'm not sure, but it may have been a while since he had a bath. . . . And he was very, very thin—and to look at [him]—he really belonged somewhere else. Steve Wozniak, on the other hand, had a full beard and he's just not the kind of a person you'd give a lot of money to.*[20]

Nevertheless, Rock invested in Apple, because Jobs was articulate. Yet how often are we swayed by soft signals?

A Harvard Business School study found male entrepreneurs were 60 percent more likely to achieve pitch competition success than female entrepreneurs. And attractive men were 36 percent more likely to achieve success than their average-looking counterparts. 68 percent of participants

---

CAN GENETIC TESTS BE A PROXY FOR DUE DILIGENCE?

Personalities are influenced by genes, and while VCs have not yet launched genetics-based due diligence, here are some variants to watch for. Business leaders tend to be unconscientious, introverted, and disagreeable. Think Steve Jobs. Genes that trigger such behavior include *DRD2* variant, which causes impulsiveness, and *DRD4*, which makes a person seek novelty. *COMT* is called the worrier gene variation that facilitates risk-taking tendencies. *HTR2A* causes persistence, and *MAOA* variation is anti-social, causing others to follow them by offering a vision of the future. Finally, *FAAH* variation reduces fear and increases reaction to money making.

Source: Scott Shane, *Born Entrepreneurs, Born Leaders—How Genes Affect your Work Life.* (New York: Oxford University Press; 2010).

chose to fund the ventures pitched by a male voice and only 32 percent of participants chose to fund the ventures pitched by a female voice.[21]

Another study conducted by two MIT researchers, Sandy Pentland and Daniel Olguin, predicted with 87 percent accuracy who would win a business plan competition.[22] But get this—neither of the researchers had read the plans or heard their pitches. So how did they predict with such high accuracy? Pentland gathered what he calls "honest signals" from these executives.

Honest signals are defined as nonverbal cues—gestures, expressions, and tone. In an interview with *Harvard Business Review*, Pentland said, "The more successful people are energetic. They talk more, but they also listen more. . . . It's not just what they project that makes them charismatic; it's what they elicit. The more of these energetic, positive people you put on a team, the better the team's performance."[23] Pentland's research did not indicate which pitch would be best—it just indicated who will win, irrespective of the quality of the idea or the pitch. VCs look for buzz and enthusiasm, "but they also need to understand the substance of the pitch and not be swayed by charisma alone," he added.

THE IMPORTANCE OF CONDUCTING BACKGROUND INVESTIGATIONS

Many venture capital funds perform detailed due diligence of potential portfolio companies prior to investments. Background checks of key portfolio company personnel are often a component of this due diligence analysis. However, while background checks will detect some issues with potential portfolio company managers, an in-depth background investigation, performed by an experienced professional, will yield a more detailed analysis of potential portfolio company managers and serve to verify the assertions and representations these individuals have made to the venture capital funds.

Background investigations include significantly detailed analyses of potential portfolio company managers. These investigations examine individuals' work history, board service, educational background, community involvement, criminal background, and, in some instances, assets. While this level of information may seem excessive, it is a necessary component of the due diligence process and serves to mitigate future issues a venture capital fund may encounter with an executive at a later date. Moreover, the reasons for conducting an in-depth background investigation as opposed to a cursory background check of a potential portfolio company manager are myriad.

Recent studies indicate that roughly 50 percent of job candidates misrepresent their job credentials, although the level and degree of misrepresentation varies widely.[24] Furthermore, misrepresentations are made by

BUT NOBODY ASKED ME IF I WAS A CRIMINAL

Smith & Wesson Holding Corporation chairman James J. Minder resigned when a newspaper report revealed he spent up to 15 years in prison for various armed robberies and a bank heist. Minder maintained he did not cover up his past. Instead, he stated that no one on Smith & Wesson's board asked about his criminal record. A background investigation of Minder could have prevented the embarrassing revelation and allowed the company to better evaluate Minder as a job candidate.

Source: "Smith & Wesson Chief Quits Over Crime." *CNN* Money.com, February 27, 2004, http://money.cnn.com/2004/02/27/news/smith_wesson/.

candidates applying for jobs at all levels of an organization's hierarchy, including its board of directors.

Background investigations can not only verify information presented by job candidates, but also they can provide insight into their personality. For example, they may potentially reveal a candidate has been a party to numerous lawsuits, experienced a corporate or personal bankruptcy, or had a personal drug habit or an extramarital affair. While some information revealed in the background investigation may be of a highly personal nature, personal issues may soon impinge on a candidate's ability to successfully perform his or her job, thus putting a portfolio company, and the entire PE or venture capital fund's portfolio, at risk.

Although events with portfolio company executives may seem rare, this is often due to the fact that many PE and venture capital funds do not want the events publicized. In reality, even the most successful PE and venture capital funds experience issues with portfolio company executives.

In another example from the venture capital industry, several venture partners interviewed a potential CEO over a period of 10 weeks. Immediately prior to presenting a final letter of employment, a background investigation was conducted. This investigation revealed that the CEO did not have the Harvard M.B.A. he claimed to possess. The venture capital fund had to restart the process of interviewing CEO candidates; 10 weeks of work could have been saved had the background investigation been conducted at the start of the interviewing process.

In addition to conducting a preliminary background investigation, experienced investigators state that PE and venture capital funds should not

> ## WOULD YOU LIKE SOME FRIES WITH YOUR COKE?
>
> Consider the case of a Kleiner Perkins Caufield & Byers–backed portfolio company and its CEO, an episode managing partner Tom Perkins described as "one of the most bizarre episodes" of his career. After a period of successful tenure, the CEO started to demonstrate paranoia, claiming his office was bugged and that he was being followed. In time, Perkins discovered the CEO's cocaine habit, and the executive was removed. However, by the time of his removal, the CEO had already exacted significant damage on the portfolio company and it soon failed.
>
> *Source:* Tom Perkins, *Valley Boy: The Education of Tom Perkins* (New York: Gotham Books, 2007), 137–138.

only perform investigations prior to hiring an individual, but investigations should also be conducted periodically throughout the individual's career. Periodic investigations maximize the possibility of detecting issues that may arise after an individual is hired and help minimize potential damage caused by an unscrupulous employee.

For instance, one experienced investigator related an experience in which she discovered Interpol was chasing a number of shareholders of a tiny start-up, as they were the target of a fraud investigation overseas. One of the shareholders was hiding in Switzerland, but all documentation he provided as a candidate stated he resided and lived in the United States. In another situation, the investigator alerted venture capital partners of the fact that a company founder had conveniently transferred assets to his partner's spouse to avoid paying federal taxes. There were numerous tax liens levied against him.[25]

In summary, background investigations are an essential component of the due diligence process. While they are more costly than a simple background check, an investigation might yield a significant piece of information that may prevent future embarrassment.

NOTES

1. Jim Rasmussen, "Billionaire Talks Strategy with Students," *Omaha World-Herald*, January 2, 1994, 178.
2. PBS, "William Shockley," accessed April 12, 2011, www.pbs.org/transistor/album1/shockley/shockley3.html.

3. Joel N. Shurkin, *Broken Genius: The Rise and Fall of William Shockley, Creator of the Electronic Age* (New York: Macmillan, 2008), 181.

4. Ibid., 251.

5. Joel Shurkin, www.pbs.org/transistor/album1/addlbios/shurkin.html, accessed February 6, 2011.

6. Geoff Smart and Randy Street, *Who: The A Method for Hiring* (New York: Ballantine Books, 2008), 160.

7. Geoff Smart (ghSMART), in discussion with the author, December 2010.

8. Smart and Street, *Who: The A Method for Hiring*, 161–162.

9. Ibid., 162.

10. Steven N. Kaplan, Mark M. Kiebanov, and Morten Sorensen, "Which CEO Characteristics and Abilities Matter?" (working paper no. 14195, National Bureau of Economic Research) 2008, accessed February 7, 2011, www.nber.org/papers/w14195.pdf.

11. Peter F. Drucker, *The Effective Executive* (New York: HarperCollins, 2002), 1.

12. Geoffrey H. Smart, "The Art and Science of Human Capital Valuation," 1998, accessed February 6, 2011, www.ghsmart.com/media/press/human_capital.pdf.

13. Ibid.

14. Ibid.

15. Ibid.

16. The Myers & Briggs Foundation, "The 16 MBTI® Types: ESTJ," accessed April 12, 2011, www.myersbriggs.org/my-mbti-personality-type/mbti-basics/the-16-mbti-types.asp.

17. Kaplan, Kiebanov, and Sorensen, "Which CEO Characteristics and Abilities Matter?"

18. Steven N. Kaplan, "Bet on the Horse: Determining Success Factors of New Businesses," *Capital Ideas*, accessed February 6, 2011, www.chicagobooth.edu/capideas/dec05/1.aspx.

19. Paul A. Gompers, Anna Kovner, Josh Lerner, and David Scharfstein, "Skill vs. Luck in Entrepreneurship and Venture Capital: Evidence from Serial Entrepreneurs," July 2006. Available at SSRN: http://ssrn.com/abstract=933932.

20. Arthur Rock, interview by Sally Smith Hughes, 2008–2009, "Early Bay Area Venture Capitalists: Shaping the Economic and Business Landscape," accessed February 6, 2011, http://digitalassets.lib.berkeley.edu/roho/ucb/text/rock_arthur.pdf.

21. Alison Wood Brooks, Laura Huang, Sara Wood Kearney, and Fiona Murray, "Investors Prefer Entrepreneurial Ventures Pitched by Attractive

Men," *Proceedings of the National Academy of Sciences of the United States of America* 111, no. 10 (March 11, 2014).

22. Alex Pentland, "Defend Your Research: We Can Measure the Power of Charisma," *Harvard Business Review*, January-February 2010, accessed February 7, 2011, http://hbr.org/2010/01/defend-your-research-we-can-measure-the-power-of-charisma/ar/1.
23. Ibid.
24. Patricia Sabatini, "Fibs on Resumes Commonplace," *Pittsburgh Post-Gazette*, February 24, 2006.
25. Interview with Theresa Mack, CPA, CFF, CAMS, CFCI, PI of Cendrowski Corporate Advisors in Chicago, Illinois, and Bloomfield Hills, Michigan.

CHAPTER 18

Diligence beyond Management

"The information required to make decisive investments in disruptive technology simply does not exist . . . it needs to be created through fast, inexpensive and flexible forays into the market."

—Clayton Christensen, *The Innovator's Dilemma*

ASSESSING THE MARKET

Successful investors know that there are good ideas aplenty—these are not necessarily good investment opportunities. Market readiness, accetance and competitive dynamics are more important. "We go to great lengths to be tuned into market trends, speaking to people in the industry, understanding the currents and identifying interesting opportunities. If you don't understand the problem firsthand, you don't have insight into creating a solution," says Roelof Botha of Sequoia Capital.[1]

In assessing markets, big data trends have intersected with venture capital investments. Ironstone is an investment firm using algorithms and the big-data approach to early stage investments. Their data say that a start-up's founding team has only 12 percent predictive value, even though most investors rank that as one of the most important factors. And just 20 percent of Ironstone's analysis focuses on the start-up itself; 80 percent is on the market it is entering, because they say start-ups are likely to change course and the market has more predictive power.[2] "It is much better to look at the contours of the marketplace and how it is shifting. Intuition has not been a great way to pick the next big thing," says Thomas Thurston of Ironstone. "We have developed disruptive algorithms to help find and predict the next big thing. We get a lot of variables from the investment pitch itself—we don't need to go out a dig for a lot more data. We look across sectors. The model is the primary driver, but we haven't given up on other traditional forms of diligence. Yet the algorithms decide if the company is in the game as opposed to our feelings or emotions."[3]

Most successful investments start with the market forces. Some ways to assess the market dynamics include the following:

- Is the market emerging, mature, or fragmented? Is there an unmet need, a pent-up demand, a potential market pull for the products? Market adoption rates differ for various technologies.
- What is the growth potential? Can the given opportunity grab a large market share quickly?
- What is the competitive advantage of the opportunity? Is it sustainable? How does it fit within the current state of competition?
- Are there any existing barriers to entry? Is there freedom to operate? Is there an existing structure of market players? Warren Buffett says, "It's no fun being a horse when a tractor comes along or the blacksmith when the car comes along." The question a practitioner needs to ask is, "Who is going to suffer the maximum pain when this product arrives in the market?"

WHEN BEING TOO FAST IS A BARRIER TO ENTRY: GOOGLE

Angel investor K. Ram Shriram recounted his initial meeting with Sergey Brin and Larry Page, cofounders of Google. He suggested that as the time for search engines had come and gone, they should sell their technology to the existing search engine companies like Yahoo!, Inktomi, and Lycos. Brin and Page demonstrated their search engine to several existing search engine companies, but nobody wanted to buy the technology. They called Shriram with the feedback: "None of them want to buy us. . . . They said that because our engine is brutally efficient, it would hurt their current businesses—it would cut their banner ad revenues by half. . . ." Shriram promptly wrote a small check that led to the first $500,000 angel round. "I still did not believe that this would succeed," he said. He cautioned, "You are up against heavy odds."

Menlo Ventures, one of the Silicon Valley's leading venture firms, uses a process called Systematic Emerging Market Selection (SEMS) for every investment. Using this process, Menlo tracks four aspects: market size, team, unique technology, and stage of product development (beta, shipping). Of these four, Menlo concluded that market size and the product's stage of development mattered the most. Seasoned practitioners are like surfers who can spot the waves and ride them. At times, a good surfer has to go a bit farther in the ocean instead of waiting for the tide to come!

EVALUATING THE IDEA OR PRODUCT

While conducting due diligence for products or technology, consider the following factors:

- *Primary value proposition*: Quite simply put, does the stated solution offer a significant advantage—a significantly quantifiable improvement over the current solution? Is it faster, better, or cheaper? Terry McGuire of Polaris Ventures says, "Early on in my career, I found every technology fascinating—my reaction would be 'You can do that, really!'—but over time, I found that you need healthy skepticism. Believe that the world can be changed, but ask all the right questions."[4]

BLOGGING IN 140 CHARACTERS: WHO WANTS THIS?

Early on, when the Twitter site went down for three hours, ardent fans sent homemade cookies to the engineers at the office with a note "We know you guys are working hard to get the site up. Thanks for everything you do."
　　—Bijan Sabet, Spark Capital, early investor in Twitter[*]
　　People wondered how we could invest in something as frivolous as Twitter. If you would have gone into a venture capital partnership and said the founder of Twitter invented Blogger, but now wants to do 140-character blogging, I do not know how it is going to make me money, but the founder is a stud, people would look at you like, "But its still 140 characters or less! Huh?[†]"
　　　　　　　　　　　　　　—Mike Maples, Floodgate Fund

---

[*] Speaking at VentureAlpha East, April 2013, Boston, MA
[†] Tarang and Sheetal Shah. *Venture Capitalists at Work: How VCs Identify and Build Billion-Dollar Successes* (New York: Apress, 2011).

- *Development stage*: Where is the idea in development? Is it a mere idea on a napkin, is it in the beta stage, is it already shipping, or are the first customers at hand?
- *Can it be protected?* How easy is it for another entrant to jump in? Is this an execution play, where better execution could lead to more market share? Or is it a secret sauce, where the patents, processes, or intellectual property can be used to build a moat around the business?
- *Market acceptance and adoption rate*: Several points of friction may come into play as the new technology/product tries to penetrate the market. While this is harder to analyze, the challenge is to ascertain the market pain and reasons for adoption. Are the needs of early adopters—the first customers—and the mass market aligned?
- *Growth potential*: What percentage of growth can be achieved in the first five years, and how does that compare with the size of the overall market? What is the effective mechanism to reach such potential? What are the points of friction in growth? Is the sales cycle long? What distribution channels exist?

Intellectual property (IP) due diligence requires some additional points:

- Are the ownership, title, assignments, and license agreements in place?
- What are the claims and scope of protection (technical and geographic)?
- Noninfringment—does the core IP address the company's primary products? Does the company have freedom to operate? Are there any blocking patents?
- Can the IP be invalidated in a litigious environment? Is any threatened or pending litigation foreseen?

It is important to consider the product in conjunction with the timbre of the entrepreneur. In a study, Saras Sarasvathy finds that "*starting with exactly the same product, the entrepreneurs ended up creating companies in 18 completely disparate industries!*" [Italics added.][5]

As the French writer Antoine de Saint Exupéry wrote, "A rock pile ceases to be a rock pile the moment a single man contemplates it, bearing within him the image of a cathedral."[6] Sarasvathy builds a theory of effectuation whereby given means can lead to several imagined end points. The means in any entrepreneurial environment are meager: personal traits, expertise, and social networks. There is no elaborate planning—to the contrary, the plans are made and unmade, recast on a daily basis as entrepreneurs uncover new information. Seasoned entrepreneurs know surprises are no deviations from the path but are the norm from which one learns how to forge a path.

Take the example of a company that had six different changes in its business plan—the last iteration was PayPal.[7] Formed on the premise of developing cryptography software for handheld devices, the model evolved to transmitting money via a handheld PDA. The final evolutionary step in the business model was Web-based payments, which allowed for rapid traction and acted as a de facto tool for processing Web payments. One of the cofounders, Max Levchin, exhibited the energy and technical acumen of a typical type A entrepreneur who goes down the wrong path on several occasions but iteratively corrects those missteps by asking the right questions. To start with, Levchin partnered with Peter Theil, a hedge fund manager who invested initial capital and complemented Levchin's technical acumen. Thiel bought into the premise that there is demand for cryptography and that it is a relatively untapped and poorly understood market. "The assumption was that the enterprises were all going to go to handheld devices . . . as a primary means of communication. Every corporate dog in America will hang around with a Palm Pilot or some kind of device." These assumptions were accurate, except that the timing was wrong—too early by about a decade. "Any minute now, there'll be millions of people begging for security on their handheld devices," Levchin would recall. But pretty soon, they realized that the market was not ready. It was a nightmare that every venture practitioner dreads—a technology in search of a market. "It's really cool, it's mathematically complex, it's very secure, but no one really needed it," Levchin would say. The battle between inertia versus changing direction and adapting flexibly to meet the market's needs paid off handsomely. Levchin started experimenting with questions like "What can we store inside the Palm Pilot that *is* actually meaningful?" and "Why don't we just store *money* in the handheld devices?" And while most venture practitioners would wring their hands at these questions and promptly kick the entrepreneur out, the early investors took a supportive approach, returns of which may have been significant. Four years from its inception, PayPal was acquired by eBay for $1.5 billion.

THE BUSINESS MODEL

A business model defines how value is created and monetized. It succinctly addresses *the who* (target customer), *the how* (distribution strategy), leading to *how much* (gross margins) and *how fast* (revenue growth).

The set of choices any company makes differentiates their business and establishes its costs and gross margins. Examples of business model jargon include "bricks and mortar" model, "razor blade" model, and "freemium" model, to name a few.

The business model determines the efficiencies of meeting the customer needs; ergo, it has an impact on the margins and costs for operating. Consider the software industry, where the products were once distributed in shrink-wrapped cases complete with manuals. Today, the cloud prevails, where no disks, installations, or manuals are necessary.

However, at the very early stages of any company, the business model may not be clear.

In an interview with NBC, Eric Schmidt, former CEO of Google, recalls his first meeting with Larry Page and Sergey Brin and subsequently his challenges with the business model.

> *Larry and Sergey were sitting there . . . they looked like children to me. I certainly did not see the success of the company and thought it was a terrible risk. I did not understand the advertising business at all and thought it was a joke. I thought there was something wrong in the cash position . . . they could never be making so much money as they claimed. My first act was to investigate the books to make sure this was legit. . . . I asked to see the money was coming in to prove that the people were actually paying for these adwords. . . . I overheard that a customer who was not getting their reports was screaming at one of the sales executives! I asked our Google sales executive, why is he screaming at you and she said, 'You don't understand Eric, their business needs cash every day and we are their business.' And then all of a sudden, I got it!" he recalled.*[8]

Schmidt joined Google and took the company public three years later when the company was valued at $23 billion. At the time of his departure, Google's market capitalization was over $180 billion.

JUST A BUNCH OF KIDS FARTING AROUND

Q: How do you get behind start-ups with no business model? With Pinterest, how do you get from zero revenue to a $3.8 billion valuation?

Marc Andreessen: "There are two categories of companies. You can guess which one I think Pinterest is in. There are the ones where everybody thinks they don't know how they're going to make money but they actually know. There's this kind of Kabuki dance that sometimes these companies put on where we're just a bunch of kids and we're just farting around and I don't know how we're going to make money. It's an act. They do it because they can. They don't let anyone else realize they have it figured out because that would just draw more competition. Facebook always knew, LinkedIn always knew, and Twitter always knew.

"They knew the nature of the valuable product they were going to be able to offer and they knew people were going to pay for it. They hadn't defined it down to the degree of being ready to ship it, or they didn't have a sales force yet, so there were things that they hadn't yet done. But they knew. They had a high level of confidence and over the passage of time we discovered they were correct.

"Now, there are other companies that honestly have no idea. Like, they really honestly have no idea. You need to be very cautious on these things because one of the companies that had no idea how it was going to make money when it first started was Google."

Source: Douglas Macmillan, "Andreessen: Bubble Believers 'Don't Know What They're Talking About'—Venture Capitalist Discusses the Current State of Tech Investing," *Wall Street Journal,* January 3, 2014.

Twitter was once in the same league, in which its business model is unclear, but the users are hooked. While the market demand and users existed, the monetization of the business did not occur for several years. According to Todd Dagres of Spark Capital, the rationale to invest was clear: "The team was great and the product seemed compelling. When we invested, the traction was largely among early, techie adopters. We thought the appeal would spread from the tech community to the general population so we invested. We were also concerned about the competitive market, but became comfortable when we decided that Twitter had the potential to be the category leader. *We were not obsessed with monetization when we invested.* [Italics added] We felt comfortable that monetization would follow if Twitter could build a large and engaged community,"[9] he remarked. Even as the company filed its public offering in 2013, the Twitter generated upward of $500 million revenues in a year.

FINANCIAL PROJECTIONS

At the very early stages of venture investment, practitioners rarely debate the financial projections. Rather, shrewd venture practitioners test the assumptions and capital required to achieve value inflection. "What are the milestones that this financing will achieve? How far are you from being cash-flow positive (in both time and money)?" are the questions Khosla Ventures team would ask of any entrepreneur.[10] As the company progresses to maturation with Series B or Series C rounds and starts to generate some revenues, the financial projections are analyzed in greater detail.

Finally, any practitioner would seek to understand the amount of capital needed to reach break-even. This is important from the perspective of reserving capital over multiple rounds for future investments. But it is foolish to expect precision when you are in this cloud of ambiguity. As Aristotle remarked, "for it is the mark of an educated man to look for precision in each class of things just so far as the nature of the subject admits; it is evidently equally foolish to accept probable reasoning from a mathematician and to demand from a rhetorician, scientific proofs."[11]

DO BUSINESS PLANS MATTER?

Practitioners do not put much emphasis on business plans, but rather use them effectively to understand aspects of the business. A business plan is more like a resume—it is used to get an interview or, in this case, a meeting with an investor. Beyond that, it becomes a fluid or at times completely irrelevant document. "I don't care much for business plans," says Brad Feld, managing director of The Foundry Group. Or consider Arthur Rock's example: When he raised the first round of capital for Intel, he "wrote the business plan myself, just two-and-a-half pages, double-spaced, which said nothing! . . . Normally I don't write business plans—the companies write a business plan. But in this case, I just felt that the investors were already there and all we needed to do was give them a little sheet of paper they could put in their files."[12]

In an interesting study of more than 100 ventures, researchers concluded there was "no difference between the performance of new businesses launched with or without a written business plan. The most widely dispensed advice for would-be entrepreneurs is that they should write a business plan before they launch their new ventures."[13] Courses are taught, business plan competitions pit universities against each other, and writing the plan takes about 200 hours. But unless a would-be entrepreneur needs to raise substantial start-up capital from angels or institutional investors, there is no compelling reason to write a business plan, aside from its use as a good strategic planning tool.

For passive investors, the business plan is a starting point, assessed by a junior analyst and eventually debated by senior partners. However, for investors who have deep domain expertise, the business plan is not of much consequence. And Jeffry Timmons rightfully argues that the business plan is obsolete the instant it emerges from the printer.[14]

NOTES

1. Tarang and Sheetal Shah, *Venture Capitalists at Work: How VCs Identify and Build Billion-Dollar Successes* (New York: Apress, 2011).
2. Claire Cain Miller, "Google Ventures Stresses Science of Deal, Not Art of the Deal," *The New York Times*, June 23, 2013.
3. Thomas Thurston speaking at Stanford Business School, October 2011, accessed on January 2, 2014, www.youtube.com/watch?v=xnIfVtsUp8Q.
4. Terry McGuire (Polaris Ventures) in discussions with the author, January 2011.
5. Saras D. Sarasvathy, "What Makes Entrepreneurs Entrepreneurial?" accessed February 6, 2011, available at www.effectuation.org/paper/what-makes-entrepreneurs-entrepreneurial.
6. Antoine de Saint Exupéry, *Flight to Arras*, trans. Lewis Galantiére (New York: Harcourt Brace, 1942), 129.
7. Jessica Livingston, *Founders at Work: Stories of Startups' Early Days* (New York: Apress, 2007). This episode has been recreated based on PayPal founder Max Levchin's interview with Jessica Livingston.
8. "Inside the Mind of Google," 2010, CNBC Interview with Maria Bartiromo.
9. Todd Dagres (Spark Capital), in discussions and e-mail communications with the author, 2008 and 2011.
10. Khosla Ventures, "What We Look For: Main Fund—What Matters," Web site, accessed February 6, 2011, www.khoslaventures.com/khosla/main_fund_wm.html.
11. *Nichomachean Ethics*, Book I, passage 3, accessed February 9, 2011, http://classics.mit.edu/Aristotle/nicomachaen.mb.txt.
12. Arthur Rock, interview by Sally Smith Hughes, http://digitalassets.lib.berkeley.edu/roho/ucb/text/rock_arthur.pdf.
13. William D. Bygrave, Julian Lange, Aleksandar Mollov, Michael Pearlmutter, and Sunil Singh, "Pre-Startup Formal Business Plans and Post-Startup Performance: A Study of 116 New Ventures," *Venture Capital Journal* 9, no. 4 (October 2007), accessed February 6, 2011, http://blog.guykawasaki.com/bygrave.doc.
14. Jeffry Timmons and Stephen Spinelli, *New Venture Creation: Entrepreneurship for the 21st Century*, 5th ed. (New York: McGraw Hill, 1999), 85.

CHAPTER 19

Structuring Investment
Transactions

"For many entrepreneurs, reading a term sheet is no more interesting than reading the latest volume of the Federal Register. And most lawyers will tell you what the terms mean but not how they can be used to screw you, how to negotiate them, and what is the 'norm.'"
—Mark Suster, entrepreneur turned venture capitalist (VC)[1]

Much has been written about term sheets, including line-by-line analysis of terms. A line-by-line analysis is helpful, but it is akin to looking at trees when the perspective of the big picture or the forest is critical. Term sheets are dense with legalese. The goal of this chapter is to simplify, prioritize, and focus on the key terms that help complete a transaction.

Investment structure is the framework that describes the flow of capital from the investor to the company and back.

THE SPIRIT OF THE TERM SHEET

After due diligence, investors propose a set of investment terms that define the transaction. At the heart of it, both the entrepreneurs and investors agree upon the following underlying spirit of the term sheet:

- The investment opportunity and market conditions are ripe for rapid growth.

- Both parties bring a unique set of elements—technology and capital—to create value.
- Together, these elements can help catalyze and create value faster.
- Both parties agree to collaborate for a meaningful period of time, ideally until exit do us part.
- Both parties understand that financial success is critical for both parties, as is the timing of returns.

While this credo can be established, there can be several points of creative tension or stress between the two parties.

NEGOTIATION STRESS POINTS

The potential stress points in any negotiation can occur around the economic or control factors. Table 19.1 identifies these stress points and the relevant terms that address them.

TABLE 19.1   Differing Goals of Entrepreneur and Investor

	Entrepreneurs Want	Venture Capitalists (VCs) Want	Relevant Terms That Come into Play
	Maximize valuation	Lower valuation; potential for up rounds and target returns	Price per share and amount of investment leading to valuation
At point of making an investment	Adequate capital to meet and exceed milestones	Capital efficiency; reach breakeven/ financial independence rapidly	Amount of investment, use of proceeds
	Avoid loss of control	Exert control if the milestones start to slip. Ensure that the team, strategy, and vision are aligned	Employment agreements, vesting of founders' stock, structure of board, independent board seat choices
	Freedom to operate their businesses. No micromanagement.	Ensure that execution is per predetermined milestones.	Board and governance matters; milestone-based financing

TABLE 19.1 Differing Goals of Entrepreneur and Investor (Cont.)

Between investment and exit	As needed, investors should assist with future financings, strategy, and customer connections	If opportunity grows rapidly, maintain pro rata ownership	Preemptive rights or right of first refusal
	Stay in control and experiment despite inefficiencies	If it doesn't grow as well and ends up in the "living dead" category, VCs should have the ability to liquidate their holdings.	Antidilution, redemption, or liquidation, drag-along rights and tagalong rights
At point of exit	May choose an early exit to accomplish personal financial goals, or delay/ avoid an exit to achieve ego-driven needs (like world domination).	Speed to exit and maximized value is critical.	Redemption, dividends, liquidation preferences, and registration rights

Types of investment structures include debt, convertible loan, and preferred stock. The simplest form of investment, a debt, would be governed by some basic parameters, such as the principle, interest rate, collateral, and schedule of payments. Debt may be secured by collateral such as assets and/ or receivables, or it may be unsecured. An unsecured debt acts as a quasi-security. In this chapter, convertible note and preferred stock structures are presented. The preferred stock is the most commonly used investment structure in venture capital investments.

But at the heart of it, investment structures are designed with two key parameters: economics and control. As Brad Feld of the Foundry Group points out, terms sheets can be simple if we focus on what matters:

1. *Ownership and economics:* Buying a meaningful slice of the company at the right price is the first step for any investor. But most savvy practitioners know that while valuation is important, the potential of the opportunity in the long run, as well as other investment terms, matters.

In some investments, such as distressed real estate, the philosophy that "you make money when you buy" may be true; with venture capital investments, that may not necessarily be the case. A pre-money value of $8 million or $10 million is not that significant when the opportunity could potentially offer a billion-dollar exit. The price-based debate creates undue tension at the point when a relationship is being established.

2. *Governance and control:* Also described as protection or control aspects of an investment, these rights minimize risks, protect against any downside, and thereby potentially amplify the upside. Governance is established by the board of directors, which typically appoints the CEO and approves an annual plan, budget, and major business decisions. The board is controlled by investors and establishes certain protective provisions to ensure that the management does not jeopardize the security interests of the investors.

Table 19.2 details the various investment terms.

STRUCTURING TERMS TO GENERATE TARGET RETURNS

A good investment structure allows an investor to double up and invest higher amounts as the opportunity progresses—or minimize the risks if it craters. Structure starts with valuation primarily, followed by liquidation and antidilution preferences (used to protect ownership), dividends, and

TABLE 19.2   Summary of Key Investment Terms: Preferred Stock

Term	What It Means	Importance to Investors	Key Negotiation Variables
Economic Terms: Those That Impact Financial Outcomes for Investors			
Valuation	Establishes value of a company	Project potential internal rate of return	Percentage of ownership, price per share
Liquidation preference	Creates a waterfall of distribution—who gets paid first and how much—when a liquidity event occurs	Improves returns at exit, protects investment at lower exit values	Multiple (1X, 2X), participating preferred, cap/no-cap

Antidilution	Prevents dilution of investors' ownership if a down round occurs	Minimizes downside/protects ownership	Weighted average/ full ratchet
Dividends	Allows investors to declare dividends	Improves potential returns	Percentage, cumulative/ noncumulative
Preemptive rights/ right of first refusal (ROFR)	Allows investors to buy additional shares in future rounds	Allows for increasing ownership if opportunity gets stronger	Time frame for decision, pro rata share
Redemption of shares	Allows investors to redeem their ownership/ shares after a certain time frame. Ensures that investors are able to trigger the timing and conditions of an exit; drag-along and tagalong rights allow one party to sell his or her shares if the other party is able to find a seller.	Allows for exits; redemption is especially important when the company has minimal upside potential. Registration rights depend on the strength of the company and state of the public markets.	Time period (number of years), fair market value.
Registration rights, conversion to common at public offering, piggyback rights, drag-along rights/tagalong rights, co-sale agreements			These are exit-related provisions, and savvy practitioners do not waste much time negotiating these boilerplate terms.

rights of first refusal. These terms combined effectively can help any investor (a) establish an ownership position and (b) build up ownership as the opportunity progresses. Let's start with the voodoo of valuation.

VALUATION METHODS AND OTHER VOODOO ARTS

Jim Breyer, when making the first investment in Facebook, remarked, "The price was way too high but sometimes that's what it takes to do the deal." Accel's $12.7 million investment to acquire 15 percent of Facebook at approximately $100 million pre-money valuation grew by 50X in six years.[2] In hindsight, the price does not seem too high. But Breyer ought to be comforted that he could make the investment. Several investors had passed on Facebook—the opportunity of the decade.

With Josh Koppelman of First Round Capital, it was another opportunity that slipped away due to valuation debates. "We offered Twitter a term sheet—$500,000 at a $5 million pre-money valuation. Evan Williams, founder of Twitter, continued to fund it. Three months later, Union Square Ventures was leading the round at a $20 million valuation. We could have participated but thought the valuation was high."[3]

While valuation is one of the important terms for the entrepreneur as well as the investors, no simple method exists to calculate valuation at the seed- and early-stage of investments.

Valuation is a function of the sector, stage of the company and the geography. Technology sectors often gain higher valuations as compared to medical devices or biotech sectors. In competitive geographies like Silicon Valley, valuations can soar quickly. In regions that suffer from paucity of capital, strong startups barely get what they deserve.

Seasoned practitioners often say, "sounds about right" when numbers are tossed around. Depending on the stage of the company, valuation can be a simple back-of-the-envelope calculation, net present value calculation, or comparable transactions, called "comps." This chapter briefly covers the approaches to valuation. However, the emphasis is more on the subjective art at an early stage of venture investing, rather than formulaic net present value (NPV)/discounted cash flow (DCF) approach.

Valuing an early-stage company is a nebulous exercise—an art form at best. Aswath Damodaran, author of *The Dark Side of Valuation*, writes, "There can be no denying the fact that young companies pose the most difficult estimation challenges in valuation. A combination of factors—short and not very informative histories, operating losses and the . . . high probability of failure—all feed into valuation practices that try to avoid dealing with the uncertainty by using a combination of forward multiples and arbitrarily high discount rates."[4]

HOW TO VALUE INTEL: LESSONS FROM ARTHUR ROCK

Bob [Noyce] called me one day and said, "We're thinking of leaving [Fairchild Semiconductor] to form a company," and I asked him how much money they thought they needed to get started, and they said, "$2.5 million." And I said, "Okay. You got it." No—first, I think we first discussed the terms—how much of the company they would be willing to give to investors for putting up $2.5 million, and we agreed on 50 percent. Then I said, "Okay, you're covered," and went about raising it.

Source: Arthur Rock, interview by Sally Smith Hughes, 2008–2009, "Early Bay Area Venture Capitalists: Shaping the Economic and Business Landscape," accessed February 10, 2011, http://digitalassets.lib.berkeley.edu/roho/ucb/text/rock_arthur.pdf.

THE DRIVERS OF VALUATION

By aligning the valuation drivers with the prior steps of the due diligence, we can see that in order of priority, the valuation will tend to be higher when all the following criteria are met:

- The opportunity serves an *attractive market* with higher *growth potential.*
- The opportunity has *an established competitive position* via patents or market share or leadership.
- A *strong team* is in place or, as Rob Hayes of First Round Capital puts it, it has "an execution machine."
- The opportunity may demonstrate *capital efficiency* (needs lower amounts of capital to achieve financial independence), revenues, gross margins.
- A meaningful *exit potential within the target time frame* can be achieved: There is a universe of strategic buyers that is large, accessible, and seeks growth opportunities via acquisition.
- Geographic supply-demand drivers: Valuation of start-ups is much higher in competitive markets like Silicon Valley.
- Finally, the state of the public markets, frothiness, or excessive capital supply can often elevate valuations across the board and trounce all of the above criteria.

THE SIMPLIFIED FORM OF THE VENTURE CAPITAL METHOD OF VALUATION

Harvard Business School professor William Sahlman's venture capital method of valuation begins with the end in mind. Consider Table 19.3. Assume you are investing $800,000 in a seed stage company, and your ownership will be in the 26 percent range. This rule of thumb works well when you are dealing with very early-stage companies with little or no meaningful comparable data.

Starting with some data, we know that

Median time to liquidity via an acquisition = 5.5 years

Median pre-money valuation of seed round = $2.3 million

Median amount of investment at seed stage = $800,000

Imputed venture capital ownership at the time of investment = 26 percent

To generate a target internal rate of return (IRR) of, say, 106 percent, you need to retain, or preserve ownership to, as much as 20 percent. On the lower end of the spectrum, with a 36 percent IRR, you would be expected to retain at the minimum of 5 percent.

Thus, the simple exercise should allow any practitioner to assess whether the investment opportunity can realistically help reach the target IRR by preserving ownership until an exit point is reached.

Preservation of equity depends on a number of variables, and not all can be predicted. Thus, while negotiating valuation, any practitioner keeps the following three variables in perspective: timing of exit, ownership at exit, and target IRR. Let's expand on these.

1. *The timing of the exit:* timing depends on several factors, both internal and external.

TABLE 19.3   Example of Simplified Valuation Method

Scenarios	Home Run	Middle of the Road	Mediocre
Estimated value of venture capital ownership at exit, assuming dilution from 26%	20%	5%	2%
IRR	106%	36%	4.5%
Cash-on-cash multiple	37.5	4.68	1.25

    a. Internal factors:

        i. Resources, including management team quality and cash resources: Any rapid churn in the management team, unforeseen uses of cash, and changes in the burn rate will significantly affect the timing and value of the exit.

        ii. Ability to execute and meet milestones.

        iii. Strategy and business model.

        iv. Investor's desire to force an exit: Many practitioners need to show exit activity to allow for future fund-raising success.

    b. External factors:

        i. Competitive threats.

        ii. Acquirer industry dynamics.

        iii. Public market/macroeconomic conditions.

2. *The estimated venture capital ownership at exit:* ownership at exit depends on value creation vis-à-vis burn rate. All practitioners aim to minimize future dilutions. Some common sources of nondilutive capital infusion include the following:

    a. *Strategic relationships:* Joint development agreements within the pharmaceutical sector are common. The start-up gets access to a funding stream in exchange for exclusive distribution rights.

    b. *Venture debt:* When Facebook wanted to raise $3 million, right after raising $12.7 million, Western Technology Investment offered venture debt. This form of financing reduces the overall cost of capital for start-ups and preserves equity for current owners. Venture debt is a hybrid form of financing available to certain types of venture-backed companies. As it is considered higher risk, venture debt financiers usually seek collateral, a higher rate of return, and warrants to sweeten their rate of return.

    c. *Federal and state grants:* A range of options are available, but are restricted to technology-intensive companies for conducting research and development activities. The Small Business Innovation Research (SBIR) and Small Business Technology Transfer (STTR) federal funding programs offer grant opportunities each year. While these depend on funding availability for agencies and are hyper-competitive, several start-ups have opportunistically gained traction with such grants.

3. *The exit value of the company:* While this value can be guesstimated, as most practitioners say, focus on building something of value, and exits take care of themselves. Practitioners typically target a minimum threshold of IRR, say, 35 percent, for each opportunity, and based on projections and exit probability, choose to invest or pass on opportunities.

In summary, the valuation economics boil down to (1) minimizing dilu-
tion and (2) maximizing exit value. Some practitioners alleviate all these
concerns and try to squeeze as much equity as possible at the early stage,
that is, maximum ownership at the lowest valuation. But this approach can
come back to bite you.

As Rick Heitzmann, managing director of FirstMark Capital, says,
"Valuation matters. But you cannot get too focused on it. You get a sense
of people when they fight for the last nickel—this is a like a marriage and
the goal is to keep the big picture in mind. Entrepreneurs do not always
take the highest offer but select the best partner, and we have found that the
combination of our experience and networks creates a far superior value
proposition to just offering money."[5]

COMPARABLE VALUATIONS OF SIMILAR INVESTMENTS (COMPS)

In the comparable valuation or comps method, valuation is determined by
comparable transactions in the marketplace. Consider Table 19.4, which
shows a typical range of values. The revenues and the acquisition price are
estimated, as these may not be declared or available publicly. A median and
mean multiple is calculated that indicates a range of multiples that could be
deployed in such a scenario.

In Table 19.5, the universe of publicly traded companies is assessed. While
the data is available, critics argue that the method does not factor in several
risks, such as technology, market adoption, and liquidity risks. Furthermore,
the growth rates and gross margins for each company are different.

While this method is used broadly in later-stage companies, it has its
own set of fair challenges:

- *The universe of comparable transactions may be broad*: As they say,
  with a large data set, you can draw any conclusion you desire. When

TABLE 19.4 Sample Comparable Method (Private Companies)

Company	Acquisition Price	Date of Acquisition	Estimated Revenue	Multiple
Tech Gizmo, USA	$550M	Jan 2013	$50M	11X
Maps-R-Us, Germany	$225M	July 2012	$28M	8X
Gemini Global, USA	$155M	Dec 2010	$26.2M	5.9X
Pantera Premier, Spain	$40M	June 2011	$2M	20X

TABLE 19.5 Sample Comparable Method (Publicly Traded Companies)

Company	TTM Revenues ($M)	TTM EBITDA	Market Cap ($M)	Enterprise Value ($M)	Enterprise Value (X Rev)	Enterprise Value (X EBIT)
Gentoo	670	73	1,640	1,323	2.0	18.1
Soup Street Group	433	99	1,776	1,220	2.8	12.3
Avalon Innovations	1229	114	4,440	3,600	2.9	31.6
Sapphire Technology	225	45	800	990	4.4	22.0

entrepreneurs present comparable transactions, and when investors dig into the data set, valuations can be surprisingly different.

■ *Lack of transparency*: While the only data available is the pre-money valuation, the data do not depict the finer nuances of strengths and risks embedded within. For example, valuation skews toward the positive when an experienced entrepreneur may be leading an opportunity. Other factors that may affect value are the quality of technology and its attractiveness to customers or existing partnerships—these factors may be invisible from the comps data set.

■ *The comparable data set in a frothy environment may create a lemming effect*: In the year 2000, the median pre-money valuation at first round was $8 million. By 2010, it had dropped to $4 million.

VALUATION AND THE ART OF GETTING A SEAT AT THE TABLE

Early-stage investors can seldom predict whether an opportunity will grow, gain momentum, and generate returns. A classic investment approach is to invest a small amount and gain a seat at the table. "You are buying an option to invest in future rounds," says Jim Plonka of Dow Venture Capital. And if the company begins to grow, investors could maintain or build up their ownership position by investing additional amounts in future rounds.

When Sabeer Bhatia, founder of Hotmail, met with Draper Fisher Jurvetson (DFJ) to pitch his idea, like most entrepreneurs, he asked for valuation in nice round numbers: $3 million. Neither DFJ nor Bhatia

(Continued)

VALUATION AND THE ART: (*Continued*)

would have the time to debate comps, develop intricate financial models, and craft the correct "ask" amount. Rather, DFJ followed the classic move of buying a seat at the table and putting in enough chips. Tim Draper asked, "How much money do you need just to prove to us that you can do this—that it's even possible to make e-mail available on the web?" Draper asked for 30 percent of the company for $300,000; Bhatia pushed back and they agreed on 15 percent, with an implied post-money valuation of $2 million. DFJ was able to invest a small amount and test the hypothesis as well as the team's mettle. DFJ invested additional capital in future rounds, and 20 months later, Hotmail was acquired by Microsoft for approximately $400 million.

Source: Adapted from Jessica Livingston, *Founders at Work: Stories of Startups' Early Days* (Berkeley, CA: Apress, 2007), 20.

DISCOUNTED CASH FLOW METHOD

If you have a master's in business administration, the DCF valuation technique will have been drilled into the depths of your cranium. Like most highly academic techniques, the DCF is irrelevant for early-stage venture capital on a number of counts. For one, at an early stage of any company, you really do not have comparable data, and the rest is projections. Thus, I have seen entrepreneurs conjure up projections and use extensive DCF models to develop precise valuation—a healthy exercise—but at the end of the day, value is what can be transacted up. A great model with multiple Excel spreadsheets is helpful, but if a transaction cannot be consummated, what good is all this idealism?

To calculate valuation of a firm using DCF, we estimate growth rate—the percentage of growth and the number of years of such growth. The entrepreneur's estimates and practitioners' estimates on growth rates can vary significantly. But let us assume that the two parties agree upon a growth rate.

The second variable is free cash flows (FCF) available during such a period. FCF seems like a novel concept when we discuss start-ups and early-stage companies.

Finally, we assume a discount rate—you consider the terminal value and those FCFs and pull them all together to the present date. That rabbit you pull out of your hat is NPV—a formula that is an amalgamation of four different projected variables: the rate of growth, the time period of growth, the cash flows, and the cost of capital.

When all is said and done, you are trying to establish a value for the existing assets and future growth. The approach is well suited for more mature companies.

Start-ups have little or no revenues, no customers, and at times, operating losses. Even those young companies that are profitable have short histories, and most young firms depend on private capital, initially, owner savings, and venture capital investments later on. As a result, many of the standard techniques we use to estimate cash flows, growth rates, and discount rates either do not work or yield unrealistic numbers.

In addition, the fact that most young companies have a high mortality rate causes further aggravation. Researchers studied the survival rate of 8.9 million firms and concluded that only 38 percent of businesses survived over a five-year period. See Table 19.6, which shows the survival rate of technology companies, which is substantially lower than health services.[6] In fact, at least two-thirds of technology companies die in five years, a higher mortality rate as compared to health services. Thus, astute practitioners factor this survival rate in the valuation negotiations.

Damodaran suggests that besides using "a combination of data on more mature companies in the business and the company's own characteristics to forecast revenues, earnings, and cash flows," we should "adjust the value for the possibility of failure."[7] He further points out that multiples of valuation should be considered at the point of exit, rather than present-day multiples. If the revenue of a start-up after year 5 were to drop to a compound annual growth rate (CAGR) of 10 percent, the multiple should reflect this growth as opposed to, say, 50 percent CAGR in earlier years. This would create an interesting conundrum where, besides revenues, practitioners would try to project the exit multiple five years down the road.

While this may not be adopted as easily, most practitioners use a rule of thumb to assert valuation while considering risks of technology failure, management churn, financing risk, and illiquidity premium.

As one venture capitalist (VC) pointed out, "I expect each of my portfolio companies to generate 10X or higher returns and make the fund

TABLE 19.6 Survival Rate of Firms

Sector	Year 1 (%)	Year 5 (%)	Year 7 (%)
Health services	86	50	44
Technology	81	31	25
Financial activities	84	44	37
Business services	82	38	31
All Firms	**81**	**38**	**31**

whole—getting caught up in discount ratios and valuation techniques does not help. I seek the best in class and work hard to make them the *numero unos* of their category." As Michael Moritz of Sequoia Capital once remarked, "We are in the business of creating a large bonfire with a small matchstick." Jim Breyer successfully accomplished that with his $12.7 million investment in Facebook.

Establishing a price for an illiquid security, with significant risk (management risk, market risk, technology risk, follow-on financing risk), is nebulous activity. At the early stages of investment, practitioners have honed the valuation process to an art form, a subjective technique at best. When valuation debates become prolonged, some practitioners consider using a blended approach that diffuses valuation issues, liquidation multiples and springing warrants, but these can create complexity in the legalese and deal structures.

For most practitioners, the ability to generate returns is what matters. For each investment, seasoned investors seek 10X or higher returns. "I want each of these to have the potential to be a 10-bagger and make my fund," one general partner (GP) remarked. As most agree, valuation is just a small, yet important part of the overall structure.

Let us look at terms beyond valuation. The convertible loan (also called convertible note) is a simple and popular investment structure that is used more often by angel investors and early-stage investors.

CONVERTIBLE LOAN

A convertible loan starts with senior position on the balance sheet and drops down, or converts to equity, when the company meets certain milestones. Primarily used as a risk mitigation tactic in the early stages of the company, a convertible note allows the investor to claim the assets of a start-up if it fails. Alternatively, in certain conditions, the note holder can "call" the note, or ask for redemption under certain trigger conditions.

Used in situations in which establishing valuation is cumbersome, a convertible note postpones the pricing of equity round until a suitable event occurs.

The key parameters that come into effect with convertible notes are principle, interest rate, and conversion trigger points. After the conversion, the interest payments are terminated, and appropriate changes on the balance sheet (the liabilities are shifted to the equity section) are duly recorded. Typical convertible note terms include the following:

- *Interest rate*: Depending on the risk investor's appetite, interest rates vary from 3 percent upward to as much as 10 percent; it is normal to accrue interest for most convertible notes.
- *Term*: Typical terms are one year, but notes can be as much as two years or longer.

- *Conversion triggers*: The note converts to preferred stock upon raising a predetermined amount in a Series A round.
- *Improving the returns:* Investors frequently add a few other terms in the mix to improve the returns.
  - *Discounts*: For example, a 20 percent discount is given to the share price of the next round.
  - *Warrants*: Warrants would act as sweeteners and help aggregate a higher ownership through additional shares at a lower price point.
- *Capped convertible notes*: A capped convertible note establishes a cap on valuation for the next round; for example, a cap at $2.5 million pre-money indirectly establishes the valuation of $2.5 million at the next round. Mark Suster warns, "A sword that can cut both ways, a convertible note with cap, could hurt the entrepreneur. It basically sets the maximum price rather than your actual price. Example: If you do a convertible note raising $400k at a $3.6m premoney, your ceiling is 10 percent of the company ($400k/$4m postmoney). But your actual next round might come in at $2 million premoney. You might have been better just negotiating an agreed price in the first place. Not always, but sometimes."[8] Capped notes work in favor of investors in such situations.

Consider Table 19.7, which assumes each investor puts in $100,000. The cap on conversion moves steadily upward from $3 million to $20 million. The final investor comes in at 12 percent discount, but no cap. The effect of cap on conversion can be seen when a Series A round is closed at a $12 million pre-money valuation with an effective share price of $1.29. Only investor 1 and investor 2 benefit from the cap. Interestingly, investor 4, who negotiated a discount on the next-round price, benefits too.

Bridge Loan

Similar to a convertible note, a bridge note is raised to meet certain short-term needs of a company. Typically used between financing rounds, a bridge loan

TABLE 19.7 Impact of Capped Conversion

Investor	Cap	Discount (%)	Conversion Price ($)
Investor 1	$3,000,000	0	0.46
Investor 2	$5,000,000	0	0.77
Investor 3	$20,000,000	0	1.29
Investor 4	None	12	1.14

JUST DON'T F— IT UP

Peter Thiel, an investor who made his money in PayPal, was one of the first angel investors in Facebook. He invested $500,000 as a loan that would convert to equity if Facebook achieved its milestone of 1.5 million users. "Just don't f— it up," Thiel said to Mark Zuckerberg at the time of investing.

Facebook did not meet the milestone of acquiring 1.5 million users, but Thiel converted his loan to equity and joined the board. Thiel's $500,000 got him 10.2 percent equity, implying a valuation of $4.9 million for the company. In six years, Facebook's value grew to an estimated $50 billion. Thiel's investment grew by a mere 10,000X in six years!

Source: David Kirkpatrick, *The Facebook Effect* (New York: Simon & Schuster, 2010), p. 89.

bridges a company between its existing cash and a future financing round. Terms are similar to a convertible note. Investors are leery of a bridge to nowhere and may build in a stair-stepped interest rate, warrants, or incentives. Thus, if the bridging event does not occur as predicted, investors gain additional ownership.

EQUITY: PREFERRED STOCK

When any corporation is incorporated, the founders contribute capital and designate a certain number of shares. While at the time of formation only one class of shares may exist, typically common shares, this may change when investors come into the picture.

Preferred stock is a separate class of shares which enjoys control and financial preferences over and above the common shareholders. As seen earlier, Table 19.2 summarizes these various aspects of a term sheet.

If the value of preferred stock grows, the ability to invest additional amounts of capital, such as with preemptive rights, helps investors maintain or build their position in a growing company. If it sours, the ability to gain control (via management changes), minimize the impact of downsides (via antidilution), and attempt to salvage the remains of the day is important. In reality, most practitioners agree that if any opportunity teeters, not much can be done to resurrect the remains. In any portfolio, at least a third of the investments will likely end up as write-offs.

KEY NEGOTIATION ELEMENTS

While negotiating equity rounds, here are the key elements to focus upon:

- Valuation or percentage of ownership at the point of investment
- Information rights/board seat
- Ability to invest in future rounds to maintain pro rata ownership
- Liquidation preferences

Most of the other terms, such as antidilution and registration rights, are pretty standard, and hence, it is best to optimize the process.

Warrants

A warrant is a right to buy a security at a fixed price: the exercise or strike price. Typically, warrants are issued in conjunction with an existing investment—a security, such as a convertible note or venture debt. For investors, warrants provide the ability to increase the overall return. Investors can improve their ownership positions at a suitable point in the future, as the opportunity matures.

A typical warrant would include terms such as the following:

- Percentage of investment or amount of investment:
  - *Percentage of investment:* If an investor issues a $500,000 convertible note with 10 percent warrants, the warrant allows the investor to invest $50,000 in the future.
  - *Amount of investment:* The warrant allows an investor to purchase shares worth $100,000.
- Strike price:
  - *Nominal value:* An example would be a value established at, say, $0.001 per share. An investor-friendly term, this would allow an investor to increase ownership at a certain point in the future.
  - *Share price of the next round:* A company-friendly term, this allows an investor to double up or increase the ownership position.
- Term:
  - *Time:* Term could be any time, say, up to 10 years; the longer the duration, the better for the investors.
  - *Event-based triggers:* Events reduce the life of the warrant upon certain trigger conditions, such as future financing or value creation milestones. Such milestones reduce the overall liquidity that would affect the founders.

Springing Warrants   At the point of entry, valuation debates are the primary cause of tension. Founders believe that the value of the company should be as high as possible. It's a technological marvel—future revenue and growth projections are just a matter of time. For practitioners who have heard ample stories and burned their capital, the skepticism is obvious.

For John Neis of Venture Investors, the answer was simple—take the middle path. When the founders of Tomo Therapies came up to discuss an investment opportunity, Neis was intrigued, but like most practitioners, he looked at the financial projections with a degree of healthy skepticism. Typically, the struggle between the buyer and the seller is evident, as each side tries to extract the maximum value up front. Not in this case—Neis developed a structure of springing warrants.

In this structure, quite simply, the venture fund's ownership decreases as the founders and entrepreneurs meet their projections and milestones. A representative example is presented in Table 19.4. It is an elegant model to balance the ownership struggles and provide adequate rewards if the founders meet their goals. The springing warrants are issued to founders, and these are exercisable (at a nominal exercise price) at certain milestones. The founders would thus acquire additional shares of common stock based on a predetermined formula. In the example in Table 19.8, if the founders believe they can generate revenues of $30 million in 2014, while the investors think it would be more like $23 million, the two parties can converge the valuation today with the assurance that as founders create value, investors relinquish a portion of their equity.

Tomo Therapies (Nasdaq: TOMO) grew to $200 million in revenues in four years of commercial launch. For Neis and Venture Investors, the largest shareholders, this investment was a barn burner—a 10X return or higher. In his modest style, John Neis says, "Tomo's technology saves lives—and bringing that to market was the important goal for all. The financial returns are always a welcome by-product of our efforts to change the world."

TABLE 19.8   Springing Warrants Can Be an Effective Way to Diffusive Valuation and Performance-Related Challenges

Revenues	2014	2015	2016
Baseline revenues	$5M	$12M	$23M
Upside case revenues	$7M	$9M	$15M
Additional equity granted to founder for meeting upside targets	3%	5%	8%

Options

The typical recipient of a stock option is an employee. A typical recipient of a warrant is an investor. This is the primary difference, beyond which the mechanics are more or less the same. It is important for any practitioner to understand the impact of an option pool on the investment structure. When exercised, options will dilute ownership for all stockholders. Employee stock options are offered as incentive tools to attract and retain talent. Incentive stock options are used for vendors, consultants, and the like. The tax implications for each need to be considered, but these are beyond the scope of this book. Typical option agreements include the following:

- Number of shares
- Strike price
- Term and vesting
- Buyback provisions

LIQUIDATION PREFERENCE

The second most important term after valuation is liquidation preference, writes Mark Suster of Upfront Ventures.[9]

Liquidation preferences, often seen as an opportunity to juice up the returns, are rights to receive a return before the common shareholders do. These preferences come into play at the time of liquidating the assets of the company. Liquidation occurs under two scenarios: a sale via acquisition (presumably a good outcome if the sale price is right) or shutting down the company (and calling it a dog).

From a negotiation perspective, liquidation preferences have the following variables:

- *Liquidation multiple:* Defined as multiple of the amount invested, practitioners set a multiple of, say, one time the value of the original investment. This essentially translates to investors recovering the amount invested. The multiple is an indicator of market dynamics, and while one time is the standard norm in a healthy market, at times the multiple has scaled up to as much as 10 times. In the third quarter of 2010, 85 percent of the transactions had a multiple of one to two times.
- *Straight convertible preferred or nonparticipating:* In a nonparticipating liquidation preference, investors are entitled to the amount they invested and dividends, if any. That is it: They do not get anything more. Under certain circumstances, where an earn-out amount has been offered upon achieving certain milestones, investors can get a

higher return when the preferred shares are converted to common. Thus, practitioners should ensure they have the option to choose the greater of the two scenarios.

- *Participating preferred (or, as entrepreneurs call it, a double dip):* In this scenario, investors first recover the amount invested, dividends, and the multiple agreed on. The double dip occurs when they participate—a much kinder term—which means the preferred shareholders get to enjoy the spoils with the common shareholders on an as-converted basis. Market trends indicate that about 50 percent of the transactions conducted fall in this category.
- *Capped participation:* A smart entrepreneur may have invented this term, which essentially caps the return any investor can get. A typical cap would be, say, 2.5X of the original amount invested. Typically, about 40 percent of participating transactions are capped.

As Table 19.9 illustrates, liquidation preferences can have a significant impact on the rate of return, but it is primarily a downside protection mechanism for investors. At larger exit values, these preferences do not demonstrate a significant impact on the common shareholders or the IRR.

Assumptions:

- Acquisition value for company = $4 million
- Investment = $900,000
- Time to exit after initial investment = 3 years
- Dividends at 8 percent per annum, noncumulative

TABLE 19.9 Liquidation Preference and Its Impact on IRR and Common Shareholders

	4×	2.5× No Cap	2.5× Capped	1×
Liquidation multiple (A)	$3,600,000	$2,250,000	$2,250,000	$ 900,000
Dividends (B)	$ 216,000	$ 216,000	$ 216,000	$ 216,000
Balance (C = Acquisition Value − (A) − (B))	$ 184,000	$1,534,000	$1,534,000	$2,884,000
As common (D = 47% of C)	$ 86,480	$ 726,631	$ 726,631	$1,366,105
Total to investors (A + B + D) =	$3,902,480	$3,192,631	$2,250,000	$2,482,105
IRR to investors	63%	52%	36%	40%
Balance for common shareholders	$ 97,520	$ 807,369	$1,750,000	$1,517,895

Stacking of Liquidation Preferences over Multiple Rounds

If you are a Series A investor and a Series B investor arrives and stacks on his or her preferences on top of yours, the scenario could get more complex due to the misalignment of interests between the various parties (two separate classes of preferred shareholders and common shareholders). Brad Feld of the Foundry Group writes:

> *As with many VC-related issues, the approach to liquidation preferences among multiple series of stock varies (and is often overly complex for no apparent reason). There are two primary approaches: (1) the follow-on investors will stack their preferences on top of each other: series B gets its preference first, then series A, or (2) the series are equivalent in status (called pari passu . . .) so that series A and B share pro-ratably until the preferences are returned. Determining which approach to use is a black art which is influenced by the relative negotiating power of the investors involved, ability of the company to go elsewhere for additional financing, economic dynamics of the existing capital structure, and the phase of the moon.*
>
> *Higher Liquidation Preferences = Demotivated Founders and Employees*[10]

Excessive liquidation preferences benefit only the investors and reduce the potential outcomes for common shareholders, including management and founders. When those who are working hard to create value see that all they would get is W2-like returns, the desire to perform and create significant value diminishes. Brad Feld explains: "The greater the liquidation preference ahead of management and employees, the lower the potential value of the management/employee equity. There's a fine balance here and each case is situation specific, but a rational investor will want a combination of 'the best price' while insuring 'maximum motivation' of management and employees. Obviously what happens in the end is a negotiation and depends on the stage of the company, bargaining strength, and existing capital structure, but in general most companies and their investors will reach a reasonable compromise regarding these provisions."

An elegant solution to protect the founders could be the founder's liquidity preference. Although rarely used, it is a creative approach to address the challenges wherein the founders can wash out completely. "Creating a special class of common stock for the founders with a special liquidation preference is not typical, but it is an option that offers investors a great deal of flexibility and creativity," writes attorney Jonathan Gworek. Gworek recommends a win-win approach where a founder's liquidity preference creates a financial threshold for the founders, especially if they have invested significant capital prior to any outside investments. Such a clause allows for the founders to retain a floor, a minimum position for value created by the entrepreneurs.[11]

Professors Colin Blaydon and Fred Wainwright, who head the Center for Private Equity and Entrepreneurship at the Tuck School of Business at Dartmouth, write that "risk-reducing mechanisms were seen to be counterproductive—an attempt to 'close the barn door after the horse was gone.'" Blaydon and Wainwright conclude, "the continued prevalence of a participation feature in deal structures today indicates that the VC community either has less confidence in the potential growth of portfolio companies or a lower appetite for risk." Furthermore, they point out that participation "sets a precedent for terms in subsequent financing rounds" and that the "VCs who funded the earlier rounds . . . will now have to transfer some of that hard won value to the new investors."[12] It becomes a karma thing, as a Series A investor tries to squeeze the entrepreneur; when the Series B investors come in, they love to jump in and do the same. Jack Ahrens of TGap Ventures says, "It is best to avoid any multiple preferences and clever terms—it becomes a rat's nest and does not do anybody any good." At the early stage of investment, simpler is better. "You are betting on the market and the CEO—let's not get too tied up in preferences and such legalese when there are no revenues and no product," says Rick Heitzmann, FirstMark Capital.[13]

Consider the typical trends of liquidation preferences. Note that these vary with market conditions.

- An average of 40 percent of financing uses senior liquidation preferences. As the series scale up to Series C and D, senior liquidation preferences grow, from 30 percent (at Series B) to 60 percent (at Series E or higher). Naturally, the later investors are risk averse and want to have the exit prior to the other investors, and thus they demand better preferences.
- At least 20 percent of the financings have multiple liquidation preferences. As much as 85 percent of the Series A financings have a multiple of 1X to 2X, with the rest being 2X to 5X. In certain market conditions, when capital supply shrinks, or if the company may have struggled, a 5X preference was observed.
- At Series A, about 50 percent of financings were participating preferred. Of these, about 25 percent to 50 percent had no cap. The rest were capped anywhere from 2X to 5X.

ANTIDILUTION PROTECTIONS

Antidilution protection is a downside protection mechanism that protects existing investors when a company is forced to accept a down round, which is a lower share price compared to what the previous investors have paid. Existing investors receive additional shares, and their position is adjusted based on the price of the down round. The common shareholders, typically the management and founders, endure the maximum pain in such circumstances. An investor-friendly term, it forces the management team to retain value, execute on its milestones, and ensure value is created in an effective and timely manner. However, down rounds can occur with changes in burn rates (as unanticipated issues occur). Poor market conditions could significantly affect a company's ability to raise future rounds of capital.

Antidilution provisions fall into three categories:

1. *Full ratchet*: An investor-friendly provision, this has the largest impact on the common shareholders. The full ratchet converts the price of *all* the previously sold shares down to the price of the current round, irrespective of the amount raised or the number of shares issued.
2. *Broad-based weighted average*: A company-friendly provision (well, a true company-friendly provision equals no antidilution provisions), this clause has the least impact of all on common shareholders as it is based on the weighted average of the outstanding shares, including options and warrants.
3. *Narrow-based weighted average*: The same as broad-based, this eliminates the options and warrants and thus has a lower impact on common shareholders.

The norm is weighted average (either broad-based or narrow-based), and thus practitioners are better off staying in the middle of the road.

As Table 19.10 illustrates, the impact of antidilution on Series A would have been significant if there were no protective provisions. This is illustrated in the line "Additional ownership due to antidilution protection." The full ratchet offers maximum additional ownership, while the weighted average drops the ownership proportionally. Notice the significant drop in ownership for common shareholders.

In this example, we assumed Series A price per share equals $9 with 100,000 Series A shares sold. We also assume Series A amount raised equals $900,000 and Series B price per share equals $4.50, with 250,000 Series B shares, with amount raised equals $1,125,000.

TABLE 19.10   Impact of Antidilution Provisions on Ownership

	Series A	Full Ratchet (%) Series B	Weighted Average— Broad (%)
Series B preferred		42.6	44.5
Series A preferred	47	17	17.8
Additional Ownership Due to Antidilution Protection		17	13.2
Common	43	18.9	19.8
Options	10	4.4	4.6

Frank Demmler, who has participated in over 200 investments, points out that if Series A antidilution leaves little ownership for common/management, the Series B investors will have a due concern. Often, Series B investors will drive renegotiation between Series A and management to find a satisfactory middle ground. "The bottom line is that under most circumstances, full ratchet antidilution protection will be completely waived, while weighted average is likely to be accepted."[14]

So why negotiate for something that will potentially be renegotiated anyway? Over 90 percent of the financing rounds used weighted average antidilution.[15] These percentages vary slightly as capital supply-and-demand conditions vary. It is best to stick with weighted average antidilution.

Dividends

While most early-stage practitioners know that dividends are neither expected nor declared by the board, the provision is included in the term sheet. The investor-friendly language is to seek cumulative dividends to juice up returns at the time of an exit. The data trends indicate that about 40 percent of Series A financings seek cumulative dividends. In some years, as much as 80 percent of Series A financings sought cumulative dividends.

As we can see in Table 19.11, liquidation preferences, combined with the antidilution provisions, impact the overall economics significantly.

Pay-to-Play

Usually, this clause comes into effect when several investors have joined the club, say at Series B, Series C, or later. The provision tries to keep the syndicate together and ensure that all investors continue to participate in future rounds, especially when times are bad. As venture funds of varying shapes, sizes, and

TABLE 19.11   Key Economic Terms and the Middle Path

Economics	Investor Friendly	Middle of the Road	Company Friendly
Liquidation preferences	2× or higher, no cap, participating preferred	1× participating preferred	No liquidation preferences
Antidilution preferences	Full ratchet	Weighted average— broad	No antidilution preferences or weighted average—narrow
Dividends (as and when declared by the board)	12% cumulative	8% noncumulative, as and when declared	None

Source: Adapted from Alex Wilmerding, Term Sheets & Valuations: An Inside Look at the Intricacies of Term Sheets & Valuations (Boston, MA: Aspatore Books, 2003).

motivations join the syndicate, it is likely that Fund A will not have as much ammunition as Fund B. Or, views of Fund A may differ with Fund B on the company's exit potential, execution plan, or business strategy. The pay-to-play provision would mean that if Fund A is unable to invest more capital in the following rounds for any reason, it will no longer play. Fund A gets kicked out of the playground wherein its ownership is converted to common stock, resulting in the loss of preferences and any substantial economic upside.

Preemptive Rights/Right of First Refusal

Seed- and early-stage investors seek a right of first refusal (ROFR) to ensure that they can maximize their upside. Thus, when a company is ready to offer additional securities, the first call would be placed to existing shareholders. In some situations, ROFR allows investors to purchase any founder's stock that may be up for sale. This tactic is used by early-stage investors who place a smaller amount of capital, and as the opportunity matures, they are able to increase their ownership and take advantage of the potential upside.

MILESTONE-BASED FINANCING: RISK MITIGATION OR DISTRACTION

Staged financing is used in seed- and early-stage investments, and the primary reason is to remove risk from the opportunity. Completion of a prototype and customer validations are a few examples of milestones that are typically used to structure investments. Recall Peter Thiel, who agreed to invest in Facebook with the precondition that his note would convert to equity after they reached a certain number of users. The company did not meet its milestone, and yet when the time came to convert, Thiel did not hold back. Staged financings can provide incentive for the teams to perform and move faster, and entrepreneurs can be assured that the tranches of capital will arrive as the milestones are completed. But is it that simple?

"Milestone-based financing forces the management to either declare victory too soon, or worse, it distracts them from a potentially bigger opportunity—in an evolutionary stage, milestones can push the founders in the wrong direction," says Jack Ahrens of TGap Ventures. If you choose to use milestone-based financing, consider the primary question: Can you disengage if the milestones are not met?

Furthermore, the caveats are as follows:

- *Definition of milestone:* Avoid ambiguity and insist on measurable and simple definitions. Instead of a broad, complete beta, it would be prudent to identify the top three key functions that the technology should meet.
- *Amount necessary to reach milestone:* If an entrepreneur prepares the budget, a practitioner needs to ensure that the resources, amounts, and line items are vetted. On the flip side, if you squeeze the amount down, be prepared to accept the blame: A common excuse from entrepreneurs can be "We couldn't meet the milestones because we did not have enough money to start with."

As with most terms, flexibility, speed, and simplicity are the keys to a successful start.

GOVERNANCE AND CONTROL: PROTECTING YOUR SECURITIES

All governance and control aspects in any term sheet are designed to protect the ownership interests of investors. Security ownership can be challenged because of internal performance issues (poor performance leads to cash challenges or lower valuation) or external financings (down rounds, debt obligations). An investor attempts to manage these conditions by controlling the board by governance and control mechanisms.

Consider the Series A investor in NewCo, who owns a 47 percent interest and thus is a minority ownership from a control perspective. But special voting rights and preferences allow such an investor to exercise control over key aspects of the company. As described in Table 19.12, typical board approval items include the following:

- *Officers and management hiring, firing, and compensation*: These provisions allow the board to select the CEO, and if necessary, replace him or her if performance is lax.
- *Stock option programs*: These have a dilutive impact on the overall shareholders if an option pool is not established. Establishing an option pool may require shareholder approval. If an option pool is established, the board would approve grant of options to key executives.
- *Annual budgets*: As the annual budgets are directly related to the direction of the company and spend rates, the board typically approves all major budget items.
- *Debt obligations*: Any secured debt creates a lien on assets of a company and can be a drain on the cash. Under the right circumstances of growth, venture-backed companies raise debt. The board would approve any debt obligations to ensure they are aligned with the CEO/CFO's plans and performance.

Protective provisions included in the term sheet would minimize any impact to the value or preferences of the security:

- *Ownership/shares*: Any issuance of stock would impact the ownership and dilute current owners. Furthermore, the pricing of stock, the amount being raised, and the type of investors are all approved by existing investors/board members.
- *Mergers/acquisitions and co-sale*: Investors and all shareholders would approve such moves, as these impact ownership and economics.
- *Changes to the certificate of incorporation, voting, and bylaws*: Any changes in the corporate structure are typically approved by all shareholders and can impact the powers of the board.
- *Changes to board or election procedures*: Existing board members typically approve any changes to the board structure (additions of seats, observers) that occur as newer investors come to the table. Investors control the board dynamics closely, especially in the early stages of the development and growth.

EXIT-RELATED PROVISIONS

These provisions come into effect at the time of the sale of the company. As very few companies go public, savvy investors do not invest too much

TABLE 19.12 Key Economic Terms and the Middle Path

Term	What It Means	Importance to Investors	Key Negotiation Variables
Governance Terms: Those That Impact Control of the Company			
Board composition	Number of seats for Series A, common, and independent shareholders	Allows for control and protection of security	Number of seats, how the board structure can be changed, rights of preferred shareholders vis-à-vis the rest
Board-approval items	Board approves hiring of executives, employment and compensation agreements, issuance of stock options, annual operating plan, and incurrence of debt obligations or contracts above a certain financial limit	To protect the ownership and equity, board would approve key business decisions that may impact the operations or the equity structure of the company.	David Cowan of Bessemer Venture Partners says, "As long as the ink is black—if the company is doing fine—I don't care much about control provisions."*
Protective provisions	Allows for protection of security interests	Preferred shareholders will approve all changes to securities, board structure, mergers, redemption of stock, and amendments to articles of incorporation	Most of these terms are standard, and very few practitioners open these up for negotiation.
Employment and vesting for management	Keeps management team focused on building the business	Aligns interests of founders and investors	Employment agreements, stock vesting, restrictions on co-sale, creation of option pool, key man insurance, noncompete provisions

*Brad Feld, "Term Sheet: Liquidation Preference," *FeldThoughts* (blog), January 4, 2005, www.feld.com/wp/archives/2005/01/term-sheet-liquidation-preference.html.

time and effort splitting hairs around these terms. For the most part, these are treated as boilerplate language. A brief description of the terms follows.

Redemption

Certain practitioners are tempted to sell the stock back to the company and redeem their investment at, say, the sixth anniversary. This provision is typically triggered when the company has made modest middle-of-the-road progress, but it is not going to be a significant exit for investors. Unkind expressions address these as the living dead. This provision implies that the investment is more a debt-like instrument and attempts to recover some or all of the investment.

Drag-Along Rights/Tagalong Rights and Co-Sale Agreements

These rights allow investors to "drag" the shareholders to an exit. The dragging comes in when a specified percentage of shareholders wants to sell the company, but another group, typically, the founders or common shareholders, refuses to sell. The price may not be right, or they may see a bigger, better opportunity in the future. The investors may have given up on the opportunity and choose to get what they can. Drag-along provisions allow investors to sell the package as a whole—if any investor is unwilling to sell, it could block an exit, and this provision allows the sale to occur. In tagalong provisions, also called co-sale agreements, the founders or management either give up or find a third party to whom they can sell their shares. The tagalong rights allow investors to tag along with the founders and offer their shares for sale as well.

Conversion to Common at Public Offering, Registration Rights, and Piggyback Rights

In the rare event a portfolio company is ready to file for an IPO, all securities convert to one class: common stock. This allows for smoother marketing and share price establishment. Thus, the preferences established will vanish. In *Venture Capital Due Diligence*, Justin Camp writes, "Convertible instruments allow investors to take full advantage of the protections offered by preferred stock . . . until they are no longer necessary, and then allow them to forgo such protections. When investors invoke registration rights, they push the company to register the stock or piggyback on other registrations. Once registered, venture capitalists are able to sell their stock in the public markets."[16] Investors can demand registration, although several factors come into play, primarily the revenues, growth rate, and state of the public markets. Piggyback rights obligate companies to let investors piggyback on the registration.

OTHER TERMS

These terms fall neither in the economic nor the governance category but are important to align the interest of investors and management.

Employment-Related Terms

All founders and key management team members should execute employment agreements. Other important terms such as stock vesting, restrictions on co-sale, key man insurance, and noncompete provisions are included to ensure management teams are aligned with the long-term goal of value creation.

Employment agreements clearly state a founder or manager's roles, responsibilities, and deliverables. These agreements incentivize the team to stay with the company, especially through tough times, and to create value. Stock vesting for founders is often negotiated aggressively to ensure that after the investment is made, the founders remain and continue to add value to the company. A separate stock option plan is typically created after investment and governed under the auspices of the board. This plan determines the dynamics of the employee stock options. Should an employee be terminated, his or her ability to exercise the balance of options will lapse.

Vesting can occur on a quarterly basis over a three- to four-year period. Acceleration of vesting upon acquisition is considered suitable to reward management for having created value. The contention is amplified when founders quit or are fired. The vesting debate can create a fair amount of distraction and hence needs to be addressed in employment agreements.

The restrictions on co-sale have been seen in a new light, especially when founders are allowed to take significant portions of their stock and liquidate it prior to a sale or IPO. Key man provisions are methods of ensuring that investors are protected if key management team members were to become unavailable due to death or disability.[17] Noncompete provisions can be enforced in certain states, but not all. The duration (number of years) and scope (geography, sector) of the noncompete agreement needs to be negotiated diligently.

The following miscellaneous conditions are prescribed in the term sheets:

- *Exclusivity and no-shop clause:* This clause is included to ensure entrepreneurs do not use the opportunity to get an auction going or to find better terms of investment by shopping the term sheet around.
- *Closing date and conditions:* This clause helps all parties, legal counsel for both sides especially, to complete the transaction on a certain date and meet any conditions prior to closing

■ *Nondisclosure, press/media:* Ensuring confidentiality, this is essentially an embargo on both parties to avoid making any premature public statements.

SYNDICATING INVESTMENTS

An analysis of more than 2,000 venture transactions shows that syndication was found to be highest in biotechnology investments (in over 60 percent of investments) and lowest in the software sector (with only 37 percent of investments). Syndication was least at the seed stages and increased in later stages.[18] Risk does bring investors together, especially in biotech sectors where capital intensity is significant.

Whether seeking syndicate investors or being asked to be one, the simple rule applies: Does the combined intellectual and financial acumen allow for the better outcomes of the investment opportunity? When inviting syndicate investors into opportunities led by Walden International, Lip-Bu Tan follows a blended approach of the heart and the head: "I look for complementary skill sets in syndicate investors so that the combined power of the board is higher in terms of value add. I am also very picky, so the core philosophy of building a company for the long term rather than the short term is important. Mutual respect is important, as is the willingness to come up with a solution that is best for the company. No ego trips!" Tom Perkins, while seeking the first round of funding for Tandem Computer, wrote about his experiences: "I showed our business plan, which I had mostly written myself, to all the local potential investors with no luck. . . . The investors' rejection was based solely on general worries over the companies in the field. . . . They had little understanding of the technical breakthrough we had achieved and how difficult it would be for those competitors to duplicate our effort and circumvent our patents. . . .These were financiers . . . who maybe were clever with money but who had no . . . confidence in technology, the kind of investors who relied on hired experts to tell them what to think."[19]

Practitioners need to conduct due diligence on each other with the same rigor they would apply to looking at new opportunities, but add a few other parameters to the mix: What are the motives of the syndicate investor? Is it a true partnership? Are their interests aligned? Do they have the ability to withstand the tremors?

Ideally, smaller funds would invite larger funds to participate with the optimistic outlook that as the capital needs for the company grow, the larger funds will be able to lead the future rounds. If a small fund invites a larger fund to come in as a syndicate partner, it creates a win-win situation for both funds. A smaller fund generates the opportunity and acts as a feeder to the larger fund. In turn, the larger fund can invest substantially higher amounts as needed by the company. The smaller fund needs to consider how antidilution and pay-to-play provisions could affect the smaller fund if the opportunity does not progress as desired. The loss appetite also differs with the size and the stage of the fund.

"It took me 15 years to crack into the inner circle of the Silicon Valley venture network. To be invited to co-invest in opportunities with the likes of John Doerr, Promod Haque, and other established practitioners takes time—you have to earn their respect as a value-add partner," says Lip-Bu Tan.

Syndication caveats include choosing your partners with care. As one practitioner pointed out, "keeping a bad venture capitalist is worse than the first time bad entrepreneur."[20] Syndicate with the ones you trust—you know how they will react in bad situations. A partnership of *unequals* can be challenging. As a practitioner remarked, "I would hope that we would get an equal ownership, but if Sequoia says they want 75 percent and we keep 25 percent, we'd be happy with that."[21]

KEEPING TERM SHEETS SIMPLE

Seed investments often focus on few key parameters such as amount of investment and valuation (and hence the percentage of investor ownership). Other terms such as liquidation preferences, antidilution, board seats, and information rights are mentioned for clarity but are not heavily negotiated (see Figure 19.1).

When Silicon Valley lawyer Ted Wang decided to simplify the standard hundred-page term sheet, he started with Mahatma Gandhi's quote: "First they ignore you. Then they laugh at you. Then they fight you. Then you win." In his uncommonly modest style, Wang wrote, "I hesitate to use a quote from one of the greatest people ever to grace planet earth, and certainly the question of how to structure early-stage investment is a laughable cause as compared to the rights that Gandhi (also a lawyer) fought to advance. That said, I think this quote accurately captures the life-cycle of creating a simple set of documents for early-stage investment."[22]

The motivation: "Start-up company lawyers are under an intense pressure to keep our fees low on these deals and we find ourselves struggling to meet our clients' expectations around pricing," wrote Wang, who represents companies like Facebook, Dropbox, and Twitter.[23] "The result is that these small Series A deals have become a source of unwanted tension between us and our clients."[24]

FIGURE 19.1 Seed investments—simpler the better. Just use a tip jar. (Seen at a Palo Alto, CA restaurant)

Wang's simplified documents are relevant to the seed-stage investors as well as being succinct. And he may have had a lot of unlearning to do, as he eliminated language that had been a part of term sheets for 20 to 30 years. The simplified term sheet, about 30 pages in all, eliminates antidilution, registration rights, and closing conditions. Even more so, it reduces the time and expenses for completing the investments.

"The big reason we are doing it is that we think for these early-stage rounds, bashing over these terms does damage and only brings mistrust," Mark Andreessen was quoted as saying. "VCs who do angel rounds should be acting like a VC in a VC round and acting like an angel in an angel round. The problems come when VCs act like VCs in angel rounds."[25]

Here is what a simple Series Seed term sheet[26] looks like:

Securities:	Shares of Series Seed Preferred Stock of the Company
Amount of this round:	$1,000,000
Investors:	Name of funds and amounts committed by each
Price Per Share:	Price per share (the "*Original Issue Price*"), based on a pre-money valuation of _____, including an available option pool of __% of the fully diluted capitalization of the Company after giving effect to the proposed financing.
Liquidation Preference:	**One** times the Original Issue Price plus declared but unpaid dividends on each share of Series Seed, balance of proceeds paid to Common. A merger, reorganization or similar transaction will be treated as liquidation.
Conversion:	Convertible into one share of Common (subject to proportional adjustments for stock splits, stock dividends and the like) at any time at the option of the holder.
Voting Rights:	Votes together with the Common Stock on all matters on an as-converted basis. Approval of majority of Series Seed required to (i) adversely change rights of the Preferred Stock; (ii) change the authorized number of shares; (iii) authorize a new series of Preferred Stock having rights senior to or on parity with the Preferred Stock; (iv) redeem or repurchase any shares (other than pursuant to the Company's right of repurchase at original cost); (v) declare or pay any dividend; (vi) change the number of directors; or (vii) liquidate or dissolve, including any change of control.
Financial Information:	Investors who have invested at least $____ will receive standard information and inspection rights and management rights letter.
Registration Rights:	Investors shall have standard registration rights.
Participation Right:	Major investors will have the right to participate on a pro rata basis in subsequent issuances of equity securities.
Board of Directors:	Two directors elected by holders of a majority of common stock, the right to elect one by investors.

Expenses:	Company to reimburse investors for fees and expenses (not to exceed _____).
Future Rights:	The Series Seed will be given the same rights as the next series of Preferred Stock (with appropriate adjustments for economic terms).
Founder Matters	Each founder shall have four years vesting beginning from the date of his involvement with the Company. Each founder shall have assigned all relevant IP to the Company prior to closing.
Closing Date	No later than 30 days from the date of this terms sheet.

This term sheet developed by Wang is an elegant solution to the classic, dense, several-hundred-page term sheet. The proposed model is better and minimizes legal expenses, particularly for smaller seed investments.

Separately, the law offices of Wilson Sonsini Goodrich and Rosati (WSGR) have developed an online tool that generates a venture financing term sheet based on inputs/responses to an online questionnaire.[27]

In 1954, Roald Dahl, popular writer of children's fiction, wrote a short story, "The Great Automatic Grammatizator," in which a mechanically minded man concludes that the rules of grammar follow mathematical principles. He creates a mammoth grammatizator—a machine that can write a prize-winning novel in 15 minutes. WSGR has developed such an engine, a term-sheetizator if you will, that takes a few inputs and develops fascinating term sheets.

The WSGR term sheet generator has an informational component, with basic tutorials and annotations on financing terms. This term sheet generator is a modified version of a tool that the firm uses internally, which comprises document automation tools that the firm uses to generate start-up and venture financing-related documents. Because it has been designed as a generic tool that takes into account a number of options, this version of the term sheet generator is fairly expansive and includes significantly more detail than would likely be found in a customized application.

THE CLOSING PROCESS: AFTER THE TERM SHEET

To approve the investment, any company would follow these steps:

- Board approval of the investment via formal resolution
- Majority of shareholders consent via vote

- Execution of final documents: Once the term sheet is executed, attorneys draft detailed documents that include:
  - Share purchase agreement or subscription agreement, including purchase details, company's representations and warranties, board composition, and voting matters
  - Investor rights agreement (IRA) including information rights, preemptive rights, registration rights, and affirmative and negative covenants[28]
    - Affirmative covenants (or actions the company should take), which include maintaining the existence of the corporation, paying taxes, maintaining insurance, complying with key agreements, maintaining accounts, and allowing access to premises
    - Negative covenants (or actions the company should avoid), which include changing the business, amending the charter, issuing stock, merging the company, conducting dealings with related parties, making investments, or incurring debt or financial liabilities
    - Modifications to the certificate of incorporation to allow for the new shareholders to be recognized, as well as ensure that the company does not take any actions that are not aligned with preferred shareholders' rights
    - Issuing of share certificates to shareholders/investors

Structuring a simple terms sheet is an art form as well as a science. The goal is to grasp the risks inherent within the opportunity and develop a set of conditions that would allow the investor to generate target returns. At the very early stages of an investment, savvy investors invest small amounts and get a seat at the table—as the opportunity grows, they double up. It is prudent to establish these terms as middle of the road. Any exotic elements would cast a practitioner in an unfavorable light.

The lead investor, the one with the maximum investment, typically sets the terms. As goes the golden rule—he who has the gold makes the rules. The other syndicate investors have a choice—to accept those terms or not—but seldom have significant negotiating leverage. In anticipation of future financing, existing shareholders, at times and without much reason, will attempt to bump up the value significantly. If the bump-up is not justified, this creates the illusion of progress and can cause more harm than any benefit in the long run.

Everything that can be renegotiated will be renegotiated. In as much as 30 percent of subsequent financing, new investors renegotiated terms established at previous rounds. The most commonly renegotiated terms are (1) automatic conversion price, (2) liquidation preferences, (3) redemption maturity, and (4) funding milestones, vesting provisions, or performance benchmarks.[29]

As follow-on rounds occur, it is typical for the new lead investor of the follow-on round to set the valuation and terms. Down-round financings are normal occurrences in the business of venture capital—companies often miss milestones and run low on cash. The only valuation that matters is the one at the time of exit.

The entire philosophy of term sheets is summarized in Steven Kaplan and Per Stromberg's words: "The elements of control: Board rights, voting rights and liquidation rights are allocated such that if a firm performs poorly, the venture capitalists obtain full control. *As performance improves, the entrepreneur retains/obtains more control rights. If the firm performs very well, the venture capitalists retain their cash flow rights, but relinquish most of their control and liquidation rights.* [italics added]"[30]

NOTES

1. Mark Suster, "Want to Know How VCs Calculate Valuation Differently from Founders?" *Both Sides of the Table* (blog), July 22, 2010, accessed January 2, 2014, www.bothsidesofthetable.com/2010/07/22/want-to-know-how-vcs-calculate-valuation-differently-from-founders.
2. David Kirkpatrick, *The Facebook Effect: The Inside Story of the Company That Is Connecting the World* (New York: Simon & Schuster, 2010).
3. Josh Koppelman, speaking at Upround Conference, San Francisco, 2013.
4. Aswath Damodaran, "Valuing Young, Start-Up and Growth Companies: Estimation Issues and Valuation Challenges," June 12, 2009, available at SSRN: http://ssrn.com/abstract=1418687.
5. Rick Heitzmann (First Mark Capital), in discussions with the author, February 2011.
6. Amy E. Knaup, "Survival and Longevity in the Business Employment Dynamics Data," *Monthly Labor Review* (May 2005), 50–56; Amy E. Knaup and M.C. Piazza, "Business Employment Dynamics Data: Survival and Longevity," *Monthly Labor Review* (September 2007), 3–10.
7. Aswath Damodaran, "Valuing Young, Start-Up and Growth Companies."
8. Mark Suster, "Is Convertible Debt Preferable to Equity?" *Both Sides of the Table* (blog), August 30, 2010, www.bothsidesofthetable.com/2010/08/30/is-convertible-debt-preferable-to-equity.
9. Mark Suster, "Want to Know How VC's Calculate Valuation?"
10. Brad Feld, *Feld Thoughts* (blog).
11. Jonathan D. Gworek, "The Making of a Winning Term Sheet: Understanding What Founders Want," Morse Barnes-Brown Pendleton PC, June 2007, accessed February 9, 2011, www.mbbp.com/resources/business/founder_termsheet.html.

12. Colin Blaydon and Fred Wainwright, "It's Time to Do Away with Participating Preferred," *Venture Capital Journal*, July 2006, accessed February 11, 2011, http://mba.tuck.dartmouth.edu/pecenter/research/VCJ_July_2006.pdf.
13. Rick Heitzmann, in discussions with the author.
14. Frank Demmler, "Practical Implications of Anti-Dilution Protection," accessed February 10, 2011, www.andrew.cmu.edu/user/fd0n/54%20Practical%20Implications%20Anti-dilution%20excel.htm.
15. Based on a survey conducted by law firms Wilmer Hale and Fenwick & West.
16. Justin J. Camp, *Venture Capital Due Diligence: A Guide to Making Smart Investment Choices and Increasing Your Portfolio Returns* (Hoboken, NJ: John Wiley and Sons, 2002), 140.
17. While this may seem unimportant, I am aware of at least one situation where the founder of a venture-backed company died in a car accident. In another situation, the founder had an ugly divorce case that caused undue distraction to the board, shareholders, and the company while his ownership in the company was being divvied up.
18. Kara Swisher, "Series Seed Documents–With an Assist from Andreessen Horowitz–To Help Entrepreneurs With Legal Hairballs," All Things Digital (blog), March 1, 2010, http://allthingsd.com/20100301/series-seed-documents-with-a-big-assist-from-andreessen-horowitz-set-to-launch-to-help-entrepreneurs-with-legal-hairballs/.
19. Tom Perkins, *Valley Boy: The Education of Tom Perkins* (New York: Gotham Books, 2007), 112.
20. Jennifer M. Walske, Andrew Zacharakis, and Laurel Smith-Doerr, "Effects of Venture Capital Syndication Networks on Entrepreneurial Success," Babson College Entrepreneurship Research Conference (BCERC) 2007, Frontiers of Entrepreneurship Research 2007, available at SSRN: http://ssrn.com/abstract=1060081.
21. Ibid.
22. Ted Wang, "Version 2.0 and Why Series Seed Documents Are Better Than Capped Convertible Notes," *Series Seed* (blog), September 2, 2010, www.seriesseed.com.
23. Ted Wang, "Reinventing the Series A," *VentureBeat* (blog), September 17, 2007, http://venturebeat.com/2007/09/17/reinventing-the-series-a.
24. Anthony Ha, "Ted Wang and Andreessen Horowitz Try to Reinvent the Seed Round," *VentureBeat* (blog), March 2, 2010, http://venturebeat.com/2010/03/02/series-seed-andreessen-horowitz.
25. Kara Swisher, "Series Seed Documents—With an Assist from Andreessen Horowitz—To Help Entrepreneurs With Legal Hairballs," *All Things*

Digital (blog), March 1, 2010, http://allthingsd.com/20100301/series-seed-documents-with-a-big-assist-from-andreessen-horowitz-set-to-launch-to-help-entrepreneurs-with-legal-hairballs/. Marc Andreessen's venture firm, Andreessen Horowitz, was the first to agree to use Series Seed documents, followed by uberangel Ron Conway and venture capital firms including First Round Capital, SoftTech VC, True Ventures, Polaris Ventures, and Charles River Ventures.

26. From Series Seed, developed by Fenwick & West, LLP, www.seriesseed.com.

27. See www.wsgr.com/wsgr/display.aspx?sectionname=practice/termsheet.htm.

28. Justin J. Camp, *Venture Capital Due Diligence: A Guide to Making Smart Investment Choices and Increasing Your Portfolio Returns* (Hoboken, NJ: John Wiley and Sons, 2002), 167–173.

29. Steven N. Kaplan and Per Stromberg, "Financial Contracting Theory Meets the Real World: An Empirical Analysis of Venture Capital Contracts" (CRSP working paper 513), April 26, 2000, accessed February 11, 2011, http://ssrn.com/abstract=218175.

30. Ibid.

CHAPTER 20

Serving on the Board

"The biggest consistent irritant were coinvestors more intent on talking over management, rather than listening to them, in the board room."

— Donald Valentine, Founder, Sequoia Capital

In a narrative account of a business, there is usually only room for one hero. When we look at the plucky start-up or entrepreneurial business venture, the company founder or CEO is deified as a visionary who forges a groundbreaking idea into reality against all odds. In this account, the CEO is described as a captain of industry, creating with mighty volition a brilliant management team that works tirelessly to craft the idea into a viable business. Cast into a secondary supporting role is the venture capitalist (VC). Despite this more marginal role, the VC's critical contributions, such as providing the capital and financing—the lifeblood of a firm—and access to a plethora of resources, from networks and contacts to mentoring and strategic guidance, can be invaluable.

Giving entrepreneurs the opportunity to cultivate an idea with the benefits of professional management and strategic guidance is a potent formula that fast-tracks ideas and products to the market. As the gatekeeper to this highly sought-after funding, a venture capitalist is someone in the business of providing financial capital and advisory assistance at every stage of development, including by serving as a board member. At the most basic level, board members are expected to adhere to duty of care and loyalty. In a venture-backed company, these duties extend to the following:

- Value identification
- Value creation
- Sustaining value
- Asserting value via an exit/liquidity event

No corporate governance textbook can prepare someone for the challenges of the boardroom.[1] However, the basics seldom change. Thus, the goal of this chapter is to help understand and appreciate the protocols and practices of board meetings.

SELF-EDUCATION: PREPARING FOR YOUR BOARD ROLE

In early-stage companies, the business, its goals, and its challenges, complete with its cast of characters, are visible. The purpose of the pointers listed here is to initiate steps into self-orientation and education. In addition to possessing a thorough understanding of the history and evolution of the company, any practitioner needs to consider the following:

- Develop a thorough 360-degree understanding of the business, including suppliers, customers, competitive threats, and replacements. The practitioner needs to understand the cycle of cash and friction therein. This is critical.
- Understand a company's strategy and key goals. Over the next 12 months and three years, how do you see your contribution vis-à-vis issues and challenges facing such a company? ("What would keep the CEO awake at night, and how can I help?")
- Ensure you have relevant expertise to affect the stated strategy. Prepare to impact the company's challenges and demands in a disciplined and consistent manner.
- Be aware of people- and cash-related challenges. Does the team need to be augmented? What is the cash position, burn rate, and timing of the next financing round?
- Understand the current board structure and how you fit in this context.
- What are the board's external and internal challenges? Examples may include the following:
  - *External:* Compliance with tax, civil, criminal, and employment laws, any legal matters or shareholder actions.

■ *Internal:* Emotional and power dynamics between board members, excessive churn of board members or CEO, strategy du jour, product development and market adoption challenges, burn rate, and cash situation.

ROLES AND RESPONSIBILITIES OF A BOARD MEMBER

It is well known that venture capital is the financial fuel that kick-started many great companies in the past decade, but there is less familiarity with what VCs do once they sit on a company's board. Beyond financing, what kinds of support do they provide to start-ups? How do they use their investment muscle to attract and win more capital? To recruit a star management team? How do they winnow and champion the most promising drivers from the rest? "As a board, your role is to prove the business plan," says Lindsay Aspegren, founder of North Coast Technology Investors "and your only two control levers are the CEO and the budget."

The boardroom is where the VC wields the greatest influence on a company's future growth. Typically, a company board is a group of people who meet periodically and provide advice and guidance on the direction of the firm. For many start-ups and younger firms, VC board members are selected based on their influence and knowledge of the industry to help companies make a clear footprint on the market. VC boards therefore do a lot: they attract, recruit, and retain an excellent management team and fellow board members; mentor and manage the executive team; provide advisory services and expertise outside the purview of the management team; and oversee adherence to fiscal, legal, and ethical governance standards. Brad Feld, managing director of the Foundry Group, points out the simple role of any board member: "With the exception of really two decisions, I'd like to think that we work for the CEO of the company. The two decisions we really make are, one, the capital allocation decision (do we want to keep funding the company?), and two, whether we keep and support the CEO."[2]

Key Roles of a Board Member

The primary role of any board member boils down to the following:

■ *Shareholder value:* Create, sustain, and enhance shareholder value.
■ *CEO selection and assessment:* Evaluate CEO performance, transition, assist in recruitment, succession planning.

- *Governance:* Manage risk via business strategy, finance, management, market insights, and legal compliance.

The board expertise, attributes, and roles of the board members shift as the company matures. Table 20.1 demonstrates the minimum attributes required as the company evolves over time.

LEGAL REQUIREMENTS OF BOARD SERVICE

"The Basic Responsibilities of VC-Backed Company Directors," a white paper developed by the Working Group on Director Accountability and Board Effectiveness,[3] provides a framework of responsibilities and duties of VC board members. Any board member must discharge his or her actions in good faith and in the best interest of the corporation at all times. The fiduciary duties—a legal relationship between the director and the corporation of confidence and trust—are described here.

Fiduciary Duties

Duty of care: Requires a director to act with the care that an ordinarily prudent person in a like position would exercise under similar circumstances.
Requires directors to:

- Obtain information they believe is reasonably necessary to make a decision
- Make due inquiry
- Make informed decisions in good faith

Duty of loyalty: Requires a director to act in the best interests of the corporation and not in the interest of the director or a related party. Issues often arise where the director has a conflict of interest.

- Where the director or a related party has a personal financial interest in a transaction with the company (e.g., the inherent conflict between venture capitalists as directors and as representatives of their fund's interests)
- Where the director usurps a corporate opportunity that properly belongs to the company
- Where the director serves as a representative of a third-party corporation and the third-party corporation's objectives conflict with the company's best interests

TABLE 20.1 Arc of Value and the Attributes of Board Members

	Seed and Early Stage	Growth Stage	Path to Liquidity
Management goals	Product development	Sales	Management of growth
Key metrics of the company	Burn rate, time to launch	Revenues, break-even	Growth, profitability, and gross margins
Evolution of management team attributes	Technical/product development, intellectual property	Operational, sales and marketing, finance, human resources	Management, investor relations, legal
Minimum board attributes	Relevant technical expertise	Business/financial expertise	Public company–like corporate governance
Number of board members	Three	Three to five	Seven or more
Culture of the board	Experimentation, nurturing, and openness	Expansion	Control and efficiencies
Governance via committees	Establish financial reporting and financial threshold levels; approval of key legal and shareholder agreements	Establish compensation and audit committee, name formal board chairman, and perform additional financial and risk reporting	Name lead director, establish public company–like internal controls and practices, and conduct Section 404 planning
Examples of board's role in value creation	Provide access to scientific and technical luminaries, identify product development guidelines, attract first beta sites, and assess/identify development partners	Advise on sales efficiencies, accelerate customer access, provide channel partnership insights, position competitively, provide access to future rounds of capital	Maintain the course and develop regulatory and financial standards, practices, and policies

Source: Adapted from Working Group on Director Accountability and Board Effectiveness, "A Simple Guide to the Basic Responsibilities of a VC-Backed Company Director," white paper, available at www.levp.com/news/whitepapers.shtml.

- Where the director abdicates his or her oversight role or does not act in good faith

Examples of not acting in good faith include the following:

- Consciously or recklessly not devoting sufficient time to required duties
- Disregarding known risks
- Failing to exercise oversight on a sustained basis

Failing to act in good faith can have serious adverse consequences to a director, such as being exposed to personal liability for breaches of the duty of care or losing coverage under indemnification provisions or insurance policies. Generally, state corporate laws have procedures for handling interested transactions and corporate opportunities, such as requiring full disclosure and disinterested director approval.

Confidentiality and Disclosure

Board members need to protect all information and at times push the management to share all material information with the shareholders. Often, first-time CEOs do not know the extent of information that needs to be shared. A prudent board lead member and lead counsel can mentor the CEO. But the judgment rule is one that needs to be exercised to ensure that board members are protected.

Duty of confidentiality: A subset of the duty of loyalty. Requires a director to maintain the confidentiality of nonpublic information about the company.

Duty of disclosure: Requires a director, pursuant to the duties of care and loyalty, to take reasonable steps to ensure that a company provides its stockholders with all material information relating to a matter for which stockholder action is sought.

Business judgment rule: Creates a presumption that in making a business decision, the directors of a company acted on an informed basis, in good faith, and in the honest belief that the action taken was in the company's best interests. The business judgment rule helps protect a director from personal liability for allegedly bad business decisions by essentially shifting the burden of proof to a plaintiff alleging that the director did not satisfy his or her fiduciary duties. This presumption and the protections afforded by the business judgment rule are lost if the directors involved in the decision are not disinterested, do not make appropriate inquiry prior to making their decisions, or fail to establish adequate oversight mechanisms.

Good governance is akin to parenting—too lax behavior or micro-management leads to dysfunctional kids. A board member represents *all* shareholders (not just their financial interests), focuses on finding the right CEO, and then offers relentless support to her. Approving key strategic directions becomes easier with the right CEO.

A good board member first orients, then engages. Experienced board members are adept at "pattern recognition," where lessons learned from various start-ups can be amalgamated to ensure mistakes are avoided.

Most rookie VCs are bad board members. Akin to a new parent who struggles to understand his or her first child, a rookie practitioner stumbles all over, eager to display his or her acumen (or lack thereof). It gets worse if the rookie has arrived with an M.B.A., ready to divide the world into four quadrants. The only training ground for the rookie practitioner is the battlefield, but a view of apprenticeship, staying humble, and serving is critical. Find the right CEO and offer her all you can. Entrepreneurs candidly describe the rookie board members by saying "He learned how to be a director. We paid the tuition," or "My strategy is to minimize the value subtracted."[4] Many CEOs joked that some VC board members were exceedingly valuable while other micro-managers were downright pains in the posterior.

And then there are times when VCs cannot help a CEO. As Norman MacLean wrote in his novella *A River Runs Through It*, "So it is, that we can seldom help anybody. Either we don't know what part to give or maybe we don't like to give any part of ourselves. Then, more often than not, the part that is needed is not wanted. And even more often, we do not have the part that is needed. It is like the auto-supply shop over the town where they always say, 'Sorry, we are just out of that part.'"

When there is ability and receptivity, any board member should, in conjunction with the CEO, identify the value creation milestones. If the CEO is on target and plan, the best way to serve is often to stay out of the way. Much damage has been done with the intention of doing good.

There are innumerable factors in determining whether or not a company succeeds—but none is as important as the role of the VC board member. By their very nature, start-ups are not meant to be structured in a top-down, hierarchical way. More team-oriented than command-control, they must be managed from the ground up. A more engaged and flexible board member, ready to embrace and see opportunities in the challenges of growing a business, can be an asset to the firm. The key is to balance the interpersonal abilities with skills in order to stay focused on those three magic words: maximize shareholder value.

NOTES

1. Brad Feld and I have co-authored *Startup Boards* (Wiley)—an essential guide to understanding the dynamics of a startup's board of directors.
2. Brad Feld (Foundry Group) in discussions with the author, December 2010.
3. Working Group on Director Accountability and Board Effectiveness, "The Basic Responsibilities of VC-backed Company Directors," a white paper, available at www.levp.com/news/whitepapers.shtml. This white paper discusses director accountability and effectiveness and was developed by a working group of leading VCs.
4. William D. Bygrave and Jeffry A. Timmons, *Venture Capital at the Crossroads* (Watertown, MA: Harvard Business Press 1992), 220.

CHAPTER 21

Board Culture, Composition, and Orientation

*"The Chairman's statements were guarded—guarded by
enormous, labyrinthine fortifications that went on and on with
such complexity and massiveness it was almost impossible to
discover what in the world it was inside them he was guarding."*
—Robert Pirsig, *Zen and the Art of Motorcycle Maintenance*

Let us assume that a board of a venture-backed company is populated with five members: three investor representatives and two management team members. "Great boards are relatively small, generally not more than five or seven people, who understand finance and technical areas," says Seth Rudnick of Canaan Partners.[1] While in the early stages of a company's evolution, board composition may be driven by the largest shareholders, it is critical to structure the board with expertise necessary for the company's growth. "The board should have one expert each at the minimum from sales, strategy, industry expertise, and marketing areas. This allows for a balanced contribution, and the CEO can reach different experts as needed," says Rick Heitzmann of FirstMark Capital.

While board-member orientation is critical, it happens in a fairly ad hoc manner in most venture-backed companies. An orientation is essential to ensure that members understand their role and that they align their agenda with the overall mission. Members may have differing agendas: investors may seek exits at varying times, while the management team may have a desire to build the company.

BOARD ORIENTATION: ON-BOARDING A NEW MEMBER

A typical orientation meeting could be one-on-one with the lead director and would include the following:

- Introduction of the company and the management/current board members, if any
- Key goals and challenges of the company
- Board structure and goals
- Review of materials: handbook, policies, evaluation, and committees

The following orientation materials can be offered to a new board member:

- Company handbook
  - Company overview/business background
  - Management team and organization chart
  - Directors' biographies, listing, and contact information
  - Financial reports and projections
  - Capitalization table
- Board policies
- Conduct
  - Frequency of meetings
  - Establishment of committees: audit, compensation, governance
  - Decision-making procedures
  - Policy on observer roles
  - Legal responsibilities
  - Liabilities and insurance coverage, indemnification, confidentiality, conflict of interest matters and resolution
- Media and press policies
- Committees
  - Description (audit, governance, compensation committees are typically formed)
  - Composition, chaired by, purpose, and authority of each committee
- Board self-evaluation process
  - Skills, knowledge, expertise of each board member
  - Membership on various committees
  - Attendance and performance

TOWARD A BETTER BOARD CULTURE

An effective board is active, one in which members know their boundaries. Boards can be categorized as active, passive, or somewhere in between. While early-stage venture boards are predictably active, some board members can be more engaged than others. In a small family of five to seven board members, each member wields significant power, which if misused leads to distraction and the destruction of value.

Healthy boards espouse key cultural aspects such as the following:

- *Deep attention to details combined with macro views:* The ability to step back and look at the forest through the trees.
- *Promote inquiry and dissent:* The ability to challenge management assumptions and to act in a nonthreatening and nonaccusatory manner.
- *Minimize the minutiae:* The ability to organize the quality of information and discuss key issues, not irrelevant ones such as leases and janitorial services.
- *Control the flow:* The ability to focus less on packaged information, leaving more room for open discussions.
- *Establish a collegial atmosphere:* The personalities promote open and honest discussions in a respectful atmosphere; the CEO feels challenged but never threatened and is viewed as an extension of this team.[2]

Board members also fall into certain categories—these create the fabric of the boardroom dynamics. These categories include the following:

- A board member who is an authoritative pit bull, perpetually demanding higher sales revenues and lower burn rates, can create a culture of fear.
- The other end of the spectrum includes an utterly disengaged, passive board member. A practitioner describes this specimen as one who "starts every meeting by asking what the company does."[3] Such an overstretched director can never add value and does harm by distraction. Not reading the board package or being prepared for the meeting is one thing; not knowing what the company does is unpardonable and is similar to the inability to recall the names of your own children.
- Somewhere between the overstretched director and the micro-meddler sits the passive-aggressive member, who can do much harm by manipulative behavior.

Experience and luminary status of other board members, interpersonal relationships between board members, and board–CEO dynamics define the underlying ethos. Like all relationships, this fragile web has a finite life span.

However, the interpersonal dynamics of mutual respect and trust, the preparedness, the energy, and the work ethic of each board member determine the duration of the relationships beyond the life of the investment opportunity.

Honest self-assessment of individual members as well as the entire board is crucial—eager beavers and passive padres can never build a company, but in all likelihood, they will promptly take credit for all successes.

Practitioners agree that irrespective of the outcomes of the investment, the interpersonal dynamics of different members, especially in critical times, allow the building of strong relationships between practitioners as well as their venture firms.

Venture capitalist (VC) board members face many pitfalls in helping govern their companies. As Andy Rappaport of August Capital noted, "A great board cannot make a great company, but a bad board can kill a good company."[4] A badly functioning board can be characterized in many ways, but the fundamental shortcoming is not performing the self-checks necessary to ensure it stays cognizant of the real-time needs of company. A savvy VC board addresses surmounting crises head-on.

In the beginning, a venture company gets by on the momentum of an exciting idea or concept. It is not unlike a heady romance, where the founder, who is consumed by passion for an idea, meets a VC interested in investing and taking the company forward. Their courtship is mostly driven by the CEO's charisma, technical expertise, and deep and narrow ambition. The VC offers a steadying foundation, the financial stability through investment rounds.

Andy Rappaport of August Capital observes that "a CEO has to be a person who . . . focuses on one issue, a single set of objectives," while a VC board member is someone "who likes to take a broad view," which "provides a check and balance" to the CEO's intensity.[5]

Very few CEOs survive the travails of a venture-backed company from seed stage to an exit. Like any relationship, the visions and plans for a company's future can become misaligned between investors and the CEO. Harvard Business School's Noam Wasserman has labeled this situation the "paradox of success," where during the course of trying to raise money, the founder-CEOs "put themselves at the mercy of capital providers, increasing the hazard of succession."[6]

As the company grows, any skill gaps between the abilities of the founder-CEOs and the organization's needs widen precariously. VCs should be quick to dispense with the unrealistic and romantic notion of the CEO who "goes all the way" in favor of a proactive approach that involves a candid evaluation of the CEO's strengths and weaknesses. Cracks in the relationship between the CEO and VC can easily lead to turmoil if not managed well.

A common mistake on boards in the venture capital business, according to Promod Haque at Norwest Venture Partners, is "not taking timely action to change a nonperforming CEO for fear that it will rock the boat."[7]

Board members can also become vulnerable to management spin on information, relying too heavily on their CEOs for the details of the business. VCs who appointed CEOs may be unable to offer dispassionate or unbiased criticism of management actions or decisions. This type of dependency quickly becomes dysfunctional and can lead to opacity and misunderstanding.

Being a good board member is simple as long as the focus is on shareholders' value maximization. However, bad board behavior abounds aplenty. Like dysfunctional families, each board has its own quirks and challenges. But where a culture of trust and open communication exists, the boardroom can be a productive arena.

Build a Trusted Partnership

Does the CEO know each board member's strengths and draw on these resources? Does the CEO feel secure and safe, discussing issues honestly and promptly? Does the CEO assign tasks to the board members effectively? "I really struggled to reconcile my role as a board member," says Brad Feld. Brad has formed companies, sat on boards and served as chair, and taken a few of the companies public. "It took me a while to firmly get my head set in one place where I focused on being the investor rather than the guy trying to run the company. It wasn't my responsibility to fix everything in the company, but to help the company win—I would provide feedback to the CEO and work for her. Trying to direct the CEO or entrepreneur does no good for any venture capitalist."

Ensure Open Communication Channels

Communication between board members needs to be open and frequent. The biggest mistake made by board members is to presume that there is consensus at the board and not bothering to ask others if they agree. "I sit on four boards and find this happens all the time," says Pascal Levensohn. If board members fail to communicate critical issues between board meetings, these can lead to surprises as well as inefficiencies. A common tactic employed is to discuss such surprises "offline" or delay the decision until a consensus is reached. Such behavior hurts the progress of the company, and very soon the CEO realizes that the board is playing the proverbial fiddle while Rome may be burning.

According to *A Simple Guide to the Basic Responsibilities of VC-Backed Company Directors*,[8] an open door policy between management and the board is equally crucial. VCs can share their wide range of experiences in other portfolios to benefit a company, particularly during critical moments of transition (e.g., when a company is about to consider an initial public offering). VCs can also give advice on organizational planning and compensation structures. They should also serve as sounding boards for their CEOs and carve out opportunities to mentor them. This means making themselves available for broad-based consultations even outside normal board meeting schedules.

As Brad Feld puts it, "With some portfolio companies, the tempo of exchange is different, it could be daily—multiple times a day. Some want to meet—it is always useful to get face-to-face, but I let the entrepreneur decide the interaction."[9]

A good board member invites and welcomes input from CEOs, non-VC directors, and other board members, including observers. Peer reviews and self-evaluations ensure greater accountability and better governance. Effective board members also avoid the distractions of boardroom intrigue and political maneuvering and focus on the operational goals of their roles: promoting the best interest of the company and maximizing value for shareholders.

Qualities to be nurtured among members for an effective, harmonious board include strong interpersonal skills to manage the team dynamics and the relationship with management; pattern recognition skills to anticipate events and make tough decisions, often with little information; partnering experience to work with other investors with different financial stakes and to manage board meetings without getting lost in the mundane details; strong networking skills to reach out to contacts in the industry; and strong mentoring and hands-on consultative skills with the CEO and top executives to maintain open lines of communication. One tool to foster openness within the organization is to hold board retreats during critical junctures in the development of the company. Unlike other board meetings, the retreat can be used to address critical issues lingering on the table with the help of an outside facilitator.

Avoid Complacency

For any portfolio company, VCs should have an understanding of the company's competitive position in the industry to help it stay nimble and to make inroads in the market. VCs are expected to keep abreast of specific industry developments, as well as the current regulatory environment; to maintain oversight of rules and regulations; and to understand the governance requirements throughout the development of the company.

Align Interests of All Shareholders and Management

In any company, the cast of characters includes various classes of share-holders, the management team, and the board. The interests of this cast, as described in the following section, can vary across the axis of time, value creation, and capital needs.

A VC REPORTS TO LIMITED PARTNERS AND THE VENTURE CAPITAL FIRM

Any practitioner primarily seeks to maximize returns, and thus timely exits are essential. Strong returns allow the practitioner to raise the next fund and ensure longevity, possibly higher fees, and improved brand stature. Conflicts can arise when the following occur.

1. *Career:* A practitioner seeks attribution quickly in anticipation of moving on from the current fund to greener pastures.
2. *Fund-raising:* The next fund needs to be raised and there are no successes to show.
3. *Exit timing:* A practitioner cannot see the growth trajectory or strong exit value within a meaningful time frame.
4. *Financial:* This company is becoming a sinkhole and the practitioner has "checked out." "Alignment does not matter when a company grows fast or craters quickly—you need alignment with the portfolio companies that are stuck in the middle," says Brad Feld.

IMPORTANCE OF INDEPENDENT DIRECTORS

The role of an independent director can alleviate any vested behavior. "Allocating a tie-breaking vote to an unbiased arbiter commits the entrepreneur and venture capitalists to more reasonable behavior and can reduce the opportunism that would result if either party were to control the board," writes Brian Broughman.[10]

Experts studied 213 VCs' investments in 119 companies and found that VCs control board seats in 25 percent of the cases, the founders in 14 percent of the cases, and neither in 61 percent of the cases.[11] In those 61 percent of the cases, the independent director acted as an adjudicator and likely brought the two sides to a common ground.

Various studies and anecdotal assessments show that independent directors were known by both parties in as many as 70 percent of the investments.

"From a value-add perspective, access to independent thought leaders and executives is important for us," says Kenneth Van Heel, director of alternative investments at Dow Chemical Company.[12]

Independent directors are brought in because they have the mutual respect of both the company and the investors, their behavior is objective and balanced, and they have strong reputations.

NOTES

1. Seth Rudnick (Canaan Partners) in discussions with the author, September 2008.
2. Allison Leopold Tilley, "Best Practices for the High Performance Board," podcast, accessed January 30, 2011.
3. Ibid.
4. Dennis T. Jaffe and Paul N. Levensohn, "After the Term Sheet: How Venture Boards Influence the Success or Failure of Technology Companies," November 2003, accessed January 30, 2011, www.equitynet.com/media/pdf/How%20Venture%20Boards%20Influence%20The%20Success%20or%20Failure%20of%20Technology%20Companies%20(Dennis%20Jaffe,%20et%20al,%202003).pdf.
5. Ibid.
6. Pascal N. Levensohn, "Rites of Passage: Managing CEO Transition in Venture-Backed Technology Companies," January 2006, accessed January 30, 2011, www.levp.com/news/whitepapers.shtml.
7. Ibid.
8. Working Group on Director Accountability and Board Effectiveness, "A Simple Guide to the Basic Responsibilities of VC-Backed Company Directors," accessed January 31, 2011, www.nvca.org/index.php?option=com_docman&task=doc_download&gid=78&Itemid=93.
9. Brad Feld (Foundry Group), in discussions with the author, December 2010.
10. Broughman, Brian J., "The Role of Independent Directors in VC-Backed Firms," October 13, 2008, available at SSRN: http://ssrn.com/abstract=1162372.
11. Steven N. Kaplan and Per Johan Strömberg, "Financial Contracting Theory Meets the Real World: An Empirical Analysis of Venture Capital Contracts," March 2000 (CRSP working paper,No. 513), available at SSRN: http://ssrn.com/abstract=218175 or doi:10.2139/ssrn.218175.
12. Kenneth Van Heel (Dow Chemical Company Pension Fund), in discussions with the author, December 2009.

CHAPTER 22

Board Value Creation and Evaluation

"A lot of VCs have a playbook of how they are going to add value. They end up in a Socratic mode—always asking for information— constantly probing and pushing, but never turning around and saying—let me help you solve that problem. It becomes a very time-consuming affair for the CEO, and it's a very selfish act on the part of the venture capitalists."

—Brad Feld, The Foundry Group[1]

To ensure that, as a practitioner, you are on the "assets" side of the board's balance sheet, you must understand the company's short-term value drivers. For early-stage companies, the immediate drivers may be product development, which calls for technical acumen. As the product gets ready for launch, access to beta sites or first customers takes priority. Risk mitigation is interwoven at all stages, with ongoing threats from competitors or substitutes. As the company grows, access to financial resources and growth management techniques comes to bear. Finally, the exit negotiation requires the ability to align all stakeholders and ensure positive outcomes. Several variables affect this complex interplay, including the stage of the company, the present and future constitution of the board, skill sets, and investor alignment and preferences.

Generally speaking, a practitioner can support the CEO of an early-stage company by following value creation steps:

- Product development
- Sales and growth of revenues
- Improved profit margins

"The only reason top-tier venture capitalists [VCs] invite you to coinvest is because of your ability to add value—be it your domain expertise or your network of contacts. You have to win their respect and gain confidence to be invited to participate in the future deals," says Lip-Bu Tan of Walden International. A board becomes a stage where relationships are forged.[2] How a practitioner engages with the company determines the strength of those relationships.

PricewaterhouseCoopers conducted a study of over 350 companies that had received seed or first-round financing.[3] There were three value creation metrics:

1. *Strategy:* Market size, competitive position, and business model
2. *Resources:* Cash flow, investor value contributed, and strength of management team
3. *Performance:* Product development, channels/alliances, and customer acquisition

The study concluded that a company that experienced a successful IPO had successfully attracted customers, built a distribution channel, achieved good cash flow, and seized a strong competitive position very early. On the other hand, a company that experienced acquisition had a smaller market and gradual progress on product development, customer acquisition, and channel development.

ON VALUE CREATION

Andreessen Horowitz has an in-house market development team, which invites Fortune 1000 corporations, such as Nike and Sprint, to meetings where small groups of portfolio companies can pitch products and develop business relationships. The firm is on pace to do 1,200 of these meetings a year.

GOOD GOVERNANCE AS THE FIRST STEP
TOWARD VALUE CREATION

A McKinsey survey of over 2,500 directors and officers concluded that institutional investors are willing to pay a 14 percent premium for shares of a well-governed company.[4] On the flip side, poor governance translates to failed investments and, even worse, lawsuits.

Depending on the stage of venture investments, the role of directors is amplified in areas such as value identification, value enhancement, sustaining momentum, and risk mitigation. The concept of value is unique to each company's stage of evolution. Exploring the fit between the company's needs and the practitioner's expertise starts with the primary driver: capital. A practitioner "buys" his or her board seat and attempts to ensure value enhancement by displaying his wares: intellectual and social capital.

BOARD BEST PRACTICES

Establish the following practices to ensure healthy board dynamics:

1. Provide an annual calendar that includes frequency of meetings, including an annual strategy session where you can "go deep," assessing the company's progress and preparing a road map for the next 12 months.
2. Ensure board materials are distributed ahead of time. Materials include the following:
   a. Agenda
   b. Minutes of the last meeting
   c. Business overview: The primary focus is on key milestones and progress thereof. Depending on the stage and evolution of the business, an overview could include the following:
      i. Progress against key milestones: Highlight delays and develop countermeasures
      ii. Product development: Present completed alpha, beta, pilot customer trials
      iii. Sales and marketing:
         - Pipeline
         - Actual sales versus budget

(Continued)

BOARD BEST PRACTICES: (*Continued*)

- Gross margins
- Competition
- Customer feedback

iv. Financial status highlights: Provide the cash position and burn rate, including an income statement, balance sheet, and cash flows.

v. Include any significant issues to be considered.

d. Resolutions

3. The secretary records the minutes of any board meeting. Generally, minutes are brief, factual statements that briefly state the resolutions and outcomes. Corporate counsel assists in ensuring the minutes are recorded accurately.

4. Records such as board books, minutes, and resolutions are available for reference in legal and acquisition-related discussions.

THE CEO'S PERSPECTIVE ON VC VALUE ADD

In an informal study, a sample of presidents and founders of venture capital–backed companies were asked to value the contributions of their VC counterparts.[5] The top three areas of contribution reported were as follows:

1. Financings, advice, and introductions
2. Strategic focus
3. Recruiting and hiring senior management—CEOs and VPs

The areas where VCs were least valued include the following:

- Selection of professionals, law, patent, accounting
- Strategic relations with other companies
- Functional advice in marketing, engineering

The challenge around functional advice on marketing, especially when practitioners do not have entrepreneurial background, is widespread. "I have seen situations where relatively junior VCs get too caught up in what-if analysis and demand that the CEO prepare these unnecessary scenarios—what

HANDS-OFF

In a survey of more than 150 CEOs, 58 percent said they want to work with venture capital firms that are entrepreneur friendly and collaborative . . . BUT they are wary of firms that are too hands-on. Only 1 percent said hands-on was an important quality.[6]

Source: NVCA, Branding and Venture Capital: Research Preview, July 2013. Survey conducted by DeSantis Breindel.

if a meteorite hits the earth and such," says Rick Heitzmann of FirstMark Capital.

Another survey of more than 300 companies shows that the best value a board member can offer is to assist with future financing. According to CEOs surveyed, industry knowledge and time commitments were identified as the top two weaknesses of boards. Aydin Senkut of Felicis Ventures says, "I think portfolio value-add can be more strategic than just a function of time spent—for instance we have been able to help founders where it really matters—making a connection that resulted in an exit or to find that super critical executive like a CFO. Those valuable connections can sometimes be achieved with a mere 30-minute phone call, but it could be transformative in value."

Industry Expertise as a Value Driver

Industry knowledge, sector/domain expertise—the terms mean more or less the same in the venture business. Some practitioners have built their expertise by doing—starting companies—while others have gained awareness by observing—reading about trends and discussing opportunities with sector experts. The CEO of a portfolio company does not care as long as a practitioner is able to deliver tangible elements.

Consider David Cowan of Bessemer Venture Partners, who was an expert on Web security but who has successfully morphed his expertise into other domains. "Over the years, Bessemer has made a number of investments in the Software as a Service (SaaS) arena. Our investments and knowledge within this arena has led to creation of unique metrics that are significant value drivers. We offer these to all our SaaS portfolio companies, and it helps them to assess their own performance vis-à-vis the rest of the SaaS universe," says Cowan.

Sales and Vendor Relationships as a Value Driver

Any venture-backed company needs rapid access to potential customers and vendors. A practitioner with a strong Rolodex can reduce some of this friction. "With one of our portfolio companies, I arranged and participated in at least 15 customer meetings in the first 12 months of our Series A investment. To get access to decision makers quickly is important for start-ups—essentially, you are accelerating the time to market." Lip-Bu Tan emphasizes that a practitioner ought to be able to play a role in every stage of evolution—product planning, customer acquisition, manufacturing, and organizational development. However, a rookie practitioner can make a classic mistake of digging too deep. A mistake I have made too often is to assess the pipeline and challenge the CEO on the probabilities and timing of the sales. This becomes an exhausting affair for both parties and yields little positive outcome. Rather, a practitioner should understand the sales dynamics, as Ravi Mohan of Shasta Ventures suggests. "I recall my first board meeting where I wanted to conduct a review of the sales pipeline. It is a very common mistake and a low-level tactical move. I am now better in serving my CEOs by focusing on the high-level quarterly goals and by understanding the sell cycle, customers' buying motivations, and any friction therein. It is important to use the board meetings wisely so that the CEO can get the benefit of the board's time and intellect."

Business Strategy as a Value Driver

"One of the companies I invested in originally planned to develop a product—I convinced its leaders to build a services company. It was pretty

---

WORK PRODUCT AS A VALUE DRIVER: BRENT AHRENS, CANAAN PARTNERS

"During my early years, one of the CEOs of our portfolio company was in my face saying 'Hey, look, when have you done this before?' and my response was honest—I have not run a company before, but let me share a specific example. I described how I had developed a marketing campaign for a certain product line and its strong impact on sales."

By demonstrating his thoughtful approach, providing a tangible example, and supporting it with numbers, Brent Ahrens was able to add value to the company while building a strong relationship with the CEO. This is by far the best way for a new board member to earn the CEO's trust and respect.

clear that a services model would function efficiently and solve the problem the company was attempting to tackle," says Todd Dagres, Founder of Spark Capital.[7] Todd got involved with Akamai's founders at a very early stage, during the Massachusetts Institute of Technology's $50K business plan competition, and helped shape the key elements of the company's business model. Akamai, which is a Hawaiian word meaning "smart," is now a publicly traded company with over $800 million in revenues.

As Brad Feld correctly points out, "Every CEO and company's needs are different, and there is no formulaic approach to value add. It is highly customized." Alex Bangash, an advisor to institutional investors, says that the channel is determined by resources available and often does not matter as much as the ability to provide value to the portfolio. "Value can be added via online tools, via conferences, and via dedicated teams. The channels are unique, yet the core remains the same across the board—firms can add value via design partners, growth hackers and hiring networks."

In a survey of more than 300 participants, the National Association of Corporate Directors (NACD) Private Company Governance Survey concluded that the three weakest areas of board effectiveness are director education and development, board and director evaluation, and CEO succession planning. Often, venture-backed boards have little or no time to indulge in the luxury of education, development, and self-evaluation.

BOARD SELF-EVALUATION

Self-evaluation of boards, while it seldom occurs, is a critical exercise. Venture-backed company boards tend to be smaller in size and are more interactive. Thus, the formal self-evaluation may never occur. Nevertheless, several CEOs of venture-backed companies express the challenges of time and attention. In a McKinsey study of 586 corporate directors, respondents pointed out that they would like to double their time on strategy and spend at least five times their time on talent management.[8]

Quotes such as "He learned how to be a director. We paid the tuition," or "My strategy is to minimize the value subtracted"[9] are indicative of fundamental challenges that exist in the boardroom. In the white paper "A Simple Guide to Basic Responsibilities of a VC-Backed Director,"[10] guidelines for an annual self-review suggest the following criteria:

- Preparedness
  - Review all board materials prior to meetings.
  - Be aware of key challenges for the company, both short term and long term.

- Communicate with other board members between meetings.
- Complete any assignments in a timely and thorough fashion.
- Alignment
  - Aligns with other board members and CEO with respect to key performance indicators and challenges.
  - Ensures other board members are aligned with CEO and supportive, as well.
  - Raises any challenging issues related to performance and conflicts, which are not to be ignored or brushed under the carpet.
- Attention
  - Attends all board meetings, is engaged in thoughtful manner without cell phone or e-mail distractions.
- Contribution
  - Proactively seeks ways of assisting the CEO to meet or exceed their goals. The CEO is at the center of the board's universe and a VC's role is to be supportive, staying behind the scenes as much as possible.

When time is the most critical resource, especially in early-stage companies, no director is going to raise his or her hand to take on any additional tasks. This is where opportunities for demonstrating leadership arise. Lindsay Aspegren of North Coast Technology Investors says, "As board members, we are charged to make decisions amidst a dynamic and fast-changing microcosm. We have to manage change effectively. It is not only understanding this role, but having the skills and the experience to do this job well. There is much emphasis on the front-end, the deal, in our business, but not enough on the postinvestment plan."

NOTES

1. Brad Feld (The Foundry Group), in discussions with the author.
2. Lip-Bu Tan (Walden International), in discussions with the author, December 2008.
3. PricewaterhouseCoopers, "Paths to Value," 2002. The Paths to Value study analyzed more than 350 R&D and services-intensive companies in the United States, Europe, and Israel that received seed or first-round private financing between 1999 and 2001.
4. McKinsey & Company, *The State of the Corporate Board, 2007: A McKinsey Global Survey*, accessed January 30, 2011. A total of 2,268 respondents, including 825 directors and officers, contributed to this survey.

5. Fred Dotzler, "What Do Venture Capitalists Really Do, and Where Do They Learn to Do It?" De Novo Ventures, accessed January 30, 2011, www.denovovc.com/articles/2001_Dotzler.pdf.

6. NVCA, Branding and Venture Capital: Research Preview, July 2013, survey conducted by DeSantis Breindel. http://nvcatoday.nvca.org/index.php/nvca-study-explores-the-importance-of-brand-management-in-the-venture-capital-industry.html (Accessed on April 8, 2014).

7. Akamai went on to become a global Internet/Web company.

8. *McKinsey Quarterly,* February 2008 Survey on Governance. Of the 586 respondents, 378 were privately held companies, making it a relevant sample for the purposes of our discussion.

9. William D. Bygrave and Jeffry A. Timmons, *Venture Capital at the Crossroads* (Harvard Business Press, 1992), 220.

10. Working Group on Director Accountability and Board Effectiveness, "A Simple Guide to the Basic Responsibilities of VC-Backed Company Directors," October 2007, www.nvca.org/index.php?option=com_docman&task=doc_download&gid=78&Itemid=93.

CHAPTER 23

Challenges in the Boardroom

"The fundamental cause of the trouble is that in the modern world the stupid are cocksure while the intelligent are full of doubt."
—Bertrand Russell

Venture-backed boards undergo considerable stresses when a portfolio company faces challenges. These manifest as:

- Resource challenges
  - Sales growth is slower than anticipated.
  - Cash position is weak.
- Performance challenges
  - Milestones have not been met.
  - Value creation steps have not occurred within projected timelines or prescribed budgets.
  - Loss of key accounts or major clientele.
  - Loss of key executives or churn of talent.
  - CEO transitions.
- Market-based/external challenges
  - Constrained market conditions affect sales or future financing.
  - Competitive forces disrupt the company's progress.
  - IP-related matters cause unforeseen issues.

When Arthur Rock resigned from the board of Apple, he was irritated by the chutzpah displayed by Steve Jobs. "They took a two-page ad in every newspaper you could think of, announcing that they were ready to ship the

PowerPC, which I did not know they were going to manufacture—but that's not important—but that they were going to kill Intel. Literally—that's what it said. At that point, I resigned," he would say.[1]

Patterns of emotional behavior manifest in wide-ranging forms, including ego games designed to impress friends, actions taken to save face, self-interested actions, and personal vendettas, according to Pascal Levensohn. Left unchecked, the force of emotion may compromise directors' abilities to promote the shareholders' best interests. An independent outside director can play a crucial role in defining the success of the company.[2]

CHALLENGES AMONG SHAREHOLDERS

Multiple classes of shares with multiple preferences stacked on each other creates a labyrinth wherein keeping track of each entity's agenda and economic interests can be challenging. Furthermore, while the terms may be static, each practitioner and his or her fund's status is dynamic.

Any venture capital fund owns preferred stock, while the management may own common stock. Thus, any exit discussions where the management or common shareholders do not benefit would lead to frustration. In a few cases, the common shareholders have successfully negotiated additional cash prior to consenting to the sale of the company. According to one entrepreneur, the carve-out was offered only because the venture capitalists (VCs) were concerned about a possible shareholder lawsuit challenging the terms of the sale. In another case where the VCs lacked board control, the VCs offered a carve-out to obtain the support of the other directors for the sale.[3]

Cash Flow–Related Matters

If the burn rate is too high, management is seen as the primary culprit. The board and the CEO may disagree on the spend rate and priorities. Tension can arise over the priority of cash distribution at exit when the numbers are mediocre—for example, should accrued dividends, which primarily benefit investors, have a priority over management performance bonuses?

Performance-Related Challenges

Are you writing checks to defend sunk capital? Or to fuel growth? Consider the example of NEON, a health care IT company backed by ARCH Venture Partners. The company had developed tools for hospitals to organize data and increase transaction speed. The target market never developed because the hospitals' IT protocol had not reached the point at which they could maximize the potential of NEON's technology. And any IT company selling to hospitals is leery about the sales cycle, which can be as long as nine months or more. NEON was one of the larger investments for ARCH, and thus, the partners were investing a fair amount of time in trying to resurrect the opportunity. This conundrum has been faced by many practitioners when the initial thesis of an opportunity does not pan out. "The technology had to have a market somewhere . . . we just hadn't found it yet," Steven Lazarus, founder of ARCH, would recall. From hospitals, where the adoption for new technologies was sluggish, the company shifted its target market to Wall Street. Its technology was ideally suited for speedier transactions and messaging, and in five years the company grew to $180 million in revenues before it was acquired.[4] ARCH continued to support the company despite market-related challenges and it paid off.

Compare NEON with the defunct online grocer Webvan—termed as one of the most epic failures in the dot-com bubble fiasco, this company sold groceries such as bread and vegetables. Within 18 months it had spent $1 billion on several futuristic warehouses, promising to offer groceries in 30 minutes or less. Webvan's investor list was the who's who of venture capital—Sequoia Capital, Benchmark Capital, and several others. The company also raised almost half a billion dollars by going public (its stock went from $30 to 6 cents in a few months). Senior executives or investors did not have any experience in the supermarket trade—Webvan went from being a $1.2 billion company with 4,500 employees to being liquidated in under two years. "The presumption that you needed to get big fast worked for Amazon.com and virtually no one else," commented Gartner analyst Whit Andrews at the time of Webvan's bankruptcy.[5] His prophetic words rang true when, in 2009, Amazon resurrected Webvan and unveiled AmazonFresh.

In each of these examples, the underlying challenges of performance exist. Neither NEON nor Webvan was able to penetrate the market. However, the market conditions—the dot-com boom and bust—and capital needs of each business (Webvan needed a lot of money, NEON did not) also act as criteria for decisions. Whatever be the reasons, the Webvan boardroom may have been much more challenging than NEON.

Pascal Levensohn, founder of Levensohn Venture Partners says, "When there is an opportunity for collusion, such challenges are likely to occur."[6] Venture capitalists, most of whom are trying to be supportive and nurturing without being overbearing, can be vulnerable to such planned attacks. GCA Savvian's Steve Fletcher is realistic about the challenges of a venture capitalist's role on the board. "If a company's executives really set out to defraud people, if they make up invoices or clients, it's difficult to detect as an auditor or a board member or an investment banker. The CEO and CFO

A TRUSTING BOARD AND FRAUDULENT CEO: A $50 MILLION LESSON

From: Paul Johnston
To: Pete Solvik; Jonathan D. Roberts
Subject: Resignation
Jonathan and Pete:
This is a very difficult e-mail to write, but effective immediately both Parrish and I are tendering our resignation. We have both made a grave mistake by misrepresenting our revenue reporting to the board. Looking back at the time, we thought we would be able to right the wrong and correct our representation, but we have not been able to do this. Revenues have been overstated with a delta of approximately $400 K a month. . . .

So began the sordid nightmare for a group of VCs who had invested $50 million in this company. Entellium, the Seattle-based company that was driving the next revolution of customer relationship management tools, came under intense fire. Entellium's four-year rise, which garnered it numerous product design awards, accolades from *Business Week* magazine and Forrester Research, and a CRM Market Leader designation, ended with the arrest of CEO Paul Johnston and CFO Parrish Jones.

The two were convicted of hatching a scheme that inflated revenue numbers to attract venture capital. The two colluded and kept separate books. Entellium's board was told that it had earned $5.2 million, when its actual revenues were around $1.7 million.[7] Like an elite athlete bafflingly tempted to take steroids, Entellium's CEO and CFO pumped up the company's success until it was almost hyperbole. Johnston and Jones put up a show that dazzled investors, who forked over about $50 million in good faith. One of the biggest venture funds lost around $19 million.[8]

are the most important executives of a company. In reality, most of your information comes from them."[9] In a small company of 15 to 20 employees, the primary board interactions are with the CEO and the CFO. To any practitioner, the Entellium case offers expensive lessons:

- *Cover the blind spots.* Blind spots in business often occur both when things are going badly and when the business is going well. Assistant U.S.

Attorney Carl Blackstone, who prosecuted the case against Johnston and Jones, called Entellium a "legitimate company with a real product and real employees" with the only discordance being the inflated revenues, from which Johnston pocketed about $1.4 million.[10] In other words, there weren't explicit red flags to board members about something fishy in the books. The numbers—even the exaggerated versions hammered up by Johnston and Jones—made sense and fit the story of a robust company like Entellium and its vibrant industry. As a VC you may find it hard to question your charismatic and driven founder and CEO, especially when the numbers look great! VCs can avoid being hoodwinked by learning to intelligently question all the facts. Safeguards like periodic in-depth reviews of sales to dig deeper into financial records can help.

- *Put healthy skepticism to work by putting periodic reviews in place.* A study found that among 1,770 VCs who have taken at least one of their portfolio firms public, 196 (11.07 percent) of them have funded a fraudulent IPO firm, and 154 (8.7 percent) of them have backed an IPO firm that committed fraud after their exit.[11] Obviously, the VCs who backed Entellium are not alone.
- *Enlist key players and enhance information flow.* In the case of Entellium, a stronger relationship with the business development team might have exposed deception sooner, since collusion was largely confined to the CEO and CFO. "You always want the perspective of people who aren't on the management team and don't have a direct interest in sticking to the management team's story," advises Justin Hibbard of the research group Quidnunc Group, which conducts due diligence for venture investors.[12]
- *Internal audits.* Ask for customer lists with purchase order amounts and corroborate details. Unfortunately, the extra costs of audits can be significant. Depending on the audit firm and the scope of work, this could be anywhere from $50,000 a year upward, and the cost rises quickly as the company grows. Still, as insurance, it is well worth the investment and peace of mind.

Although the CEO is essential to the company's success, his or her leadership should be subject to checks and balances.

CEO Transitions

Author and professor Noam Wasserman writes in his book, *The Founder's Dilemma*,[13] "Entrepreneurs face a choice, at every step, between making money and managing their ventures. Those who don't figure out which is more important to them often end up neither wealthy nor powerful." Several CEO behavioral characteristics act as warning signs leading to a potential transition. Pascal Levensohn points out that the CEO:

- Repudiates board input and stays the wrong course
- Is often missing in action
- Is defensive and combative with the board, stonewalling board inquiries
- Is not proactive in keeping the board informed
- Shirks responsibilities or passes the blame

If ignored, these warning signs can deteriorate into more serious mismanagement problems, such as revenue shortfalls, gaps, and delays in meeting purchase targets or in completing contracts, and an exodus of employees. Valuation is often impacted negatively when the CEOs do not relinquish control, as seen in Table 23.1.

MANAGING CEO TRANSITION

Almost two-thirds of all venture-backed start-up companies replace their founding CEOs or top executives, as seen in Table 23.1. Initiating and managing transitions during the changing of the guard is one of the most important decisions VCs will make as board directors or members. Friction between the VC board members and CEO generally arises during these times. As CEOs build management teams by recruiting trusted team members, the risk of implosion during such times can be high. With their broader perspectives, VC board members can lobby to add talent outside the CEO's circle. This kind of strategic recruiting may call for the difficult task of moving

TABLE 23.1   Impact on Valuation When CEOs Gave Up Both Board Control and CEO Role

	Share of company valuation ($m) N = 230	Share of company valuation ($m) N = 219
Gave up both CEO role and board control	6.5	9.5
CEO role only	5	7.2
Board control only	4.1	6.1
Kept both CEO role and board control	3.3	4.8

Source: Founder's Dilemma, Noam Wasserman

founding members out of management seats and into more supportive, advisory roles.

Such transitions can be challenging for both sides—in the formative stages, the VCs mentor the CEO, act as sounding boards, and even joke that they act as corporate shrinks. This build-up leads to deepening personal ties, but a practitioner needs to realize the consequences of any friendship. "One of the mistakes I made early on was trying to become friends with the entrepreneurs. You eventually learn that you can like them and admire them, . . . and you get too close to them, and it sort of inhibits you in some ways," James Swartz of Accel Partners once stated.[14]

Table 23.2 shows how founders change over rounds. The best way to manage these changes is to anticipate them, monitoring for early signs of leadership problems, and acting quickly and decisively before any shortfalls lead to irreparable damage. One way to do this is for both parties to establish specific performance expectations. Annual reviews of CEO performance, including management team feedback, board member feedback, and input from other key stakeholders, are critical.

Besides value creation, the role of the board member is critical in assessing the performance of the CEO and helping identify and recruit other suitable members of the management team. Studies have shown that in venture-backed companies, management turmoil and change is constant, and roughly half of the CEOs step away. Founders are unable to retain their roles as CEOs during the rapid evolution stages of the company—managing people, budgets, and technology in a rapidly evolving marketplace is rare. Thus, a practitioner needs to be prepared to identify and recruit key management talent. John Doerr of Kleiner Perkins Caufield & Byers (KPCB) identifies himself as the "glorious recruiter." Benchmark Capital went on to bring a top recruiter as a full partner in the firm. Leonard Bosack, along with his wife Sandy Lerner, formed Cisco Systems. Their tenure with Cisco lasted for four years after they raised their first $2.5 million Series A round from Sequoia Capital.[15]

In venture jargon, change management does not mean managing change, but quite literally, changing a member of the management team. "It's a tough

TABLE 23.2   CEO Changes over Series of Investments

	A Round	B Round	C Round	D Round
Founder still CEO	75%	62%	48%	39%
On 2nd CEO	19%	29%	35%	38%
On 3rd or more CEO	6%	9%	17%	23%

Source: Founder's Dilemma, Noam Wasserman

decision and very disruptive," says Deepak Kamra of Canaan Partners. He adds, "It's much easier to assume that the CEO will eventually work out, so let's keep him."

Thomas H. Bredt, formerly of Menlo Ventures, points out that one of his portfolio companies had a very effective CEO who was able to build a world-class product. "The product risk was overcome and the team surpassed our expectations—the CEO was a great engineer who could get a product to market. After the IPO, we agreed that the founder would be better suited in the capacity of the chairman. Solidifying the company's position post-IPO required a different skill set." Organizational development and management, sustained growth, defending competitive jabs—all under the public glare of analysts—calls for a different timbre.

As John Kenneth Galbraith once remarked, "The great entrepreneur must, in fact, be compared in life with the male 'epis mellifera.' He accomplishes his act of conception at the price of his own extinction."[16] People seldom grow from managing product development, to managing people, to eventually managing expectations in the post-IPO public glare. As human beings, we rarely recognize our own shortcomings and inabilities when it comes to managing people, products, and capital.

Management of communication around this subject is critical. When the decision to replace the CEO is finalized, the board and the CEO would also agree on a clear message to be communicated to employees, customers, investors, and other stakeholders to assure everyone of the continuity and integrity of the company during the transition period.

BEST PRACTICES IN MANAGING TRANSITIONS

While every investment starts with the assumption that the team will perform, in cases where a transition needs to be planned, a practitioner can manage this effectively:

- Prioritize skills and experience essential to build the company.
- Enlist support from the board as well as the existing CEO.
- Establish a new role for the founder ahead of time. If the CEO himself initiates the change, as seen in Table 23.3, they stay in other executive roles and can continue to add value.
- Make the search priority one. One board member should lead the process.
- Choose the closer: Prime candidates usually need persuasion. One board member—the best closer—works with the dream candidate to close.

TABLE 23.3 Triggers of Change and CEO Transitions

	Moved to CTO or CSO	Other C Level role	Left the company immediately	Lower Level Executive role
Trigger of change = Board	26%	25%	37%	13%
Trigger of change = Founder CEO	24%	49%	24%	2%

Source: Founder's Dilemma, Noam Wasserman

- Ensure that the founder and the new CEO are aligned and an effective "hand-off" process is established.
- Stay close to the new CEO: To ensure a smooth transition, maintain a high touch relationship in the first few months. Avoid complacency after the CEO arrives.

As Thomas Bredt points out, "by far, this is the biggest service any venture practitioner can do for the CEO is to educate and alert the CEO, preferably prior to making the investment, that transition is normal."[17]

ALIGNMENT OF EXIT METHOD, TIMING, AND EXIT VALUE

Successful VC board members have alignment and clear understanding of exit strategies as well as a strong sense of when a company has matured or is languishing toward failure. If a company fails to accomplish milestones, encounters dwindling resources, or suffers from competitive pressures—the exit method and value may be severely compromised. On the other hand, selling to a corporate buyer or going public on the stock exchange at the right time is expected to yield a strong outcome.

But timing matters on exits, as does alignment of the stakeholders. If one venture investor is under more pressure to achieve an exit quickly than are other investors, the misalignment can impair the exit value. Further, if the CEO or the management team does not want to exit, the investors end up with another set of challenges.

As the company evolves into maturation, it is rare and even unlikely that one individual will encompass all the skills necessary to guide the CEO and enhance value at every stage. Board members' ability to add value may diminish, and they need to cede their positions to more suitable peers within the firm. This rarely happens in practice—board members embed themselves within the company, especially as the company ascends to rapid growth. It's only during a crisis that disemboweling occurs.

At the heart of the challenge is the hero-worship *rock star* culture—practitioners become stars when huge exits and payoffs occur. The board members at the time of the exit are the heroes who cross the proverbial finish line and enhance their resumes. But rotation for the sake of rotation can be challenging as well—a company may lose much-needed talent. Education of new members and their ability to build the right chemistry is critical. In the larger context, the rotation challenge may be less of an issue, but it still is a pertinent one.

NOTES

1. Arthur Rock, interview by Sally Smith Hughes, 2008–2009, "Early Bay Area Venture Capitalists: Shaping the Economic and Business Landscape," accessed January 30, 2011, http://digitalassets.lib.berkeley.edu/roho/ucb/text/rock_arthur.pdf.
2. Pascal Levensohn, "The Problem of Emotion in Boardroom," *Directors and Boards,* Spring 1999.
3. Brian J. Broughman and Jesse M. Fried, "Renegotiation of Cash Flow Rights in the Sale of VC-Backed Firms," *Journal of Financial Economics,* Vol. 95, pp. 384–399, 2010; UC Berkeley Public Law Research Paper No. 956243. Available at SSRN: http://ssrn.com/abstract = 956243.
4. Robert Finkel and David Greising, *The Masters of Private Equity and Venture Capital* (McGraw-Hill; First edition November 2009), 216.
5. "The greatest defunct Web sites and dotcom disasters," CNET. 2008–06–05. Archived from the original on 2008–06–07. Accessed March 21, 2011, www.cnet.com/news/the-greatest-defunct-web-sites-and-dotcom-disasters/.
6. Pascal Levensohn (Levensohn Venture Partners) in discussions with the author, August 2010.
7. Dan Richman, "Former CEO of Entellium Pleads Guilty to Wire Fraud," *Seattle Post-Intelligencer,* December 11, 2008, accessed January 30, 2011, www.seattlepi.com/business/391777_entellium12.html.
8. Kristie Heim, "Entellium CEO Pleads Guilty to Wire Fraud," *Seattle Times,* December 12, 2008, accessed January 30, 2011, http://seattletimes.nwsource.com/html/businesstechnology/2008499215_entellium120.html.
9. Constance Loizos, "Could It Happen to You?" *Venture Capital Journal,* November 1, 2008, accessed January 30, 2011, www.jphibbard.com/uploads/VCJ%2011-01-08.pdf.

10. Christie Heim, "Entellium CEO Pleads Guilty to Wire Fraud."
11. Xuan Tian, Gregory F. Udell, and Xiaoyun Yu, "Disciplining Delegated Monitors: Evidence from Venture Capital," January 23, 2011. Available at SSRN: http://ssrn.com/abstract = 1746461.
12. Constance Loizos, "Could It Happen to You?"
13. *Harvard Business Review*, February 2008.
14. James R. Swartz, interview by Mauree Jane Perry, 2006, "National Venture Capital Association Venture Capital Oral History Project," accessed January 30, 2011, http://digitalassets.lib.berkeley.edu/roho/ucb/text/rock_arthur.pdf.
15. Pete Carey, "A Start-up's True Tale: Often-Told Story of Cisco's Launch Leaves out the Drama, Intrigue," *Mercury News*, December 1, 2001.
16. John Kenneth Galbraith, *The New Industrial State* (Boston: Houghton Mifflin, 1971).
17. Thomas Bredt (Menlo Ventures), in discussions with the author, July 2008.

CHAPTER 24

Exit Strategies

"For I must tell you friendly in your ear
Sell when you can: you are not for all markets."
　　　　　—William Shakespeare, *As You Like It*, act 3, scene 5

A portfolio company is acquired, or its stock trades on the public exchanges; those rare (and hopefully happy) moments are when the practitioner celebrates or, possibly, heaves a sigh of relief. Capital invested comes back and completes a full circle—an investor "exits the investment" by selling the stock of the portfolio company.

The two primary exit options, acquisitions and initial public offerings (IPOs), are reviewed, along with private exchanges—an emerging option with implications for some highly sought-after technology companies.

- *Mergers and acquisitions (M&A or trade-sale):* Mergers and acquisitions is the most popular path of exit for a venture-backed company. Also called *trade sale*, a portfolio company is sold to a larger company. The transaction nets a return for investors, who in turn share the spoils with their limited partners.
- *Initial public offering:* An IPO is a highly desired badge of honor; investors list a company on a publicly traded stock exchange and sell privately owned shares for the first time to the public. Of course, fewer companies can demonstrate the growth and value to be considered IPO ready. And after they are ready, the Securities and Exchange Commission (SEC), the

federal regulatory body, prescribes rules and regulations on public offerings to keep everyone honest. Some venture practitioners treat the public offering as a financing event and not an exit. Compared to acquisitions, IPOs typically deliver a higher return to investors, as seen in Table 24.1.

- *Private exchanges:* SharesPost and SecondMarket have sprung up, offering shares of sought after start-ups to eager buyers. After all, who does not want a piece of Facebook?
- *Redemption of shares:* Remember that redemption clause you negotiated—the one where you can treat your equity much like a debt instrument and trigger the repayment after 5 years? That is technically an exit, but no venture practitioner worth his IRR speaks of redemption in public.

And yes, a write-off is technically an exit, but it doesn't need much deliberation in this chapter. Be assured that in your portfolio, the lemons, as depicted in Figure 24.1, will always ripen much faster. Stated differently, the losses occur much faster.

A good practice for general partners (GPs) is to track the losses in a systematic manner. Limited partners (LPs) certainly seek to understand the conditions and lessons learned with write-offs. After all, the goal is to avoid making the same mistakes again, or to make new mistakes each time! Each exit path has its own advantages and challenges, as seen in Table 24.2.

PRECONDITIONS FOR AN EXIT

Certain preconditions need to be established prior to any exit overtures. These are discussed in Table 24.3.

TABLE 24.1 Returns: Or Why an IPO Is Better

Exit Path	Observations	Median IRR (%)	Mean IRR (%)	Standard Deviation
IPO	108	58.39	123.42	207.97
Trade-sale	423	18.32	75.32	408.27

Source: Data from Center for Private Equity Research, Frankfurt. Period from 1971 to 2003. Carsten Bienz and Tore E. Leite, "A Pecking Order of Venture Capital Exits" (April 2008). Available at SSRN: http://ssrn.com/abstract=916742.

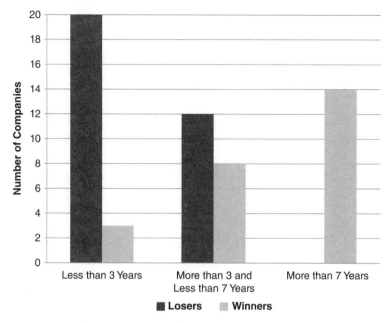

FIGURE 24.1   Lemons ripen faster than pearls
Source: Jeffry Timmons, *New Venture Creation: Entrepreneurship for the 21st Century*, 5th ed. (New York: McGraw Hill, 1999).

Alignment of Interests of Stakeholders

Alignment of interests of various stakeholders can determine whether passage of an exit will be smooth or be a joyride to the suburb of hell. The cast of characters includes the following:

- Board of directors, presumably with multiple investors, each with varying degrees of motivations and investor preferences
- Founders/chief executive officer motivations
- Common shareholders' interests

Naturally, the board exerts the maximum influence, but the role of other stakeholders is important as exits are being planned. Consider a Cisco executive who, while conducting due diligence, assesses the quality and character of the target company's management team. Cisco interacts with the executives in an informal manner to explore short-term and long-term goals. "We look for culture, qualities, and leadership style. We don't care about the product that

TABLE 24.2 Pros and Cons of Exit Methods

Method of Exit	Pros	Cons
Acquisition (trade-sale)	Speed. Reduced regulatory challenges. (Assuming the FTC does not get involved!) Value can be lower in comparison to an IPO, but as many practitioners point out, it is efficient.	Takes two to tango. In some cases, earn-outs may be beyond the control of current management or existing investors. Founders or any other shareholders cannot retain partial ownership.
Listing on public exchange or an IPO (initial public offering)	Larger valuation in stronger market conditions. Can use stock for acquisitions. Improves stature and morale. Founders can retain partial ownership.	Company needs to achieve growth rates that are higher than average. Expensive process. Regulatory and market challenges.
Private exchanges	Rapid liquidity. Higher valuations.	Awareness and demand for the companies needs to be high. No one is looking to invest in no-name companies. Value is determined by sheer frothiness and public market-like speculation.
Redemption	Ability to recover at least some capital, assuming company has some cash at hand at the time of redemption.	Dependent on company's ability to redeem, as well as other balance sheet obligations and board composition. Payouts could be spread out over time to minimize cash impact, further reducing any IRR.

TABLE 24.3 Preconditions for an Exit

Preconditions for an Exit	Favorable Conditions	Unfavorable Conditions
Value drivers	Rapid sales and expansion, market leadership and proprietary position.	Flat growth, limited potential. Sagging morale. A dog. A distraction.
Board-investor alignment	Board members/investors are aligned with respect to timing and value of exit.	The largest investor wants that quick hit—a fund-raise cycle is coming up and we need that IRR! You want to stay! Or the largest investor (and the chair of the board) is fatigued and wants to get rid of this dog. You, on the other hand, are a seed investor and control a fraction of the shares. The common shareholders want to block the sale because those 3X liquidation preferences do not leave any crumbs for them.
Board-management alignment	Board and CEO/founders are in agreement with respect to timing and value of exit.	The investors want to sell. The CEO wants to grow. Investors sell—unhappy CEO ends up writing a book. What a wicked world! The CEO wants to sell—the investors want to hold and build value. A premature liquidity event for venture capitalists (VCs)!
Market demand	Buyers are kicking the doors down. A nice auction process is driving price and IRR to all-time highs. Sell this—and get that private placement memorandum ready for the next fund raise?	No market demand, but we want to sell. Hire an I-Banker, prepare a book, and start the selling process. With no bites and sinking cash position, attempt to raise a bridge note or a swallow a down round. Eighteen months later, shut the company down.
Macro conditions	Strong public markets and economic conditions.	Competition, erosion of margins, regulatory changes

is on the manufacturing floor . . . the second- and third-generation product is locked up in their heads," a Cisco executive points out.[1] John Chambers, the CEO of Cisco, laid out five guidelines for acquiring companies, including the "chemistry between companies has to be right" and "long-term win for all four constituencies—shareholders, employees, customers, and business partners."[2] If the founders and CEO of the target company do not see the exit as a win, it may show during buyer diligence. When Ted Dacko, CEO of HealthMedia, was getting ready to complete the sale of his company to Johnson & Johnson, he was not worried about the exit value as much as the team culture. "I wanted to ensure everyone understood the exit strategy and was aligned—we did not have any passive aggressive behavior," he says.

> *We had a tough time convincing our board of directors who were also our investors to embrace many of our activities that would help build the Zappos brand and make the world a better place. The directors didn't fully understand or were convinced of things like brand or culture, dismissing many of these as "Tony's social experiments." Sequoia expected an exit in five years and hadn't signed up for these additional things. I was pretty close to being fired from the board. I was learning that alignment with shareholders and board of directors was just as important.[3]*

Exit strategies, value, and timing evolve as the company matures. Practitioners have a strong sense of when a company has matured or is languishing toward failure. If a company fails to accomplish future-financing rounds, misses milestones and targets, exhausts ideas and resources, or sees its market shrink or shift, then it is critical to close down operations rather than to slowly wither into oblivion.[4] Conversely, selling to a corporate buyer or going public at the right time is certainly expected as a strong outcome. Timing matters. Premature efforts to drive exits can lead to depressed value, or worse, no buyer interest. Sell too late and the dynamics may shift—potential buyers, market conditions, and the arrival of competition could impair the value. Mitch Lasky of Benchmark Capital points out that the window of exit opportunity can be narrow. "Look for that S curve when growth and exit multiples are on your side," he says. See Figure 24.2.

Alignment of Exit Value: What's a Few Hundred Million, Anyway?

At an appropriate time, specific exit values should also be discussed openly to ensure alignment with various stakeholders. For example, different investors may have conflicting valuations in mind. Examples abound where one

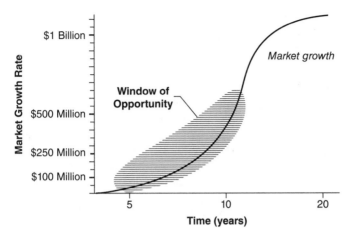

FIGURE 24.2 The S Curve of Exit Opportunities

venture capitalist (VC) was happy to part with the company for $100 million and another was expecting to turn at least $300 million.[5] If the liquidation preferences come into play and impact the common shareholders, unpleasant situations, such as holdup of the voting process or, worse, lawsuits, can ensue.

For any practitioner (and any LP), the exit of an investment is a much anticipated event. However, as many as 30 percent of all venture capital–backed companies were either still hanging around in the portfolio or had quietly shut down.

Savvy practitioners do not necessarily aim for premature exits; rather, they work toward building companies that generate value for customers and are financially sound. For such companies, exit options are always plentiful and never at the mercy of markets. Alternate exit options, such as sale of the company to a private equity group, or redemption, are likely scenarios as well.

SECONDARY MARKETS

Private exchanges, such as SecondMarket and SharesPost offer liquidity to private investors. In the past, employees in private companies couldn't sell their shares, but thanks to private exchanges and secondary markets, early liquidity is now possible. VC funds are 10-year closed-end funds. Finally, in an economic environment unfriendly to IPOs, cashing out via secondary markets makes sense.

Private exchanges generally function by having an intermediary take shares from sellers or companies and actively find buyers, a process that

ANALYZING THE CAUSE OF DEATH

In hospitals and doctors' residency training programs, a morbidity and mortality (M & M) conference is held. Surgeons and residents candidly discuss complications and deaths. Students are often present as this is a great learning opportunity. The resident practitioner who performed the operation presents the summary of the case, pertinent history, physical examination findings, lab results, and images. Cases are presented and critiqued by the participants. Questions are asked regarding why the case was managed in a certain way. Other surgeons often chime in to share their views and what they learned from similar cases. Often, a consensus may be reached if the complication could have been prevented. Such honest and robust conversations often prevent the same mistakes from occurring and can save lives in the future. The atmosphere can be rich with debates, but the goal is not to blame any one person nor is it retribution. Every attendee learns from the mistakes. The focus of such a conference is on education, improving quality of care, and saving lives.

When it comes to analyzing the cause of start-up failures, a venture capitalist can learn from this model. They may save some LP capital and prevent the same mistakes from occurring time and again.

can drag into weeks—completely out of sync with the fast-paced world of trading. SecondMarket and SharesPost simplify the process by offering an auction-style system, formalizing the market-clearing process with more ease and transparency. Besides VCs, angel investors and senior management of private companies are potential users. "Those people are not necessarily looking to sell all of their position in a company, but want some amount of liquidity for their shares."[6] Early investors are especially keen on the legitimate transition/exit as a way to cash in some of their earnings. Accel Partners sold about 15 percent of its stake in Facebook, then valued over $500 million via secondary markets.[7] While still a fraction of what is traded in public exchanges such as the New York Stock Exchange and NASDAQ, private exchanges have brought a much needed third exit option to venture practitioners.

The two companies SharesPost and SecondMarket deliver their services in distinct ways, and their models will continue to evolve. SharesPost works by connecting buyers and sellers through bulletin boards. Every private company on the site is represented on its own bulletin board, where requests are posted "with the highest price posting for shares at the top of the list for buyers, and the reverse for sellers."[8] Interested parties who want to buy or sell then visit the bulletin board, find the most attractive bid, and ask prices—a process dubbed as "price discovery."[9] While there are no limitations on sellers wanting to unload stock, buyers generally have to have substantial invested assets and experience under SEC Regulation D. SharesPost charges a basic site user fee, and revenue is indifferent to whether the stock is sold. SecondMarket employs a more traditional broker-dealer arrangement, overseeing trading and taking in commissions in the amount of 2 to 5 percent, depending on the deal, equally split between buyer and seller.[10] While SharesPost uses a more hands-off, bulletin-listing system, Second-Market can be likened to a trading floor, with brokers waiting in the wings. Using the online bulletin board, sellers post their stocks. SecondMarket grades buyers based on the type and volume of deals they have done in the past or deals in which they have demonstrated an interest. Buyers with the strongest grades get a call from a SecondMarket rep and begin the negotiation process. Like SharesPost, SecondMarket sorts out the paperwork, but it also pockets a commission. Barry Silbert, SecondMarket's CEO, has boasted that this embodies "Wall Street 3.0"—defined as "using technology and doing things in a transparent way to bring trust back into the system."[11]

Widespread online sales of private shares placed the burden on companies to approve scores of transactions and brought in an unwieldy mass of shareholders with varying agendas. Such trading avenues also impacted employee morale and caused distraction when employees would sell their shares and quit. Companies now allow employees and other stakeholders to sell shares in narrow windows of time. SecondMarket estimates there will be about 30 to 40 large, company-organized "invitation only" controlled sales of early investors' and employees' stock, up from 10 to 15 a year ago. According to reports in the *Wall Street Journal*,[12] companies have attempted to control pre-IPO trading because online trading could lead to speculative swings in share price, affecting companies' stock-based incentives for employees, and spreading information about privately held companies too widely. Individual investors are often excluded from purchasing shares of some of the most popular private technology companies before they have held an IPO, with institutions preferred as buyers.

Any investor would welcome these models where friction in venture capital transactions is minimized and holdings need not be locked up for as much as 10 years. As one LP remarked, such exchanges have a remarkable effect in smoothing out the J curve.

NOTES

1. David Mayer and Martin F. Kenney, "Economic Action Does Not Take Place in a Vacuum: Understanding Cisco's Acquisition and Development Strategy" (BRIE working paper 148), September 2002.
2. Glenn Rifkin, "Growth by Acquisition: The Case of Cisco Systems," *Strategy and Business* 7 (Second Quarter, 1997), accessed December 13, 2010, http://www.strategy-business.com/article/15617?gko = 3ec0c.
3. Tony Hsieh (CEO, Zappos), *Delivering Happiness: A Path to Profits, Passion, and Purpose* (New York: Hachette Book Group, 2010), 209–211. Tony tried to buy Sequoia's stock for $200 million, but eventually Zappos was sold to Amazon for $1.2 billion.
4. Paul Stavrand, "Best Practice Guide for Angel Groups—Post Investment Monitoring," July 2007, accessed January 30, 2011, www.angelcapitalassociation.org/data/Documents/Resources/AngelCapitalEducation/ACEF_BEST_PRACTICES_Post_Investment.pdf.
5. Working Group on Director Accountability and Board Effectiveness, "A Simple Guide to the Basic Responsibilities of VC-Backed Company Directors,"www.nvca.org/index.php?option=com_docman&task=doc_download&gid = 78&Itemid = 93.
6. Benjamin F. Kuo, "Interview with Greg Brogger, SharesPost," June 17, 2009, socaltech.com, accessed February 11, 2011, www.socaltech.com/interview_with_greg_brogger_sharespost/s-0022276.html.
7. Pui-Wing Tam and Geoffrey Fowler, "Hot Trade in Private Shares of Facebook." The *Wall Street Journal*, December 2010.
8. Benjamin F. Kuo, "Interview with Greg Brogger, SharesPost."
9. Rafe Needleman, "SharesPost Lets You Buy the Un-buyable." CNet, June 30, 2009.
10. Ibid.
11. Kathryn Glass, "Building a SecondMarket to Make Way for Wall Street 3.0." *Fox Business*, July 16, 2010
12. Yuliya Chernova, "Trading Pre-IPO Shares Gets Trickier—Investors Wanting to Get in Early on the Next Twitter Find a Tougher Path," *The Wall Street Journal*, October 29, 2013.

CHAPTER 25

Acquisitions: The Primary Path to an Exit

"Fighting and scars are part of a trader's overhead. But fighting is only useful when there's money at the end, and if I can get it without, so much the sweeter."

—Isaac Asimov, *Foundation*

In a study of 11,500 venture capital–backed companies that raised capital between 1995 and 2008, 65.21 percent exited through either an initial public offering (IPO) or mergers and acquisitions (M & A). Within this universe, the vast majority of the exits were acquisitions, and only 9.61 percent of them achieved exit via a public offering.[1]

As seen in Figure 25.1, acquisitions are significantly larger as compared to public offerings.

Acquisitions are the preferred path for most venture-backed companies due to speed and efficiency, as well as minimal regulatory challenges. Acquisitions offer larger companies much needed growth and expansion opportunities. Figure 25.2 shows median sales at IPO for VC-backed companies.

As seen in Figure 25.3, only about 10 percent of all acquisitions offer more than 10X returns.

IBM acquired 70 companies in seven years, spending about $14 billion.[2] By pushing these newly acquired products through an existing global sales force, IBM estimates it increased its revenue by almost 50 percent in the first two years after each acquisition and an average of more than 10 percent over the next three years.[3]

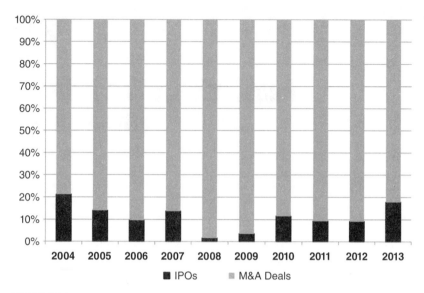

FIGURE 25.1   Liquidity events of VC-backed companies.
Source: NVCA

By rough estimates, Cisco acquired more than 120 companies over a 15-year span—an average of 8 to 12 companies each year. The first 71 companies acquired within an eight-year period[4] were at an average price of approximately $350 million. In that same period, Cisco's sales increased over 35X from $650 million to $22 billion, with nearly 40 percent of its 2001 revenue coming directly from these acquisitions.[5] By 2009, Cisco had more than $36 billion in revenues and a market cap of approximately $150 billion.

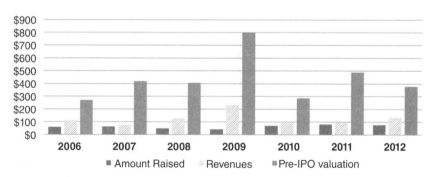

FIGURE 25.2   Median Sales at IPO
Source: Preqin

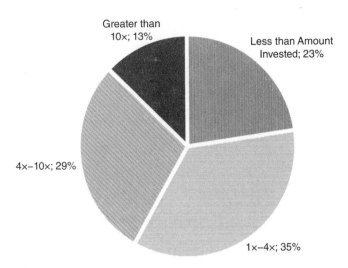

FIGURE 25.3   Acquisitions exit ranges.
Source: NVCA, Exit Data (2010–2013)

Google has acquired 131 companies[6] at an average of 10 companies a year. For Google, the technology drivers have opened up new revenue sources. Its acquisition of Applied Semantics helped Google develop a text-advertising network called AdSense, now a multi-billion-dollar revenue generator. Andy Rubin's start-up, Android Inc., was snapped up by Google and led to the development of what is now a leading operating system for smartphones.[7]

Acquisitions are seen as the fastest way for larger companies like Google, IBM, and Cisco to expand, whether vertically or horizontally. Such diversification strategies can bolster companies' revenues and profitability and can fuel growth in new markets, or often fend off competition. Venture capital–backed companies make strong acquisition candidates, as they "offer an established revenue/customer base and proprietary technology, are profitable and receptive to fair valuation metrics, have a unique and defensible market position, and employ strong management teams."[8] For larger companies, especially the ones with significant cash, stagnant revenues, and limited growth potential, acquisitions is a core component of their growth strategy.

Key drivers for acquisitions, as seen in Table 25.1, are as follows:

- *Improved revenues and profitability:* As discussed earlier, Cisco's sales increased 35X from $650 million to $22 billion, with nearly 40 percent of its revenue coming directly from these acquisitions.

TABLE 25.1   Exit Drivers

Acquirers	Sellers
Growth and increased revenues via access to new products, geographic markets	Positive market/macroeconomic conditions
Operational synergies and reduced risks through diversification	Financial trade-offs: time and capital required to create future value versus present value
Accelerating innovation, minimizing research and development risks	Investor liquidity
Access to talent (or acqui-hires)	Inability to raise capital to fuel additional organic growth
Industry consolidation	Reduced pace of growth
Defensive/competition	Ability to sustain competitive pressures
	Margin erosion
	Reduced pace of growth
	Intellectual property landscape

- *Operational synergies:* Larger companies seek to reduce costs and expand revenues and profitability by seeking synergistic companies that feed their value chain.
  - *Vertical:* Vertical synergies occur when an acquirer moves vertically—up or down the value chain or supply chain. Also called *forward integration* or *backward integration,* examples include HP's acquisition of 3PAR to move into cloud computing, or Cisco's acquisition of Webex to expand its networking gear and voice-over-Internet protocol tools to Web presentation tools.
  - *Horizontal:* Horizontal synergies occur when an acquirer moves to buy another company within a similar domain, For example, Oracle acquires Sun Microsystems.
  - *Diversification of product lines to increase revenues:* Google, a search engine, acquires YouTube, an online video repository, to establish its ad revenues in the online video market. Amazon acquires Diapers. com and Zappos to expand its offerings. Rich Levandov, an investor in several technology start-ups says, "Venture capital is about asymmetrical information and value—you know something that the buyer does not and you have something that a buyer wants—and wants it now," he says. One of his portfolio companies, a start-up with an

investment of $2 million, has no revenues. Yet five buyers jostled to snag the company at $40 million. Another example of asymmetrical value is StubHub. "Before StubHub, there was an opaque and muddy view of the secondary market for tickets. We were able to create value for both sides of the market, so revenues and growth followed. It was a good model." The company was profitable, with $15 million of total capital invested. "It is better to be bought rather than to sell, and we lived that cliché." When eBay came knocking, Heitzmann politely demurred, "We do not wish to sell, but if you are aggressive about buying, let's see your offer." Ultimately, StubHub was sold for $310 million.

- *Geographic penetration:* Access to a new geographic territory, when conducted internationally, is also referred to as cross-border transactions.
- *Quash any rising threats:*
  - Apple bought Lala, a cloud-based Web streaming music service and within a few months shut it down. Lala users are angry; yet Apple bought Lala simply to take it offline because it didn't like the price erosion—Lala was charging 10 cents per track as compared to 99 cents at the iTunes music store.[9]
  - Google snapped up reMail, a popular iPhone application that provides "lightning fast" full-text search. reMail was yanked from the iTunes App Store soon thereafter, and no predictions were made on the future of reMail. As TechCrunch's M.G. Siegler predicted, "Google is just as happy to kill one of the best e-mail applications on the iPhone—much better than the iPhone's native e-mail app."

OPERATIONAL SYNERGIES? IMPROVED REVENUES? REALLY!

HERE ARE THE REAL REASONS WHY COMPANIES ARE ACQUIRED.

Warren Buffett describes the three primary drivers of acquisitions: animal spirits (Don't just stand there, do something. Buy a company); bigger is better (Ego. Larger acquisitions are better); and undue optimism on postmerger integration (It will all work out—if not, all we lose is shareholder capital). Buffett writes, "We suspect three motivations—usually unspoken—to be, singly or in combination, at work in high-premium takeovers. Leaders, business or otherwise, seldom are deficient in animal spirits and often relish increased activity and challenge."

(Continued)

OPERATIONAL SYNERGIES?: (*Continued*)

"All the other kids have one, what about me?"

When a CEO is encouraged by his advisors to make deals, he responds much as would a teenage boy who is encouraged by his father to have a normal sex life. It's not a push he needs. Some years back, a CEO friend of mine—in jest, it must be said—unintentionally described the pathology of many big deals. This friend, who ran a property–casualty insurer, was explaining to his directors why he wanted to acquire a certain life insurance company. After droning rather unpersuasively through the economics and strategic rationale for the acquisition, he abruptly abandoned the script. With an impish look, he simply said: "Aw, fellas, all the other kids have one."

I am bigger . . .

Most organizations, business or otherwise, measure themselves, are measured by others, and compensate their managers far more by the yardstick of size than by any other yardstick. (Ask a *Fortune 500* manager where his corporation stands on that famous list, and invariably, the number will be ranked by size of sales; he may not even know where his corporation places on the list by profitability.)

Kissing toads, optimistically . . .

Many managers apparently were overexposed in impressionable childhood years to the story in which the imprisoned handsome prince is released from a toad's body by a kiss from a beautiful princess. Consequently, they are certain their managerial kiss will do wonders for the profitability of Company T(arget). Such optimism is essential. Absent that rosy view, why else should the shareholders of Company A(cquisitor) want to own an interest in T at the 2× takeover cost rather than at the x market price they would pay if they made direct purchases on their own? In other words, investors can always buy toads at the going price for toads. If investors instead bankroll princesses who wish to pay double for the right to kiss the toad, those kisses had better pack some real dynamite. We've observed many kisses but very few miracles. Nevertheless, many managerial princesses remain serenely confident about the future potency of their kisses—even after their corporate backyards are knee-deep in unresponsive toads.

Source: www.berkshirehathaway.com/letters/1994.html, accessed March 5, 2011.

If acquisitions offer an efficient mechanism for generating returns, who are GPs to judge these human fallacies of ego, mindless activity, and undue optimism? As cash piles are hoarded by public companies, the animal spirits for acquisitions will continue.

THE SELL PROCESS

Should the board decide to put the company on the block for sale, the process, as depicted in Figure 25.4, starts with dipping your toe in the water.

Step 1: Test the Waters

Companies considering a sale generally hire a "sell side" investment bank to oversee the process of the company in a timely and efficient manner. Investment bankers charge a fee, typically, around 4 percent to 7 percent of the transaction amount, along with a retainership. At this stage, a company would invite investment bankers to propose terms and timelines and to demonstrate their industry awareness and connections. While these discussions ensue, the ineffective bankers will be eager to take the assignment and, after collecting substantial retainer fees, fail to deliver value. The low-level tactics include proposing significantly higher valuations to snag the assignment, and later point to the buyer universe for poor outcomes. On the other hand, the best of the breed may not be willing to engage or sell something unless they believe the opportunity is meaningfully attractive to the universe of acquirers, and if they do, they may propose a lower number to get the

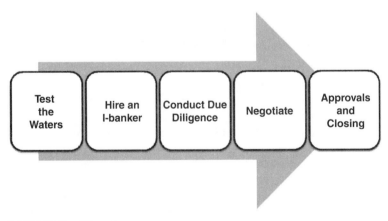

FIGURE 25.4   The sell process.

transaction completed fast. The company should seek the right balance between investment banker industry expertise, fee structures, target valuation range, and target time lines of transaction.

Company boards identify the investment bankers who have relevant knowledge of the challenges and opportunities of a particular sector and market conditions. Investment bankers are able to gauge the field, identify potential buyers, and know the potential hurdles and buyer objections. In determining the company's selling price, investment banks can provide fair assessments of value by analyzing the company's long-term prospects and current financials. Beyond providing these financial advisory services, investment banks identify potential buyers, solicit bids, and review proposals; help companies select the most attractive candidates; and participate in the negotiations with interested parties.

At times, the value and visibility of the company may be such that an investment banker may be unnecessary. Or consider the approach of Heitzmann, who sold StubHub to eBay: "We deliberately built a board with tentacles in the potential buyer's market. You generally know someone—first-time entrepreneurs do not have much of a network—and that's where we come in. One of our board members knew people at eBay, and that's how it started," he says.

Bankers also bring about a degree of laziness in VCs, says Brad Feld of the Foundry Group. "On most occasions, with an investment banker, the price goes down," says venture capitalist Lindsay Aspegren. Lindsay, who was once with Goldman Sachs, has been an investor in technology start-ups for over a decade.

Also, many buyers do not view the smaller investment bankers as credible, and if the process is unsuccessful, the company is scarred—likely to be treated as damaged goods.

Step 2: Formalize the Process—Hire an Investment Banker

At this stage, the board would hire an investment banker (I-banker), who will proceed within the following framework:

- *Process metrics and timelines:* The I-banker will establish valuation guidelines, universe of potential acquirers, and steps/timelines for the process.
- *Presentation materials*: A teaser sheet, a set of slides, and relevant information memorandum will be created.
- *First contact*: At this point, the I-banker blasts e-mails to the universe of acquirers, using teasers, which provide high-level information to acquirers. Teasers are typically a page or two long, with key highlights

of the technology, revenues, and growth potential. Teasers do not disclose the name of the company and offer only some key points that get the buyers to the door to sign a nondisclosure agreement.

- *Screening the parties interested in the company*: Once the interested parties have been identified and have signed nondisclosure agreements, these would be prescreened. This can be a nebulous step, as the goal of prescreening is to eliminate those who are merely seeking information without providing any insights into their process, motivations, or criteria. And beware of tire kickers. Brad Feld cautions that expressions of interest occur many times along the way. "It could well be corporate development guys from large companies just sucking info from entrepreneurs, or staying busy, doing their job. They may have no money but are wasting an entrepreneur's time. We see many tire kickers and can help our entrepreneurs to cut through the noise—we know a lot of natural acquirers, and we don't hesitate to call them when the time comes." Also, after the prescreening stage, companies choose to negotiate the terms themselves, without any substantial involvement from the I-bankers. Many intermediaries prefer to offer advice on the various potential outcomes based on negotiation parameters—mature I-bankers will seldom prescribe one path over another. The ultimate decision lies with the company.
- After a suitable buyer has been identified, the parties proceed to stage two of the process.
  - *Execute a letter of intent*: A letter of intent (LOI) establishes a level of commitment on both sides to proceed in a diligent and a timely fashion to finish what has been initiated. An LOI would include the following:
    - *Exclusivity*: The seller is engaging with only one party. This clause tilts the axis in favor of the buyer.
    - *Confidentiality*: This clause protects the seller's information. This is a must-have clause that does not impact the economic terms.
    - Broad parameters of transaction terms are established.
      - Due diligence
      - Conditions to closing
      - Employee matters
    - Timelines are suggested.
- Buyers may choose to offer a nonbinding LOI, which is a two-edged sword. Furthermore, a weak yet binding LOI does not accomplish much for the seller.
- Once the LOI has been executed, the buyer is aware of the negotiating advantage that starts therein. Other suitors usually step back at this point, and the dance frenzy intensifies. A seller needs to ensure that the

LOI has enough teeth in it to protect valuation and ensure that the diligence is completed with a sense of urgency.

Step 3: Conduct Due Diligence

Larger companies and the buyer's counsel will engage in deep due diligence. Sellers establish a data room with relevant documents, which include the following:

- *Corporate records*: Certificate of incorporation, bylaws, board minutes, shareholders list.
- *Business records*: All material contracts of purchase, sale and supply agreements, research agreements, licensing and distribution agreements and government contracts, list of all assets and intellectual property.
- *Financial records*: All financial statements, receivables, loan and equity agreements, tax records. Copies of all placement memorandums, capitalization schedules, and equity amounts.
- *Employee records*: All employee agreements, consultant agreements, details of option plans and benefits (pension, health care) offered.
- *Legal*: Details of any litigations, pending or foreseen.

Step 4: Negotiate/Structure the Transaction

Typical elements of negotiation during the sell process include, besides valuation, the following:

- Asset purchase versus stock purchase:
  - Most acquisitions occur as asset purchases. This eliminates any unknown or contingent liabilities that a seller may assume as a result of stock purchase. Assets can be chosen ("You keep those desks and phone systems, we keep the IP and the customers") and allow for depreciation, which is a tax advantage.
  - In a stock purchase, the buyer can assume net operating losses (NOLs) that the seller may have accrued, which may reduce the buyer's tax liabilities and augment the value. On the flip side, the buyer also assumes all liabilities, known or unknown. And yes, those old desks and archaic phone systems are a part of the deal.
- Cash offering, part cash and part stock, or all-stock transaction:
  - An all-cash transaction is preferred by sellers and venture investors. Buyers can finance such transactions via external financings.
  - Stock transactions allow the seller to gain long-term economic advantages and to be a shareholder and enjoy any advantages.

■ Earn-outs and escrows: A buyer may believe that the value of the company lies in executing certain orders that generate revenues and cash flows or profits. Furthermore, a buyer may establish certain targets and milestones for such an earn-out. Jack Ahrens of TGap Ventures tries to minimize any earn-outs: "The company is going to be controlled largely by the acquirer and so are the resources—people as well as cash. Things can get sticky pretty quickly when motivations change," he says. Depending on the sector, practitioners advise that approximately 15 percent of the value in earn-outs is acceptable. In the pharmaceutical sector, these percentages vary significantly and depend on the stage of drug development. Escrow percentages range from 5 percent to 15 percent, and periods (12 to 24 months) are negotiated as the buyer attempts protection from any surprises and contingencies.

■ Other terms are as follows:
  ■ Representations and warranties made by the target company.
  ■ For the employees, who stays, who goes.
  ■ Employee options, such as vesting schedule and acceleration.
  ■ Indemnities offered by the target company.

Step 5: Approvals and Closing

The board and shareholders approve the transaction. The closing, a process during which the attorneys and key stakeholders execute final agreements, occurs on a set date. While these would historically happen in person, typically at an attorney's office, many of these are done virtually nowadays. After all, if signatures can be scanned and money can be wired, we do not need the general assembly.

WHEN AN ACQUIRER COMES KNOCKING

As they say, companies are always bought, never sold. Here are some points to consider when a potential acquirer comes calling:

■ Technology companies seek to acquire innovative start-ups because larger companies are unable to innovate at a rapid pace.

■ Acquisitions or acqui-hires are a tactical way to recruit high-powered talent.

■ Price, although important, is seldom a primary consideration in the acquisition. Several practitioners affirm that in many negotiations, the price effectively doubled by the time the transaction was consummated. This was not without due theatrics and emotional drama, but the sellers who held their ground and knew how to play the game were richer in the end.

■ Eventually, acquisitions are a primary mechanism of growth for public companies.

THE BUY-SIDE ACQUISITION PROCESS

While larger companies seek certain features, product lines, or technologies, the first choice may be to build it internally. Any chief technology officer (CTO) of a company like Microsoft, Google, or Yahoo! will assert that his team can develop product internally, and do it faster and cheaper. However, in decisions where larger corporations look at make-versus-buy options, the CTO's ego and insecurities are not high up on the list. The potential for increased revenues, competitive dynamics, and financial growth and market timing comes into play. Often, this is where the CFO and the corporate development team display their acumen. At a very primal level, every CEO seeks to deploy excess cash to build a larger empire and demonstrate King Arthur-like prowess. Warren Buffett's wisdom shows here: "Of one thing be certain: if a CEO is enthused about a particularly foolish acquisition, both his internal staff and his outside advisors will come up with whatever projections are needed to justify his stance. Only in fairy tales are emperors told that they are naked."

Whatever the motivation—technological, market driven, or ego driven—target companies and venture practitioners benefit from such behavior. The search process starts where the acquirer establishes certain criteria to narrow down the universe of potential targets.

Besides technological and market fit, examples of search criteria may include the following:

■ *Size of transaction*: Consider the fact that Google has historically acquired a number of companies that are below the $30 million price tag. Examples include Adscape, now called Adsense ($23 million), and Blogger and WritePost, both rumored to be in the $10 million to $20 million range.

■ *Geographic location*: Cisco is known to focus on the Silicon Valley area. John Chambers once stated in his acquisition strategy that "Geographic proximity is important. If the newly acquired firm is located close to Cisco, interaction will be easier."[10] The location also drives other intangibles—for example, Groupon's founders wondered whether this Midwest-based company would culturally integrate with Google!

But information flows both ways, and the process of acquiring companies does not necessarily follow a prescribed, linear path. Many larger corporations rely on a network of relationships. For example, numerous Cisco executives serve on boards/advisory boards of start-ups. Such relationships provide key insights on technological developments. Investors too have found out that networks are an excellent mechanism to sell companies and generate returns in a consistent fashion.

Larger companies also ask their sales team to keep an eye out for new entrants who may threaten their position. Cisco heavily relies on its sales force to watch for new developments.

And of course, VCs are a great source of information. Of the various acquisitions made by Cisco, Sequoia—which originally invested in Cisco—had invested in at least 12 of them.[11] Sequoia was also an investor in YouTube, which was acquired by Google, one of its earlier portfolio companies. A study shows what most practitioners would intuitively know—an acquisition is likely when there is a common venture capital investor linking the acquirer and the target.[12]

A BIG FISH SWALLOWS A SMALL FISH

Acquisitions are seldom completed in five easy steps as described, followed by hugs and a friendly dinner. Often, people threaten, lose sleep and fret, and wave their arms. It's a storm of greed, fear, and the desire to win. The stakes are high.

When Quidisi, a company that operated Diapers.com, reached $300 million in sales in a few years, Amazon took notice. Over an introductory lunch, an Amazon executive ominously informed the founders of Quidisi that the giant was getting ready to start selling diapers. They should consider selling to Amazon.

Quidisi had raised over $50 million from leading VCs in Silicon Valley. The founders didn't jump in, and a few months later they noticed something strange—Amazon had dropped prices on diapers by as much as 30 percent. As an experiment, Quidisi changed prices, and voila: Amazon's tracking bots monitored and changed its prices too. For Quidisi, this price drop impacted growth and started to erode into profit margins. Worse, their ability to raise additional equity capital or possibly consider an IPO was now slimmer than ever.

In the meantime, Walmart made an acquisition overture to Quidisi, and offered $450 million. Quidisi founders flew to Seattle to meet with

(Continued)

A BIG FISH SWALLOWS A SMALL FISH: (*Continued*)

Jeff Bezos, chair and CEO, to discuss Amazon's interest. To keep the heat, that morning Amazon announced a service called Amazon Mom, where it offered a 30 percent discount and free shipping. When Quidisi factored these maneuvers in the costs of selling diapers, Amazon was on track to lose $100 million in three months on diapers alone. Amazon was doing about $34 billion in revenues, and Bezos wanted Diapers.com at a price. He was also not going to let this slip to Walmart, which did over $400 billion in revenues. Amazon's $540 million offer was open for 48 hours, and even as the offer was tentatively accepted, Walmart countered with $600 million. Executives at Amazon let Quidisi know that Bezos was such a furious competitor that he would trigger a "thermonuclear" option and drive diaper prices to zero if they sold to Walmart. A lot of Amazon Moms would have been happier at free diapers. The move paid off, and Quidisi was sold to Amazon, largely out of fear.

Source: Brad Stone, "The Secrets of Bezos," *Bloomberg Businessweek*, October 2013.

When any acquisition-related discussions occur, practitioners point to their duty to shareholders to maximize the outcome for all. Thus, in certain situations, bringing in an investment banker would be appropriate. For the investment banker, the goal of such an exercise is to drive the price up, or run an auction. Daniel Axelsen of New Enterprise Associates (NEA), a Silicon Valley venture firm, has performed financial and strategic analysis as investment banker for leading technology companies. His experience at Qatalyst, a leading investment bank, included the sale of publicly traded companies such as 3PAR, a data storage and systems company that was acquired Hewlett Packard after a fierce auction with Dell. "The company and the board have a fiduciary obligation to all shareholders to maximize value. This process was like a three-dimensional game of chess," Axelsen says. The role of the investment banker here was to move the needle effectively from $1.15 billion to $2.4 billion, all in a matter of a few weeks. The following events occurred, according to public records:

- Dell announced that it would acquire 3PAR in a transaction valued at approximately $1.15 billion.
- A week later, Hewlett-Packard (HP) announced it had offered $1.5 billion, or 33 percent higher than Dell's offer to acquire 3PAR.

- Three days later, 3PAR said it accepted Dell's revised offer for $1.6 billion.
- A day later, both parties reoffered their bids, with HP offering more than $2 billion. A week later, Dell declined to revise its bid after HP upped its bid to $2.4 billion. HP completed the acquisition.

If Google wants to buy a company, surely some competitors, say Microsoft, would love to jump into the fray. Recall that when Google did a $900 million deal with MySpace, Microsoft followed soon thereafter and did a $300 million deal with Facebook. Investment bankers know who the interested parties are and who is seeking suitable acquisition opportunities. They can rush to gather additional interest from various acquirers and juggle with different buyers, all the time pushing the price as high as possible. The frenzy would culminate with a letter of intent with one of the suitors. At times, the buyer promptly locks up the game by proposing a "no shop" clause, where the target cannot indulge in the abovementioned exercise. "Exclusive processes are lot harder and don't necessarily yield the best results," says Daniel Axelsen, formerly with Qatalyst Partners.

A buyer's due diligence process will occur in phases. The primary goal of the buyer is to ensure that the technology and teams are a suitable fit within its existing fabric. Thus, while the product lines, revenues, and markets are tangible, the softer challenges of postmerger integration are important as well. For example, Cisco sets short-term and long-term joint initiatives with the target's management team as a way to assess culture, management qualities, and leadership styles. They look for softer cues: Does one person speak over everyone else? Do some people roll their eyes when the other is talking? Cisco negotiates directly with key individuals to identify their postacquisition intentions and also insists on employees waiving their accelerated vesting rights to ensure that they stay with the company after integration.

Valuation is not the most important negotiating point.[13] One Cisco executive remarked, "*Acquisitions are not financial—we do not do them because we can swing a good deal—they are strategic and help grow our company in the right direction* [italics added]."[14] When a buyer seeks to make a strategic acquisition, the price is no longer a multiple, but could be significantly higher.

"As a practitioner, your goal is to understand that universe of strategic buyers," says Lindsay Aspegren of North Coast Technology Investors. For larger companies, effective integration is key, or else the entire exercise is deemed a failure. Cisco has as many as 60 employees to manage the postintegration process. An integration leader is appointed, and within 30 days of announcement, the human resources team lays out compensation plans for the team so that the talent pool can avoid uncertainty, stays, and focuses on creating value.

After the board approval and shareholder consents, the closing process begins.

DEAL KILLERS

Acquirers often walk away from opportunities for several reasons, but the most critical deal breakers are often alignment of interests and financial terms. For investors, the primary deal killer is the value of an exit, yet a young CEO may find a $30 million *acqui-hire* offer appealing.

Understanding the buyer's motivations is critical. The value of the acquisition, pace of transaction, and terms and conditions are often driven by the buyer's ambitions.

Good record keeping is often underestimated by start-up CEOs, and it's often the onus of the board and investors to ensure that all records are up to date. Material contracts, cap tables, intellectual property assignments, and even timely payment of taxes can cause irritants in this process.

I'LL DO THE MACARENA FOR 17X IN 17 MONTHS

Link Exchange, an online banner exchange company, was acquired by Microsoft for its technology and customers. After Sequoia invested in Link Exchange, Tony Hsieh asked Michael Moritz of Sequoia to attend an initiation meeting with its six employees. After the introductions, the team decided they wanted to "move together in unison" and someone brought out a boom box. They started clapping, cheering . . . and as the song "Macarena" started, Moritz participated in the dance, as any good VC would. "I don't think words can truly describe what watching Moritz being forced to do the Macarena was like. It ranks up there as one of the strangest sights to behold," wrote Hsieh. "I had tears streaming down my face from laughing so hard."

Seventeen months after Sequoia invested $3 million, Link Exchange was acquired by Microsoft for $265 million. Moritz collected $50 million—a return of 17 times his initial investment in 17 months. Time to do that Macarena again . . . and Moritz's turn to laugh.

Source: Adapted from Tony Hsieh, *Delivering Happiness: A Path to Profits, Passion, and Purpose* (New York: Hachette Book Group, 2010), 45–46.

NOTES

1. Xuan Tian, Gregory F. Udell, and Xiaoyun Yu, "Disciplining Delegated Monitors: Evidence from Venture Capital," January 23, 2011, available at SSRN: http://ssrn.com/abstract = 1746461.
2. Between 2002 and 2007.
3. Marc Goedhart, Tim Koller, and David Wessels, "The Five Types of Successful Acquisitions," *McKinsey Quarterly*, July 2010, accessed February 10, 2011, www.mckinseyquarterly.com/The_five_types_of_successful_acquisitions_2635.
4. Between 1993 and 2001.
5. David Mayer and Martin F. Kenney, "Economic Action Does Not Take Place in a Vacuum," (BRIE working paper 148), September 2002.
6. Between 2001 and 2013.
7. Amir Efrati, "Google Cranks Up M&A Machine," *Wall Street Journal*, March 5, 2011.
8. Montgomery & Co., "The Return of M&A: An Outlook for the Venture Industry," June 2009, accessed February 10, 2011.
9. Eliot Van Buskirk, "Apple Kills Lala Music Service," April 30, 2010, accessed February 21, 2011, www.wired.com/2010/04/apple-kills-lala-music-service.
10. Glenn Rifkin, "Growth by Acquisition." April 1, 1997, www.strategy-business.com/article/15617?pg = all.
11. David Mayer and Martin F. Kenney, "Economic Action Does Not Take Place in a Vacuum."
12. Paul A. Gompers and Yuhai Xuan, "Bridge Building in Venture Capital-Backed Acquisitions," (AFA 2009 San Francisco Meetings Paper), February 1, 2009, available at SSRN: http://ssrn.com/abstract=1102504.
13. David Mayer and Martin F. Kenney, "Economic Action Does Not Take Place in a Vacuum."
14. Ibid., attributed to Michael Volpi, Chief Strategic Officer.

CHAPTER 26

Initial Public Offering

"The canvas isn't empty. It's full of whatever you imagine it to be full of. My art is so conceptual that not only do I not tell, but I don't even show. All I do is sign the canvas and try to sell it."
—Jarod Kintz, Author

Making the announcement to issue common stock on the public exchange, or "going public" for the first time, holds a special cachet in the world of venture capital–backed companies. It often marks the coming of age of companies, so entrepreneurs see it as the epitome of success. But the regulatory and market complexities are significant and have impacted the initial public offering (IPO) dynamics significantly.

A decade ago, an IPO was within reach for companies with annual revenues between $30 million and $50 million that showed a profitable quarter and had a good board and management team. After the dot-com crash, it was the larger, more mature companies with revenues of $150+ million that were seen as suitable candidates for public offering. This, combined with regulatory challenges, had the effect of stretching out IPO timelines for companies.

If the company is ready and the markets are favorable, the public offering is certainly a better option, because most acquisitions don't generate the killer returns that public offerings do. Because IPO-ready companies can be affected by market downturns and regulations, the volume of investment returns for investors may be driven more by acquisitions than public offerings. Consequently, acquisitions are efficient and faster exit options.

When a company decides to file for a public offering in United States, it registers its securities with the Securities and Exchange Commission (SEC) for sale to the general public. From a business perspective, it is a culmination of a longer strategic plan for the company. For entrepreneurs, the priority is to expand capital resources by tapping into the public equity markets for additional investors.

The benefits and costs are manifold. The advantages are evident, including enabling access to capital, exposure, and prestige; facilitating future acquisitions of other companies (via partial payments in shares); enjoying access to multiple financing opportunities such as equity, convertible debt, and cheaper bank loans; and developing increased liquidity.[1] The costs are also not to be ignored: loss of privacy as to matters regarding business operations; competition; disclosure of executive officers' compensation, material contracts, and customers; pressure from shareholders to perform and meet market expectations; and time-consuming diplomacy in undergoing periodic reporting to investors and shareholders and regulatory compliance. Across three decades, from 1980 to 2010, venture capital–backed IPOs as percentage of all IPOs is a mere 35 percent.[2]

THE IPO PROCESS: THE LONG AND WINDING ROAD

The IPO journey can be divided into many different phases in which the actual IPO is seen as a significant milestone in an otherwise complex structural transformation. According to *Ernst & Young's Guide to Going Public*, there are essentially three main stages:[3]

1. A planning stage, where the company commits to diligent preparation that includes conducting feasibility studies and readiness checks on the business and financials itself, as well as the market.
2. An execution or implementation stage takes place, where the right management and advisory teams are established; financial infrastructure and accounting, tax, operational, and information technology processes and systems are assessed; corporate structure and governance are established; and investor relations and corporate communication strategies and plans are managed.
3. Finally, the company reaches a realization phase, where shares are priced and the IPO transaction closes.

In this preparatory stage, which takes place about one to two years before the IPO is set to take place, a company does its homework to assess the readiness to go IPO:

- *Prepare a compelling business plan.* The business plan should be long term, covering 24 to 36 months before and after the IPO to provide a clear road map that can be embedded early in the organization.
- *Benchmark the portfolio company's performance.* Before deciding to go public, companies monitor their performance, tracking growth rates, sales performance, profitability, and market share. Companies should also measure themselves on other benchmarks, such as ensuring that their products and services are well-defined and assessing their reputation among various market stakeholders (e.g., customers, analysts, and investment banks). Aside from financials, reputation and brand name are important intangibles for leveraging a company's strength in the public markets.
- *Is this a public-ready company?* A compelling business track record and a plan to demonstrate how IPO funds will fuel growth is key. Is there growth? Rising profits? In the management team, what expertise gaps need to be filled for operating a public company? Also, does the company have adequate budgetary systems in place with financial information readily available on a monthly and quarterly basis? What are the states of investor relationships and the corporate structure for transparent reporting to shareholders? In a survey of global institutional investors, respondents ranked the top nonfinancial factors leading to IPO success.[4] In order of priority, these are as follows:
  - Management credibility and experience
  - Quality of corporate strategy and its execution
  - Brand strength and market position
  - Operational effectiveness
  - Corporate governance practices

In reviewing IPO trends of more than 7,500 companies from 1980 to 2010, the median age of a company is 8 years. The lowest median age during these three decades was 5 years and the highest median age was 15 years.[5]

After this soul-searching stage, it is in the second stage that the company begins the practical preparation toward going IPO.

STEPS TO AN IPO

After an IPO readiness assessment is completed, the steps to an IPO, as presented in Figure 26.1, include selection of underwriters, conducting the road show, and demand assessment.

Consider the road map to IPO for Google. To comply with SEC rules, Google had to consider disclosing its financial information. It found itself in a position where it had more than 500 shareholders and had 120 days

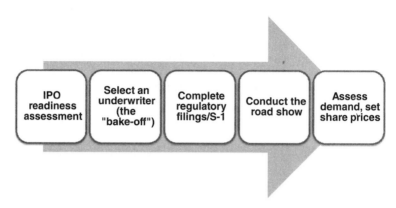

FIGURE 26.1 Steps to an IPO.

from the end of the year to file the financial statements. Google faced three choices: buy back shares from some shareholders, report financials publicly without selling any shares, or go public. Google had to present its financials by 2:00 P.M. and three hours ahead of this deadline, at 11:00 A.M., the company announced that it would be going public.[6]

Prior to filing, Google realized neither of the exchanges, NASDAQ nor NYSE, would list the offering, as they were short of three board members. Companies preparing for IPO should take special care in building an independent and a strong company board that offers a broad mix of skills—from industry networks, technical knowledge, and expertise in business development to acquisition integration and financial analysis. Google was able to add three heavy hitters quickly—the president of Stanford University, the president of Intel, and the CEO of Genentech.

The "Bake-Off"

Investment banks compete for the issuing company's business during a process known as the *beauty contest* or *bake-off*. The investment banks present their credentials to the company's board of directors, as well as their view of market conditions and challenges.

Hire an Underwriter

The word *underwriter* is said to have come from the practice of having each risk taker write his or her name under the total amount of risk that they were willing to accept at a specified premium. In a way, this is still true today. An underwriting syndicate brings new issues to market. Each firm takes the responsibility (and risk) of selling its specific allotment.

Underwriters or investment banks are hired to raise investment capital from investors on behalf of the company. This is a way of selling a newly issued security, such as common stock, to investors. Syndicates of banks (the lead managers) typically underwrite the transaction, which means they have taken on the risk of distributing the securities. Underwriters make their income from the price difference (the underwriting spread) between the price they pay the issuer and what they collect from investors or from broker-dealers who buy portions of the offering.

Google ended up with 31 underwriters—a long list, indicative of the eagerness of the middlemen. Several would drop off eventually. Credit Suisse and Morgan Stanley ended up with their names on the S-1 filings.

File the S-1/Prospectus

Any company intending to go public is required to file a legal document known as the prospectus with the SEC. Registration is a two-part documentation process that involves Form S-1. Part 1 covers the prospectus, which serves as the primary documentation of disclosure to investors, detailing the operations and financial conditions of the company. Part 2 covers the supplemental information furnished to the SEC (copies of contracts, etc.). Once the SEC approves the company's registration statement, a final prospectus is released to investors.

The prospectus, which reads much like a business plan, includes the company's financial history and growth strategy, the details of its offering, and information on company management. It also outlines industry competition and other risk factors that investors would want to know in advance. In essence, the prospectus provides all the information investors need to know in order to decide whether to participate in the IPO. The preliminary prospectus is also known as a red herring because of the red ink used on the front page, which indicates that some information—including the price and size of the offering—is subject to change.

Quiet Period Begins

As soon as a company files a preliminary prospectus with the SEC, the quiet period begins. The company is prohibited from distributing any information not included in the prospectus. This period lasts for 25 days after the IPO, after the shares start trading.

Sergey Brin and Larry Page did several things noteworthy at the time of the Google IPO, but the *Playboy* interview was the one that almost got them crossways with the SEC during the quiet period. A week before its celebrated IPO, the SEC caught wind of this interview, which had been conducted about five months prior. Eventually, this interview was included in its entirety in the S-1 Prospectus as Appendix B. *Playboy* lost the exclusive interview to an inane SEC rule, and the media made some hay about it, as did the late-night comedians. As CEO Eric Schmidt quipped, it was a generic article, "without any pictures, I might add."[7] Phew!

The Road Show: Which City Are We In, Again?

Google did not have to struggle much with a road show as it decided to go down the Dutch auction path for selling its shares to the public. But the underwriter typically schedules dozens of meetings across the country. The CEO and his team, typically the CFO and other key executives, will join the tour during which the company pitches its business plan to institutional investors: mutual funds, endowments, or pension funds. At these meetings, the underwriter attempts to gauge the level of interest in the IPO, which helps lead to a decision on how to price the stock offering.

Book building is the process by which an underwriter attempts to determine at what price to offer an IPO based on demand from institutional investors. An underwriter builds a book by accepting orders from fund managers indicating the number of shares they desire and the price they are willing to pay. The book runner is the managing or lead underwriter who maintains, or runs, the books of securities sold for a new issue. Often the book runner is given credit for the total size of the deal.[8]

Following the road show, the company prints its final prospectus, distributes it to potential investors, and files it with the SEC.

Great Demand, or Put It on Ice?

And after all the road show presentations are complete, if the demand from the institutions is feeble, the underwriters will recommend that you put the offering on ice. Let it chill. And someday, it is hoped, it will be springtime.

NOT AN ENDGAME, BUT A FINANCING EVENT

According to Ernst & Young, around 70 percent of start-up companies fail before they reach their IPO potential, with the majority of successful IPOs mostly around for at least five years before the transition.[9] Once on the public market, these companies must compete with other IPOs. Only 8 percent of offerings are competitive in terms of value and fair market value offered by peers in the industry.[10]

The metamorphosis from a private company to a publicly listed company is a daunting process, requiring massive strategic planning and cost-benefit analysis of markets and products, value chain activities, infrastructure (e.g., business information systems, compensation, plans, and redundant assets), governance and management structures, and other business components—from both financial and legal perspectives.[11] The process itself, timed from the decision to go public to the day the IPO transactions are closed, varies significantly. Several factors will affect the timeline, such as how well the process is planned, how well the company is positioned in the market, and the abilities of the management team and advisors, as well as factors outside the control of companies, such as market conditions and the current regulatory environment.[12]

TIMING THE MARKET

Researchers point out that when public markets are favorable, the experienced venture capitalists (VCs) are quick to take advantage. After assessing more than 40,000 transactions spanning two decades, authors Paul Gompers, Anna Kovner, Josh Lerner, and David Scharfstein concluded that not only are the investments of the specialized venture capital organizations more successful, but there is no appreciable degradation with changing conditions.[13]

IPO UNDERPRICING AND DUTCH AUCTIONS

IPOs generate strong returns for investors, as seen in Figure 26.2. But IPOs can be underpriced by as much as 15 percent, thanks to an incestuous relationship between underwriters and institutional investors.

The goal, when pricing an IPO, should be to establish an offering price that is low enough to stimulate interest in the stock but high enough to raise an adequate amount of capital for the company. The process of determining an optimal price usually involves the underwriters (syndicate) arranging share purchase commitments from leading institutional investors.

In order to balance the needs of the investor and the issuing company, the investment bank traditionally tries to price a deal so that the first-day pop is about 15 percent.[14] This is a nice gift that benefits underwriters (the company pays the price) and their institutional investor friends—this incestuous cycle may seal the next investment opportunity that may be led by the underwriter.

Underwriters may claim that the effect of initial underpricing of an IPO generates additional interest in the stock when it first becomes publicly traded. But in reality, those institutional friends make an instant 15 percent. This results in money left on the table—lost capital that could have gone to the company, had the stock been offered at a higher price. The company all along believes that the underwriters are representing its interests, but really

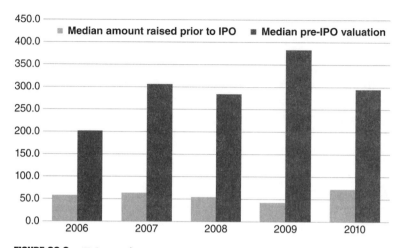

FIGURE 26.2 IPO trends.
Source: Dow Jones VentureSource

the underwriters just want to get the deal done quickly—the costs can be borne by the company, after all.

According to professor Jay Ritter, over 50 years, IPOs in the United States have been underpriced by 16.8 percent on average. This translates to more than $125 billion that companies have left on the table. IPO pricing is also a worldwide phenomenon. In China, the underpricing has been severe, averaging 137.4 percent from 1990 to 2010. This compares with 16.3 percent in Britain from 1959 to 2009. In most other countries, IPO underpricing averages above 20 percent.[15]

Table 26.1 outlines a few examples where either underpricing or frothy market conditions led to instant transfer of wealth from a company to those institutions that received IPO allocations.

TABLE 26.1 Money Left on the Table: Instant Transfer of Wealth from Company to Those That Received IPO Allocations, Thanks to the Underwriters

Company	IPO Offer Price	First Closing Market Price	Shares	Money Left on the Table ($M)
VMWare	$29	$51	33,000,000	$726
Akamai Technologies	$26	$145.1	9,0,00,000	$1,072
Goldman Sachs	$53	$70.3	55,200,000	$959
Blackstone Group	$31	$35.6	133,333,000	$622

Source: Prof. Jay R. Ritter, University of Florida, "Money Left on the Table in IPOs."

IT'S ALL GOOD . . . EVEN IF LINKEDIN LEFT $130 MILLION ON THE TABLE

Investment bankers set LinkedIn's share price at $45 when they could have asked for $90, the media argues, and thus effectively cheated LinkedIn out of over $130 million. On the opening day, shares jumped up to $94.25, popping over 100 percent.

The New York Times noted that while there is "nothing wrong with a small 'pop' in the aftermath of an IPO," such a tremendous rise in stock price indicates "in reality, LinkedIn was scammed by its bankers."

Joe Nocera of the *New York Times* pointed out that "the fact that the stock more than doubled on its first day of trading—something the investment bankers, with their fingers on the pulse of the market, absolutely must have known would happen—means that hundreds of millions of additional dollars that should have gone to LinkedIn wound up in the hands of investors that Morgan Stanley and Merrill Lynch wanted to do favors for. Most of those investors, I guarantee, sold the stock during the morning run-up. It's the easiest money you can make on Wall Street."

Others debated that IPO pricing is the epitome of highly educated guessing, and there is no simple way of estimating the supply-demand.

Source: The New York Times and the Wire

The danger of overpricing is an important consideration for venture investors. If a stock is offered to the public at a higher price than the market will pay, the underwriters may have trouble meeting their commitments to sell shares. Even if they sell all the issued shares, if the stock falls in value on the first day of trading, it may lose its marketability and hence even more of its value. This can have emotional consequences, and hence most companies would rather succumb to the 15 percent loss.

INFORMATION ASYMMETRY: THE BIGGER FOOL THEORY OF IPO UNDERPRICING

Kevin Rock of Harvard Business School pointed out that IPO price is observable and does not correspond to a unique level of demand, which is unobservable. Like a one-sided marketplace, buyers still don't know who is willing to buy at the set share price and if the offering will be accepted en masse or selectively. The informed investor has an opportunity to profit from his knowledge by bidding for "mispriced" securities. In this way, the informed investor is compensated for his due diligence into the asset's value and obtains some upside for showing where capital should best be allocated. The uninformed investors compete with the informed, and the issuer must ultimately compensate them for their disadvantage. In other words, the bigger fools pay the price. But we need the fools so that the smarter can make money.

"The underwriters, however, need the uninformed investors to bid since informed investors do not exist in sufficient number. To solve this problem, the underwriter re-prices the IPO to bring in these investors and ensure that uninformed investors bid. The consequence is underpricing," writes professor Steven Davidoff.[16] If the investment bankers tilt the scale to only the smarter buyers, the advantages evaporate: for the pop to occur, you need the foolish and the greedy in large quantities. Davidoff writes, "When investment banks can allocate shares in greater measure to informed investors, the underpricing is reduced since the compensation needed to draw uninformed investors is lower. Underpricing has also been found to be lower when information about the issuer is more freely available so that uninformed investors are at less of a disadvantage."[17]

THE DUTCH AUCTION: ELIMINATE THE POP AND THOSE MIDDLEMEN

Google is an unconventional company in every way—even its IPO was a case study of sorts. Eric Schmidt, CEO of Google, did not like this pop—this 15 percent that should be in the hands of the company—and pushed for a Dutch auction. "I know this may sound like baloney, but we settled decisively on the Dutch auction after we got a letter from a little old lady who asked why she couldn't make money from the IPO the way the stockbrokers would. We thought she had a point about the basic fairness of the system," he wrote.[18]

A Dutch auction is an attempt to minimize the extreme underpricing that underwriters establish. In a Dutch auction, individuals could log on to their brokerage accounts and bid for a certain number of shares, say 500 shares. Or bid for shares for a certain amount, say $1,000. After the auction was completed, the company would establish a price and the individual bidders would receive a certain allocation of shares. "We liked this approach because it was consistent with the auction-based business model we used to sell our ads—it had a strong intuitive appeal for us," Google CEO Eric Schmidt would say.[19]

Such auctions threaten large fees otherwise payable to underwriter syndicates. Google had as many as 31 underwriters at the table when contemplating the IPO path, but ignored the conventional. Although it was not the first company to use Dutch auction, no company the size of Google had ever done such a thing. Google's share price rose 17 percent in its first day of trading despite the auction method. Wall Street was angry—it felt left out of one of the biggest IPOs of the time. "Don't bother to bid on this shot-in-the-dark IPO," said *BusinessWeek*. The *Wall Street Journal* ran a front page article: "How Miscalculation and Hubris Hobbled Celebrated Google IPO." Miffed underwriters actively discouraged institutional investors from buying, to punish Google, reduce demand, and send the initial price down. But for Google, a successful IPO was one where average investors, not necessarily big institutions, eventually gained from the underpricing.

POST IPO: SHOULD VCs STAY ENGAGED?

After the rapture and thrill of the IPO settles, and the tombstones have been proudly distributed, a question comes up: Should a VC stay involved with a public company? A successful IPO outcome is a financing event and not a guarantee of long-term success of the company. With analysts and shareholders eagerly watching the ticker price run across the board at the stock exchange, the CEO is under pressure to deliver consistent earnings and growth. And this leads to an interesting conundrum for any practitioner: Should I stay and help the CEO become successful? Or should I keep my fiduciary responsibility to my limited partners (LPs) and move on to the next portfolio company? No easy answers here. Lip-Bu Tan of Walden International says, "I think it is a big mistake when a VC resigns from the board when a company is going public. That's when the CEO needs the most help. Being a public company is very unforgiving—the CEO is in the public eye and trying to live life by the quarterly earnings, and with a VC's skills and expertise, you can help the CEO and the company to become a stable and a strong company."[20]

Seth Rudnick of Canaan Partners, who has led at least half a dozen companies to the IPO stage, differs in his views. "As a venture investor, you're looking at a number of metrics: What's best for the company, what's the IRR that you're getting for your investors? How do all the other investors in the company benefit? And those are all very complicated decisions. Frankly, at Canaan Partners we strongly urge all of our partners who are in companies that go public to get off the boards so that the decisions then become simply those that you would make as an investor rather than as a board member," he says. "I think you get too confounded, you know, you love the company, you want to stay on it, you want to stay involved but the dynamics are much different now."[21]

For Brad Feld of the Foundry Group, the choice is easy. "Forget your ego, do what your LPs want you to do," he says.[22] For a VC who is engaged with a public company, the responsibilities and liabilities become significant. Reporting, disclosures, insurance, insider trading issues—the game changes substantially. Factors such as the performance of the company, publicity, and liability risk are key parameters of consideration for any VC who wishes to stay on the board of a publicly traded company. In the proverbial limelight, public companies have a strong incentive to avoid any negative publicity that will adversely affect the stock price. Delivering financial statements in a transparent and timely way, whether annually or quarterly, gives investors and analysts continued assurance and confidence in the company.

As companies are traded publicly, LPs often pressure VCs to sell these stocks and return capital to investors. While these dynamics are dependent on limited partner–general partner terms, investors are eager to gain liquidity, especially after a long investment horizon. On the flip side, the VCs may believe these stocks have latent value and the price can only go up. For some VCs, their IRR, and their careers, are also at stake. The timing and decision of sale is a perennial debate. Diana Frazier of FLAG Capital, a fund of funds managing more than $6 billion, points out, "There were two venture funds that had significant investments in Google. One fund sold their stock at the time of the IPO, the other one held on for much longer. No marks for guessing who made more money."

While IPOs are the pinnacle of all exits, secondary sales and private exchanges have evolved. Early investors and founders can enjoy partial liquidity, thanks to these exit options.

PICK YOUR LPS WITH CARE

"We decided we wanted to have all tax-exempt sources as limited partners. This was to avoid difficulties such as selling securities to pay for taxes—our limited partners are all tax-exempt sources such as U.S. and European Foundations."

—Don Valentine, Sequoia Capital

Source: Don Valentine, "Target Big Markets," www.youtube.com/watch?v=nKN-abRJMEw#t=368.

NOTES

1. KPMG, LLP, *Going Public*, accessed February 11, 2011, www.kpmg .com/Ca/en/IssuesAndInsights/ArticlesPublications/Documents/ Going%20Public.pdf; *Ernst & Young, Ernst & Young's Guide to Going Public: Lessons from the Leaders*, accessed February 11, 2011.
2. Jay R. Ritter, Cordell Professor of Finance, University of Florida, *Initial Public Offerings:1980–2010,Tables Updated through 2010*,as of January 2011.
3. Ernst & Young, *Ernst & Young's Guide to Going Public*.
4. Ibid.
5. Jay R. Ritter, *Initial Public Offerings*.
6. This was announced on April 29, 2004.
7. Eric Schmidt, "Google's CEO on the Enduring Lessons of a Quirky IPO," *Harvard Business Review*, May 2010.
8. Investopedia, definition of Book Runner, accessed February 21, 2011, www.investopedia.com/terms/b/bookrunner.asp.
9. Ernst & Young, *Ernst & Young's Guide to Going Public*.
10. Roman Binder, Patrick Steiner, and Jonathan Woetzel, "A New Way to Measure IPO Success," *McKinsey Quarterly*, January 2002, accessed February 11, 2011.
11. KPMG, LLP, *Going Public*.
12. Ibid.; Ernst & Young, *Ernst & Young's Guide to Going Public*.
13. Paul A. Gompers, Anna Kovner, Josh Lerner, and David Scharfstein, "Venture Capital Investment Cycles: The Impact of Public Markets" (NBER working paper series, vol. w11385, May 2005, available at SSRN: http://ssrn.com/abstract = 731040.
14. Frontline, PBS, "An IPO Primer," accessed February 22, 2011, www.pbs .org/wgbh/pages/frontline/shows/dotcon/thinking/primer.html.
15. Steven M. Davidoff, "Why I.P.O.'s Get Underpriced," *The New York Times*, May 27, 2011.
16. Ibid.
17. Ibid.
18. Eric Schmidt, "Google's CEO on the Enduring Lessons of a Quirky IPO."
19. Ibid.
20. Lip-Bu Tan (Walden International), in discussion with the author, August 2008.
21. Seth Rudnick (Canaan Partners), in discussion with the author, August 2008.
22. Brad Feld (The Foundry Group), in discussion with the author, December 2010.

CHAPTER 27

Human Psychology

"It has been said that man is a rational animal. All my life I have been searching for evidence which could support this."
                                                        —Bertrand Russell

Every practitioner should aim to be a student of human behavior. We are primal beings, and we function in ways that cannot be fully explained within the logical construct. A few challenges are likely to occur while making investment decisions, primarily due to randomness of human psychology and emotions.

Let's start with David McRaney's observations in his book *You Are Not So Smart*. His book points out as many as 48 ways we delude ourselves. But for the sake of brevity, let's focus on the few that are relevant in the context of venture capital investments.

EMOTIONS VERSUS LOGIC

In any investment decisions, practitioners create elaborate logical labyrinths to minimize risk or justify actions; but as human beings, we are equal parts emotion. Or mostly emotions, if you start to scratch beneath the surface. We have a tendency to ignore odds in our favor and often rely on gut feelings. Snap judgments. Love at first sight. You had me at hello. We could go on and on. At work, we do stuff because we like someone. We want to earn points or be liked. Or we want to reciprocate, to feel good about ourselves. Research shows that when it comes to identifying risk, our brains are hardwired to respond from the gut. In his book *How We Decide*, author Jonah Lehrer points out that "our best decisions are a finely tuned blend of both feeling and reason—and the precise mix depends on the situation." Now, there is nothing wrong in healthy emotions, but as students of human behavior, we need to recognize that sometimes it's not necessarily logic that's at work. "Without emotion, it becomes incredibly difficult to settle on any one opinion. We would endlessly pore over variables, weigh the pros and cons in an endless cycle of computations," writes McRaney.[1] Thus, in any situation where the decisions don't add up, know that emotions—not logic—may be at work.

RECIPROCATION, OBLIGATIONS, AND INDEBTEDNESS

In a classic book on human psychology, *Influence—Science and Practice*, author Robert Cialdini writes that reciprocity is one of the most widespread and basic norms of human culture. Quite simply put, reciprocity is exchange: If someone wishes you happy birthday, you do the same for theirs. Holiday cards, dinner invitations, horse-trading where politicians vote on bills just because the other politician supported their bill are all examples of reciprocity. Lobbyists play this game pretty well. Pharmaceutical companies are especially notorious and curry favors at the cost of innocent patients: leading doctors snag consulting agreements or paid vacations to Hawaii, where they are gently reminded to prescribe more medication. It even extends to international aid. So why is this relevant to venture capital investments?

Most venture capitalists (VCs) have relationships, investors who are often aligned philosophically, intellectually. Such investors often syndicate investments and may have made (or lost) money standing side by side. If a VC "refers" or "brings you in" on a deal, this ritual of reciprocity starts. This creates a web of obligations that you may not necessarily want to be a part of. This obligatory dynamic could very well impact decisions and returns, especially when coinvestments occur with a big fish and a small fish—a multi-billion-dollar fund and a smaller fund. In such situations, more often than not, the smaller fish pays the price. The best antidote is to ensure that the relationship is indeed trustworthy and is then supported by a strong legal framework.

A VC WITH EGO: WHY SHOULD I EAT YOUR LEFTOVERS?

VCs tend to compete, often mindlessly. Paul Graham, founder of Y Combinator, one of the world's leading accelerators, writes: "A while ago an eminent VC firm offered a series A round to a start-up we'd seed funded. Then they heard a rival VC firm was also interested. They were so afraid that they'd be rejected in favor of this other firm that they gave the start-up what's known as an 'exploding term sheet.'" An exploding term sheet is time sensitive and pressures founders to make a decision in a short time frame, often to their disadvantage. Graham called this firm to find out if they would still invest if the rival firm did not invest. In what seems like a mindless move, they said no. "What rational basis could they have had for saying that? If they thought the start-up was worth investing in, what difference should it make what some other VC thought? Surely it was their duty to their limited partners simply to invest in the best opportunities they found; they should be delighted if the other VC said no, because it would mean they'd overlooked a good opportunity. But of course there was no rational basis for their decision. They just couldn't stand the idea of taking this rival firm's rejects."[2]

CONFORMITY (OR GROUPTHINK)

In groups, we like to conform rather than act independently. Time and again, studies have shown that our behavior changes, at times dramatically, when we are in groups. And this might explain why you have some investors who say one thing in a one-on-one session but change their views when they are in a group. It's group dynamics at work, and they don't want to be seen as renegades. Conformity is default behavior in human beings; indeed, as it's seen as essential to survival in tribal contexts. McRaney points out that our desire for conformity is strong and unconscious, like the desire to keep everyone happy around a dinner table. But *beware of the other side, the dark place conformity can lead to.* The Enron debacle, in which a publicly traded company with over $60 billion in assets was bankrupted, is a fine example where conformity prevailed and no one dared ask questions. Enron even dragged down Arthur Andersen, one of the five largest audit and accounting firms in the world. Shareholders lost $11 billion, and the CEO landed in jail. Collaboration increases dishonest behavior, and that's conformity's dark side. If you see groupthink and weak spines around the table, raise your hand and ask, "Are we conforming to look good to each other? Or do each of us believe this is a good decision?"

The other interesting aspect of group dynamics is that it can decrease the quality of decisions, writes Dan Ariely in his book *The (Honest) Truth about Dishonesty.* We have all seen this happen in large organizations and government entities: it's called bureaucracy and decisions are made using the lowest common denominator approach. No one gets fired, it's all good, but nothing ever gets done. It is rare for such a challenge to occur in a start-up, but be watchful.

ROCK STARS IN THE BUSINESS

The lead singer of rock band U2, Bono, is a VC. He is managing director and cofounder of a Silicon Valley–based venture fund, Elevation Partners. While we have not seen such star power in a start-up's boardroom, it would be fun to speculate what a board meeting would be like. Bono walks in, sits down, removes his shades, and says, "We really should move away from iOS and look at Android." There would be a chorus of "ayes," followed by, "And now can we get your autograph, picture, and a hug?"

"We, more often than not, subconsciously gravitate towards people who look like us, who agree with or compliment us, or are physically attractive," writes Robert Cialdini. It's called similarity, compliance, association, and cooperation. Such psychological nuances often make one board member persuasive over others, creating a halo effect. These aspects of human behavior may be especially troubling in the context of venture capital. While such behavior cannot be avoided, we need to recognize it, and make sure that we can tackle this behavior effectively. Watch for pandering when one board member excessively grovels at the feet of another VC demigod. They are setting the stage for groupthink.

THAT OVERHYPED ROLODEX IS NOT AS USEFUL AS YOU THINK

VCs may have 1,000-plus connections on LinkedIn, but a human brain has the capacity to keep track of only about 150 connections. Beyond that, it's all a pile of data. Research shows that the size of our brain determines the size of our "active" network, where we maintain these relationships in a meaningful fashion. And our prefrontal cortex can process only about 150 connections. Noted author Malcolm Gladwell pointed out in *The Tipping Point* that in companies, productivity declines once the size of the company grows beyond 150 people.[3] In such networks, the grease of information and activities—getting together for a beer, a hike, or a game—keeps it running smoothly. The power of reciprocity works well, and the network is "alive." But if we try to expand the network without being able to nourish it meaningfully, the ability to impact and reciprocate in such a network crumbles. The bottom line is, don't believe in your own ability to tap in your 1,000-plus LinkedIn contacts: keep your expectations low.

We are complex, emotional beings, each motivated by different drivers and insecurities. Is your investment decision and thesis driven by independent, honest analysis and facts? As noted entrepreneur and investor Peter Thiel points out, "Humans are massively cognitively biased in favor of near-term thinking. VCs are no different."[4] Or as McRaney would put it, the misconception is that we calculate what is risky or rewarding and always choose to maximize gains while minimizing losses. The truth is, we depend on emotions to tell us something is good or bad, greatly overestimate the rewards, and tend to stick to our first impressions.

NOTES

1. McRaney describes the case of a patient with a brain tumor who lost his emotional responses and became a complete wreck, as he could not make any decisions.
2. Paul Graham, "The Hacker's Guide to Investors," April 2007, www.paulgraham.com/guidetoinvestors.html.
3. Malcolm Gladwell, *The Tipping Point: How Little Things Can Make a Big Difference* (New York: Little, Brown and Company, 2000).
4. Peter Thiel, Stanford CS183 Class Startup, as recorded by Blake Masters, http://blakemasters.com/post/22271192791/peter-thiels-cs183-startup-class-8-notes-essay accessed on January 2, 2014.

Afterword

"**Y**ou're still here?" asks the perplexed protagonist in the post-credits coda to the 1986 comic masterpiece, *Ferris Bueller's Day Off*. Shuffling closer to the camera, a befuddled Ferris tells the audience, "It's over. Go home." Then walking away, he gives one final backwards glance and echoes, "Go" with a dismissive wave of his hand.

Now those of you who've made it this far in this book have been exposed to a soup-to-nuts look at the innards of the venture capital business. You're now equipped with a roadmap for becoming a venture capitalist (VC). "Go," says Ferris.

But wait a second! Not so fast! This book, as comprehensive as it may be, is but one of dozens of books that give a roadmap for *how* one might become a VC, but none of these books really ask a far more daunting question: *why*?

After all, as an institutional investor in venture capital funds, I am evermindful that I'm signing up for illiquid, opaque, difficult-to-exit partnerships that typically last twice as long as the average American marriage. In *whom* I'm investing becomes almost as important as in *what*. After all, I'm one degree attenuated from the actual assets. You invest in the company, but I invest in you.

And indeed, when I consider a fund investment, my own idiosyncratic evaluation process focuses on four things: the people, the strategy, the portfolio, and the track record. Of these, track record can be the least instructive, as it is often a lagging indicator, not a leading one (I'll note that's an uncommon viewpoint, as conventional wisdom holds that winners repeat). The extant portfolio, on the other hand, embodies the people and the strategy in action. It is in understanding the portfolio on a first-hand basis that one can get a sense for the resonance of the investor and the strategy.

But understanding the people becomes the greatest challenge. What motivates them? What are they afraid of? How do they define success? What have they learned from failure? What risks are they willing to take? Which are beyond the pale? What are their rules? When do they break their rules? And so on. . . .

Add into the mix that people's behavioral footprints can vary with time, based on their own personal growth and the disparate things going on in their professional or private lives—although nothing is private when you're managing money with which I've entrusted you—and it can be pretty challenging to triangulate how well-armed for success one person will be. By the way, it's a daunting task to understand just one person; add into the mix the cross product of interactions among a team of partners and the "soft" evaluation of partnerships become an almost impossible task.

But try we must.

Therein lies the essence of the voodoo that we do. And at long last, after years of thinking about these issues in an unstructured way, I stumbled across a philosophical concept that gave an organizing principle to the people evaluation process: *eudaemonia*. Now that may seem like a ten-dollar word from my five-dollar mouth, but it's an important idea. Aristotle's theory of human happiness arises from this word, but *eudaemonia* itself connotes much more than happiness. A more authentic translation is "human flourishing." Lacking context, human flourishing is an incomplete concept. That's where *arete* comes in. *Arete's* headline definition is excellence, but a deeper understanding of *arete* includes the concept of fulfillment of purpose or function, that is, being the best you can be.

As the venture capital business has contracted over the past several years, many young partners have come to me in what I call the "parade of the LIFOs [last in-first out]." Since these LIFOs tend to be the youngest folks at their firms, they stand to be the first out the door as fund-raises fail to fulfill the expectations of the partners and salaries need to be cut. One thing that amazes me is how many of these younger VCs entered the business in 1999 or 2000 because it was The Thing To Do for a strapping Stanford grad, much like investment banking or consulting had been for me when I graduated from college or business school. Yet, the deep dissatisfaction they harbor is palpable; it's been a tough dozen years, and the winning investments haven't come as easily as one might have thought. It's been a demoralizing slog for many. In their dismay, they are living *dis-daemoniously*.

To be sure, there are today an innumerable number of satisfying, high-performance careers for dynamic individuals, and the perception of venture capitalism as a "glamorous" gig overstates the reality. While the definition of wild "success" in baseball is getting one hit in every three at-bats, VCs often define victory as finding that one-in-a-generation company. The odds of that happening are almost infinitesimal. Compensation can be good in the interim, but there are lots of other good ways to earn a living that offer better chances of personal fulfillment.

And that's where *eudaemonia* comes in. The highs of venture capital can indeed be high, but the tough slog of waiting for portfolio companies to emerge and become game-changers can be protracted and exhausting. It is during that time that patience can be tested, and one is forced to look deep within oneself and ask, "Am I fulfilling my purpose? Am I being the best I can be?" If the answers to those questions are affirmative, you're halfway home. In the negative, the dissonance can be excruciating, particularly because you made a promise to me, your shareholder, to stick it out to the end. We're all lashed to the mast together.

Venture capital can be an all-consuming endeavor; it can be more of a lifestyle than a profession. Happiness and success are closely linked, while unhappiness and frustration weigh on the psyche and impair one's effectiveness. Over time, these negative sentiments threaten to seep into all crevices of one's life. So think deeply about the journey upon which you're about to embark before you follow Ferris's advice to "go," having been armed by the knowledge in this book. You owe it to yourself, your customers (entrepreneurs), and your shareholders (limited partners) to take an introspective look at yourself and strive for your own unique *eudaemonia*.

Acknowledge Socrates's assertion that the only true wisdom lies in knowing that you know nothing. Free yourself from the conceit that you can outsmart some of the smartest folks around, and focus on the particular wisdom that you can uniquely offer. Drop the pretense and be genuine. Entrepreneurs will appreciate it, and potential investors will be grateful that they don't have to fight through a thicket of inauthenticity.

—Chris "SuperLP" Douvos, CFA,
Palo Alto, California

About the Author

Mahendra Ramsinghani has invested in more than 50 seed stage companies and has more than a decade of experience in fostering the growth of early-stage technology businesses. As Director–Venture Capital Initiatives for Michigan Economic Development Corporation (MEDC), Mahendra led the legislation for two fund-of-funds programs that deploy $200+ million in venture capital funds in Michigan.

He is also the co-author of *Startup Boards* (Wiley, 2014) with VC and author Brad Feld.

His writings have been featured in MIT's Technology Review, Forbes, and Thompson Reuter's peHub.

Mahendra's background includes a bachelor's degree in electronic engineering and an M.B.A. with a major in marketing & finance. He lives with his wife, Deepa, and daughter, Aria, in San Francisco, California.

About the Companion Web Site

The companion web site (www.wiley.com/go/businessofvc2e) offers various tools such as LP-GP Fund Due Diligence Checklist, Investment Due Diligence Checklist, Investment Summary format, and more.

The companion site also includes external links to white papers and other industry guidelines.

The password to enter the site is: venture123.

If you have comments, updated links, or corrections, you can send them to the author at mr@thebusinessofvc.com.

Index